APPLIED SYSTEMS ANALYSIS
Engineering Planning and Technology Management

APPLIED SYSTEMS ANALYSIS
Engineering Planning and Technology Management

Richard de Neufville
*Massachusetts Institute
of Technology*

McGraw-Hill Publishing Company

New York   St. Louis   San Francisco   Auckland   Bogotá   Caracas   Hamburg
Lisbon   London   Madrid   Mexico   Milan   Montreal   New Delhi   Oklahoma City
Paris   San Juan   São Paulo   Singapore   Sydney   Tokyo   Toronto

This book was set in Times Roman by Publication Services.
The editors were B. J. Clark and John M. Morriss;
the production supervisor was Janelle S. Travers.
The cover was designed by John Hite.
Project supervision was done by Publication Services.
R. R. Donnelley & Sons Company was printer and binder.

APPLIED SYSTEMS ANALYSIS
Engineering Planning and Technology Management

3 4 5 6 7 8 9 0   DOC DOC   9 5 4 3 2

ISBN 0-07-016372-3

Library of Congress Cataloging-in-Publication Data

de Neufville, Richard, (date).
    Applied systems analysis: Engineering planning and technology management /
    Richard de Neufville.
      p.   cm.
    Includes index.
    ISBN 0-07-016372-3
    1. Engineering economy.   2. Systems analysis.   3. Operations
research.   I. Title.
TA177.4.D45   1990
658.4'032—dc20   89-12094

ABOUT THE AUTHOR

Professor Richard de Neufville is Founding Chairman of the Technology and Policy Program at the Massachusetts Institute of Technology (MIT). This innovative curriculum in systems planning and management received the Sizer Award for the Most Significant Contribution to MIT Education.

Professor de Neufville received his bachelor of science, master of science, and doctorate in civil engineering from MIT.

He has taught Applied Systems Analysis at MIT since 1968, in both the School of Engineering and the School of Management. He has also held visiting appointments in Engineering at the University of California, Berkeley, and the Ecole Centrale de Paris, and in Management at the London Graduate School of Business and the Master's in International Business Program in France. His previous book for McGraw-Hill, *Systems Analysis for Engineers and Managers,* was awarded a NATO Systems Science Prize.

His work in decision analysis and strategic planning is widely recognized for its impact on professional practice. His experimental research won the Alpha Kappa Psi and the Risk and Insurance Awards. Most recently, the Australian Institution of Engineers cited his work on the Second Sydney Airport for Engineering Excellence.

The author of two other textbooks, *Airport Systems Planning* (MIT Press and MacMillan in England) and *Systems Planning and Design* (Prentice-Hall), Professor de Neufville was named as a U.S.-Japan Leadership Fellow in 1989. Previously he was a Guggenheim Fellow and served as a first White House Fellow for President Johnson.

CONTENTS

Part 2 System Evaluation 195

PREFACE

THE TOPIC

Applied Systems Analysis is the use of rigorous methods to help determine preferred plans and designs for complex, often large-scale systems. It combines knowledge of the available analytic tools, understanding of when each is more appropriate, and skill in applying them to practical problems. It is both mathematical and intuitive, as is all planning and design.

Systems Analysis is a relatively new field. Its development parallels that of the computer, the computational power of which enables us to analyze complex relationships, involving many variables, at reasonable cost. Most of its techniques depend on the use of the computer for practical applications. Applied Systems Analysis may be thought of as the set of computer-based methods essential for the planning of major projects. It is thus central to a modern engineering or business curriculum.

Applied Systems Analysis covers much of the same material as operations research, in particular linear and dynamic programming and decision analysis. The two fields differ substantially in direction, however. Operations research tends to be interested in specific techniques and their mathematical properties. Applied Systems Analysis focuses on the use of the methods.

Systems Analysis includes the topics of engineering economy, but goes far beyond them in depth of concept and scope of coverage. Now that both personal computers and efficient financial calculators are available, there is little need for professionals to spend much time on detailed calculations. It is more appropriate to understand the concepts and their relationship to the range of techniques available to deal with complex problems.

Applied Systems Analysis emphasizes the kinds of real problems to be solved; considers the relevant range of useful techniques, including many besides those of operations research; and concentrates on the guidance they can provide toward improving plans and designs.

Use of Systems Analysis instead of the more traditional set of tools generally leads to substantial improvements in design and reductions in cost. Gains of 30% are not uncommon. These translate into an enormous advantage when one is considering projects worth tens and hundreds of millions of dollars.

SCOPE OF TEXT

The object of this book is to help the student and practitioner learn to apply Systems Analysis successfully and productively. It is addressed to the user, who has to know how to select the techniques appropriate in any situation, to apply them to real problems, and to interpret their results intelligently. It is also addressed to the customer, the person responsible for large projects, who has to know how to evaluate the results and proposals generated by systems analysts. To meet their needs, the text presents the techniques and concepts that have been found to be most important in practice.

The text presents the fundamental topics of optimization and evaluation. Each is treated differently, according to the state of analytical and conceptual progress in the area.

Optimization focuses on linear and dynamic programming as the central methods of interest in practice. Insofar as standard computer programs are available to execute these methods, the emphasis here is on how to formulate problems correctly and efficiently, and on how to translate the mathematical results into improved designs. Procedures that are not used in practice, such as the simplex method, are bypassed so that time can be spent productively on important considerations. The presentation is integrated with the classical techniques of engineering and economics so that students can learn to exploit the range of methods according to their needs.

Evaluation features decision analysis as the principal means to identify optimal strategies in the risky environment that is necessarily part of complex, long-term projects. Indeed, use of this approach is leading to fundamental improvements in the way we plan such developments. The presentation here is unique in the way it integrates decision analysis into the hierarchy of evaluation techniques. Each of these, particularly including engineering economy and cost-benefit analysis, is described in sufficient detail.

The text does not cover two topics sometimes included in systems analysis: dynamic systems and statistics. Dynamic systems are not treated because their applicability to problems of management and design, as distinct from mechanical systems, is minimal. Research into the possibility that large-scale physical systems and organizations can be described with feedback loops and the like is suggestive but still too speculative for actual practice. Classroom experience, on the other hand, indicates that statistical procedures are extremely difficult to integrate effectively with optimization and evaluation: A careful treatment of the methods and issues requires more understanding of probability and causal mechanisms than is generally available.

A major strength of the text, as emphasized by reviewers, is the way it effectively integrates the broad range of methods available to the user. The idea throughout has been to help the user understand the relative strengths and weaknesses of alternative methods, to indicate when they are best used, and to provide guidelines for application.

PRESENTATION

The presentation of the techniques differs substantially from that of competitive texts. It particularly features

Application to real problems, drawn from an extensive range of practical work over the last 20 years.

Synthesis of the methods, ordinarily treated quite distinctly in separate texts, into an integrated framework.

Consideration of multiple objectives, as a realistic feature of the actual nature of planning and management.

The text is easy to use for teaching and learning because it does not require extensive mathematical skills. Because people who need to apply Systems Analysis come from a wide range of backgrounds, every effort has been made to avoid unnecessary mathematical complexity. The idea is to teach, not to impress. Readers should, however, be familiar with

Elementary Calculus, so that they can deal with the classical techniques of optimization.

Vectors and Matrices, the basic means of describing problems to computers.

Elementary Probability, to work with expected values.

They should also have some acquaintance with real-world problems, so that they can appreciate when and why some techniques are better than others.

Making the material easy to learn and to teach has been a leading consideration. Great care has been devoted to defining concepts clearly and consistently, to giving and explaining examples, and to making the text completely self-contained. The language and sentences are also kept as simple and as direct as possible, in recognition that a text may be used as much at one in the morning as at one in the afternoon!

The format uses three special devices to make learning easier. These are

Boxes, self-contained blocks of material inserted in the text, that highlight examples.

Semantic Cautions, indented sections drawing attention to potential ambiguities caused by conflicting definitions used in different disciplines.

Italicizing of definitions where they first appear, to help readers locate and refer to important concepts.

Additionally, references to detailed case studies easily available in the literature are provided where appropriate.

Both conceptually and pedagogically, *Applied Systems Analysis* is a complete rewrite of my previous textbook *(Systems Analysis for Engineers and Managers,* coauthored with Joseph Stafford). It includes many case studies, drawn from a second text *(Systems Planning and Design: Case Studies in Modeling Optimization and Evaluation,* coauthored with David Marks) and two decades of worldwide professional experience. It incorporates recent developments while dropping topics that have proven to be of little use in practice. It offers a wider, more instructive range of problem sets. Finally, it is written to be clear, even on the most difficult points.

The text reflects the current pervasive use of personal computers throughout, in its choice of topics and their use. The material on sensitivity analysis, multiobjective optimization, and system optimization procedure can only be applied to realistic problems when computers are available. Likewise, topics such as the evaluation of cash flows are best done in practice by spreadsheet programs. As a practical matter, however, specific programs have not been incorporated into the text, because of the enormous, ever-changing variety of software available. Experience suggests that instructors will find it easiest to use the programs with which they and the students are familiar. Alternatively, if there is not enough time to go into the mechanics of specific software, the material may be covered completely without computers.

SUGGESTED USE

The material works well for the wide range of users who need a comprehensive introduction to Applied Systems Analysis. It provides in one text the material ordinarily found only in several specialized subjects. Years of classroom experience indicate that introducing students to Systems Analysis in this way, with many examples of real applications, is highly motivational: It encourages students to select the more advanced topics that will be most useful to them.

Juniors and seniors in engineering follow the mathematics easily and are challenged by the references to practice. Entering graduate students who have not previously had Systems Analysis appreciate the way the applications motivate the study of the techniques.

The text is also appropriate for first-year students in management, provided they have had a reasonable grounding in mathematics. It is routinely used in this context both at the Massachusetts Institute of Technology and in the Master's in International Business Program in France.

Experienced professionals appreciate the way the material applies to real problems. Although some may have to brush up analytic skills, many have used the material for self-study and reference. The predecessor text, *Systems Analysis for Engineers and Managers,* was adopted by the Open University in Britain for nationwide educational television. It was also awarded the NATO Systems Science Prize.

At the Massachusetts Institute of Technology we now present the material in two kinds of subjects. In the fall, it is given as a schoolwide elective taken by seniors and graduate students in all fields of engineering. During the spring and summer it is given to professionals entering business school programs.

McGraw-Hill and I would like to thank the following reviewers for their many helpful comments and suggestions: William O'Neill, University of Illinois; Elizabeth Paté-Cornell, Stanford University; Robert Stark, University of Delaware; E. Earl Whitlatch, Ohio State University; and Jeff Wright, Purdue University.

Richard de Neufville

APPLIED SYSTEMS ANALYSIS
Engineering Planning and Technology Management

PART
1

SYSTEM
OPTIMIZATION

CHAPTER

1

INTRODUCTION

The design of a system represents a decision about how resources should be transformed to achieve some objectives. The final design is a choice of a particular combination of resources and a way to use them; it is selected from other combinations that would accomplish the same objectives. For example, the design of a building to provide 100 apartments represents a selection of the number of floors, the spacing of the columns, the type of materials used, and so on; the same result could be achieved in many different ways.

A design must satisfy a number of technical considerations. It must conform to the laws of the natural sciences; only some things are possible. To continue with the example of the building, there are limits to the available strength of either steel or concrete, and this constrains what can be built. The creation of a good design for a system thus requires solid technical competence in the matter at hand. Engineers may take this fact to be self-evident, but it often needs to be stressed to industrial or political leaders motivated by their hopes for what a proposed system might accomplish.

Economics and values must also be taken into account in the choice of design; the best design cannot be determined by technical considerations alone. Moreover, these issues tend to dominate the final choice of a design for a system. As a general rule, the designer must choose between many possible designs, each of which appears equally effective technically. The selection of a design is then determined by the costs and relative values associated with the different possibilities. The choice between constructing a building of steel or concrete is generally a question of cost, as both can be essentially equivalent technically. For more complex systems, political or other values may be more important than costs. In planning an airport for a city for instance, it is usually the case that several sites can be made to perform technically; the final choice hinges on societal decisions about the relative importance of ease of access and the environmental impacts of the airport, in addition to its cost.

The centrality of economic considerations in the design of engineering systems needs to be stressed. The recognition that economic theory is essential to engineering practice is relatively new, and thus relatively limited. This new relevance results from the evolution in engineering from the detailed design of devices to the design of systems.

As engineering more explicitly deals with the design of systems, we must deal with new issues and incorporate suitable new means of analysis. Traditionally, engineering education and practice have been concerned with detailed designs. At that level technical problems dominate and economics are often secondary. In designing an engine for example, the immediate task—and the trademark of the engineer—is to make the device work properly. In systems designs however, economic considerations can become most important. Thus the design of a transportation system generally assumes that engines to power vehicles will be available, and focuses attention on such issues as whether service can be provided at a price low enough to generate sufficient traffic to make the system worthwhile.

Applied systems analysis thus differs from traditional engineering in that it explicitly includes a great deal of economics. The importance of this discipline to systems analysis is particularly strong because one of the economists' main concerns has been with what they call "resource allocation." This is the problem of determining how to apply different resources to achieve any given objective at least cost. From the theoretical point of view, this problem is exactly that faced by the systems designer. Economists have therefore developed a body of theory and means of analysis particularly suited for applied systems analysis.

Systems optimization, the topic treated in the first part of the text, is the prime instance of how economic theory has been incorporated into engineering systems analysis. Many of the key concepts have been adapted with little modification. In particular, the basic model of the way we can transform resources to achieve objectives, the production function, comes directly from economics. So does marginal analysis, which is the basic method for solving the resource allocation—or design—problem.

The treatment of systems optimization starts in Chapter 2 with the description of the production function as the underlying model of any system. Chapter 3 then briefly covers the mathematical theory of optimization with constraints. This section forms the basis for all that follows. Chapter 4 covers marginal analysis, a simple method that is not only useful in many complex situations but that provides substantial perspective on the nature of optimal solutions. Chapters 5 to 7 then cover the most important methods of modern, computer-based systems analysis.

Chapter 5 covers linear programming, the most widely used and effective means of optimization. Chapter 6 describes sensitivity analysis, an essential ingredient to any practical optimization since our mathematical descriptions of reality are inherently inexact. Chapter 7 covers dynamic programming as the most important example of the enumerative class of optimization techniques that complements linear programming. Chapter 8 introduces the essential elements of multiobjective analysis, an activity that is still very much in the process of development. Finally, Chapter 9 integrates the preceding material into a coherent procedure for optimizing the design of systems, and provides an extended example.

REFERENCE

Miser, H. J., and Quade, E. S., eds., (1985). *Handbook of Systems Analysis,* Elsevier Science Publishers, New York.

CHAPTER
2

PRODUCTION FUNCTIONS

2.1 CONCEPT

Production functions constitute the most basic models of applied systems analysis. They are attractive because they are both simple and powerful. They are simple in that they may consist of only one formula or computer routine; yet they are powerful in that this single expression can effectively summarize an enormous amount of detailed engineering data. Production functions thus serve as a fundamental means to discuss alternative designs of a system.

A *production function* represents the *technically efficient* transformation of *physical resources* into *products*. The words stressed are important to the definition and need to be carefully understood.

A production function is an engineering model first of all. It represents a relationship between physical quantities. Specifically, it describes how various resources—the inputs to the process—combine to form some products—the outputs of the transformation. A production function for air transportation, for example, would relate the several inputs to the process (aircraft of different types, fuel, pilots, ground equipment, etc.) to the various outputs (number of passengers, tons of cargo carried, etc.)

A production function represents *technically efficient* combinations of resources. It is technically efficient in that each point on the production function represents the maximum product that can be obtained from any given set of resources. The production function therefore excludes any lesser amount of product that would come from a wasteful or technically inefficient use of these resources. The production function for air transportation thus expresses the maximum that can be carried for any number of pilots, aircraft, and so on—not the lesser amount that would arise if management were careless, pilots were lazy or the aircraft were flown in circles. By definition, a production function is the locus of all technically efficient combinations of resources.

> **Semantic caution:** Ordinary language confuses two distinct concepts: *technical efficiency*, described here, and *economic efficiency*, which in brief is whether a design is best economically (see Chapter 4). The one does not imply the other. Technical efficiency is a necessary but not a sufficient condition for economic efficiency. The latter can clearly only be obtained if resources are not wasted. A design may be technically efficient but economically inefficient, however. For example, a design for a steel building might be technically efficient in that it could carry the most load for the least steel, and yet be economically inefficient compared to a concrete structure—due perhaps to the much higher cost of steel in that region.

The production function can represent very complex situations. It quite easily incorporates hundreds and even thousands of different resources, as for example in a linear programming problem (see Section 5.2). More commonly, production functions deal with only a handful of variables. This is because of our own desire to simplify the description of the design into something we can easily comprehend.

The principal limitation of the production function is that it can now, as a practical matter, only handle a limited number of products. Production functions are thus typically expressed in terms of a single product. This limitation is in part due to the lack of appropriate theory to describe processes that create multiple products, as Section 2.5 describes. It is also due to our limited ability to optimize efficiently over multiple products or objectives, which Chapter 8 describes.

In view of this limitation, most of the subsequent discussion focusses on production functions for single products. This does not mean that production functions can in practice only describe situations with one product; it does mean that they apply principally when—as is generally the case—different products can be aggregated into a single category. A production function thus would describe an automobile factory in terms of its production of "cars" rather than in terms of two-door cars, four-door cars with and without automatic transmission, and so on.

2.2 SINGLE OUTPUT

Single-output production functions are both the most common kind and the easiest to describe. Mathematically, they are of the form

$$Y = g(\mathbf{X}) = g(X_1, \ldots, X_i, \ldots, X_n)$$

where Y is the product and $\mathbf{X}$ is the vector of n different resources X_i.

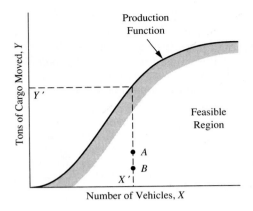

FIGURE 2.1
The production function is the upper bound to the feasible region of production.

By definition, the production function is technically efficient. This means that Y is the maximum product that can be obtained for any set of resources **X**. To illustrate this, consider the hypothetical production function in Figure 2.1, describing the "tons of cargo moved" as a product in terms of the "number of vehicles" as the single resource. For any set of resources X', there are many levels of product that could be achieved, depending on how efficiently the system is organized. One might get as little as A or B. The maximum one can obtain, Y', is the point on the production function corresponding to X'. The entire production function itself is the locus of all points Y'. It is the solid line in Figure 2.1.

The production function is thus the bound to the feasible region of production. This *feasible region* consists of all the levels it is possible to produce with each X'. It thus includes levels A and B as well as Y'. When products and resources are shown as in Figure 2.1, the feasible region is below the production function.

A production function in terms of many resources is a surface. In three dimensions (one product, two resources) this is easy to visualize: it is a shell or dome of some sort. In a higher number of dimensions—in *hyperspace*, that is— the nature of the surface is more difficult to imagine. Yet it always has the same kinds of properties as in conventional space.

2.3   MATHEMATICAL REPRESENTATIONS

There are two basic ways of representing production functions: the deductive and the inductive. Each has quite different implications for the cost and accuracy of the analysis. Both are useful in practice.

The deductive approach uses a convenient functional form, whose parameters are subsequently estimated statistically to reflect reality as closely as possible. The advantage of this approach is that the choice of the right form leads to relatively simple calculations and to results that are easy to interpret. The disadvantage is that any chosen functional form implies a number of restrictions; it is a pattern that has only a limited number of shapes. The choice of a functional form thus will distort our view of reality to some degree and may hide important features of the production function.

The inductive approach synthesizes the production function from a detailed understanding of the physical processes involved. The mathematical representation may be in some explicit functional form, but it is more likely to be generated by extensive calculations that simulate the performance of different designs. This approach can have the merit of being much more accurate. It has the twin disadvantages of requiring far more detailed, laborious efforts, and of not having a functional form that can be easily interpreted.

Deductive models. The best-known and most widely cited deductive model of the production function is the Cobb-Douglas model:

$$Y = a_0 \prod X_i^{a_i} = a_0 X_1^{a_1} X_2^{a_2} \ldots X_n^{a_n}$$

[Note: the symbol $\prod$ represents the multiplication to all i terms. It is similar to $\sum$. Both will be subscripted only where several possible indices for terms might cause ambiguity.]

The Cobb-Douglas model dominated the literature and practice until the early 1970s, until its deficiencies became too obvious and practical alternatives became available through the development of high-speed computers. It has several attractive features:

- It can, by suitable choice of the parameters a_i, represent a broad range of the important characteristics of production functions (see Section 2.4).
- These parameters can be immediately interpreted in terms of the characteristics of the production functions, which is a great pedagogical and practical advantage.
- It is easy to estimate statistically. This is because the multiplicative equation can be transformed into a linear function by expressing variables in terms of their logarithms:

$$\log Y = a_0 + \sum a_i \log X_i$$

The parameters can then be estimated by statistical regression analysis designed to find the best fit of a line to data.

The weakness of the Cobb-Douglas function lies in its inability to represent real situations fully. The model inherently implies that certain features of the production process—as defined by the a_i as described in Section 2.4—remain the

Examples of Cobb-Douglas Model

A classic use of the Cobb-Douglas model was Nerlove's (1965) analysis of the production of electric power. He related output to the inputs of labor, capital, and fuel. By statistical regression he obtained

$$\text{output} = a_0(\text{labor})^{0.78}(\text{capital})^{0.00}(\text{fuel})^{0.61}$$

Further analysis underlines the difficulties created by the Cobb-Douglas requirement that its parameters be constant throughout the range of inputs and output. When Nerlove divided his analysis by level of production he obtained quite different results. For the lowest levels of production he obtained

$$\text{output} = a_0(\text{labor})^{1.45}(\text{capital})^{0.18}(\text{fuel})^{1.29}$$

and for the highest levels he got

$$\text{output} = a_o(\text{labor})^{0.84}(\text{capital})^{0.10}(\text{fuel})^{0.75}$$

These later results indicate that the first model simplified the real situation by, in effect, imposing single values of the a_i parameters (such as the 0.78 exponent for labor) when different values should apply for different sizes of plants.

---

same regardless of the level of production. These constancies may not exist (see box).

The model that is now widely recommended is the translog model:

$$\log Y = a_0 + \sum a_i \log X_i + \sum \sum a_{ij}(\log X_i)(\log X_j)$$

It is essentially the Cobb-Douglas model supplemented with interaction terms between resources.

The translog model overcomes the obvious disadvantages of the Cobb-Douglas formulation, while maintaining most of its advantages. The extra interactive terms make it possible to represent processes with complex features that the Cobb-Douglas model cannot cope with. Yet its linearity permits estimation of the parameters by standard techniques. The calculations are extensive, but proceed quickly on modern computers. The principal drawbacks of the translog model are that the characteristics of the production function cannot be read directly from the model, and it does require considerable effort and data to obtain.

Inductive models. Inductive models of the production function are based on a detailed understanding of the mechanisms that produce a particular product. Typically this perspective is gained by use of technical relationships. These models are thus widely known as engineering models of the production function.

The technical relationships can sometimes be expressed analytically, in terms of one or more explicit equations. These situations are convenient because they make it possible to compute the production function rapidly with the assistance of modest computers or even calculators. Unfortunately, such analytic situations are relatively rare; they mostly occur when the production process occurs in a fairly homogeneous, continuous force field. Moving cargo up a river is a classic example of this (see detailed discussion in Section 2.6).

Most frequently, the engineering production functions have to be simulated through quite extensive computer programs. These are typically expensive since they require enormous effort to identify the relevant data and create the program. The actual calculations may not be too difficult once the program is finished, but a substantial overall effort is required in any case. The simulations typically mimic the detailed design an engineer would have to undertake to establish the result or product of a particular design or combination of inputs. The computer program must thus include all the information required, specifically, extensive tables of discrete data (e.g., strength of specific sizes of steel plate) or non-analytic experimental results (e.g., engine performance). The production function is established by generating hundreds, if not thousands, of designs and identifying the envelope to the production possibilities. This outer limit is, by definition, the production function.

Examples of both an analytic and a simulation engineering production function appear in the accompanying box. Since the models cannot be expressed in a simple equation, they are shown graphically by means of contour lines of equal levels of productions. These contours, known technically as isoquants, are described in detail in the next section.

Inductive Models of Production Functions

A. Analytic Model: Cargo Transport in a River
The basic equation is that the effective push generated by the engines in the barges must equal the resistance of the water to the barges. Both elements can be expressed in terms of the design parameters of the barges: their horsepower, length, width, and depth. Hoffmeister and de Neufville (1973, 1976) solved the equation to obtain the product, ton-kilometers per hour, as a function of the horsepower and size of the barge (see Figure 2.2a and Section 2.6).

B. Simulation Model: Thermal Efficiency in Electricity
In another classic example, Cootner and Lof (1965, 1975) established the production function for thermal efficiency in steam generation of electricity in terms of boiler temperature and pressure. The isoquants, in Figure 2.2b, were obtained from engineering data and industry estimates. Note that the scales are logarithmic.

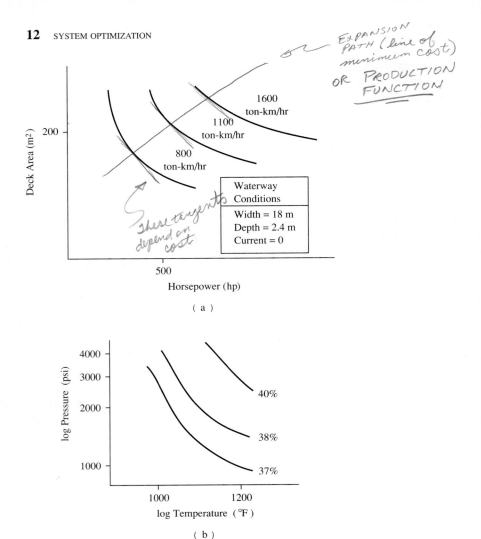

FIGURE 2.2
Examples of engineering production functions.

2.4   CHARACTERISTICS

The characteristics of the production function—its shape, slope, and smooth-ness—are important determinants of the kind of optimization techniques that can be usefully applied. It is therefore necessary to understand these characteristics both in general and in detail. Descriptions of production functions use a wide range of expressions that differ from those traditional in mathematics. They are based on concepts that have specific physical and economic interpretations, and are particularly useful for our purposes. Because they are different, they require particular attention. The following paragraphs develop these concepts.

Note carefully that few of the expressions used to describe production functions apply naturally, if at all, to situations where there are several products. This is a reflection of the fact that the profession has only recently begun to analyze systems in their full detail.

Isoquants. An isoquant is a locus on the production function of all equal levels of product. The term "isoquant" is, in fact, simply a word constructed to mean "equal quantity." Isoquants are easier to visualize when the production function is a shell in three-dimensional space: they are then simply cuts of the shell at specified levels of product. Figure 2.3 illustrates this for a hypothetical production function describing ton-kilometers per hour produced by barges built with different horsepower and deck area. As the figure suggests, the isoquant is like a contour on a mountain.

Isoquants are useful for describing production functions, particularly those that do not have convenient functional forms. They are thus almost always used to illustrate engineering production functions, as was done for the models illustrated in Figures 2.2.

The isoquants also illustrate an important phenomenon: any level of product can in general be obtained by many different combinations of resources, each technically efficient. Figure 2.2a shows that one can move a given amount of cargo either by moving a small barge quickly or a larger barge more slowly. Both these combinations, indeed all those on an isoquant, are technically efficient. There are thus no technical grounds to choose between the designs. The choice then rests with economic considerations, as Chapter 4 explains.

Isoquants for real situations often have a distinct shape: they tend to be asymptotic to the axes of the inputs, as indicated in Figure 2.2. This shape

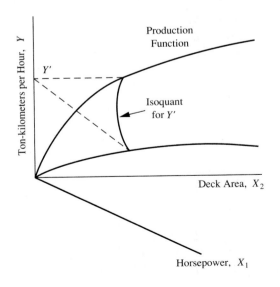

FIGURE 2.3
Example of an isoquant.

reflects the general necessity of having some of each input in the process in order to attain the production. Thus in the production function for river transport shown by Figure 2.2a we must have both capacity (represented by deck area > 0) and propulsion (horsepower > 0) in order to attain any output. In a few cases, inputs can substitute absolutely for each other. Either copper or aluminum can, for example, be used to make electric cable. In cases involving the possibility of absolute substitution, the isoquants can intercept the axes of the inputs. The general rule in practice, however, is that they do not intercept the axes but move away from them as they do in Figure 2.2.

Marginal products. A marginal product is the change in output due to a unit change in a specific input. Formally, for the production function $Y = g(\mathbf{X})$, the marginal product MP_i for input X_i is

$$MP_i = \frac{\partial Y}{\partial X_i}$$

This concept now only applies to single output production functions. No practical equivalent term has been developed for multiple-product models.

Empirically, marginal products typically follow a distinctive pattern, that of diminishing monotonically as X_i increases. This phenomenon results from the fact that the first additions of an input to a process generally do the most good; additional quantities gradually have less and less beneficial effect. Using again the example of moving cargo through a stream, greater amounts of horsepower in the engine do not increase speed proportionately since resistance grows exponentially with speed: the marginal product of horsepower thus diminishes steadily. Figure 2.4 illustrates this behavior.

This trend is known as the "Law of Diminishing Marginal Products." The term is inaccurate, unfortunately, and can be misleading. There is nothing formal or necessary about the pattern; exceptions to the "Law" exist. The counterexamples are usually found at relatively low levels of production, when a particular

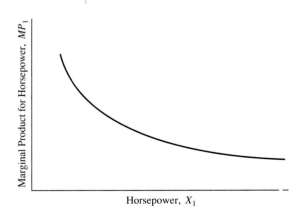

FIGURE 2.4
An example of diminishing marginal product.

input does not contribute significantly until a "critical mass" of it exists. The marginal product of uranium in terms of nuclear power is an obvious instance of this situation. The marginal product of some catalysts is another, and there are many others.

Marginal products can be easily calculated if the production function has a convenient form (see box). Otherwise, they may have to be calculated using small increments of X_i and the corresponding changes in product.

Marginal rates of substitution. A marginal rate of substitution is a special relationship between two inputs. It is the rate at which marginal increases in one input must substitute for marginal decreases in another input so that the total product remains constant. Figure 2.5 illustrates the definition in two dimensions. As the figure suggests, the marginal rate of substitution can be interpreted as the slope of the isoquant.

Any marginal rate of substitution can be expressed in terms of marginal products, and this is the form most useful for practice. Since by definition the changes in each input X_i and X_j lead to no net change in product, we can write:

$$\Delta X_i MP_i + \Delta X_j MP_j = 0$$

Marginal Products for a Cobb-Douglas Production Function

Consider a production function in the general Cobb-Douglas form:

$$Y = a_0 X_1^{a_1} \dots X_i^{a_i} \dots X_n^{a_n}$$

The marginal products are

$$MP_i = a_0 X_1^{a_1} \dots a_i X_i^{a_i-1} \dots X_n^{a_n}$$

This may also, and more conveniently, be expressed by extracting the term a_i/X_i and writing $MP_i = (a_i/X_i)Y$.

The marginal product MP_i is diminishing with X_i whenever the coefficient $a_i < 1.0$. This is because the expression is multiplied by $X_i^{a_i-1}$, which diminishes in X_i when $(a_i - 1)$ is negative.

A quick inspection of a Cobb-Douglas production function thus determines which marginal products are diminishing. Notice that some may diminish and others might not. Notice also that the Cobb-Douglas form implies that these relationships are constant throughout the function.

For Nerlove's basic model of the electric power industry

$$\text{output} = a_0(\text{labor})^{0.78}(\text{capital})^{0.00}(\text{fuel})^{0.61}$$

all marginal products are diminishing. This is also true for the higher level of production. But for the lowest level of production, this is not so (see Section 2.3). This model represents a typical result.

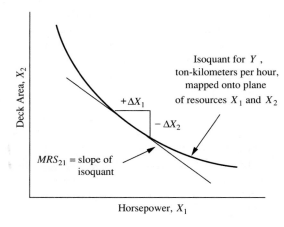

FIGURE 2.5
The marginal rate of
substitution is the slope of the
isoquant in two dimensions.

so that the marginal rate of substitution of X_i for X_j is

$$MRS_{ij} = \frac{\Delta X_i}{\Delta X_j} = -\left(\frac{MP_j}{MP_i}\right)$$

Two points are to be noted here: first, the marginal rate of substitution is the
inverse ratio of the marginal products; second, the slope is negative as suggested
by Figure 2.5 (see box). The marginal rate of substitution is useful in defining
optimum combinations of resources, that is optimum designs (see Section 4.4).

Returns to scale. The returns to scale describe how fast output changes relative
to the size of the production process. Formally they are defined as the ratio of the
rate of change in output due to a proportional change in all inputs simultaneously,

---

Marginal Rates of Substitution for a Cobb-Douglas Production Function

For the model

$$Y = a_0 \prod_i X_i^{a_i}$$

the marginal rate of substitution is

$$MRS_{ij} = -\left(\frac{MP_j}{MP_i}\right) = -\left(\frac{a_j}{a_i}\right)\left(\frac{X_i}{X_j}\right)$$

The model implies that this ratio is constant for any given ratio of X_i and X_j in
the design. This may not actually be the case. In Nerlove's model for electric
power, the marginal rates of substitution were different at low and high levels of
production.

---

and of that proportional change. The mathematical expression thus refers to an initial level of production, $Y' = g(\mathbf{X})$, a constant indicating the increase in scale or use of all inputs, s, and a consequent second level of production, $Y'' = g(s\mathbf{X})$. The returns to scale of the production function are thus

$$RTS = \left(\frac{Y''/Y'}{s}\right) = \frac{\{g(s\mathbf{X})/g(\mathbf{X})\}}{s}$$

Both returns to scale and marginal products refer to rates of change in the production function. But their concepts differ substantially. Most importantly, returns to scale characterize the variation in the production function along rays drawn through the origins of the inputs, rather than in specified directions parallel to the axes of the inputs. Figure 2.6 depicts this distinction (see box). Marginal products also are explicitly expressed in units of product, whereas returns to scale refer to a nondimensional rate.

In practice, the relevant question about the returns to scale is whether they are greater, equal to, or less than one. That is, whether the returns to scale are increasing, constant, or decreasing. The answer has important implications for the strategy to be followed in creating large systems.

The most interesting situation is that of increasing returns to scale, $RTS > 1.0$. This means that bigger production processes, bigger plants specifically, are inherently more productive than smaller ones. For a production function with increasing returns to scale, doubling all inputs would, for example, more than double the output. More would thus be produced by using available resources in one larger plant than in two smaller ones half the size. Increasing returns to scale thus indicate that, purely from the point of view of the production technology, it is advantageous to consolidate production in large plants rather than disperse it in a few small ones.

These implications of increasing returns to scale for design strategy generally hold when the economic factors are incorporated into the analysis. They may not, however, for either of two significant reasons. Firstly, the costs of the inputs

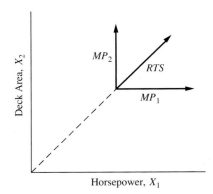

FIGURE 2.6
Directions in which the rate of change in output is measured for marginal products and returns to scale.

Returns to Scale for a Cobb-Douglas Production Function

For the model

$$Y' = a_0 \prod_i X_i^{a_i}$$

a scale increase by a factor of s of each input X_i increases the product to

$$Y'' = s(\exp \sum a_i)Y'$$

[Note $s(\exp)$ should be read as "s to the power of."] The returns to scale are

$$RTS = \frac{s(\exp \sum a_i)}{s}$$

For the Cobb-Douglas production function, the returns to scale are thus increasing if $\sum a_i > 1.0$, constant if $\sum a_i = 1.0$, and decreasing if $\sum a_i < 1.0$. In the electric power industry analyzed by Nerlove, the returns to scale were increasing.

The Cobb-Douglas model implies that returns to scale are the same throughout the process. This may not be so; Nerlove found that $\sum a_i = 2.92$ for lower levels of production and 1.69 for the higher levels.

---

may also increase with scale, thereby counterbalancing the physical advantages of the increasing returns to scale. Secondly, the concept of returns to scale is not properly defined for multiple output processes, since the "product" is not unique. Attempts to apply the concept of returns to scale to such situations can thus give misleading results. Section 4.5 describes these problems in detail.

Increasing returns to scale are systematically inherent in a broad range of technologies. Many of these have the common characteristics that their products are a function of volume whereas the inputs vary with surface. One example is shipping, in which the amount carried is a volume and the effort required is principally a function of the wetted surface of the ship; hence the motivation for supertankers and other very large ships. Other examples are pipelines, the production of electricity using boilers, and especially the chemical industries whose plants are typically combinations of pipes and containers.

Constant returns to scale are typically associated with processes in which higher levels of output are achieved by replicating some basic unit of production, rather than by increasing the size of this unit. The trucking industry thus normally shows constant returns to scale: the size of its vehicles is limited by both traffic regulations and the designs of roads and bridges, so that to move more one generally has to use more vehicles rather than to increase their size.

Decreasing returns to scale are also possible, although apparently rare in practice. They can exist when the production is so large that it is difficult to coordinate and control. Such might be the case of a large, nationwide industry.

To the extent that the causes of the decreasing returns to scale are administrative and organizational, however, they may be solved. This might be done by breaking up the large production process into many smaller units, each with no less than constant returns to scale. If it were possible to operate with these smaller units, then the overall production function would have constant returns to scale, and the single large unit of production would simply be technically inefficient (that is, at some interior point of the feasible region of production—as point A in Figure 2.1).

Convexity of the feasible region. The overall shape of the production possibilities is of interest to the analyst because it indicates which methods can be used to optimize the system, and whether this process will be difficult or not. Specifically, for example, this shape crucially determines whether we can optimize a system using linear programming (Chapter 5) or dynamic programming (Chapter 7). The essential issue with regard to the shape is whether the feasible region is convex.

A *convex feasible region* is one that has no reentrant boundaries, no edges that intrude into or dent the space. Figure 2.7 illustrates the situation. It is to be stressed that the convexity of the feasible region does not simply depend on the shape of its boundary. Indeed, the same boundary can be associated with both convex and nonconvex feasible regions. Figure 2.8 illustrates this case, with feasible regions for production (left) and for cost (right). The feasible region for costs is above the boundary, since it is always possible to pay more. Cost functions are discussed in detail in Section 4.4.

Formally, a feasible region is convex if every straight line between any two points in the region lies entirely in the region. Mathematically, if **A** and **B** are vectors to two points A and B on the function that bounds the region, the vector **T**:

$$\mathbf{T} = w\mathbf{A} + (1 - w)\mathbf{B} \qquad 0 \le w \le 1$$

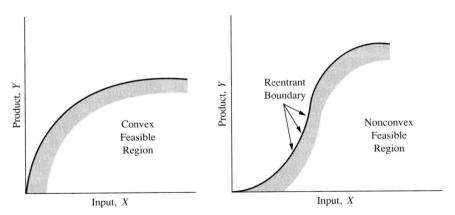

FIGURE 2.7
Convex and nonconvex feasible regions for production functions.

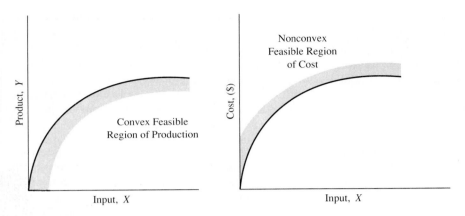

FIGURE 2.8
Convexity of the feasible region depends on the shape of the space.

represents every point on straight line between A and B, and all **T** must describe points inside the region for it to be convex. This property defines a test to distinguish between convex and nonconvex regions. Figure 2.9 indicates the situation.

Convexity of a feasible region is highly desirable because it facilitates optimization. This property guarantees that the function being optimized will be unimodal, that there will be only one optimum set, either a point or a surface. Where there is convexity, the optimization process does not have to be concerned about local optima that could be suboptimal globally: the optimum found will be the global optimum. This result leads to great efficiency in computation: it

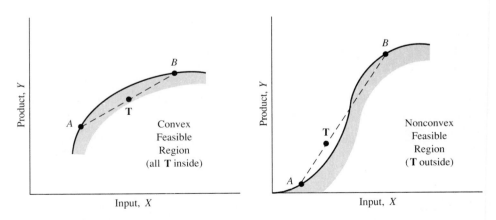

FIGURE 2.9
The test for convexity of the feasible region is that all T be part of the region.

Compatibility of Diminishing Marginal Products and Increasing Returns to Scale

Consider Nerlove's basic model of the electric power industry

$$\text{output} = a_0(\text{labor})^{0.78}(\text{capital})^{0.00}(\text{fuel})^{0.61}$$

All marginal products are diminishing, $a_i < 1.0$. However, the returns to scale are increasing, $\sum a_i = 1.39 > 1.0$.

This result leads to great efficiency in computation: it means that the optimization does not have to search the entire feasible region to obtain the optimum, it can simply start anywhere and follow any single path of gradual improvements, which necessarily lead to the optimum (see Chapter 4).

Production functions bound convex feasible regions if both the marginal products and the returns to scale are monotonically decreasing or constant with increasing inputs. The role of returns to scale is to be emphasized, as beginners frequently assume that decreasing marginal products imply that the production function flattens out in all directions, as a dome does. This is not correct. It is possible to have both decreasing marginal products and increasing returns to scale (see box). The production function associated with this situation is saddle-shaped, and the feasible region is not convex.

2.5 MULTIPLE OUTPUTS

It is often necessary to deal with the fact that a production process results in not just a single but multiple outputs. The difficulty in this regard is that the tools for dealing with such situations are not well developed. This section thus merely presents some of the issues, laying the basis for further discussion of analytic methods in later chapters.

Examples of multiple output processes abound. For example: refining crude petroleum leads to gasoline, fuel oil, and tars; metallurgical processing of zinc also produces cadmium, a close chemical relative; et cetera. Sometimes the several products are fairly subtle. The transportation of passengers by some scheduled service, say an airline, produces the trips or the movement of people, and a frequency or convenience of the service. In general then, the output of a production process is a vector of products:

$$\mathbf{Y} = (Y_1, \ldots, Y_j, \ldots, Y_m)$$

The description of a multiple output process is complicated by the fact that it is often difficult to distinguish between inputs and outputs. Consider the development of an airport in a region. One of the consequences of the operation of this facility, in addition to the air transport, is noise. As a result of the process, noise is in some sense a product. On the other hand it could equally be argued that one of the inputs to the production of air transport is a loss of quiet. Because of these kinds of ambiguities analysts now tend to avoid the explicit distinction between inputs and outputs.

The general mathematical form of a production function for a process with multiple outputs is thus

$$g(\mathbf{Y}, \ \mathbf{X}) = 0$$

This formulation simply describes the relationships between characteristics of the process, and avoids the need to apply the label of input or output to any of the factors involved.

A great difficulty in working with a multiple output production function is that the classical concepts used to describe production functions are unavailable. Indeed, since there is no single product, since in fact it may not be quite clear what is a product, the concept of marginal product does not apply. Likewise, it is difficult to define returns to scale since the multiple outputs may not all change at the same rate as the scale of inputs varies.

In practice, the standard way of analyzing production processes with multiple outputs has been to focus on a single major product, and to treat the other consequences as by-products of secondary importance. More recently, a variety of multiobjective methods of analysis have become available, and these are discussed in Chapter 8. Neither of these approaches is fully satisfactory so far, and much research is being done on the topic.

2.6 APPLICATIONS

To optimize the design of river transportation, engineers at the Massachusetts Institute of Technology developed a production function for the system of towboats and barges. This case indicates how such functions can be derived, and illustrates the concepts of marginal products and returns to scale. The use of this production function for optimization is shown as an application in Section 4.6.

Inland water transportation, on both rivers and lakes, is used worldwide. It is often the most heavily traveled form of communication in developing regions where roads are sparse or nonexistent. It is thus frequently critical to define the right system for its particular context.

A system of inland water transportation typically consists of towboats and flat-bottomed barges. Barges can be self-propelled but this design is inefficient since it keeps the expensive propulsive unit idle when the barge is being loaded and unloaded; it is only really justified when the cargo must cross extensive open water and each barge requires power for safety.

The physics of combinations of barges and towboats have been extensively documented by analysis and experiments in tow-tanks. These studies have led to empirical equations from which it is possible to predict the performance of any system in a specific stream—as defined by its width, depth, and current. The purely technical aspects of the system can be considered well-known. But these do not themselves provide any useful guidance on how to select the best power plant for a raft of barges, let alone the best combination of both for a given situation. To get this guidance, one can build on the technical details to construct the production function.

The essence of the technical equations is that the effective push of the towboats equals the resistance of the flotilla as it moves through the water. The empirical equations describing these terms are very messy to write (see Hoffmeister and de Neufville, 1973 for details) but can be solved quickly by computer for any combination of the design parameters.

The two key design parameters for the system are the size of the barges, as represented by the deck area, and the horsepower of the towboats. These can be considered the two inputs to the system. The output is then the weight of cargo involved in any period, expressed in ton-kilometers/hour for example. The production function is then the locus of optimal outputs for each combination of horsepower and deck area.

As the production function consists of an infinite number of points, it is difficult to deal with in detail. Designers need to define overall views of the production function as expressed by the marginal products and returns to scale. When each point on the production function is generated individually by a computer program from given inputs, these views are easy to generate.

The marginal products are simply defined by varying one parameter when the others are held constant. For our case, for example, Figure 2.10 gives the output for a given deck area and varying horsepower; this is, in effect, a

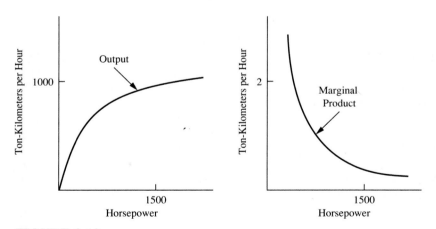

FIGURE 2.10
Total output of River Transport (left) and marginal product (right) for horsepower for a specified level of the other design parameters (Deck Area = 200 m^2), and specified water conditions (stream width = 30 m, stream depth = 6 m, current = 0).

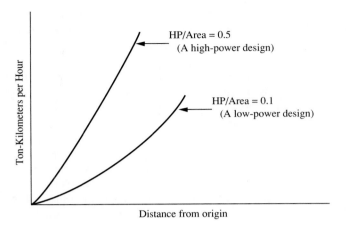

FIGURE 2.11
Increasing returns to scale for River Transport for designs with different Horsepower/Deck Area ratios, for specified water conditions (stream width = 18 m; stream depth = 2.4 m; current = 0).

"vertical slice" through the production function viewed as a "dome" of output rising from different combinations of inputs. From this curve the marginal product is derived by either calculating the slope or taking the derivative. In this case they are uniformly decreasing, as should be expected.

The returns to scale can be explored simply by plotting the change in output obtained by scaling up uniformly all parameters of a particular design. If these plots bend upward, as they do in Figure 2.11, then larger designs give greater output per unit input and there are economies of scale. The results here are again in the expected direction of economies of scale for ships, but are limited because the constraints of the river limit the benefits of larger size of the flotilla of barges. (Experienced mariners will note that uniformly scaling up all aspects of a design is not the best way to proceed in a real situation—the application in Section 4.6 makes this point in detail).

From the nature of marginal products and returns to scale the analyst can determine whether the feasible region of the production functions is convex or not. In this case it is nonconvex because of the increasing returns to scales. This fact limits the kinds of optimization techniques that can be used on the production function (specifically, linear programming of Chapter 5 is excluded).

REFERENCES

Cootner, P., and Lof, G., (1965). *Water Demand for Steam Electric Generation*, Johns Hopkins, Baltimore, MD. Also Chapter 7 in de Neufville and Marks (1974).

de Neufville, R., and Marks, D. H., (1974). *Systems Planning and Design: Case Studies in Modeling, Optimization and Evaluation*, Prentice-Hall, Englewood Cliffs, NJ.

Hoffmeister, J., and de Neufville, R., (1973, 1974). Chapter 6 in de Neufville and Marks (1974), also "Optimizing the Supply of Inland Water Transport," *ASCE Water Resources Journal*, 99, August 1973, p. 293–308.

Nerlove, M., (1965). *Estimation and Identification of Cobb-Douglas Production Functions*, Rand McNally, Chicago, IL. Also Chapter 9 in de Neufville and Marks (1974).

Pindyck, R. S., and Rubinfeld, D. L., (1989). "Production," Ch. 6, and "The Cost of Production," Ch. 7, in *Microeconomics*, Macmillan, New York.

Sage, A. P., (1983). "Production and the Theory of the Firm," Ch. 2, *Economic Systems Analysis*, North Holland, New York.

PROBLEMS

2.1. *Feasible Regions*

State what types of returns to scale and marginal products each of the following functions exhibit: (assume $X, Y \geq 0$)

(a)	$23X^{0.3}Y^{0.4}$	(b)	$12X^{1.6}Y^{0.5}$
(c)	$2X^{0.4}Y^{0.8}$	(d)	$5X + 3XY - 4Y - 2Y^2$
(e)	$X + 2Y^4 - Y^2Z^3/3$	(f)	$7X^{0.3}Y^{0.5}$
(g)	$16X^{1.1}Y^{0.5}$	(h)	$X - 4Y^2 + 2XY$
(i)	$10X^{0.1}Y^{0.3}$	(j)	$5X^{0.3}Y^{0.4}Z^{0.4}$
(k)	$1.1X^{1.3}Y^{0.3}$	(l)	$2Xe^Y$
(m)	$X + Y^2 + 1$	(n)	$4X + Y$

Which of the above functions define convex feasible regions over their entire range?

What can you conclude in your own words about the relationship between returns to scale and marginal products?

2.2. *Thought Problems*

(a) A chemical plant uses heat to convert raw materials (A and B) into a product. The reaction must take place at a certain high pressure, which is maintained by a spherical reaction chamber. What sorts of marginal products would you expect for each of the four resources (A, B, heat, and chamber size)? Note that for a sphere,

$$\text{volume} = (4/3)r^3, \qquad \text{surface area} = 4r^2$$

and (since pressure is independent of chamber size) the thickness of the chamber wall is also independent of size. What can you say about returns to scale in this process?

(b) Two major inputs in Midwestern Plains farming are land and labor. What would you expect about the marginal returns on the inputs? (For example, Soviet farms frequently employ an order of magnitude more people per acre than would a typical Minnesota farmer. How would the marginal benefit of employing one more person on the Soviet farm compare to that of one more person on the Minnesota farm?) Looking at historical trends, what are the returns to scale like in Plains farming? Would you expect the same results in an area characterized by fertile valleys and rocky hillsides? Why?

(c) Transoceanic shipping companies can obtain ships of differing weights and horsepower to achieve an output of tons-mi/yr carried. From what you know about trends in ship size over the last 20 years (tankers are one well-publicized example), would you expect that there are economies of scale, diseconomies of scale, or constant returns to scale? How would you expect productivity to change as ship weight is increased for a given horsepower engine? As horsepower is increased, for a given ship weight? What does this imply about the marginal returns for weight and horsepower?

(d) In American trucking, all operators have essentially the same kind of trucks, with size and axle load limited by regulation. Employees tend to receive the same wages, depending on whether they are in unions or not. What sort of returns to scale would you expect in the size of trucking firms? Why? What sort of marginal returns would you expect for the number of employees and the number of trucks used by the company?

(e) An advertising campaign is being organized for a new product. TV minutes and magazine inches will be purchased and the advertiser wants as many people as possible exposed to the product's name. What marginal returns and returns to scale would you expect?

2.3. *Translations*
For each part, describe the production function in equation form and draw it, indicating key points.

(a) A trade journal shows that the watermelon output per acre is roughly the square root of the number of seeds planted, for outputs between 50 and 300 watermelons per acre. The cost of seeds is $2/1000 seeds for the first 10,000 seeds and $1.50/1000 seeds after that. Watermelons sell for about $5 each.

(b) For small buildings, construction of a housing unit (Y) requires the use as primary materials of either 5 tons of cement for a concrete house, or of 3 tons of structural steel for a metal frame house. When, however, more than 10 units are built together, the construction code requires additional facilities, such as parking lots. The output per unit material is then reduced by one-third. The unit prices of cement and steel in place are $1000 and $2000, respectively. The value of a housing unit is $40,000.

2.4. *Production Function I*
(a) Describe the marginal products, marginal rates of substitution, and the returns to scale for the production function:

$$Z = 10X^{0.1}Y^{0.3}$$

(b) Is the feasible region convex? Explain.

2.5. *Production Function II*
Same as 2.4 (a), for: $Z = 10X^{0.2}Y^{0.4}$

2.6. *Production Function III*
As 2.4 (a), for: $Z = 2 \log_e X + 4 \log_e Y$

2.7. *Production Function IV*
As 2.4 (a), for: $Z = 0.3X^{0.8}Y^{0.6}$

2.8. *Vi-Tall Cereal*
Tab Booleigh, chief cook at Health Foods Inc., makes Vi-Tall Cereal from rye and bran. Her recipe is as follows: 1 lb of Vi-Tall requires either 1 1/2 lbs of rye

or 1 lb of bran. For batches of 10 lbs or more, spoilage reduces the output per unit of grain by 1/3. The prices per pound of rye and bran are $2 and $4 respectively. A pound of Vi-Tall sells for $7.50.

(*a*) Does the production function define a convex, feasible region?
(*b*) Plot the isoquants for 4 and 12 lbs.
(*c*) What is the *MRS* of rye for bran?
(*d*) What are the *MP*s with respect to rye and bran?

2.9. *Plywood Factory*

Charles B. Ord, known to his friends as Chip, makes plywood from hard and soft wood using either of three processes with the following characteristics:

Process	Hard	Soft	Ply
	Board Feet of Wood		
1	1000	500	1333
2	1000	1850	2500
3	1000	3200	4000

ASSUME PROCESS 3

(*a*) What is the *MP* for soft wood when Chip has 1000 bd. ft of hard and 3200 of soft wood?
(*b*) How much hard and soft wood would Chip use if the factory manager assigned 500 bd.ft of hard wood each to Process 1 and Process 2?   *½ of softwood*
(*c*) Establish and draw the isoquant for 10,000 bd. ft of plywood.   *combi. of*
(*d*) What is the *MRS* between hard and soft wood at (1000, 1850)?   *hard & soft to get 10,000*

2.10. *Timothy Burr*

Tim operates a logging mill that chews up pine and balsam. Having analyzed its records, Tim finds that the marginal product of pine is inversely proportional to the square root, and that the marginal product of balsam varies with the inverse 1/4 power. What is the marginal rate of substitution? What can you say about the returns to scale of the operation?

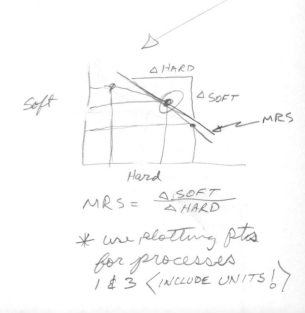

$$MRS = \frac{\Delta SOFT}{\Delta HARD}$$

* we plotting pts for processes 1 & 3 (INCLUDE UNITS!)

CHAPTER
3

INTRODUCTION TO CONSTRAINED OPTIMIZATION

3.1 THE PROBLEM

In practice, systems engineers always have to make their designs conform to a variety of constraints. They generally have to work within a budget. They will have to satisfy engineering standards designed to ensure the quality, the performance, and the safety of the system. They will also have to meet legal restrictions the community has imposed to achieve its health and other objectives. The design of the primary water supply system for New York City, for example, had to provide water at a minimum pressure of 40 psi (pounds per square inch) as measured at the curb, with less than a legal maximum for parts per million of various chemicals.

Constraints generally express some objectives for the system which could not be dealt with analytically in an obvious way. Setting constraints on a system is an alternative to the difficult problem of dealing explicitly with the multiple outputs of a system, which has been very difficult to do (see Section 2.5). Thus New York City's standard of 40 psi at the curb represents an effort to ensure that the water pressure will be adequate for all residents of the city.

The analysis will often demonstrate that many of these restrictions do not make much sense in detail. They may easily cost far more to meet than is worth spending on the objective they represent. New York's standard of 40 psi for water pressure thus entailed enormous extra costs for the construction of its huge underground aqueducts. Tens of millions of dollars could have been saved in the design if even slightly lower pressures had been permitted in a few areas. While agreeing with the principle behind the restrictions, in this case the idea that water pressure should be "adequate," there is generally much scope for improvements at the level of detail (perhaps 38 psi would have been a better standard than 40 psi).

The reason that many restrictions on design do not make sense in detail is that they were never established on the basis of an analysis of the system. New York's standard of 40 psi was certainly not based on a demonstration that it was the optimum level, or that it was functionally preferable to 39 or 41 psi; it was almost certainly agreed to because it was somewhere in the right region and because it was a nice round number.

Part of the systems engineer's job in the future should be to help define the appropriate levels of restrictions or, even better, to optimize the multiple output production process directly (see Chapter 8). Meanwhile, however, the designer often will simply have to meet the restrictions.

The difficulty in meeting restrictions on the design is that they complicate the optimization process. To see this consider some function of many variables:

$$g(\mathbf{X}) = g(X_1, \dots, X_i, \dots, X_n)$$

which we assume to be continous and analytic in that it has first and second derivatives. If this function is unconstrained, the necessary conditions for its optimum (a maximum or a minimum) is that all the first derivatives with respect to its arguments equal zero:

$$\frac{\partial g}{\partial X_i} = 0 \quad \text{all } i$$

On the other hand, if the function is constrained, these conditions for optimality may or may not apply. The optimum may then be at the intersections of the function with the constraint. Figure 3.1 makes the point. In a large scale system with hundreds of variables and constraints, the optimum could be located at an infinity of points.

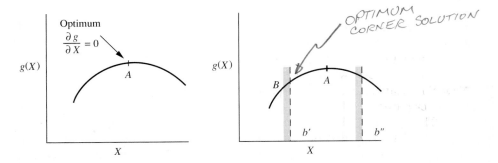

FIGURE 3.1
In unconstrained situation (left) the maximum is at A; with constraints (right) it is either at B, if $X \le b'$, or at A again if $X \le b''$.

The problem is then to find ways to define optimality conditions which can pinpoint the optimum when there are constraints. For analytic functions there are two principal means of doing this, Lagrangeans and the Kuhn-Tucker conditions. These are explained in detail in Sections 3.3 and 3.4.

3.2   OBJECTIVE

The purpose of this chapter is to provide insight into the nature of the optimal design of constrained systems. It develops two key concepts that are essential in the practical application of optimization, particularly in sensitivity analysis (Chapter 6). These concepts are those of shadow prices and complementary slackness, defined in Sections 3.3 and 3.4 respectively.

These key ideas are developed by an incremental process. The presentation builds on the common understanding of unconstrained optimization in two steps of increasing complexity. The first, that of equality constraints solved by Lagrangeans, brings out the concept of shadow prices. The second, involving inequality constraints and the Kuhn-Tucker conditions, introduces complementary slackness.

This process focuses on the necessary conditions for optimality, as these are the ones that bring out the key issues. It avoids the second-order sufficiency conditions for optimality. These are both complex and beside the point since systems analysis essentially never uses these conditions in practical situations.

3.3   LAGRANGEANS

Lagrangeans constitute the easiest solution to optimization subject to constraints. Historically they are also the first. They may be considered an intermediate step to the general optimality conditions published by Kuhn and Tucker in 1951.

Lagrangeans solve the problem of optimizing a function subject to *equality constraints*, ones that must be met exactly. These routinely occur in practice. A standard example is the requirement to use one's budget entirely—otherwise it might be cut in the following period. Formally, the Lagrangean addresses the problem of optimizing $g(\mathbf{X})$ subject to a series of constraints $h_j(\mathbf{X}) = b_j$. Putting the matter into the standard vocabulary used with optimization, we call the function to be optimized the *objective function*. We then write the problem as

Optimize: $g(\mathbf{X})$

Subject to: $h_j(\mathbf{X}) = b_j$ and $\mathbf{X} \geq 0$

The condition that all $\mathbf{X}$ be positive is a standard assumption that in no way limits practical applications: variables can always be redefined to meet this requirement. The purpose of this condition is to simplify the second order, the sufficiency conditions of optimality. In linear programming, discussed in Chapter 5, this sign convention is also exploited to facilitate the optimization procedure.

The problem is solved by constructing a new function to be optimized. This is called the *Lagrangean* and is

$$L = g(\mathbf{X}) - \sum \lambda_j[h_j(\mathbf{X}) - b_j]$$

Each parameter λ_j is a constant associated with a particular constraint equation, and is to be solved for. These parameters are known as the *Lagrangean multipliers*.

The marvelous aspect of the Lagrangean is that it simultaneously permits us to optimize $g(\mathbf{X})$ and to satisfy the constraints $h_j(\mathbf{X}) = b_j$. All we do is to apply the conventional process for unconstrained functions to the Lagrangean. The difference is that whereas in considering $g(\mathbf{X})$ we had i variables, one for each X_i, we now have $(i + j)$ variables, including one for each of the λ_j multipliers associated with the j constraints.

Applying the standard method of optimization to the Lagrangean we set all first derivatives equal to zero and obtain:

$$\frac{\partial L}{\partial X_i} = \frac{\partial g}{\partial X_i} - \frac{\sum_j \lambda_j \partial h}{\partial X_i} = 0$$

$$\frac{\partial L}{\partial \lambda_j} = h_j(\mathbf{X}) - b_j = 0$$

The $(i + j)$ set of X_i and λ_j that satisfy these $(i + j)$ equations will determine the optimum. This solution will be designated (X^*, λ^*) where the *superscript* * indicates optimality.

Notice that the optimal solution to the Lagrangean clearly satisfies the constraints placed on the original problem; they are identical to the $\partial L/\partial \lambda_j$ equations that help define the optimal solution. Likewise, this solution also maximizes $g(\mathbf{X})$ since, at optimality where the constraints are met, the second term in the Lagrangean equals zero and optimizing L is then equivalent to optimizing $g(\mathbf{X})$ (see box on following page).

The Lagrangean multiplier has a most important interpretation. It gives the systems designer valuable information about the sensitivity of the results to changes in the problems. At the optimum, the Lagrangean multiplier λ_j equals the rate of change of the optimum objective function $g^*(\mathbf{X})$ as the constraint $b_j = h_j(\mathbf{X})$ varies. To see this, take the partial derivative of the Lagrangean with respect to this constraint and obtain

$$\frac{\partial L}{\partial b_j} = \lambda_j \quad \text{all } j$$

Now since the constraints are identically equal to zero at the optimum,

$$g^*(\mathbf{X}) = L \quad \text{and} \quad \frac{\partial g^*}{\partial b_j} = \frac{\partial L}{\partial b_j} = \lambda_j \quad \text{all } j$$

In the vocabulary of economics and systems analysis, the Lagrangean multiplier is known as the *shadow price* of the constraint. This neatly describes the parameter: it is the implicit price to be paid, in terms of changes of $g(\mathbf{X})$, per unit change of the constraint b_j. Being a derivative, the value of the shadow price

Example Use of Lagrangeans

Consider the problem:

Maximize: $g(\mathbf{X}) = 3X_1X_2^2$ *OBJECTIVE FUNCTION*

Subject to: $h(\mathbf{X}) = X_1 + X_2 = 3$ and $X_1, X_2 > 0$ *PRODUCTION CONSTRAINT FUNCTION*

The Lagrangean is

$$L = 3X_1X_2^2 - \lambda(X_1 + X_2 - 3)$$

There is only one λ because there is only one constraint.

There are $(i + j) = 3$ equations defining the optimal solution. These are

$$\frac{\partial L}{\partial X_1} = 3X_2^2 - \lambda \quad = 0$$

$$\frac{\partial L}{\partial X_2} = 6X_1X_2 - \lambda \quad = 0$$

$$\frac{\partial L}{\partial \lambda} = X_1 + X_2 - 3 = 0$$

The first two equations imply that $X_2^* = 2X_1^*$. The third then leads to

$$\mathbf{X}^* = (1, 2) \quad \text{and} \quad \lambda^* = 12$$

The optimum is

$$g^*(\mathbf{X}) = 12$$

---

in general varies with the value of the constraint; the values calculated are thus instantaneous, at the margin, for any given value of the constraint.

> **Semantic caution:** Although the Lagrangean multiplier is called the shadow *price*, it has no necessary connection with money. Its units are always in terms of those of the function to be maximized, $g(\mathbf{X})$, divided by those of the relevant constraint. Thus for the design of New York City's water supply system: when the objective was to maximize the capacity to deliver water subject to constraints on the pressure, the shadow price of the pressure standard was in terms of gallons per psi. The shadow price is expressed in terms of money only when $g(\mathbf{X})$ is some monetary amount such as dollars of benefit from a system.

The shadow price on a constraint is the quantitative indication of whether it is worthwhile to alter this requirement. It is the information that allows the designer to judge to what extent each of the constraints on a system make sense in detail. For New York City's water supply system, for example, the shadow price on the requirement that water be delivered throughout the city at a minimum pressure of 40 psi at the curb was extremely high; unless the community for some reason thought this was an absolutely vital threshold, it would be reasonable to lower this standard for the areas of highest elevation so that the resulting improvements to the overall system could be shared by the whole community.

This issue of sensitivity of the optimum to changes in the definition of the problem is one of the central topics of all practical applications of systems analysis (see Section 3.1). Chapter 6 is devoted to this topic, and Sections 6.2 and 6.3 particularly focus on shadow prices.

3.4 KUHN-TUCKER CONDITIONS

The most usual situation in practice is that we have to deal with *inequality constraints*. Our plans must perform at least as well as some standards, but can also perform better if that is convenient. Thus New York City's standard for water pressure of 40 psi at the curb does not mean that pressure everywhere must equal 40 psi at the curb; it simply means that it can not be less and therefore that it may in many places actually be more than 40 psi.

The existence of inequality constraints significantly increases the number of solutions that we have to consider. They are not restricted to lie on a line or function, but may be anywhere inside the space defined by the restrictions. Figure 3.2 illustrates this point.

A formal statement of the optimization problem with inequality constraints is

Optimize: $g(\mathbf{X})$

Subject to: $h_j(\mathbf{X}) \leq b_j \qquad \mathbf{X} \geq 0$

The inequality constraints are written as "less than or equal" because this form

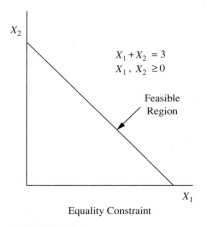
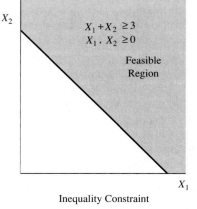

FIGURE 3.2
The feasible region defined by an inequality constraint is larger than that defined by an equality constraint.

leads to a simple statement of the Kuhn-Tucker conditions, adequate to the purpose of this chapter.

The real inequalities can always be generalized to this form. In practice, constraints are often "more than or equal" to some quantity. New York City's water pressure standard is that way:

$$\text{pressure} \geq 40 \text{ psi}$$

This can also be written as

$$- \text{pressure} \leq - 40 \text{ psi}$$

Formally, a constraint that requires an expression to be "less than or equal" to some amount is an *upper bound* in that it prescribes a maximum. Conversely, a "greater than or equal" constraint is a *lower bound*.

The strategy for solving the problem with inequality constraints is simple: we transform it into a problem we know how to solve. This is exactly the same path that Lagrange took in developing the Lagrangean; by means of some additional variables he changed the constrained problem to one that looked like an unconstrained problem.

The key to the solution for the problem with inequality constraints lies in changing these inequalities to equalities. This is done by introducing new variables, S_j, defined as the amount required to make up the difference between the constraint and the value of $h_j(\mathbf{X})$. They are thus called *slack variables*. The inequalities can then be written as equalities:

$$h_j(\mathbf{X}) + S_j^2 = b_j$$

where the slack variable is introduced as a squared term to ensure that it is a positive quantity.

The solution then consists of solving a Lagrangean to the revised problem:

Optimize: $g(\mathbf{X})$

Subject to: $h_j(\mathbf{X}) + S_j^2 = b_j$ $\mathbf{X} \geq 0$

This function is called the *generalized Lagrangean* and is

$$L = g(\mathbf{X}) - \sum \lambda_j(h_j(\mathbf{X}) + S_j^2 - b_j)$$

This equation involves $(i + 2j)$ unknowns with the addition of the j slack variables. The optimization proceeds as with standard Lagrangeans except that we now have j additional equations relating the Lagrangean and the slack variables. The new equations introduced in the generalized Lagrangean are

$$\frac{\partial L}{\partial S_j} = 2\lambda_j S_j = 0 \quad \text{all } j$$

They imply in general that either $\lambda_j = 0$ or $S_j = 0$. For this reason they are known as the *complementary slackness* conditions.

These complementary slackness conditions have important consequences for analysis and design. Their interpretation is as follows:

- If the optimal solution $\mathbf{X}^*$ lies right on the constraint, $h_j(\mathbf{X}^*) = b_j$, then $S_j^* = 0$ and the shadow price $\lambda_j^* \neq 0$. In this case there is some value, in terms of better $g(\mathbf{X})$, to changing the constraint. Technically, we say this constraint is *binding*, and that the objective can be increased by changing this constraint.
- If the constraint is not binding, $h_j(\mathbf{X}^*) \leq b_j$, then $S_j^* \neq 0$ and $\lambda_j = 0$. That is, the nonbinding constraints do not affect the value of the objective $g(\mathbf{X})$.

These ideas are pursued in detail in Chapter 6, which discusses sensitivity analysis, and particularly in Section 6.2.

The *Kuhn-Tucker conditions* themselves are the entire set of equations associated with the generalized Lagrangean:

$$\frac{\partial L}{\partial X_i} = 0 \qquad \text{all} \ \ i$$

$$\frac{\partial L}{\partial \lambda_j} = 0 \qquad \text{all} \ \ j$$

$$\lambda_j S_j = 0 \qquad \text{all} \ \ j$$

Given the sign convention adopted with the original statement of the problem, we can also include nonnegativity conditions on the shadow prices:

$$\lambda_j \geq 0 \qquad \text{all} \ \ j$$

Since $\lambda_j = \partial g^*(\mathbf{X})/\partial b_j$, and since increasing b_j increases the feasible region and can thus only make $g(\mathbf{X})$ bigger, then λ_j must be positive. If we had a minimization problem or lower bound constraints, different restrictions on the shadow prices would exist. These are, in effect, part of the second-order conditions of optimality.

A more compact form of the Kuhn-Tucker conditions can be obtained by combining the complementary slackness and the constraint equations, $\lambda_j S_j = 0$ and $\partial L/\partial \lambda_j = 0$, into

$$\lambda_j [h_j(\mathbf{X}) - b_j] = 0$$

This is obviously true if $\lambda_j = 0$. It is also true if $\lambda_j \neq 0$ since then $S_j = 0$, and so $h_j(\mathbf{X}) = b_j$. This form obscures the meaning of the conditions; it is, however, the standard form the reader is likely to encounter elsewhere.

3.5 APPLICATIONS

Textbook. The following box provides a straightforward application of the Kuhn-Tucker conditions to a simple mathematical problem. Two points deserve particular attention. Notice first that the different combinations of ways of meeting the complementary slackness conditions must each be examined for feasibility, and then for optimality if feasible. Secondly, note that the restrictions on the shadow prices must be taken into account to determine which feasible solutions are optimal.

Example Use of Kuhn-Tucker Conditions

Consider the problem:

Maximize: $g(\mathbf{X}) = X_1 + 2X_2$

Subject to: $h_1(\mathbf{X}) = (X_1 - 1)^2 + (X_2 - 2)^2 \leq 5$
$h_2(\mathbf{X}) = X_1 \qquad\qquad\qquad \leq 4$

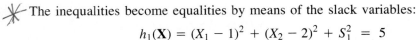 The inequalities become equalities by means of the slack variables:

$$h_1(\mathbf{X}) = (X_1 - 1)^2 + (X_2 - 2)^2 + S_1^2 = 5$$

$$h_2(\mathbf{X}) = X_1 + S_2^2 \qquad\qquad = 4$$

The corresponding Lagrangean is

$$L = (X_1 + 2X_2) - \lambda_1[(X_1 - 1)^2 + (X_2 - 2)^2 + S_1^2 - 5] - \lambda_2[X_1 + S_2^2 - 4]$$

The Kuhn-Tucker conditions are

$$\frac{\partial L}{\partial X_1} = 1 - \lambda_1(2)(X_1 - 1) - \lambda_2 = 0$$

$$\frac{\partial L}{\partial X_2} = 2 - \lambda_1(2)(X_2 - 2) \qquad = 0$$

$$h_1(\mathbf{X}) = 5$$

$$h_2(\mathbf{X}) = 4$$

$$\lambda_1 S_1 = \lambda_2 S_2 \qquad\qquad = 0$$

$$\lambda_1, \lambda_2 \geq 0$$

The complementary slackness conditions offer the possibility of various combinations of λ_j, S_j being equal to zero. These must be investigated. Thus:

- If $S_2 = 0$, then $X_1 = 4$ from $h_2(\mathbf{X})$. However, this is infeasible from $h_1(\mathbf{X})$. Therefore, $S_2 \neq 0$ and $\lambda_2 = 0$.
- Since $\partial L/\partial X_2 = 0$ and $\lambda_1 \neq 0$, therefore $S_1 = 0$.

The first two conditions can thus be solved as $\lambda_1 = \lambda_1$

$$\lambda_1 = \frac{1}{2(X_1 - 1)} = \frac{2}{2(X_2 - 2)}$$

Thus, $X_2 = 2X_1$.

Substituting the previous in $h_1(\mathbf{X})$, knowing that $S_1 = 0$, we obtain

$$(X_1 - 1)^2 + (2X_1 - 2)^2 = 5(X_1 - 1)^2 = 5$$

Thus, $X_1 = 0$ or 2.

These solutions lead to

$$\lambda_1 = -\frac{1}{2} \quad \text{or} \quad \frac{1}{4}$$

However, since $\lambda_j \geq 0$, the only feasible solution is

$$\lambda_1^* = \frac{1}{4} \qquad X_1^* = 2 \qquad X_2^* = 4 \qquad g(\mathbf{X})^* = 10$$

Note that if we used $\lambda_1 = -\frac{1}{2}$, we would obtain

$$X_1 = 0 \qquad X_2 = 0 \qquad g(\mathbf{X}) = 0$$

which is not optimal.

[handwritten annotations in right margin:]

MAXIMIZE
$= X_1 + 2X_2$
$= 2 + 2(4) = 10$
$X_1 \leq 4$
$X_1 + S_2^2 = 4$
$S_2^2 = 2$
$\lambda_2 = 0$

Real-world. The problem of determining what price to charge for the products of a system illustrates the use of the generalized Lagrangean and the Kuhn-Tucker conditions in a practical setting. This is a most important issue in systems design. Although pricing may appear to be an economic issue quite distinct from engineering, the fact is otherwise. The demand for the products of a system, and thus the load on a system, depends on their prices. As it is not possible to design a system without considering its load, a full systems design, correctly done, will consider the prices that will be charged for the products of the system being designed.

The specific problem to be considered concerns the pricing of air transportation in an uncongested, developing area. It is drawn from a large study done by de Neufville and Mira (1975) for the United States and Colombian governments.

The problem assumes that the system uses a number of aircraft flights F, to transport a number of people, P. The value $V(\cdot)$ of the system, to the society as a whole, is a positive function of both F and P: it is better to serve more people and to have the greater convenience of more flights and higher frequency. On the other hand the system has a cost, taken to be the number of flights times their average cost, c. The net value of the system, the objective function $g(\mathbf{X})$, is then:

$$g(\mathbf{X}) = V(F, P) - Fc$$

The constraint on the system is that the capacity of the aircraft, C, cannot be exceeded by the number of persons per flight:

$$\frac{P}{F} \leq C$$

The preceding two equations constitute the statement of the problem, where net value is to be maximized.

The generalized Lagrangean is

$$L = V(F, P) - Fc - \lambda\left(\frac{P}{F} + S^2 - C\right)$$

so that the Kuhn-Tucker conditions are

$$\frac{\partial L}{\partial F} = V_F - c + \frac{\lambda P}{F^2} = 0$$

$$\frac{\partial L}{\partial P} = V_P - \frac{\lambda}{F} = 0$$

$$\frac{\partial L}{\partial \lambda} = \frac{P}{F} + S^2 - C = 0$$

$$\frac{\partial L}{\partial S} = 2S\lambda = 0$$

where the subscripted variable indicates the partial derivative with respect to that variable.

The solution is obtained by substitution. First we can recognize that

$$\lambda = FV_P \neq 0$$

since neither the number of flights nor the incremental value per passenger equals zero. This then implies that $S = 0$ and $P/F = C$: it would be better for society overall if planes flew full and empty seats were not wasted. Substituting the value of the shadow price in the first equation leads to

$$V_F + CV_P = c$$

Economic theory indicates that the price, p, charged for a service should be its marginal value to people, $p = V_P$. Therefore, the analysis defines the optimum price to charge a person for a flight is

$$p^* = V_P = \frac{1}{C}\{c - V_F\}$$

The implications of the formal analysis are quite interesting. Firstly, we may see that when there is a positive value to greater frequency, $V_F > 0$, as there is in a developing area, the optimum price for a ticket is less than the average cost:

$$p^* = \frac{1}{C}\{c - V_F\} \leq \frac{c}{C}$$

A subsidy to the system is thus in order to ensure that, from the point of view of society, adequate transportation services tie the region together. The optimal amount of this subsidy per flight is the difference between the average cost and the amount paid per flight:

$$\text{optimal subsidy} = c - Cp^* = V_F$$

the value to society of the extra flight.

When there is sufficient frequency so that $V_F = 0$, then the optimal price for a ticket is its average cost. Finally, if the air traffic system is saturated so that extra flights cause delays, $V_F \leq 0$, then the optimal price is greater than its average cost: the optimal policy is to tax the system to dampen demand, lessen congestion, and improve the overall performance of the system.

REFERENCES

Baumol, W. J., (1977). *Economic Theory and Operations Analysis*, 4th ed., Prentice-Hall, Engle-wood Cliffs, NJ.

de Neufville, R., and Mira, L.-J., (1974). "Optimal Pricing for Air Transport Networks," *Transportation Research*, September, pp.1–11.

Winston, W.L., (1987). "Non-Linear Programming," Ch. 11, *Operations Research: Applications and Algorithms*, PWS Publishers, New York.

PROBLEMS

3.1. *Constrained Optimization I*
Given the problem:

Maximize: profit $= XY$ \$

Subject to: $X + 4Y \leq 12$ (units of resource) $X, Y \geq 0$

(a) Formulate the problem, state the optimality conditions, and solve for the optimal values of X, Y and profit.

(b) If you were offered another unit of resource for \$8, would you buy it? Why?

(c) What is the maximum you would pay for a unit of resource?

3.2. *Constrained Optimization II*
Given the problem:

Maximize: $Z = 2X + 3XY$

Subject to: $XY + X^2/9 = 13$ $X, Y \geq 0$

(a) Formulate the problem, state the optimality criteria and solve.

(b) What is the practical significance of the Lagrangean multiplier λ?

(c) How would the formulation change if the constraint were $XY + X^2/9 \leq 13$?

3.3. *Constrained Optimization III*
Formulate the problem, state the optimality criteria and solve:

(a) Maximize: $Z = XY$

Subject to: $X + Y^2 \leq 48$ $X, Y \geq 0$

(b) Maximize: $Z = XY$

Subject to: $X + Y^2 = 12$ $X, Y \geq 0$

(c) Maximize: $Z = X^2 + 3Y^2$

Subject to: $X + Y^2 \leq 10.5$ $X, Y \geq 0$

3.4. *Constrained Optimization IV*
Solve the following optimization problem by Lagrangean analysis, not graphically. Clearly indicate the value of all variables and the objective function at the optimum.

Maximize: $Z = 4ab^2$

Subject to: $3a + b \leq 10$ $a, b \geq 0$

3.5. *Road Work*
Assume that the number of highway miles that can be graded, H, is a function of both the hours of labor, L, and of machines, M:

$$H = 0.5L^{0.2}M^{0.8}$$

(a) Minimize the cost of grading 20 miles, given that the hourly rates for labor and machines are: $C_L = \$20$; $C_M = \$160$.

(b) Interpret the significance of the Lagrangean multiplier.

3.6. *Power Plant*
A cooperative operates an oil-fired power plant, selling electricity and steam to its members. The value of a unit of electricity, e, is a constant P_e per unit, which is its price from an alternative supplier. The value of steam, s, is a monotonically decreasing function $P_s(s)$. The cooperative wishes to maximize the net benefits of its members:

$$Z = P_e(e) + \int_0^s P_s(s)\,ds - P_q Q$$

where P_q and Q are the unit price and quantity of oil used in the plant.

The technical constraints on the operation are that the electricity and steam produced are less than their thermal efficiency times the quantity of oil used:

$$e \leq E_e Q \qquad s \leq E_s Q$$

and that maximum production of electricity and steam are incompatible:

$$\frac{e}{E_e} + \frac{s}{E_s} \leq 1.5Q$$

(a) Formulate the problem and state the Kuhn-Tucker conditions.

(b) By setting various combinations of the $\lambda_i = 0$, eight potential solutions are logically possible. Examine each to determine which are feasible, and explain their significance.

3.7. *Tim Burr, Jr.*
See Problem 2.10. Junior, happy with his father's identification of significant returns to scale, is all set to maximize production to take advantage of their benefits. Do so for him, with a budget B and input costs for pine and balsam proportional to the $\frac{5}{4}$ power of their quantity—since Tim can only get more lumber by acquiring it further away. Do his economics improve as he builds a larger plant?

3.8. *Heat Exchanger*
160 m of tubes must be installed in a heat exchanger to provide the necessary surface area. The cost of the installation is the sum of the cost of the tubes, the shell of the exchanger, and of the floor space it occupies:

$$\text{Cost} = 700 + 25\,D^{2.5}L + 12.5\,DL$$

where D and L are the diameter and the length of the cylindrical exchanger. No more than 20 tubes can fit into 1 m^2 of cross-section. Find the dimensions that minimize cost.

4

MARGINAL ANALYSIS

4.1 CONCEPT

Marginal Analysis is a basic form of optimization of design. It is a means of selecting the best choice from among many technically efficient ways to achieve a stated objective or product.

Marginal analysis combines two sorts of models, as all procedures for optimizing design must. One model represents the technical possibilities; the other represents the relative values of the several inputs of the production process. Specifically, marginal analysis combines the production function, which represents only the technically efficient production possibilities; and the *input cost function*, which describes the cost of the inputs used (see Section 4.2).

Marginal analysis is based on three specific assumptions. The first is that the feasible regions are convex for the portions of both models being considered. A key word in this statement is "portion." As Sections 4.2 and 4.3 explain, this qualification permits the application of marginal analysis even for processes that have increasing returns to scale, and for which the entire feasible region is not convex.

The second assumption of marginal analysis is that the only constraint on the system is the amount of money available, the budget. The resources themselves are presumed to be available indefinitely, provided there is enough money to buy them. This situation is quite common in practice, since the materials required for any one system are generally far less than the supply available. A company setting out to build a factory can thus presume that there will be as much steel and concrete available for purchase as it might require, and that it can thus optimize its design for the factory as if the supply were unconstrained.

Exceptions to this pattern are common, however. It may frequently happen that the quantity of some particular resource available is small compared to a large system. A computer manufacturer might have to recognize that his production was limited by the supply of advanced chips; a development program in bioengineering might similarly have to recognize that the number of qualified researchers was limited. A key effect of such constraints is indicated at the end of Section 4.3.

The third assumption of standard marginal analysis is that the models are analytic, that is, that they are continuously differentiable. This premise smooths the mathematics and justifies specific results. In several respects it is not a crucial assumption. The general results of marginal analysis can often still be applied even when this condition is not met. The applications in Section 4.6 illustrate this fact.

Marginal analysis is both a useful practical tool and a good basis for further analysis. Many of the ideas introduced by this method apply to more complicated situations.

4.2   OPTIMALITY CONDITIONS

Any particular objective or Product, Y', can in general be obtained in many ways. Moreover, there are also in general many technically efficient designs that will achieve that objective; these are all represented by the isoquant for Y'.

The optimal design for any Y' will be the one that provides the best value. It is the optimal configuration of inputs $\mathbf{X}^*$ that defines the point on the isoquant which delivers the product at the least cost. This cost can be defined either narrowly in terms of money alone, or more broadly in terms of social values such as environmental effects. For this discussion it does not matter which definition applies, the main result is the same. In practice, one should use the definition appropriate to the designer of the system.

Mathematically, the optimization of the design consists of minimizing the cost of the product $C(Y')$, subject to the possibilities defined by the production function $Y = g(\mathbf{X})$. The cost of the product is itself the cost of the inputs used. This is defined as the *input cost function*, $c(\mathbf{X})$. When it is assumed that there is no practical limit to the availability of any of the resources, the complete problem is

Minimize: $C(Y') = c(\mathbf{X})$

Subject to: $g(X) = Y'$

The optimization is solved by the Lagrangean:

$$L = c(\mathbf{X}) - \lambda\,[g(\mathbf{X}) - Y']$$

The key result is that, at the optimum,

$$\frac{\partial c(\mathbf{X})}{\partial X_i} = \lambda \left(\frac{\partial g(\mathbf{X})}{\partial X_i} \right) \qquad \text{all } i$$

This will define an overall or global optimum insofar as the feasible region defined by the isoquant for Y' is convex, that is, so long as there are diminishing marginal products.

This result is easily interpreted. The rate of change on the right hand side is the marginal product, $MP_i = \partial g(\mathbf{X})/\partial X_i)$ (see Section 2.4). The quantity on the left hand side is, by definition, known as the *marginal cost*, MC_i. It is the rate of change of $c(\mathbf{X})$ with respect to a single input X_i, as stated. The Lagrangean thus leads to the *Optimality Conditions of Marginal Analysis*:

$$\frac{1}{\lambda} = \frac{MP_i}{MC_i} \qquad \text{all } i$$

The optimality conditions imply balanced design, in which the contribution of each resource X_i is equally effective per unit cost as any other resource X_j. The best design is one in which each input finally provides, at the margin, the same "bang for the buck," the same MP_i/MC_i.

The nature of the input cost function needs to be considered carefully in this context. It can be quite complex. The simplest version of the cost function is one that supposes that each resource X_i has a specific unit price, p_i, which is the same regardless of the quantity purchased. This leads to a simple linear model:

$$c(\mathbf{X}) = \sum p_i X_i$$

This simple model is the one most often used in economic analysis. It frequently does not apply in systems design, however. Attempts to buy large quantities of any resource may easily lead to prices quite different from those that prevail for small quantities. At higher volumes the trend of unit costs may be either higher or lower. One may benefit from advantages such as volume discounts and wholesale prices, or one may encounter higher prices as local supplies are exhausted. The latter is a common phenomenon in the construction of large systems, for example: wage rates for workers rise enormously as labor must be either imported or paid higher rates for extra hours.

The optimality conditions are easily applied in practice when the functions are analytic (see box). They can also be used when the production function does not have continuous derivatives. This may occur, for example, when the resources are only available in specific sizes, for example, of pipe diameters for a plant, of aircraft, or steel beams. In such cases one can obtain an optimum design by tentatively adjusting the design until the MP_i/MC_i ratios are approximately equal and the optimality conditions are met approximately (see application in Section 4.6).

The optimality conditions can be manipulated to give a useful graphical interpretation. To see this, we must first illustrate the input cost function. We do this by plotting curves of equal cost, much as we plotted isoquants for production functions. These curves of equal costs are called *budget curves*, because they show how much $\mathbf{X}$ can be obtained with any specific budget. Figure 4.1 presents budget lines for both a simple linear input cost function and a more complex one, showing unit costs increasing with quantity. Note that the feasible region for costs

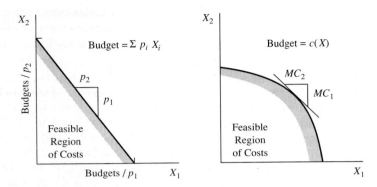

FIGURE 4.1
Budget lines for a simple linear cost function (left), and for a more complex one, showing increasing marginal costs with quantity (right).

are inside of the curves: it is always possible to obtain less, difficult to obtain the most for your money.

The graphical interpretation of the optimality conditions thus follows directly. From

$$\frac{MP_i}{MC_i} = \frac{MP_j}{MC_j} \qquad \text{all } i, j$$

we write

$$-\frac{MP_j}{MP_i} = MRS_{ij} = -\frac{MC_j}{MC_i}$$

where MRS is the marginal rate of substitution, as defined in Section 2.4. This is to say that, at optimality, the slope of the isoquant should equal the slope of the budget line. Both functions should be tangent to each other, as Figure 4.2 shows.

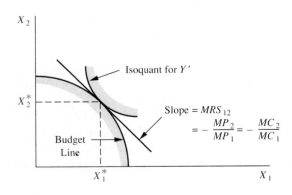

FIGURE 4.2
Graphical interpretation of the optimality conditions.

Application of Optimality Conditions

Assume a simple Cobb-Douglas production function:

$$Y = a_0 X_1^{a_1} X_2^{a_2}$$

Also, assume that the input cost function is a simple function of unit prices p_i:

$$c(\mathbf{X}) = \sum p_i X_i$$

The optimality conditions are then:

$$\frac{MP_1}{MC_1} = \frac{MP_2}{MC_2}$$

Since in this case $MP_i = (a_i/X_i) Y$ we can state that at the optimum:

$$\frac{a_1}{p_1 X_1^*} = \frac{a_2}{p_2 X_2^*}$$

For any specific Y', this can be solved explicitly for the optimum amount of each resource, X_i^*, and design $\mathbf{X}^*$.

4.3 EXPANSION PATH

The *expansion path* is the locus of all the optimum designs for every level of output Y. It represents the optimal sequence of designs as the scale of the desired production increases.

The expansion path is an important concept for the designer. Indeed, it should not be supposed that the best way to increase the output is to increase all inputs proportionately. While this may be so, it is in general not the case. The optimal ratio of inputs more usually changes as the size of the design changes. For example, the optimal crew for a 200,000 ton tanker is not 10 times greater than that for a 20,000 ton tanker; it is closer to being the same.

The expansion path is not an inherent property of the technical process. It is defined by the optimality conditions and thus depends on the ratios of the prevailing prices for the resources as well as how they may change with the quantities of resources. The concept is perfectly general, and expansion paths exist even when they cannot be defined by marginal analysis.

In marginal analysis, the expansion path is obtained simply by solving the optimality conditions for any resource X_i in terms of the others. Since there are $(N-1)$ independent conditions on the N resources, the path is a curve in N-dimensional space. Note that when we construct the expansion path from the optimality conditions of marginal analysis, we do not require that the feasible region of the production function be convex as regards scale. The expansion path, constructed for different sizes of production, is simply a chain of optimal solutions obtained for each level of product. We can thus use marginal analysis to construct an expansion path when there are increasing returns to scale (and the feasible region of the production function is nonconvex) so long as there are diminishing marginal returns and convexity of the feasible region defined by the isoquants. (See box for an example in two dimensions.)

Whenever constraints on the resources make it impossible to achieve the optimal design defined by the optimality conditions of Section 4.2, the expansion path diverts from what it would otherwise be. Figure 4.3*b* illustrates the phenomenon. This shows what happens when a constraint is imposed on the situation described in the box. In this case we suppose that there is a fixed limit on the amount of X_1 available: $X_1 \leq 10$. The expansion path proceeds normally (as

---

Expansion Path

A. *Linear Input Cost Function*
Using the optimality conditions obtained earlier for the two resource production processes, the expansion path is

$$X_1^* = \left(\frac{1}{p_1}\right)\left(\frac{a_1}{a_2}\right)p_2 X_2^*$$

In this special case, it is a straight line indicating the same ratio of inputs, regardless of size. This would be unusual in practice.

B. *Non-Linear Input Cost Function*
Consider a Cobb-Douglas production process with increasing returns to scale:

$$Y = 2X_1^{0.48} X_2^{0.72}$$

and an input cost function:

$$c(\mathbf{X}) = X_1 + X_2^{1.5}$$

The optimality conditions can be stated as

$$\frac{MP_1}{MP_2} = \frac{MC_1}{MC_2}$$

to give

$$\frac{0.48/X_1}{0.72/X_2} = \frac{1}{1.5X_2^{0.5}}$$

which defines the expansion path as

$$X_2^* = (X_1^*)^{2/3}$$

a situation in which larger designs optimally use proportionately less and less X_2 compared to X_1. Figure 4.3*a* illustrates this situation.

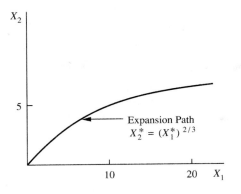 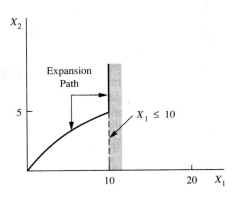

FIGURE 4.3
(*a*) **Unconstrained nonlinear expansion path for example problem (left); and** (*b*) **expansion path constrained by the limit on a resource (right).**

in Figure 4.3*a*) until this constraint makes it impossible to use more X_1. At this juncture, the optimal designs, the ones that achieve the highest output with the resources available, are located along the constraint, with ever more use of the other resource.

4.4 COST FUNCTION

The *cost function* describes the optimal, the least cost of producing any level of product *Y*. It follows directly from the optimality conditions and the expansion path. Each optimal design $\mathbf{X}^*$ has a cost, $c(\mathbf{X}^*)$ associated with the product Y'. The locus of all these points is the cost function, $C(Y)$. By means of the optimality conditions it can be defined solely in terms of costs and product, without reference to any of the inputs.

> **Semantic caution:** The cost function as defined above is to. be carefully distinguished from the input cost function that characterizes the cost of any set of resources. These two functions refer to different quantities. The former defines an optimal cost; whereas the latter defines any cost; and their functional forms will generally be different (see box on following page).

The cost function is very useful and important in practice. It helps the system designer focus on and answer the vital question of how large a system to create. It is the means of deciding what size of system we want to have—a most crucial piece of information before we engage in any specific configuration of a system.

The information conveyed by the cost function is particularly valuable because it fills a relative void in systems engineering. Indeed, while designers typically have considerable experience in designing systems of various sizes, and may often be able to outline an optimal configuration for any size, they typically

Cost Function

Consider as before the Cobb-Douglas production process with increasing returns to scale:

$$Y = 2 X_1^{0.48} X_2^{0.72}$$

and the input cost function:

$$c(\mathbf{X}) = X_1 + X_2^{1.5}$$

for which the expansion path is as shown in the previous box:

$$X_1^* = (X_2^*)^{1.5}$$

Stating Y in terms of X_2^* we obtain

$$Y = 2(X_2^*)^{1.44}$$

This leads to

$$X_2^* = \left(\frac{Y}{2}\right) \exp\left(\frac{1}{1.44}\right) = \left(\frac{Y}{2}\right)^{0.69}$$

Stating the input cost function in terms of X_2^* we obtain

$$c(\mathbf{X}^*) = 2(X_2^*)^{1.5}$$

Expressing X_2^* as a function of Y we get the cost function as

$$C(Y) = c(\mathbf{X}^*) = (2^{-0.04})Y^{1.04}$$

do not have either much experience or basis for specifying the optimal size of the system. The cost function is a means to explore this question.

The cost function has the advantage of being a particularly easy tool to use in practice. This is because, in any specific situation, it is expressed in just two dimensions: cost and product. It thus can be easily displayed and discussed with all kinds of decisionmakers, even those who are not technically trained. Being in just two dimensions, it also permits anyone to grasp the salient points.

A typical cost function appears in Figure 4.4. This presentation, with costs on the vertical axis, is the form most often used by economists. This is the way it is generally displayed in the discussion of economics issues. Notice that the feasible region for the cost function is above the curve in this case; it is always easier to spend more than required. (See also the discussion of convex feasible regions in Section 2.4.)

In engineering and other applied discussions, the cost function is generally presented as a *cost-effectiveness function*, as in Figure 4.5. Here the emphasis is on what can be obtained for any specific cost or budget. The name is different, also. One refers to effectiveness rather than product because the output of a system is often some measure of performance rather than a product to be sold. The output

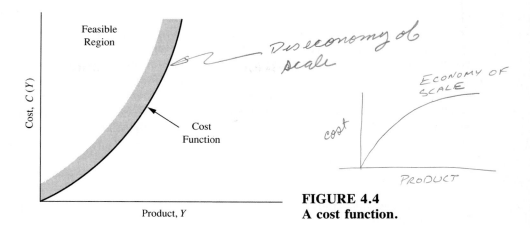

FIGURE 4.4
A cost function.

of a process for desulfurizing smokestack gasses might be "reductions in sulfur in parts per million," for example. The concept of cost-effectiveness is discussed further in Section 13.3, which covers criteria of evaluation.

One way to use the cost or cost-effectiveness function is to focus on the amount of money available. One can ask: How much can we obtain with a given budget? This information is often desired by many decisionmakers and planners. It also leads to more interesting questions of: How much more effectiveness could we obtain with a greater budget? How much more effectiveness would we have to give up if the budget were smaller?

The answers to these questions define a ratio of change in total cost, $\Delta C(Y)$, to change in effectiveness, ΔY; this is the

$$\text{Cost-Effectiveness Ratio: } \frac{\Delta C(Y)}{\Delta Y}$$

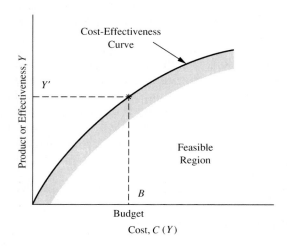

FIGURE 4.5
The cost-effectiveness curve,
an alternate view of the cost
function.

This gives the designer the unit cost of extra units of effectiveness. This actual cost can be compared to the value of effectiveness to determine whether one is paying too much or too little. The size of the design can then be adjusted to the right amount. Section 4.6 gives an example of an application of this analysis.

The cost function can be derived analytically whenever the production function and the input cost function are both known and analytic. To do this, one simply uses the information contained in the expansion path to state both production function and the input cost function in terms of a single X_i^* above. Thus:

$$c(\mathbf{X}^*) = c(X_i^*)$$
$$Y = g(X_i^*)$$

The production function thus stated can be inverted to obtain an expression for X_i^* in terms of output:

$$X_i^* = g^{-1}(Y)$$

This result, substituted in the input cost function gives the cost function:

$$C(Y) = c(\mathbf{X}^*)$$

The box on page 48 gives an example of the procedure for obtaining the cost function. The cost function for a Cobb-Douglas production process and a simple linear cost function has a particularly convenient form. Its derivation is as in the box, but as it requires a messy notation, it is omitted. The result is simply

$$C(Y) = \left(A \prod p_i^{(a_i/r)} \right) Y^{1/r}$$

where $r = \sum a_i$ and indicates whether the returns to scale are increasing or not (see Section 2.4), and A is a constant. The above equation is an important result both theoretically and practically.

> **Semantic caution:** The parameter r is defined in agreement with the traditional form used in the economic literature. It should not be confused with the discount rate, also usually referred to as r in the relevant literature, as well as in Chapters 11 through 14.

Economists use the cost function to determine the nature of the production function. They do this statistically from observation on the prices, p_i, prevailing in different locations and times for each resource X_i, the amount of product and the total cost. The statistical analysis then generates estimates of the exponents of the prices, a_i/r, and of the product, $1/r$. The estimates then permit one to derive estimates of each a_i and thus to characterize the Cobb-Douglas production function that has been presumed to underlie the situation. This process is in fact how most analytic production functions are deduced.

In practice, engineering handbooks and similar references for a particular discipline frequently state the cost function for a process as

$$C(Y) = A_0 Y^a$$

where the (A_0, a) parameters have been chosen to match experience in the field. Such formulas can be good rules of thumb for a specific time and place. They are not valid in general, however, since they do not reflect prices specifically. Relative prices of resources such as labor and materials do indeed vary substantially from country to country and over time. These changes would change the parameter A_0. The exponent of Y in the cost function should remain valid, so long as the production function itself does not change, that is, so long as there is no substantial technological advance.

4.5   CHARACTERISTICS OF COST FUNCTIONS

Cost functions can have special characteristics important for design. The most significant feature concerns "economies of scale." As this concept does not apply conveniently to production processes with multiple outputs, two new concepts are also being developed and applied; those of "economies of scope" and "advantages of scale." The following paragraphs define all three, plus the complementary concept of the learning curve.

Economies of scale. Economies of scale exist for a production process when it is cheaper to produce in quantity. Formally, they exist when the average optimal cost per unit of output decreases as the level of production increases.

Mathematically, a cost function with economies of scale is generally expressed in the form:

$$C(Y) = A_0 Y^a \qquad a < 1.0$$

The average cost per unit of output, AC_Y, is then

$$AC_Y = A_0 Y^{a-1}$$

and decreases with greater Y. It should also be noted that the incremental cost for each additional unit of production, that is the marginal cost MC_Y, is both decreasing and less than the average cost:

$$MC_Y = aA_0 Y^{a-1} < AC_Y$$

Figure 4.6 illustrates these relationships.

> **Semantic caution:** Economies of scale are similar to increasing returns to scale, but these two concepts are definitely not identical. The one does not imply the other. See discussion in text.

The concept of economies of scale is closely related to—but different from—that of increasing returns to scale (see Section 2.4). Both refer to the idea of somehow getting proportionately more as the scale of production increases. Their principal difference arises from the fact that the notion of economies of scale incorporates information about the input cost function, $c(\mathbf{X})$. The form of this function can thus affect the increasing returns to scale.

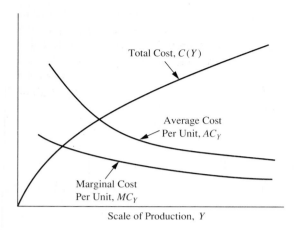

**FIGURE 4.6
General relationship
of total, average, and
marginal costs of
production for a process
with economies of scale.**

Economies of scale imply increasing returns to scale only in one class of situations: when the production function is Cobb-Douglas and the input cost function is linear. In this special case, the cost function is

$$C(Y) = \left(A \prod_i p_i^{(a_i/r)} \right) Y^{1/r}$$

and increasing returns to scale on the production process imply $r = \sum a_i > 1.0$ and thus decreasing average costs, since $1/r < 1.0$.

For the more general case in which the input cost function is nonlinear, increasing returns to scale do not imply economies of scale, or vice-versa. The box on cost functions in Section 4.4 provides an example of this possibility. In that case a production process with increasing returns to scale:

$$Y = 2X_1^{0.48} X_2^{0.72}$$

combines with a nonlinear input cost function:

$$c(\mathbf{X}) = X_1 + X_2^{1.5}$$

to define the cost function:

$$C(Y) = (2^{-0.04}) Y^{1.04}$$

which does not have economies of scale. In fact, this situation illustrates *diseconomies of scale*, where increasing the size of the production process leads to higher average costs.

The concepts of economies of scale and increasing returns to scale differ in yet another respect. Returns to scale reflect the proportionate increase in output when all inputs to the design change proportionately. Economies of scale describe what happens when the scale of the output changes, whatever the optimal design and its ratio of inputs may be. Indeed, the optimal design for a larger version of the production process is often, possibly generally, not simply a scaled up version of a smaller process. For example, the optimum design for a small 20,000 ton tanker might involve a crew of 12 whereas the optimum design for a much larger 200,000 ton tanker might have a crew of only 30 rather than 120; only one captain, first mate, radio operator, et cetera may be necessary regardless of size. The Cobb-Douglas production function combined with a linear input cost function do not reflect this reality; they imply that the expansion path is a straight line with constant proportions of inputs.

Economies of scale occur in many industries. In engineering practice these are usually expressed by empirical equations of the form:

$$C(\text{Capacity}) = (\text{Constant})(\text{Capacity})^a = A_0 Y^a$$

In different fields the exponent a has been observed to vary from about 0.4 to 0.9. For example:

- In chemical engineering it often seems that $a = 0.6$; this relationship has been known as the "six-tenths rule."
- A common rule of thumb for computers has been that Cost = $(\text{Constant})(\text{Capacity})^{1/2}$, which is known as "Grosch's Law."
- In analyzing large water tunnels over 10 ft in diameter for New York City, we found that Cost = $(\text{Constant})(\text{Cross-Sectional Area})^{0.6}$.

Economies of scale may occur in all industries for which there are increasing returns to scale, but—as previously indicated—they do not necessarily. The physical increasing returns may be counterbalanced by the economic disadvantage of input costs that increase exponentially. As indicated in Section 6.6, economies of scale are frequently also obtained by shifting to a different technology.

The existence of economies of scale in a situation or industry has significant implications both for design and policy. For design, it means that there is an important reason to concentrate production in big units: concentration drives the average cost of production down. This is the principal reason why electric generating facilities, refineries, and chemical plants tend to be so large.

For national or international policy on the organization of industry, economies of scale imply that the company that can build the largest facilities will be able to produce products cheaper than its competitors, and therefore will have a definite financial advantage over them. The largest companies can therefore drive the others out of business and will tend toward monopolies. Industries characterized by economies of scale are thus said to have *natural monopolies*, the situation in which a monopoly might be in the consumer's best interests, because it could produce at the lowest average cost. But a company with a monopoly might also be able to raise prices excessively, because it would have no competition.

Economies of scale in an industry thus present a difficult policy issue: how does society ensure the most efficient solution? Should it grant franchises to a single producer, and then regulate the industry to insure that the consumers are charged a fair price? This solution is typically implemented for electric power and communication utilities. Or should the government prohibit monopolies and

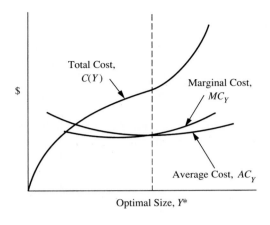

FIGURE 4.7
General relationship of total, average, and marginal costs of production for a process with an optimal size.

cartels, counting on competition to force prices down to some reasonable if not minimum level? This is the solution embedded in the "antitrust" legislation in the United States and applied to virtually every major American industry. There is no clear answer to this dilemma; each solution has its advantages. The problem must be faced whenever economies of scale exist.

Economies of scale may exist in an industry up to a certain size. Beyond this point, average costs may rise. The industry is then said to have an optimum size of plant or process. Figure 4.7 illustrates how the costs would vary in such a situation. Notice that the curve of marginal cost crosses that of average cost at the optimal size, that is, the point of lowest costs. This is because average costs decrease so long as marginal costs are less. In practice, the optimal size is nearly impossible to determine with any certainty. The existence of an optimum size is, however, important in principle: it indicates that a natural monopoly does not exist in this industry, and therefore that monopolies cannot produce and sell to the consumer more cheaply. The manufacture of automobiles is almost certainly an industry with an optimum size of production: large economies of scale to a point, and then diseconomies of scale.

Learning curve. The concept of the learning curve reflects another way in which the marginal costs of a product decrease as we manufacture more. It is, however, quite different from economies of scale in a subtle way. This must be carefully noted as it has substantially different implications for design.

> **Semantic caution:** The learning curve is also known as the "experience curve," particularly in management consulting.

The learning curve embodies the idea that any person or any plant becomes more efficient as it gains experience. The producers learn how to organize their work better, discover acceptable short cuts, and generally become more skilled. Consequently, their cost of production decreases as they produce more and more.

The strength of the learning curve effect is commonly stated in terms of the ratio, expressed as a percentage, of the marginal costs as the total number of units produced doubles between time $t = 0$ and $t = 1$. Thus:

$$\left(\frac{MC_1}{MC_0}\right) = \text{Percent Learning Curve}$$

In practice, we may hope to observe 70% to 90% learning curves.

To compare the effect of the learning curve to that of economies of scale, it is useful to express the total cost of production as

$$C(Y) = (\text{Constant}) \, (\text{Number Produced})^u$$

where u is the learning curve exponent. The marginal cost of any unit at time t is then

$$MC_t = (\text{Constant}) \, (\text{Number Produced})_t^{u-1}$$

This defines the percent learning curve as

$$\left(\frac{MC_1}{MC_0}\right) = (2)^{u-1}$$

For a median 85% learning curve, this implies: $(2)^{u-1} = 0.85$ and then $u = 0.78$. The effect of learning is thus comparable to that of economies of scale.

To determine the learning curve experimentally, one plots the marginal costs against the total number produced over time. This is usefully done on a logarithmic scale, in which a constant exponent for the learning curve would imply a straight line (see Figure 4.8).

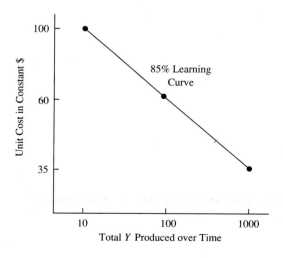

FIGURE 4.8
Typical learning curve, plotted on logarithmic scales.

When comparing the learning curve to the decreasing costs associated with economies of scale, we should carefully note the different causes of the economies, as indicated by the horizontal axes in Figures 4.6 and 4.7. With economies of scale, the costs are reduced because larger plants or facilities increase productivity; with the learning curve, the costs depend on the total number produced over time. Thus, with "learning," a smaller plant may produce more cheaply over time as it gains experience.

The learning curve effect is obviously most important in new industries, such as electronics and other producers of high technology. Correspondingly, it is less likely to be apparent in established, traditional industries, such as brick manufacture.

The implications of the learning curve for the design of systems are parallel to those of economies of scale. For new industries where the learning curve effects are strong, it is advantageous to be the first and largest producer: it enables one to produce more cheaply than competitors, thus to undersell them and gain a larger share of the market in both profits and volume. Some experts argue that the Japanese have been successful in many industries by following the policy of exploiting the learning curve effect.

Since the two effects, economies of scale and "learning," stem from independent causes, note that they can exist separately and jointly. An industry may face the possibility of both economies of scale and learning.

Economies of scope. Economies of scope is one of two ways of referring to advantages of larger size for systems producing multiple outputs. This concept is quite similar to that of economies of scale, the difference being in the nature of what causes decreasing average costs.

Economies of scope exist when the average cost of a unit output decreases with the "scope" rather than with the scale or size of output. Scope is a rather loose term embodying notions of the spread or the distribution of the production process, as distinguished from scale, a precise term relating strictly to the number of units produced. To illustrate the distinction between scale and scope, consider a transportation system for freight. Its costs in fact do depend both on the amount carried (the size or scale of the operation) and on the geographic distribution served (the scope). Both elements are in fact outputs of the transport system. The cost function would thus be

$$C(Y) = c(\text{ton-miles; mileage})$$

Economies of scale would refer to $\partial C(Y)/\partial(\text{ton-miles})$ whereas economies of scope would refer to $\partial C(Y)/\partial(\text{mileage})$.

Economies of scope exist in a number of industries where economies of scale do not. Air transport is a prime example. In air transport, the basic unit of production is the aircraft; to get more product one has to replicate this unit, so that the average cost for the output is essentially constant: there are no economies of scale. On the other hand, there may be economies of scope. If the average length of an airline's flights increases, for example, it becomes cheaper to carry a ton-mile of cargo because the processes of take-off and landing use a lot of fuel, and average costs decrease when these portions of the flight take a smaller fraction of the time. There are thus economies of scope in airlines with respect to stage length. Current research indicates that economies of scope may generally be quite significant, even when economies of scale do not exist.

Advantages of scale. Advantages of scale is the other way of referring to the benefits that may be associated with a larger system producing multiple outputs. This concept differs from those of economies of scale and of scope in that it does not describe changes in average cost.

Advantages of scale exist when the production of more units concurrently improves the quality of the service. The customers may then see that for a given price of output they get better value for money as scale increases. Strictly speaking, the cost per unit may be constant (as the price does not change), but to the customer getting better quality, advantages of scale are quite comparable to economies of scope.

To illustrate this difficult concept, consider a mass transit system operating buses in a fixed route. Because the production process simply consists of replicating identical units, by putting more buses on the line, one may presume that this system has no economies of scale, that average costs per seat-mile are constant. Yet as the size of the operation increases, the quality of the service increases: more buses on the line mean a greater frequency of service and less wait. The bigger the operation, the better it seems to the customer.

Advantages of scale occur most frequently in service industries, in which the simple fact of producing more insures a more accessible, reliable service. Examples are transportation, as just discussed; communications; banks with many branches; and so on. Formally, they are likely to occur if the multiple outputs of the production process, Y = (Quantity, Quality), are closely connected, if greater quantity implies greater quality.

The policy implications of advantages of scale are similar to those of economies of scale. This is natural, since both concepts reflect better value for money with increasing size of the operation. Advantages of scale provide a strong rationale for concentrating production in an industry.

4.6 APPLICATIONS

This section provides three applications to illustrate the use of marginal and cost-effectiveness analyses in practice. They deal with river transportation, as a continuation of the application for Chapter 2; the supply of water for a city; and the design of a safety system. Yet the principles used are applicable to many situations.

River transportation. In designing inland water transportation for the U.S. Agency for International Development and Colombia particularly, we built on the production function described in Section 2.6. To obtain the optimal, most cost-effective design, we had to incorporate the costs of the two main inputs, the horsepower and deck area of a system of barges and a towboat.

The key description of costs for any situation is the ratio of prices of the inputs. In this case we have

$$\frac{MC_{HP}}{MC_{DA}} = \frac{\text{(unit price of hp)}}{\text{(unit price of deck area)}}$$

This can be expected to vary widely from situation to situation, from country to country. In eastern Colombia, for example, the cost of constructing barges was low but the cost of engines that had to be transported over mountains was high, so the ratio was quite high.

We solved for the expansion path for any situation by using our computerized production function. Specifically, we identified the point on several isoquants at which the ratio of marginal costs equalled the marginal rate of substitution or ratio of marginal products of horsepower and deck area:

$$\frac{MC_{HP}}{MC_{DA}} = -MRS = -\frac{MP_{HP}}{MP_{DA}}$$

The results of the analysis defined different expansion paths—and thus quite different designs—for different conditions. Figure 4.9 shows typical results. In this case, as it happened, the expansion paths for water with no current (lakes, for example) were approximately straight lines through the origin. This means that there is an optimal design ratio valid for the entire range of design. The situation can be different for other cases, though. Where the current is strong, much more horsepower is required to obtain any specific output and the production function is changed. So then are the expansion paths. These are shifted to the right, as compared to Figure 4.9, when there is current and the expansion path no longer is a straight line through the origin. The optimal ratio of the inputs then changes drastically as greater output is needed.

Water supply. A cost-effectiveness analysis led to major improvements, worth hundreds of millions of dollars, in the design of the water supply system for New York City. This case provides a good example of the strengths and possibilities of marginal analysis. (See de Neufville, 1970 for full details).

The water supply system for New York City consists of several distinct elements: a series of dams in the mountains 100 or more miles (150 to 200 km) away from the city, aqueducts that bring this water to reservoirs in the hills at the edge of the city, a primary distribution network consisting of a few enormous

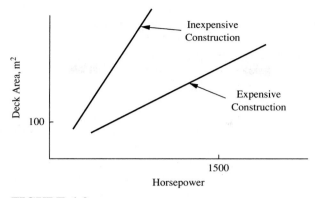

FIGURE 4.9
Expansion paths and associated optimal designs for River Transport differ
according to the ratio of costs of inputs. (Results are for specific water
conditions: stream width = 18 m; depth = 2.4 m; and current = 0.)

tunnels, a much more extensive secondary distribution network of pipes up to
a few feet (about 1 m) in diameter, and finally the detailed distribution to each
individual user.

The focus of the analysis was on the primary distribution network. As of
1975 this system consisted of City Tunnels Number 1 and 2. Each is about 20
mi (30 km) long, stretching from the Croton reservoir throughout the city, and
around 15 ft (5 m) in diameter. Because of their size, the water flows through
them quite slowly at about 3 ft/s (1 m/s) or approximately 2 mi/hr (3.2 km/hr).
The tunnels can be visualized as large, slow-moving, underground rivers, almost
as lakes.

The reason the tunnels are so large is to minimize the energy required to
push the water through the system. This energy equals the frictional resistance of
water in the tunnel, and is proportional to the square of the velocity of the water.
For any given amount of flow, the velocity is inversely proportional to the cross-
section of the stream, and thus to the square of the diameter. The net result is that
the energy required to distribute the water is inversely proportional to the fourth
power of the diameter:

$$\text{Energy Lost} \sim \text{Order of} \left(\frac{1}{\text{diameter}}\right)^4$$

Large tunnels thus conserve energy. For New York City, where water is distributed by gravity and all the energy comes from the elevation of the Croton
reservoir, the large tunnels ensure that the pressure throughout the city will be
sufficient.

City Tunnels 1 and 2 are becoming obsolete. Since they were built around 1910 and 1925, there is reason to believe that they might soon fail in some way through old age: the concrete linings of the tunnels might collapse somewhere, or valves might jam. Because the distribution of industry and residences have altered substantially in the last half century, it is also certainly true that the existing network is not optimal for the current pattern of loads on the system.

To ensure an adequate water supply for the future, New York City's Board or Water Supply thus proposed to construct a new tunnel. This new tunnel would both provide an adequate margin of safety in case of difficulty with the older tunnels, and would distribute the water more efficiently to where it is now required. Specifically, the Board of Water Supply proposed to construct the Third City Tunnel; it would be up to 28 ft (8.4 m) in diameter and cost about 1 billion dollars.

The mayor and central government of New York City were concerned about this enormous expense and wondered if it were really a good idea. They thus called in a team from the Massachusetts Institute of Technology. The questions put to us were: is the proposal from the Board of Water Supply optimal? Does it represent the best use of our money? This is a classic basis for a cost-effectiveness analysis.

Our first step was to construct the relevant production function. In doing so, the initial issue was to define its terms. The output of the system was easy to specify in principle—it was the pressure delivered by the tunnel system when supplying the demand for water. The practical difficulty is that the pressure varies throughout the system, specifically between each node at which water is taken from the tunnel system when supplying the demand for water. This is because the water is flowing and there are pressure drops. The problem was resolved by defining the output as an average of the pressure delivered at each node, weighted by the volume of water used at that node:

$$Y = \text{Average Pressure}$$

$$= \frac{\sum (\text{Pressure at node})(\text{Volume at node})}{\sum (\text{Volume at all nodes})}$$

The inputs to the system were the several sections of tunnel that could be constructed:

$$\mathbf{X} = (\text{Sections of Tunnel})$$

Each section could be varied from a diameter of zero, meaning that it would not be used, to as large as liked.

The production function itself then described the average pressure based on the design, consisting of some specification of tunnel sections. This relationship is highly complex. It is nonlinear first of all, being in fourth powers. Secondly, the equilibrium solution for the system results from the solution of differential equations describing the conservation of flow at each node. There is no direct solution to the governing set of nonlinear differential systems; an iterative solution must be obtained. The situation was thus represented by an inductive engineering production function. Specifically, we used a computer program that generated the technologically efficient output, in terms of average pressure, for any specified set of **X**. At the time this program was created, about two decades ago, this production function was at the forefront of research. Production functions of this sort are now relatively common.

The input cost function for tunnel sections of different sizes was derived from detailed engineering data available from the Board of Water Supply and their technical consultants. This has the form:

$$c(\mathbf{X}) = A(\text{Length})(\text{Cross-Sectional Area})^{0.6}$$

indicating economies of scale. The result is typical for tunnels, pipelines and similar items (see Section 2.4).

The optimal design for any level of output was defined iteratively. The optimality conditions could not be defined directly, because the production function was not analytic. They were therefore defined indirectly. To do so we had to calculate the ratio of marginal product, in terms of pressure, to marginal cost for each section of tunnel. We then developed a balanced design by adjusting a trial design until the (MP/MC) ratios were approximately equal for all sections. The exact procedure consisted of the following steps:

1. Pick a trial design.
2. Estimate (MP/MC) ratios.
3. Identify which sections have high (MP/MC) ratios and are thus undersized and require a larger diameter; conversely, identify the sections with low (MP/MC) ratios, which are oversized and should have smaller diameters.
4. Define and test new designs.
5. Iterate until a balanced—and therefore optimal—design is achieved.

The expansion path was likewise defined iteratively. Because the production and input cost function were highly nonlinear, the optimal design for a larger tunnel system was not a simple scaling up of a smaller design.

The cost-effectiveness function resulting naturally from the above information was as shown in Figure 4.10. This had several key features. First, it would be necessary to spend a great deal, about a quarter of a billion dollars, to obtain any significant result, as shown by point A in the figure. Second, the function eventually indicated strong diseconomies of scale. This is because, when the tunnel is very large, the flow is very slow and the pressure loss minuscule, so that an even larger tunnel then does very little to decrease pressure loss. Thirdly, the original design of the Board of Water Supply was at the far end of the cost-effectiveness curve.

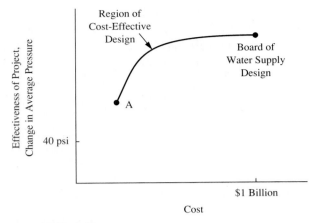

FIGURE 4.10
Cost-effectiveness function for Third City Tunnel in New York City.

The cost-effectiveness function became the focus of the determination of the optimal design. The object was to determine the right size to build and the right amount to spend. The essential criterion for determining this result was the cost-effectiveness ratio. We could use it to determine whether a larger size produced results appropriate to their costs. As Figure 4.10 demonstrates, a really small design, such as *A*, was not as cost-effective as a larger one; by doubling the costs one would really get a significant improvement. Conversely, a really large design was also cost-ineffective, only small improvements would finally be achieved at tremendous extra cost. The optimal, most cost-effective design was somewhere in between, around the "knee" of the cost-effectiveness function as indicated in Figure 4.10. It could not be pinpointed more precisely, as nobody had any reasonable basis for determining a precise value for the safety and convenience represented by a higher average pressure in the system. Finally, the City and the Board of Water Supply agreed on a design in which the diameter of the Third City Tunnel was to be around 21 ft (6.3 m) instead of as large as 28 ft (8.4 m). This design was then committed to construction.

This cost-effectiveness analysis led to significant savings. The revised design, featuring a tunnel up to 25% narrower, and thus over 40% smaller in cross-section, could be estimated at 20 to 25% less expensive to build. As the final cost of Third City Tunnel is well over a billion dollars, our cost-effectiveness analysis implies savings in the hundreds of millions of dollars.

Railroad crossings. A cost-effectiveness analysis was used to define the optimal allocation of safety devices to railroad crossings for the state of California. The issue was that the state wanted to reduce accidents, to lower the number of deaths at unprotected crossings. They faced several issues:

How many lives can we save with our existing budget?
How much better could we do with a bigger budget? Is this worthwhile?
How much would we lose if the budget were cut?
What is the best way to allocate the safety devices for any budget?

Based on a statistical analysis, the hundreds of different crossings could be classed into a few groups (such as "rural, medium traffic") and all locations in a group were presumed (as a reasonable approximation) to behave similarly. Several devices were available to reduce accidents; to illustrate the analysis, consider two in particular: gates and grade separations (tunnels or bridges). Gates are cheaper but not accident-proof, grade separations offer complete security at great cost. Again, as a first-order approximation the state estimated that gates and grade separations would not vary in cost by location.

This problem can be analyzed by marginal analysis even though the production process (saving lives by spending resources) is neither analytic nor continuous. It is suitable because the resources have diminishing marginal products: intelligent, technically efficient design uses each input in its most productive situations first, then in its next best, and so on. This defines diminishing marginal products by construction.

To conduct the cost-effectiveness analysis we construct a table that gives the ratio of marginal product to marginal cost for each possible type of investment at each location. In our case this ratio is simply

$$\left(\frac{MP}{MC}\right) = \left(\frac{\text{Lives Saved}}{\text{Unit Cost}}\right)_i \qquad \text{for each device } i$$

At the start of the analysis we then have something like Table 4.1.

To conduct the analysis we use the simple principle of using resources, of placing investments where they are most effective. The optimal design explores all the best opportunities first, then the next best, and so on. This procedure generates a cost-effectiveness curve that constantly flattens as in Figure 4.5. The

TABLE 4.1
Initial Matrix for Cost-Effectiveness of Railroad Crossings: each A_{ij} represents the *MP/MC* ratio for an investment at a location.

Device Type	Location Class		
	1	2	...
Gates	A_{11}	A_{12}	...
Grade separations	A_{21}	A_{22}	...

TABLE 4.2
Second Matrix for Cost-Effectiveness of Railroad
Crossings: The A_{ij} have been renewed to take into
account prior designs.

Device Type	Location Class		
	1	**2**	**...**
Gates	0	A_{12}	...
Grade Separations	A'_{21}	A_{22}	...

expansion path is then simply the sequence of placements that constitute the optimal strategy.

In our case, suppose that the most cost-effective investment, the one with the greatest MP/MC ratio, is gates at locations of class 1 (i.e., $A_{11} > A_{12}, A_{21}, A_{22} \ldots$). This means that we can reduce deaths by $(A_{11})N$ for N locations of class 1 at a cost of N gates. Having fully exploited the possibility of gates at this location we proceed to look for the next best possibility. Before we do so, we must revise our table to take into account the use of gates at location of class 1; specifically, we must recognize that the use of another device at these locations will no longer be as effective as when they had no protection: the A_{ij} for location of class 1 must be reduced as in Table 4.2.

This kind of analysis can be applied quite generally in many practical situations. The Railroad Crossing problem (4.17) attached to this chapter is a good exercise to fix the procedure in mind.

REFERENCES

Baumol, W. J., (1977). *Economic Theory and Operations Analysis*, 4th ed. Prentice-Hall, Englewood Cliffs, NJ.

de Neufville, R., (1970). "Cost-Effectiveness Analysis of Civil Engineering Systems—New York City's Primary Water Supply System," *Operations Research*, Vol.13, September–October, pp. 758–804.

Hax, A., and Majluf, N. S., (1984). "Competitive Cost Dynamics: The Experience Curve," Chapter 6, *Strategic Management, An Integrative Approach*, Prentice-Hall, Englewood Cliffs, NJ.

PROBLEMS

4.1. *Marginal Analysis I*
Using the input cost function: $C = 2X + 3Y^2$; and the results from Problem 2.4:
(a) Write the equation for the expansion path and sketch it.
(b) What is the significance of the expansion path?

(c) Find and sketch the cost-effectiveness function.
(d) Given a budget of $C \leq \$80$, what is the maximum output you can achieve? What combination of inputs achieves this result?
(e) What is the maximum output that can be achieved if, with no budget constraint:

$$X \leq 2 \quad \text{and} \quad Y \leq 8?$$

4.2. *Marginal Analysis II*

Do (a) to (c) as above for Problem 2.5, using the input cost function

$$C = 6X + 4Y^3$$

4.3. *Marginal Analysis III*

Given the production function: $\quad Z = 10X^{0.3}Y^{0.4}$
and the input cost function: $\quad C = 3X + 2Y^2$
(a) Find the marginal products and costs.
(b) State the optimality criteria for this situation.
(c) Write an expression in X and Y for the marginal rate of substitution of X for Y.
(d) Find the expansion path.
(e) Find the cost-effectiveness function.

4.4. *Marginal Analysis IV*

Given the production function: $Z = 2X^{0.5}Y^{2.5}$
(a) Are the marginal products increasing or decreasing? Over what ranges?
(b) What type of returns to scale does this function exhibit?
   Given the input cost function:

$$C = (64/3)X^3 + (5/3)Y^3 + 17 \qquad \text{for } X, Y > 0$$

$$C = 0 \qquad \qquad \qquad \qquad \text{for } X, Y = 0$$

(c) What is the equation of the expansion path?
(d) Write an equation for the cost-effectiveness function.

4.5. *Marginal Analysis V*

Given the production function: $Z = X^{0.7}Y^{1.4}$
(a) Are the marginal products increasing or decreasing?
(b) What types of returns to scale does this function exhibit?
Given the input cost function: $C = X^3/3 + 16/3Y^3, \qquad X, Y \geq 0.$
(c) What is the equation of the expansion path?
(d) Write an equation for the cost-effectiveness function.

4.6. *Marginal Analysis VI*

The technology of a process is represented by: $Q = 2XY$
(a) Does the production function display increasing returns to scale?
(b) Find the marginal productivity with respect to X, to Y.
For a particular island with limited resources: $C = 6X^2 + 3Y^4 + 5$
(c) Write an equation that defines the expansion path.
(d) Write an equation describing the cost-effectiveness function.

4.7. *Marginal Analysis VII*
For Problem 2.6 and the input cost function $C = 2X + 4Y$, determine the expansion path and the cost-effectiveness function.

4.8. *Marginal Analysis VIII*
For Problem 2.7 and the input cost function $C = 2X^2 + Y$:
(*a*) Determine the expansion path and the cost-effectiveness function.
(*b*) Reconcile the result with the returns to scale defined by Problem 2.7.

4.9. *Vi-Tall Again*
Plot of the expansion path for Problem 2.8.

4.10. *Economies of Scale?*
Given: $Z = X^{0.3}Y^{0.8}$
(*a*) What are the marginal products?
(*b*) Are the returns to scale increasing? Why or why not?
For the input cost function $C = X^3 + 4Y^2$
(*c*) Write an equation defining the expansion path.
(*d*) Write an equation defining the cost-effectiveness function.
(*e*) Does the cost-effectiveness function show economies of scale?

4.11. *More Road Work*
(*a*) Use the optimality criteria to solve Problem 3.5.
(*b*) Explain the relation between the optimality criteria and the Lagrangean multipliers obtained in Problem 3.5.

4.12. *Timothy Burr, III*
Bothered by the lack of economies of scale (see Problem 3.7), TB the Third decides to investigate the advantages of experience. He looks over the production figures for the last eight years:

	Year							
	1	2	3	4	5	6	7	8
Product	1700	2900	2500	1400	1800	2400	2600	2700
Av. cost	3.00	2.65	2.55	2.40	2.35	2.30	2.15	2.10

Estimate the percent learning curve for the logging operation.

4.13. *Efficient Design*
Given the production function: $Z = 4^{0.7}X^{0.3}Y^{0.5}$
and the input cost function: $C = 38 + 3X + 10Y^2$
(*a*) Does the production function define a convex feasible region? Explain.
(*b*) What type of returns to scale does the production function exhibit?
(*c*) Define and calculate the marginal rate of substitution.
(*d*) Determine the expansion path.

(e) Given a budget of $C = \$60$, what is the maximum output that can be achieved? What combination of inputs is required to achieve this output at $C = \$60$?

4.14. *Chemical Plant*

There are economies of scale if chemical reactor tanks are placed in series. A liquid waste passes through this system of tanks at a constant flow rate and chemicals are added to each tank to reduce the concentration from S_0 to S_n. The control variables for tank reactors in series are:

$n = $ number of tanks

$v = $ volume of each tank, where all tanks have the same volume

The cost of this setup may be expressed as: $C = 0.1\ n^{0.4}v^{0.6}$

The quantity produced may be approximated as: $Q = \dfrac{10v}{(10 - n)}$

(a) Compute the values of the control variables that minimize cost, as functions of Q^*, the target production volume.
(b) Compute the minimum cost as a function of Q^*.

4.15. *Potamia*

The production function for unpaved roads in Potamia is approximately:

$$M = 1.8L^{0.2}B^{0.8}$$

where: M is the length of road constructed
L is labor used (in 1000 person-hours); and
B is the machine-hours of bulldozers

(a) When labor costs \$500/1000 hr and bulldozers \$500/hr, in what ratio should labor and bulldozers be used?
(b) If L is constrained (≤ 100), how would this change the optimal ratio of L to B? (You may find it useful to graph the expansion path).
(c) At the invitation of the Prime Minister, you attend a meeting of the Potamian cabinet. The Minister for Industrial Development observes that, in developed nations, the B/L ratio is higher than it is in Potamia, and that progress is synonymous with increasing that ratio. The Labor Minister disagrees—the M/L ratio is the one that Potamia must increase, at almost any price, if it is to join the technically advanced world. Comment.

4.16. *Electric Company*

The Electric Company's oil-fired generating plant is currently operating near design capacity. More power can be generated by the plant but not very efficiently.

$Z = 10F^{0.4}L^{0.1}$ $Z = $ extra megawatts
$C = $ extra cost in dollars/hr

$C = 24F + 6L$ $F = $ extra barrels of oil
$L = $ extra operating and maintenance employees

(*a*) Find the marginal costs and marginal products.
(*b*) Determine the expansion path (optimal combinations of inputs).
(*c*) Write an equation describing the cost-effectiveness function for extra electricity generation from the current plant.
(*d*) Over the next five years, the company can supply additional power (above the present level) to its customers from three sources:

1. Extra capacity can be wrung from the current plant, as previously described.
2. Power can be bought in any quantity from the regional power grid at $6/ MW-hr.
3. An antiquated hydro-electric facility can be put back in service, to produce up to 20 MW. The cost of having the facility in service is $60/hr, regardless of the amount of electricity generated.

Construct the company's cost-effectiveness function for supplying additional power.

4.17. *Railroad Crossing*
You have been appointed project manager to work out the region's railroad crossing protection plan for the new high-speed rail line. At present, all of the 100 intersections along this line are protected by flashing lights. You must decide which crossings should have the additional protection of automatic gates and which should have grade separations.

Your staff has given you the following data describing the options and likely effects for each of the 100 crossings along this line. These are divided into three groups according to such factors as amount of traffic.

Crossing group	Number of crossings	Estimated annual number of accidents avoided per crossing by installing	
		Gates	Grade separations
A	20	0.5	0.8
B	50	0.2	0.6
C	30	0.12	0.3

The annual cost of each gate is $100K and $400K for each grade separation.
(*a*) What is the implied product of this system?
(*b*) What would be the logical resources for this problem?
(*c*) Given parts (a) and (b), what are the axes of the production function?
(*d*) Draw the isoquant passing through the point that represents building a gate at eight of the crossings in group A; draw the isoquant associated with an annual reduction of 22 accidents; and draw the line representing a budget of $4000K.
(*e*) What points on the above isoquants are on the expansion path?
(*f*) If $2M or less is to be spent annually, the most effective way to spend it is by installing gates at the crossings in group A, where 0.5 lives are saved for every $100K commitment. How many lives are saved per $100K for the five other options?

If $2.3M is to be spent, either one of the group A crossings can be redesigned as a grade separation or three of the group B crossings can be supplied with gates. Which is a more effective use of the marginal $300K expenditure? What is the marginal benefit per $100K for each alternative?

(g) Examine the marginal benefit of competing uses of succeeding increments of money, and construct the cost-effectiveness function.

(h) Describe a few ways to decide what crossing protections should be built. Which method is optimal? Which method would you expect to see used in practice? Are the results the same?

CHAPTER
5

LINEAR PROGRAMMING

5.1 CONCEPT

Linear programming (LP) is the most powerful method of constrained optimization available. Its power is staggering when compared with other approaches. Linear programs routinely deal with problems involving tens of thousands of variables and thousands of constraints. These kinds of problems are virtually intractable by other methods of analysis. The traditional methods of constrained optimization, for example, require the solution of systems of partial differential equations, notoriously time-consuming and difficult even for small problems.

Linear programming is also particularly attractive for design because it automatically provides extensive information on the sensitivity of the optimal design to different formulations of the problem. This feature is most important, because of our inherent uncertainty about the precise parameters of any situation, as discussed in Chapter 15. This sensitivity analysis is presented in Chapter 6.

Linear programming is so powerful because it exploits the computer's ability to execute simple calculations, such as additions and multiplications, very quickly. By representing a design problem by a system of linear equations it implies an optimization procedure that consists of a long series of solutions to these linear equations. This task is both simple-minded and tedious—an ideal combination for a digital computer.

> **Semantic caution:** Linear programming is called "programming" for historical reasons. It is one of a series of techniques referred to collectively as *mathematical programming*, which also includes integer programming (Section 5.9) and dynamic programming (Chapter 7). None of these techniques usually requires the user to write programs for the computer in the sense now commonly used. The mathematical programming techniques are typically available in convenient packages.

As with all mathematical programming techniques, linear programming works because it assumes that certain assumptions can be made about a problem. These assumptions establish a mathematical structure for the problem which can be solved by a particular process. Linear programming assumes that the problem can legitimately be described or approximated by linear, additive and continuous functions (see Section 5.2). Linear programming, as any other mathematical programming technique, is thus limited to specific classes of problems, those that meet its assumptions.

The standard form for a linear program consists of two parts, an objective function and constraints. The *objective function* is an equation that defines the quantity to be optimized. For linear programming this quantity must be a one-dimensional scalar quantity such as:

$$Y = \sum c_i X_i$$

The variables in the objective function, the X_i, are known as *decision variables* because we seek to make decisions about them so as to optimize the objective. This name is useful because it focuses attention on the idea that the arguments of the objective functions are the decisions we have—this is most helpful when we try to formulate a real problem.

The constraints are of the form:

$$\sum_i a_{ij} X_i \gtrless b_j$$

where the b_j are the upper or lower bounds on a particular feature of a problem and the a_{ij} parameters define the contribution of each decision variable to that feature.

> **Semantic caution:** Note that the coefficients of the decision variables in the objective function are labeled c_i, instead of a_i as in previous chapters and in the more general economic literature. This is the traditional format for linear programming, which was initially mostly applied to problems of minimizing costs. In linear programming the "a" coefficients are traditionally reserved for the matrix of constraints, and the "b" parameters for the constraints. In discussing linear programming it is useful to maintain this tradition to facilitate discussions with professionals in operations research.

Both maximization and minimization problems can be handled by linear programming. A typical maximization problem is to

- maximize output or profit
- subject to a budget and other constraints

The question here is "how much can we obtain (from this factory, mine, system) with the amount of money and resources available, given that we must operate within technical, legal, economic, and political realities?" Conversely, a typical minimization problem is to

- minimize costs
- subject to requirements on the output and other constraints

Here the question is "how cheaply can we produce our output while meeting all the technical and other standards?"

Because linear programming problems in practice typically deal with a very large number of variables, X_i, and constraints, b_j, they are almost invariably presented in vector and matrix notation. Thus:

Max or Min: $Y = \mathbf{CX}$

Subject to: $\mathbf{AX} \geqslant \mathbf{B}$

where $\mathbf{C}$, $\mathbf{X}$, and $\mathbf{B}$ are row and column vectors, and $\mathbf{A}$ is the matrix of a_{ij} parameters of the variables in the system of constraints. Note that in accordance with traditional practice, the symbols for the vectors are capitalized although the b_j and c_i are normally not.

5.2 ASSUMPTIONS

The power of linear programming is a consequence of the assumptions it makes about a problem. If these assumptions are not met, even approximately, by a problem, then linear programming will not provide a useful analysis. Linear programming is definitely not a method that is universally applicable. It does not apply in many situations, which is why other, less powerful methods such as dynamic programming are useful.

The central assumption of linear programming is that the objective function and all constraints are linear. Additionally, the decision variables are assumed to be continuous and nonnegative.

Linearity. The concept of linearity has a precise meaning that needs to be carefully understood. This idea is much more specific, and limited, than the general idea that most people have that a linear equation is some kind of summation of variables all to the power of one.

Formally, a function $f(\mathbf{X}) = f(X_1, \ldots, X_n)$ is *linear* if, for all variables X_i and constants S_i:

$$f(S_1X_1, \ldots, S_nX_n) = S_1f(X_1) + \cdots + S_nf(X_n)$$

This definition can be divided into two equivalent statements.

Constant returns. First of all, a linear function must have constant returns or economies of scale. The definition indeed implies that

$$f(S\mathbf{X}) = Sf(\mathbf{X})$$

that is, that multiplying every decision variable by a common factor S leads to

Nonlinearity of Fixed Charge Equations

The expression

$$f(\mathbf{X}) = a_0 + \sum a_i X_i$$

with the fixed charge a_0 can be seen to be nonlinear by testing the condition that

$$f(S\mathbf{X}) = Sf(\mathbf{X})$$

Multiplying each X_i by S thus leads to

$$f(S\mathbf{X}) = a_0 + S \sum a_i X_i$$

This is evidently not equal to

$$Sf(\mathbf{X}) = Sa_0 + S \sum a_i X_i$$

Thus, the expression with the fixed charge is not linear.

---

an S-fold change in the objective function or constraint. In this connection, you should carefully note that the function:

$$f(\mathbf{X}) = a_0 + \sum a_i X_i$$

is not linear (see box above). Problems involving such expressions are known as *fixed charge* problems, due to the presence of the fixed amount a_0, and are discussed in Section 5.8.

The restriction on constant returns or economies of scale can be significant in practice. Many important industries do in fact exhibit increasing returns, as Section 4.5 indicates. Linear programming must be used carefully, if at all, for those kinds of problems. For situations involving decreasing returns, however, the situation is not so drastic; it is possible to represent the situation to the accuracy desired by using piecewise linear approximations (see Section 5.7).

Additivity. Secondly, a linear function must be *additive*. This means that the value of the function with all X_i simultaneously is equal to the sum of the values of that function with each X_i by itself:

$$f(X_1, \ldots, X_n) = f(X_1) + \cdots + f(X_n)$$

The implication is that the contribution of each X_i to $f(\mathbf{X})$ should not depend on the presence or absence of any others. Such situations in fact exist quite commonly in practice (see following box). However, the difficulty is avoided quite easily in practice by formulating the linear program using what is known as "activities" as decision variables, a device explained in Section 5.6.

Examples of Non-Additive Situations

The transport of air cargo requires both pilots and fuel. Both must be available simultaneously; each alone achieves nothing. Thus:

$$\text{Air Cargo Carried} = f(\text{Pilots, Fuel})$$

but:

$$f(\text{Pilots, Fuel}) \neq f(\text{Pilots}) + f(\text{Fuel})$$

since:

$$f(\text{Pilots}) = f(\text{Fuel}) = 0$$

Similarly, the production of calves as a function of the number of bulls and cows is also clearly not additive. Bulls or cows by themselves will not ordinarily produce calves.

Continuity and nonnegativity. Finally, as previously indicated, linear programming assumes that the decision variables X_i are both continuous and nonnegative. Neither assumption is particularly limiting in practice, however.

The assumption that the decision variables are continuous means, as a practical matter, that the physical realities do not restrict them to integer or discrete values. This restriction could be seen as a considerable difficulty because many systems do indeed consist of design elements that can only be integer or discrete. For example, the number of ships in a fleet must be integer, as must be the number of warehouses in a distribution system. Similarly various components of a system, say the computers or memories in a communication network, may only come in standard sizes.

In practice the assumption of continuity is generally not a difficulty. This is for two reasons. On the one hand we can simply assume that integer variables are continuous and round off our results. In many instances this will be quite satisfactory since the possible error of a few percent is well within the accuracy with which we can formulate any real problem, as Chapter 6 indicates. On the other hand there are ways to formulate linear programs that can cope with integer values. These techniques, known collectively as integer programming, are reasonably expensive and should be avoided unless necessary. Yet, as described in Section 5.9, they do provide a means to use most of linear programming for those situations.

The assumption that all of the decision variables should be nonnegative:

$$X_i \geq 0 \qquad \text{all } i$$

is a technicality imposed by the way a linear program finds the optimum. This requirement does not restrict us in practice; we can always define variables so

Making Decision Variables Nonnegative

This can be done in two ways. The simpler case is when a variable appears to be consistently negative. In this situation we simply define a new variable, X_i', which is the negative of the other:

$$X_i' = -X_i$$

We then use X_i' in the linear program. For example, suppose that in a safety program one of the arguments is the number of accidents, measured from a previous high level, and that this variable is consequently negative. By simply focusing on the alternative variable:

Accidents Prevented $= -$(Accidents from High Level)

we could define a nonnegative variable.

The second case occurs when a variable is expected to be both positive and negative. In this situation we could achieve nonnegativity by redefining a new base of reference for measuring the quantity sufficiently low so that all readings for our problem would be positive. Thus:

$$X_i' = X_i + \text{(Large Amount)}$$

For example, if the variable were temperature, which might fluctuate above and below freezing and thus be both positive and negative on the Centigrade scale, we could redefine the temperature measurements in terms of degrees Kelvin and be sure that all temperature readings were positive on this absolute scale.

---

that they are not negative (see box above). This assumption thus merely requires that we be careful in the way we formulate a linear program.

5.3 SOLUTION CONCEPT

The way a linear program finds the optimum is fundamentally very simple, despite the potentially enormous size and complexity of the actual problem. The solution is based on two consequences of the fundamental assumption of linearity of the objective function and the constraints. As with all mathematical programming techniques, linear programming achieves its power by exploiting the consequences of the assumptions it makes about the situation.

To describe the solution concept it is first necessary to explain the consequences of the linearity assumptions, which provide the basis for all linear programming procedures. The nature of these methods is described afterwards.

Effect of linearity assumption. The two consequences of the linearity assumption are that

- the feasible region is convex, if it exists at all.
- the optimum must be located at an edge of this region, specifically at one of its corner points.

As will be explained soon, these facts reduce the optimization procedure to a search through a limited set of well-defined combinations, which is very small compared to the infinite number of design possibilities.

To understand these results, it is first of all useful to imagine the feasible region to be composed of two parts: the space defined by the constraints and the volume defined by the relationship of the decision variables to the objective function.

The region defined by linear constraints must be convex if there is any feasible region at all. This is because any two points that satisfy any linear constraint must be on one side of it and any line between them must also be entirely in the feasible region. The operational definition of convexity of the feasible region (see Section 2.4) is therefore met. Figure 5.1 illustrates the situation in two dimensions.

It is possible, both mathematically and in practice, for there to be no feasible region at all. This occurs if the constraints are mutually contradictory and there is no possible set of the decision variables X that will satisfy all constraints. For example, it might simply not be possible to meet some environmental standards with available resources or technology. In such cases the solution is *infeasible*.

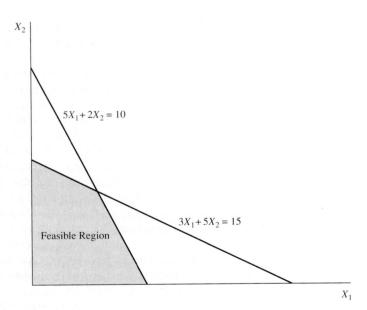

X_2

$5X_1 + 2X_2 = 10$

$3X_1 + 5X_2 = 15$

Feasible Region

X_1

FIGURE 5.1
The feasible region is convex when defined by linear constants. (Here
$5 X_1 + 2 X_2 \leq 10; \quad 3 X_1 + 5 X_2 \leq 15; \quad X_1, X_2, \geq 0).$

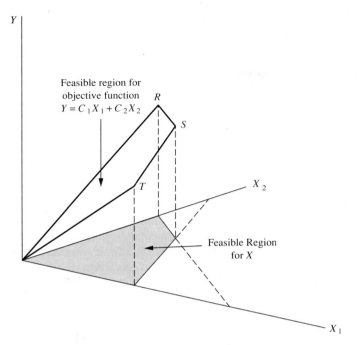

FIGURE 5.2
The feasible region for the linear objective function is also convex.

The volume defined by the linear objective function and the constraints is then also convex, by the same argument as before. Figure 5.2 illustrates the situation.

It follows from the above that the optimum solution to a linear program must be located at an edge to the feasible region, specifically at one of its corner points. Since the objective function is linear, the rate of change from any point interior to the region in any direction is constant. Thus, there is an edge that has a value of the objective function equal to or greater than any interior point. (The exception, in theory, occurs if the problem is *unbounded* so that it is possible to increase the objective function infinitely; the real world, however, does not provide this kind of luxury.) Similarly, since the rate of change of the objective function along every edge is also constant, the value of the objective function must be equal to or greater at one of the corner points to that edge than anywhere in the middle of the edge. An optimum solution must therefore lie at a corner point. For example, in trying to maximize the objective function shown in Figure 5.2, the highest point must be at R, S, or T.

Multiple optimal solutions to a linear program are possible. This occurs if the rate of change of the objective function along an edge is zero. Then the entire edge, including its corner points, constitutes a set of optimal solutions.

Every optimal solution to a linear program is a true, *global optimum*. It is the best maximum or minimum possible throughout the set, it is not a local optimum better than points in its vicinity but less desirable than some other point further away. This fact again results from the linearity of the objective function and the convexity of the feasible region, for the same reason that the optimum is at a corner point. The net effect of the linearity assumption is that a global optimum exists at a corner point of the feasible region. This provides the basis for all solution procedures.

Solution concept. The essence of all algorithms for solving linear programming problems is an organized search through the corner points. As it turns out, this is relatively easy to do, because of the nature of these points.

The corner points are defined by the intersections of the constraints. Each corner point is thus a solution to a set of linear equations. Solving such problems is easy in principle, being a system of elimination of unknowns and of substitutions, but tedious. It is an ideal task for high-speed computers.

The search through the corner points is facilitated by the fact that every corner point is linked to another by a constraint. Thus if you have solved for one corner point, for example point S in Figure 5.2, you can find others, such as R and T, by following the equations for the constraints to adjacent corner points.

The general procedure for finding the optimum solution to a linear program is thus:

- Find one corner point as a feasible solution to the constraints.
- Proceed sequentially to other corner points that provide better solutions.
- Stop when you arrive at a corner from which no adjacent corner leads to a better value of the objective function—this is the global optimum.

In practice, there are many different ways to execute this general procedure, as indicated next.

5.4   SOLUTION IN PRACTICE

A wide variety of computer programs are available to solve linear programming problems. They range from smaller routines that work on personal computers to very sophisticated programs that deal with thousands of variables to optimize the operation of huge enterprises. The suppliers of linear programming packages are in fact quite competitive so that the systems analyst can really pick and choose.

The systems analyst interested in solving problems does not have to be concerned with the exact details of the algorithms that actually do the linear program. The user of linear programs can now simply focus on the speed and capabilities of the alternatives, and only needs to be aware of the general possibilities. In this spirit this chapter does not spend any time on the actual details of any of the many algorithms for solving linear programs.

The most basic linear programs are based on the *simplex method*, which is the standard procedure described in textbooks. In its pure form the simplex method proceeds from corner point to corner point by the path that gives the greatest improvement in the value of the objective function. From any corner it thus examines the rate of change of the objective function toward all adjacent corners. This approach is in fact quite inefficient for the kind of large problems found in practice, and is thus rarely used in sophisticated programs.

The simplex method is inefficient for two principal reasons. More obviously, it involves examination of all adjacent corners which, when dealing with thousands of variables and constraints, may be quite time-consuming. It can be much faster to consider only one or a few corner points that lead to improvements in the objective function. Depending on the exact nature of the problem you are dealing with, there are other algorithms that may be faster.

The simplex method is also inefficient because it does not deal explicitly with the nature of real problems in systems design. In practice, any system typically consists of many components, such as factories in an industry. There will be constraints on each of these components by themselves, constraints that do not affect other components of the systems. The net effect is that the matrix $\mathbf{A}$, that describes the relationship of the decision variables $\mathbf{X}$ to the constraints $\mathbf{B}$, will have a lot of empty spaces in it as suggested by Figure 5.3. This structure of the problem provides an opportunity for substantial savings in computer costs.

The computer effort required to solve a linear program is a function of the number of constraints involved. This is because the major task involved in any algorithm involves the solution of corner points, which requires the solution of a system of equations of the constraints. As a rough rule of thumb,

$$\text{LP Computer Effort} = f(\text{Number of Constraints})^2$$

The technical basis for this empirical function is that the solution of the equations requires the inversion of matrices of constraints.

The costs of solving real problems can thus be drastically reduced if we can break these big problems into a series of small problems. This is precisely

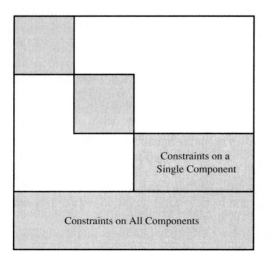

Constraints on a
Single Component

Constraints on All Components

FIGURE 5.3
The A matrix of constraints on a real system involving components, typically having many zero entries.

what can be done when the structure of the problem leads to a matrix **A** similar to that shown in Figure 5.3. This *decomposition* can lead to an order of magnitude increase in speed of the linear programming procedure. Advanced linear programming algorithms can decompose large problems automatically. Most interestingly, decomposition appears to work particularly well on the new parallel processor computers.

The simplex algorithm is thus rarely used in practice for significant problems. Most of the methods actually used are beyond description because the developers of particularly efficient procedures like to keep them secret so that they maintain their advantage over the competition.

What the user must realize in this situation is that

- many different algorithms are available for solving linear programs.
- the efficiency of these algorithms depends both on the precise mathematical structure of the problem and the special tricks used by the algorithm.

Users must therefore explore the possibilities available to them and find which one best suits their needs.

5.5 BASIC FORMULATIONS

Linear programming can be used to optimize the design of many different kinds of systems. In practice, however, a large fraction of its applications has been directed toward two classes of problems, those known as "blending" and "transportation" problems. Each is described in turn to illustrate these basic formulations.

Blending problems. These optimize the mix of ingredients in a product, that is its blend, that will minimize the cost of production while meeting all constraints. The question here is essentially how to select from a very large menu. The optimum design will specify the amount of each ingredient to be selected or, alternatively, the percent of each ingredient in the product.

The blending problem is in the standard form:

Minimize: $\quad\quad\quad\quad\quad$ Cost $=$ **CX**

Subject to: $\quad\quad\quad\quad\quad$ **AX** $\geqq$ **B**

The decision variables, **X**, are the quantities of each ingredient selected. The constants, **C**, are the unit costs or prices of each ingredient. The constraints, **B**, are limits on various aspects of the product contributed by each **X** as defined by the matrix **A**. See box for an example of a blending problem.

The design of many products can be viewed as blending problems. These include the making of steel and other alloys from a wide variety of ores and recycled scrap; the production of fuels and petrochemicals from crude and feedstocks

A Typical Blending Problem

Suppose a food company wants to make sausages as cheaply as possible. Their ingredients are various meats, grains, spices, et cetera. Their constraints are industry and legal restrictions on the amount of fat, water, meat, and so on that can be in the sausages; and also the technical realities of the production process.

This problem can be formulated in several equivalent ways. We will define the decision variables as the weight of each ingredient in a standard batch of sausages.

- The objective is

    Minimize: Cost of Batch = **CX**

    where the **C** are the unit costs by weight of each ingredient.
- Each constraint is of the form

$$\sum_i a_{ij}X_i \geq b_j$$

    where the a_{ij} represent the contribution per unit weight of each X_i to the factor constrained by b_j. Thus, if b_j is the maximum weight of fat in the batch of sausages, the a_{ij} are the percent of fat in each unit of weight of the X_i.
- There is also at least one technical constraint, that the weight of the ingredients including changes in processing has to add up to the total weight of the batch of sausages.
- Finally, the ingredients cannot be negative, so that

$$X_i \geq 0 \qquad \text{all } i$$

If the weight of the batch is defined as 100 units (kilograms or pounds, say) then the decision variables and the constraints are conveniently expressed in terms of percent.

---

of quite different constituents; the production of foods, such as bread, cereals, or hot dogs from grains and meats of quite different protein, moisture, and fat content; et cetera.

Industries faced with blending problems in fact use large linear programs routinely, sometimes daily. It must be realized that these industries are constantly redesigning their blends, to account for weekly or seasonal changes in the quality of their ingredients (scrap iron varies in chrome content, say, according to whether it comes from cars or ships; wheat has more water in the summer than in the winter), and to take advantage of even daily fluctuations in the prices of the ingredients. The optimal design of their products can typically be quite sensitive to small changes in the possible ingredients, and sensitivity analysis as described in Chapter 6 is most important in these industries.

Transportation problems. These optimize the distribution of a single product or commodity over some network. The question is where to send things, from what origin to what destination. The optimum design defines the quantities moving between any two points on the network.

These problems are called "transportation" problems because of their historical association with shipping. In fact, they relate to a wide class of situations where decisions have to be made about distribution over a network. The optimization of the development of a river basin or of an irrigation scheme are thus classically done as "transportation" problems—in these cases it is the water that is to be distributed or shipped over a series of paths.

The transportation problems use the standard form:

Minimize: $\qquad\qquad$ Cost $=$ **CX**

Subject to: $\qquad\qquad$ **AX** $\geqq$ **B**

The decision variables, X_{ij}, are the quantities of a product shipped from origin i to destination j, and the c_{ij} are the associated costs of making this shipment. The constraints may be both legal and technical, but the technical ones are most interesting in the transportation problem. These technical constraints are of two types:

- The total supplied from an origin i cannot exceed its inventory or capacity:

$$\sum_j X_{ij} \leq \text{Supply at Origin } i$$

- The total amount received at destination j should just equal the required demand since unnecessary shipments waste money:

$$\sum_i X_{ij} = \text{Need at Destination } j$$

- Finally, shipments cannot realistically be negative, so

$$X_{ij} \geq 0 \qquad \text{all } i \text{ and } j$$

The particularly interesting aspect of the transportation problems is that the matrix **A** is especially full of zeros. This is because each X_{ij} appears only twice in the matrix, once for the constraint on the origin and once for constraint at the destination. It then appears rather as in Figure 5.3. Moreover, all the nonzero entries in **A** are 1 as the preceding constraint equations show.

Special algorithms are available to solve the transportation problem. They exploit the special characteristics of the problem as contained in the matrix **A**, along the lines described in Section 5.4. These algorithms can be particularly fast and efficient compared to the standard simplex methods.

5.6 ACTIVITIES

This and the following two sections present several ways to formulate real problems into forms suitable for linear programming. The difficulty arises from the fact that whereas linear programming requires that a problem be described by a system of linear equations, the reality is that actual problems are generally nonlinear. The essential issue is: how can we adequately represent nonlinear situations with linear approximations?

The concept of an "activity" provides the basic method for representing a nonlinear model of a system through a set of linear equations. An *activity* is a specific way of combining basic materials or resources to achieve some objective or output. For example, the activity "flying Boeing 747 aircraft" is a specific way of using jet fuel and aircraft to accomplish the output of transporting passengers. An activity thus represents something intermediate between resources and output.

The concept of activities is subtle. Most people find it difficult to understand at first. Experience suggests that this is because we are used to thinking in terms of direct linkages between cause and effect, between resource and output, and thus have to make an extra effort to appreciate the idea and usefulness of activities.

To motivate the understanding of the usefulness of activities in linear programming, it is helpful to see what happens when we try to formulate a realistic problem without them. Consider the maximization of the output using several resources:

Maximize: $\quad\quad\quad\quad Y = g \text{ (Resources)}$

This problem involves a production function that generally, in a real situation, has isoquants asymptotic to the axes of the inputs (refer back to Figure 2.2 and the discussion in Section 2.4). If we try to represent this problem with a linear combination of resources:

$$g(\text{Resources}) = \sum (\text{Constant } i)(\text{Resource } i)$$

we obtain isoquants that are straight lines intercepting the axes, as shown in Figure 5.4. This representation is unrealistic. The concept of activities allows us to represent the production function with the curving, asymptotic isoquants it should realistically have. The demonstration is by example.

Consider a production function describing the creation of some automobile part, fenders for example, using labor and energy. Consider that there are two kinds of machines that can make these parts. Normally, these machines have a specific output, and require fixed amounts of labor and energy in any period. Table 5.1 shows the combinations assumed.

Use of either of the machines constitutes an activity. Each unit of an activity, for example, machine-hours of use, produces the same output and uses the same resources. The total result of any number of units of any activity is thus a linear function of the resources used. Other machines, using resources in a different ratio, would provide the basis for different activities.

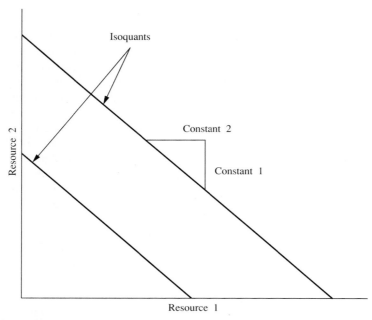

FIGURE 5.4
Isoquants for a production function represented as a linear combination of resources.

Consider now what the use of activities does to the representation of the isoquants of the production function. As Figure 5.5 indicates, each activity can be shown in the space of resources as a ray directed out from the origin at the constant angle, defined by the ratio in which they use resources. The use of a single machine of each type is defined by a point on these rays, in the figure by points A and B, and normally leads to different amounts of production. In this case point A is associated with an output of 50 fenders and point B with an output of 25. To obtain an isoquant we will thus have to use different quantities

TABLE 5.1
Production and Resources associated with each machine in a period.

Name of Machine	Resource 1 Energy Used (kwh)	Resource 2 Labor (person-hours)	Production Fenders
Activity 1	40	20	50
Activity 2	60	6	25

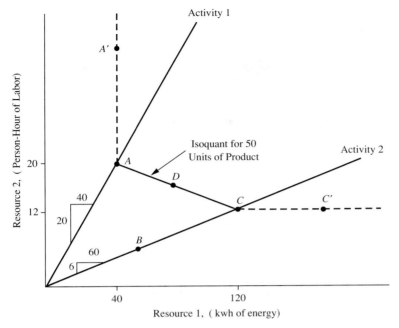

FIGURE 5.5
Isoquants for a production function represented as a linear combination of activities.

of each activity. For example, we can use either 1 unit of Activity 1 or 2 units of Activity 2, the latter being represented by point C. The isoquant passes through these two points.

What does the isoquant look like beyond the activity rays? The answer depends on whether one is between the activity rays, or between a ray and an axis. Between any two activity rays the output is simply a linear combination of the production of each type of activity. This means that the isoquant is simply a straight line between appropriate points on two rays. Caution: when several activities are used, each of the several different activities can combine, and the isoquant is represented by the line segments that imply the use of the least resources (those that lie closest to the origin). In our case, it is represented by the segment AC. For example, use of 1 unit of Activity 2, involving 60 kwh and 6 person-hours and giving a product of 25; plus half a unit of Activity 1, involving 20 kwh and 10 person-hours and also giving a product of 25; results in a total product of 50 using 80 kwh and 16 person-hours—as represented by point D. More generally, any point on the segment AC is a vector sum of some fraction of Activities 1 and 2.

The isoquant in the region between an axis and a ray is simply parallel to the axis. Consider point C' representing resources of 150 kwh and 12 person-

Formulation of LP Using Activities

Consider the problem of minimizing the cost of making a mixture, specifically an alloy, using different ores. Each ore is composed of various elements. The final alloy must have a definite chemical composition with upper and lower limits on the percentages of the various elements.

Each ore is an "activity" in that it is composed of a definite ratio of elements. The objective function is thus:

$$\text{Minimize:} \qquad\qquad \text{Cost} = \mathbf{CX}$$

where X_i is the quantity of ore i and c_i is its cost per unit weight. The set of constraints is

$$\mathbf{AX} \geq \mathbf{B}$$

where the b_j represent, first of all, a limit on the percent of some element that can be in the alloy. The a_{ij} then represent the percent of this element in ore i.

In this type of problem there is an additional constraint that must be introduced to reflect conservation of mass. The contribution by weight of each ore must sum to the total weight of alloy. If there are no losses in the smelting the conservation of mass is simply expressed as:

$$\sum X_i = \text{weight of alloy}$$

If, however, there are losses or impurities that burn off, this final constraint is:

$$\sum w_i X_i = \text{weight of alloy}$$

where each w_i represents the fraction that ore i contributes to the alloy.

---

hours: using the most energy-intensive activity available, we can only use up to 120 kwh for the labor available, additional power provides no extra product. A similar argument applies to A'.

The complete isoquant for 50 units of output is the broken line segment $A'ADCC'$. As more activities are used, the isoquant they portray will approximate a smooth curve more closely. We thus see that a linear combination of activities can correctly portray a realistic production function.

In practical problems, activities can represent a wide variety of technical possibilities. Here are some examples:

- Different types of machines, as previously discussed
- Different ways of organizing a production, for example the use of express trains or local trains

- Different materials used in a mixture or alloy, such as ores with various percentages of metals or grains with different protein and water contents

A linear program formulated using activities has the same form as any other linear program. The difference lies in the interpretation of the variables. Given a problem stated as

Optimize: $\qquad\qquad Y = \mathbf{CX}$

Subject to: $\qquad\qquad \mathbf{AX} \leq \mathbf{B}$

the decision variables X represent quantities of activities, and the constraints typically include limitations on the quantities of resources available or that must be used. See previous box for an example.

Notice that the use of activities also provides a way to deal with resources that are nonadditive, as defined in Section 5.2. We could not, for example, express the production of a transportation system for linear programming directly in terms of pilots and fuel—each alone achieves nothing. We could express this transport in terms of the use of different types of aircraft, each using standard ratios of pilots and fuel. This formulation would be additive, as the amount carried by one type of aircraft is independent of the amounts carried by other types.

5.7 NONLINEARITIES OF SCALE

The objective function for real problems is often nonlinear with respect to the scale or quantity of one or more of the decision variables X_i. Such situations commonly arise because of increasing or decreasing returns to scale, and economies or diseconomies of scale. Figure 5.6 illustrates the proposition. In such situations a simple linear representation of the form $Y = \sum c_i X_i$ may not be adequate.

Nonlinear objective functions $f(X_i)$ can be represented in linear programming by *piecewise linear approximations* consisting of a sequence of line segments. Linear programming modified to incorporate piecewise linear functions is called *separable programming* by some practitioners.

There are two difficulties in using piecewise linear approximations. The first is that the mathematical expression for the approximation is not obvious; indeed, it is arbitrary. Secondly, the approximation is only guaranteed to lead to a correct optimum, and should only be used when the feasible region is convex.

The piecewise linear approximation to a nonlinear function $f(X_i)$ consists of line segments that abut at *breakpoints*, as Figure 5.7 illustrates. The analyst must define these breakpoints, both in terms of X_i and $f(X_i)$. Unfortunately there are many equally acceptable ways this can be done, and each may lead to a different optimum solution. Greater accuracy can be obtained by using more line segments, but the best practical result is still an approximation.

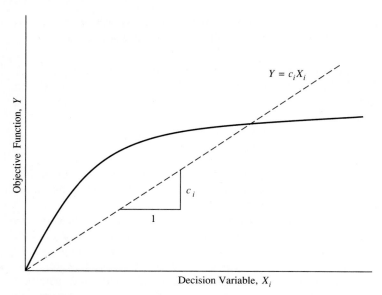

FIGURE 5.6
A simple linear representation may be an inadequate approximation to a nonlinear objective function.

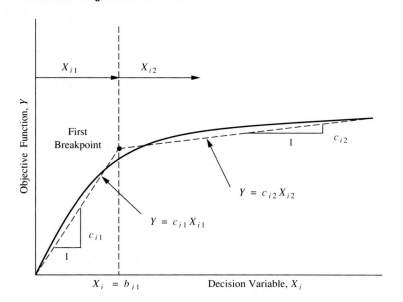

FIGURE 5.7
A piecewise linear approximation to a nonlinear objective function, illustrating the breakpoint; the new parameters c_{i1}, c_{i2}, and b_{i1}, and new variables X_{i1}, X_{i2} that must be introduced.

The use of piecewise linear approximations increases the number of variables and constraints. Specifically, each breakpoint used in the approximation requires one new variable and one new constraint. This fact limits the accuracy one may want to achieve by having the approximation consist of more line segments and breakpoints; this is because the cost of getting the solution is proportional to the square of the number of constraints (See Section 5.4).

The way the piecewise linear approximation increases the variables and constraints is a bit complicated. The central idea is that the expression for Y is no longer in terms of a single representation of X_i, as in Figure 5.6, but in terms of as many X_{ij} as there are line segments. The contributions to Y will be linear, of the form

$$Y = \sum_j c_{ij}X_{ij}$$

so long as the X_{ij} are defined to start from zero at the breakpoint beginning the line segment. Thus X_{i2} starts at b_{i1} as indicated in Figure 5.7. Concurrently, it is necessary to ensure that as each X_{ij} starts the preceding one stops—otherwise one would be double-counting the quantity of X_i. This is accomplished by placing a constraint on the X_{ij} up to the breakpoint defining the next line segment. Thus, $X_{i1} \leq b_{i1}$.

A linear program can be formulated for nonlinear returns to scale for the decision variables X_i provided that we:

1. Define each X_i as a $\sum_j X_{ij}$, $X_{ij} \geq 0$.
2. Define $f(X_i)$ as $\sum_j c_{ij}X_{ij}$ with the c_{ij} determined by the breakpoints selected.
3. Constrain the X_{ij} to the length of the associated line segment, $X_{ij} \leq b_{ij}$.
4. Incorporate the X_i in the matrix of constraints by multiplying each a_{ij} by X_{ij}.

See following box for example.

This formulation leads to a successful optimization only if the feasible region is convex. If it is not, the optimization cannot be depended on to succeed, and should not be tried. This follows generally from the theoretical basis of linear programming, which is that the global optimum can be obtained because the feasible region is convex. It is also interesting to see in detail why the piecewise linear approximation fails when the feasible region is not convex.

Consider first the convex feasible region below the curve in Figure 5.7, which might be associated with the maximization of the production $Y = f(X)$. As the computer seeks to maximize, it will choose initial amounts of X_{ij} whenever possible, for example X_{i1} over X_{i2}. This is because $c_{i1} > c_{i2}$ and thus that X_{i1} contributes more to Y than X_{i2}. Meanwhile X_{i1} meets the constraints as well as and no more than X_{i2}. Eventually, if the computer arrives at a solution that requires an $X_i > b_{i1}$, the quantity of X_{i1} in the solution will be limited and X_{i2} will be selected. The final solution will make sense in terms of X_i because a continuous amount of it will be specified: from 0 to b_{i1} by X_{i1} and from b_{i1} on by X_{i2}, and so on.

Formulation of LP Using Piecewise Approximation

Consider the problem of minimizing the cost of production involving labor, X_1, and materials X_2. Labor costs \$10 an hour up to 6000 hours a month for the 40 person work force; beyond that salaries are \$15 an hour (that is, time and a half for overtime). Suppose also that the production, defined by $a_1X_1 + a_2X_2$, must meet its quota of 400.

The feasible region is convex; we have diseconomies of scale and are minimizing costs. We can thus proceed with the approximation, substituting (X_{11}, X_{12}) for X_1.

The objective function is

Minimize: $\text{Cost} = 10X_{11} + 15X_{12} + c_2X_2$

The constraint on production is

$$a_1X_{11} + a_1X_{12} + a_2X_2 \geq 400$$

There is the constraint associated with the breakpoint,

$$X_{11} \leq 6000$$

as well as the usual:

$$X_{11}, X_{12}, X_2 \geq 0$$

Consider now the nonconvex feasible region above the curve in Figure 5.7, which might be associated with the minimization of costs. In trying to minimize Y, the computer will select X_{i2} before X_{i1}, because $c_{i2} < c_{i1}$. It is then entirely possible to have a result come out of the computer which makes no sense at all in that the quantity of X_i starts at b_{i1} with nothing before it! In short, if you use a piecewise linear approximation on a nonconvex feasible region, you may get an answer from the computer which superficially looks reasonable but is actually garbage.

5.8   INTEGER PROGRAMMING

Real problems are often discontinuous. Most typically this occurs when the inputs occur in integer amounts. For example, aircraft in an airline fleet are clearly integer. These kinds of discontinuities are frequently ignored in practice, especially when numbers are large. Thus, if the solution specifies 56.2 aircraft it is usual to round off this result. This is all the more appropriate when we realize that the formulation of the linear program is an approximation to reality, and that its results must be further tested, as Chapter 6 describes.

Optimization over convex feasible regions with discontinuous variables can also be solved formally by *integer programming*. This is a variation of linear programming which forces the solution to be integer by defining additional variables and constraints. There are several versions of integer programming. They are all relatively expensive in terms of computer time and are thus avoided if possible. If they must be used, they can be found in software libraries, combined with regular linear programs, in what are then typically called *mixed integer programs*. As far as the user is concerned, they operate pretty much like standard linear programs, except for the cost of computation.

5.9 FIXED CHARGES

A particular, common form of discontinuity requiring special attention is the fixed charge problem. A *fixed charge* is a specific amount, typically a cost, associated with any level of a decision variable. For example, the cost of X_i might be of the form

$$\text{Cost of } X_i = c_0 + c_i X_i$$

Fixed charges occur in practice when there is a basic cost of operating a facility, regardless of its level of activity. The cost of a warehouse, for instance, may involve fixed charges for rent and taxes, independent of the number of tons stored.

The difficulty with a fixed charge arises because it is often possible to avoid the charge entirely. We might, for example, have the option of establishing a warehouse or not having one at all. The cost associated with X_i is then more properly stated as

$$\text{Cost of } X_i \begin{cases} = c_0 + c_i X_i & X_i > 0 \\ = 0 & X_i = 0 \end{cases}$$

This situation, illustrated in Figure 5.8, causes difficulty because the optimization

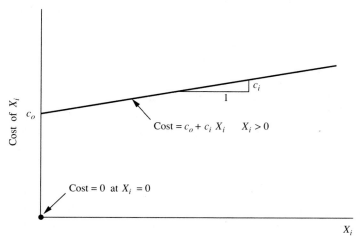

FIGURE 5.8
Graphical representation of a cost function with an avoidable fixed charge.

procedure in the linear programming chooses to include decision variables in the solution based on the coefficients c_i and does not have a way of appreciating the significant increase in cost c_0 that arises from the introduction of X_i into the solution. Linear programming simply does not handle fixed charges in the form given previously.

In the form in which fixed charges usually arise, the problem cannot be solved directly. This is because it involves minimizing cost, and the feasible region—above the line in Figure 5.8 and at the origin—is not convex. The only situation in which the fixed charge problem can be solved directly is when the charge cannot be avoided:

Minimize: Cost $= g(c_0 + c_i X_i)$ $X_i \geq 0$

One can then subtract the fixed charges from both sides of the equation and optimize the remainder:

Minimize: $(\text{Cost} - c_0) = g(c_i X_i)$

The solution to this problem is the solution to the simpler problem when the fixed charge cannot be avoided.

If the fixed charges are in fact unavoidable, there are three possible ways to look for a solution:

- Neglect the fixed charge, assuming that it is small compared to the total costs.
- Use a simple, straight-line approximation, which may be rather crude (Note that a piecewise linear approximation could not be used to represent the cost function with the fixed charge because the feasible region would not be convex).
- Run the problem with and without specific facilities in several passes.

The last approach works in principle but is only practical if the number of activities with fixed charges is very small, so that a manageable number of runs of the linear program are involved.

5.10   DUALITY

Duality is a mathematical concept of great importance to anyone who wants or needs to become involved in the details of any of the algorithms for linear programming. A person who wishes simply to apply the techniques to solve real problems could get by without knowing anything about duality. However, since much of the literature on linear programming refers to duality, and because understanding duality can help one develop a more intuitive feel for linear programming and sensitivity analysis, it is appropriate to explore this concept.

Duality in mathematics refers to cases in which there are two quite different ways of representing a problem or situation, both of which provide all the same kind of information and detail, but in a different form. These two representations are known as *duals* of each other.

Duality is usually a difficult concept to explain, although it is in fact quite simple. It is perhaps best introduced by specific examples:

Use of Duality for Editing Cartographic Data Bases

The nature of maps is changing fundamentally. The Gutenberg era is fading and electronic or computer-based maps are coming in. These cartographic data bases have enormous potential because they can be combined with all kinds of other files that can be flagged by address or location (such as the entire U.S. Census) to provide cartographic spread sheets in which data is displayed geographically rather than in a tabular form with no particular organization.

The computer maps are created by encoding the latitude and longitude of every intersection on the map, together with indications of their connections to other points. This process of digitizing is subject to a lot of error that is very difficult to correct by itself.

The standard way of editing these cartographic data bases is by exploiting the duality between boundaries and surfaces. This is known as the DIME (Dual Integrated Map Encoding) procedure. It uses the fact that areas within a boundary should only touch certain other areas; if they do not, this signals an error. The process can locate errors efficiently.

- A photograph and its mirror image are duals of each other, the difference between them is that all features are transposed left to right.
- A negative of a photograph and its positive are likewise duals, here the transposition is between light and dark tones.
- The boundaries to areas or spaces and these spaces themselves are duals, here the transposition is between the shell and its content.

These examples illustrate two aspects of duality. First, a dual is not simply a change in scale, it is a structurally different way of representing the same idea. Thus an enlargement of a print is not its dual, but its mirror image is. Secondly, a dual can be constructed from the original one once one knows the rules of transposition that are to be used.

Duals have a number of practical applications in many different fields besides linear and mathematical programming. An important use is in automatic editing and correction of complicated systems. Because duals are completely redundant representations of an original problem in every respect, they provide an ideal basis for verifying an original (see above box for an example).

All linear programs have duals. If the original problem is a maximization the dual is a minimization, and vice-versa. The first formulation, whether a maximization or minimization, is called the *primal* and its mirror image the dual.

The rule for defining a dual linear program from its primal consists of two parts: the transposition of the structure of the primal to a different form, and the introduction of a new objective function and set of decision variables. Thus, if we start with the problem

Maximize: $$Y = \mathbf{CX}$$

Subject to: $$\mathbf{AX} \geq \mathbf{B} \qquad \mathbf{X} \geq 0$$

its dual is

Minimize: $$Z = \mathbf{B}^T\mathbf{W}$$

Subject to: $$\mathbf{A}^T\mathbf{W} \geq \mathbf{C}^T \qquad \mathbf{W} \geq 0$$

where $\mathbf{W}$ denotes the new decision variables and Z is the new objective function. [Note: superscript T indicates that the vector or matrix has been transposed.] Particularly observe that the inequality signs in the dual are reversed. See box for an example.

Writing the Dual from the Primal

Suppose the primal problem is

Minimize: $$4X_1 + 12X_2 + 10X_3$$

Subject to:
$$
\begin{aligned}
2X_1 + X_2 \qquad &\geq 2 \\
X_1 + 2X_2 + X_3 &\geq 5 \\
X_3 &\geq 1 \\
X_1, \qquad X_2, \qquad X_3 &\geq 0
\end{aligned}
$$

In vector notation we have $\mathbf{C} = [4,12,10]$

$$
A = \begin{bmatrix} 2 & 1 & 0 \\ 1 & 2 & 1 \\ 0 & 0 & 1 \end{bmatrix} \qquad B = \begin{bmatrix} 2 \\ 5 \\ 1 \end{bmatrix}
$$

To write the dual we have to transpose the matrices. This operation rewrites the row vectors as columns and vice-versa, and rotates a matrix. This leads to

$$
\mathbf{C}^T = \begin{bmatrix} 4 \\ 12 \\ 10 \end{bmatrix} \qquad \mathbf{A}^T = \begin{bmatrix} 2 & 1 & 0 \\ 1 & 2 & 0 \\ 0 & 1 & 1 \end{bmatrix}
$$

$$\mathbf{B}^T = [2, 5, 1]$$

The dual problem is then

Minimize: $$2W_1 + 5W_2 + W_3$$

Subject to:
$$
\begin{aligned}
2W_1 + W_2 \qquad &\leq 4 \\
W_1 + 2W_2 \qquad &\leq 12 \\
W_2 + W_3 &\leq 10 \\
W_1, \qquad W_2, \qquad W_3 &\geq 0
\end{aligned}
$$

It should particularly be noted that the inequality signs are reversed in the dual.

A most important feature of dual problems is that the optimal answer to the primal and the dual is identical:

$$Y^* = Z^*$$

This follows from the fact that the dual problems represent the same problem, even though in a different view.

The fact that you get the same result whether you solve the primal or the dual problem makes it possible to construct linear programming algorithms that may be particularly efficient. Indeed, it is often the case that solving the dual is an order of magnitude easier than solving the original, primal problem.

The potential advantage of solving dual problems derives from the possibility that the dual may have far fewer constraints than the primal. Since the cost of solving linear programs is approximately proportional to the number of constraints squared (see Section 5.4), this difference may lead to significant savings.

The difference in the number of constraints in the primal and dual follows from the way the dual is constructed. Going from the primal to the dual, the number of decision variables in the primal (the entries in $\mathbf{C}$) becomes the number of constraints (the entries in $\mathbf{C}^T$). Conversely, the number of constraints in the primal (indicated by $\mathbf{B}$) becomes the number of decision variables in the dual ($\mathbf{B}^T$). If our primal problem has few decision variables and many constraints, it would be far easier to solve by its dual, which would have few constraints.

In practice, we really only have to know about the possible advantage of solving the dual if we are using unsophisticated linear programming packages. The most advanced versions will automatically work on the dual problem if that is advantageous; moreover, some of them work back and forth between the primal and the dual because this tactic may provide some advantages.

Finally, the elements of dual problems have some useful physical interpretations. These are explained in detail in the discussion of sensitivity analysis in Chapter 6.

5.11   APPLICATIONS

This section focuses on the practical questions that must be confronted when trying to analyze a real system using linear programming. The particular application concerns the minimization of costs in a transportation problem, and thus represents one of the most common uses of linear programming. Specifically, the example deals with the development of the Jordan river basin around Salt Lake City. This case, being in the public sector, has the advantage of being well-documented, in contrast to industrial applications which are usually confidential.

As for all transportation problems, the design of the system requires the analyst to specify which flows will go from the sources of supply to the intermediate and final destinations. In general, we may think of shipments being made from factories to users through warehouses and stores. For a river basin, the many sources are rivers and wells, supplemented by water imported by aqueducts or obtained by desalting. The uses are mostly residential or municipal; industrial, as for cooling power systems; agricultural; and hydroelectric power. Additionally, of course, the upstream users normally must deliver a fair share of the water supply to users downstream. Finally, the intermediate destinations and sources of supply are the facilities for recycling municipal and industrial wastes and the runoff from irrigation systems.

The network of flows in a river basin is quite complex whenever water is scarce. The planner must then anticipate that with recycling and pumping, every user is also a potential source of water. Virtually all combinations of sources and users may be linked. Such is the situation for Salt Lake City, especially as population growth puts pressure on a normally arid region.

The basic linear program for this situation was set up as a transportation problem as described in Section 5.5. As normally true for any real situation, this formulation has to be augmented to incorporate the particular features of the problem. The ones of interest here are those that apply generally to many cases. These concern the nature of intermediate operations, infeasible paths, losses, and blending operations.

Intermediate operations are bound by continuity and capacity. Continuity means that, over time, what flows in must flow out. This leads to a constraint for each intermediate facility of the form

$$\sum (\text{flows in}) - \sum (\text{flows out}) = 0$$

Similarly, any treatment plant or reservoir (or warehouse) may have fixed capacity, for example

$$\sum (\text{flows in}) \leq \text{Capacity}$$

When the optimal capacity is to be determined, however, the flows through the intermediate point can be unconstrained. This allows the linear program to set the flows at the level required to minimize costs and thus provides insight into the optimum capacity of these intermediate facilities.

In some cases, limitations may make it impractical to have flows between a source and a use. The flow may be physically impractical (as over a mountain) or politically infeasible due to legal agreements or environmental regulations (untreated municipal wastes cannot be used for irrigation). Infeasible flows can be handled in two ways: they can either be excluded from the formulation or included in a way that precludes their use. Superficially it would seem simpler to exclude impossible flows. As a practical matter, this may not be the case for large systems: the task of describing the matrix of constraints (possibly 1000 × 5000, say) may best be done by an automated preprocessor. It then may be easier to leave all flows in and to exclude those that are infeasible by assigning them extraordinarily high costs that will prevent them from being incorporated into the optimal plan.

Losses in the system, as through evaporation or stealing, can be incorporated easily into the linear program. They are simply defined as a final use or outflow from the system.

Blending operations mix flows with different characteristics, such as salt content, to achieve an acceptable product. Thus rain water might be mixed with some salt water to obtain a larger amount of drinkable water. This situation is handled by a constraint involving the maximum blending ratio of the pure and salty water:

$$\text{(Blending Ratio)} \sum \text{(Pure Flows)} - \sum \text{(Salty Flows)} > 0$$

The coefficients defining the specific problem must be detailed once its overall structure is set. This requires considerable hard work, often very much more than needed to formulate the linear program. For the river basin, flows, uses, and costs needed to be estimated. Here, and in general, the parameters selected are approximate at best.

Rain and other natural sources of water are inherently variable. Over time their distribution may be quite stable, as field measurements can document, but their level in any year may fluctuate widely. This difficulty is normally handled by assuming that the available flow is somewhere toward the conservative side of the distribution. In planning flood control reservoirs, it is usual to estimate the flow as the "100-year flood", thus including about 99% of the distribution. For drinking water, one looks at the "safe yield" which is normally greater than the lowest 1% of the possibilities. In short, normal practice is to define the flow using judgements about what appears to be a reasonable value from the distribution of possibilities.

Future uses must likewise be approximated. These estimates are necessarily worse than those of the flows. Uses, unlike flows, are not drawn from a stable distribution. They tend to grow, with unpredictable spurts and lags due to economic ups and downs, population shifts, and technical changes. Costs are also difficult to estimate satisfactorily, as Chapter 14 explains in detail.

In planning developments involving long-term investments, such as reservoirs and aqueducts (or mines and factories), it is necessary to make sure that the system performs well throughout its lifetime. For the Jordan River, the analysts projected the uses for the years 1980, 2000, and 2020, and defined optimal flows for each of these scenarios.

The solution for any year depends directly on the values assumed for the parameters of the problems. Since these are estimates, one can only obtain estimates of what would be the optimal design in fact. To give oneself confidence that the projected systems will perform satisfactorily for the various values of the parameters that may occur, it is necessary to explore the sensitivity of the solutions to these values. Chapter 6 indicates how to do this systematically.

The solutions for different periods typically vary significantly from each other. For the Jordan River, for example, no desalting is necessary immediately— but seems vital for the next century. Likewise the optimal pattern of flows may change: whereas now it is most economical to pump groundwater directly to households, it soon would appear necessary to blend it with rainwater. This difference in optimal designs presents planners with a problem: to what extent should investments be made in facilities needed now but not in the future? This kind of issue is best dealt with by dynamic programming, which Chapter 7 presents in detail. Ultimately, the design of a complete system may require the complementary use of both linear and dynamic programming, as Chapter 9 indicates.

REFERENCES

Bishop, A. B., and Hendricks, D. W., (1971, 1974). Chapter 12 in de Neufville and Marks (1974). Also "Water Resources Systems Analysis," *Journal of the Sanitary Engineering Div.*, ASCE, 99, February 1971, pp.41–57.

de Neufville, R., and Marks, D. W., (1974). *Systems Planning and Design: Case Studies in Modeling, Optimization and Design*, Prentice-Hall, Englewood Cliffs, NJ.

Wagner, H. M., (1975). "Sensitivity Testing and Duality," Chapter 5, *Principles of Operations Research*, 2nd ed., Prentice-Hall, Englewood Cliffs, NJ.

Williams, H. P., (1985). *Model Building in Mathematical Programming*, 2nd ed., Wiley, New York.

PROBLEMS

5.1. *Feasible Regions*
Which of the following problems can be solved by LP? Explain your answer.

(a) Maximize: $\qquad Z = X + Y$
    Subject to: $\qquad 4X + 3Y \leq 2 \qquad 2XY \leq 3 \qquad X, Y \geq 0$

(b) Maximize: $\qquad Z = 4X + Y$
    Subject to: $\qquad X + Y = 2 \qquad 0.5X + Y \geq 0 \qquad X, Y \geq 0$

(c) Minimize: $\qquad Z = X + Y$
    Subject to: $\qquad X \leq 4 \qquad X + Y \leq 7$

(d) Maximize: $\qquad Z = X + 9Y$
    Subject to: $\qquad 2X - Y \leq 2 \qquad -5X + 2.5Y \leq 1 \qquad X, Y \geq 0$

(e) Minimize: $\qquad Z = X + 9Y$
    Subject to: $\qquad 2X - Y \geq 2 \qquad -5X + 2.5Y \geq 1 \qquad X, Y \geq 0$

(f) Maximize: $\qquad Z = X + Y$
    Subject to: $\qquad X - Y \geq 0 \qquad 3X - Y \leq -3 \qquad X, Y \geq 0$

5.2. *Feasible Region I*
Consider the constraints:

$$3X_1 + 4X_2 \geq 12 \qquad 5X_1 + 4X_2 \leq 40$$
$$X_1 - 3X_2 \leq 3 \qquad 0 \leq X_1 \qquad X_1 \leq 6 \qquad X_2 \leq 6$$

Sketch the feasible region, label each extreme point, and find the extreme point(s) that

(a) Maximize(s): X_1; $\quad X_1 + X_2$; $\quad X_1 - 2X_2$; $\quad 10X_1 + 8X_2$
(b) Minimize(s): X_2; $\quad X_1 + X_2$; $\quad X_1 - 2X_2$

5.3. *Feasible Region II*

Show graphically the feasible region for the constraint set:

$$2X_1 + 3X_2 \leq 18$$
$$2X_1 + X_2 \leq 12$$
$$3X_1 + 3X_2 \leq 24$$
$$X_1, \quad X_2 \geq 0$$

Do these equations define a convex region? With what linear objective function, if any, will (2,2) be optimal?

5.4. *Graphic Interpretation*

Given the linear programming problem:

Maximize: $\qquad Z = 4X_1 + 3X_2$

Subject to: $\qquad 5X_1 + X_2 \leq 40$
$$2X_1 + X_2 \leq 20$$
$$X_1 + 2X_2 \leq 30$$
$$X_1, \qquad X_2 \geq 0$$

(*a*) Draw the feasible region in the resource space.
(*b*) Label the extreme points.
(*c*) Solve the problem for the maximum Z by inspection.
(*d*) Write the dual of the above problem.

5.5. *Meat Market*

Annette's Meat Market sells two kinds of hamburger, both of which are ground fresh daily. The regular grade contains 20% ground beef and 80% oatmeal, while the deluxe grade is 30% beef and 70% oatmeal. The regular grade sells for p_1 cents/lb; the deluxe grade sells for p_2 cents/lb. Annette can buy up to L pounds of beef per day at c_1 cents/lb, but she must pay c_2 cents/lb for each additional pound beyond L per day ($c_2 > c_1$). Oatmeal costs c_3 cents/lb, regardless of quantity purchased.

Annette can spend a total of D dollars per day on the ingredients. Her problem is how much of each ingredient she should purchase daily and how much regular and deluxe hamburger she should make. We are assuming that the customers will buy all of the hamburger she can grind. Carefully formulate as a linear programming problem. This involves: Clear definition of variables; Specification of an objective function, and of constraints.

Include in your answer a succinct explanation of the meaning of the objective function and constraints.

5.6. *STOMP Manufacturing*

STOMP, Inc., buys bulk metal (rods, strips, and so on.) and runs it through processing machines to produce parts, which are then sold to consumer products manufacturers. One stamping machine may be used to produce bird-cage hinges, nameplates for hi-fi speakers, or a mix of the two. A case of the hinges requires 15 min of time on the machine, 5 lbs of metal, and sells for $150. A case of the nameplates, requiring 20 machine min and 10 lbs of metal, sells for $300. Any number of hinges, but only 75 cases of nameplates, may be sold per week.

The metal used costs $20/lb, and is available in any desired quantity. The marginal costs of running the machine (power, use-related maintenance, and so on.) are about $25 hr. The machine operator is on a 40-hr/wk union contract which must be paid anyway, but is willing to work overtime at $12/hr.

Due to delays in receiving payments from customers, STOMP cannot afford to lay out more than $30,000/wk for metal, machine costs, and overtime. Formulate this as a linear programming problem.

(*a*) Define the variables.

(*b*) Specify the objective function and explain its meaning.

(*c*) Specify the constraints and explain their meaning.

5.7. *Mountain Movers*

The Mountain Movers truck company has $1,200,000 to replace its fleet. The company is considering three different truck types:

	Truck type		
	A	B	C
Carrying capacity (tons):	10	20	18
Average speed (mph):	40	35	35
Price ($1,000):	48	78	90
Drivers required:	1	2	2
Shifts per day:	3	3	3
Hours per day:	18	18	21

Type C is the improved model of type B. It has sleeping space for one driver. This reduces its carrying capacity to 18 tons and increases the price to $90,000. The company employs 150 drivers every day, has 50 overnight parking spaces, and wishes to maximize the delivery capacity of its fleet (in ton-mi/day).

(*a*) Define the selection of the trucks as an optimization problem. Explain the decision variables, objective function, and constraints.

(*b*) What assumptions, if any, did you make in this problem?

5.8. *Alloy Optimization*

Suppose a manufacturer must make the decision to use one or more of three different production processes, each yielding the same item. The inputs for each process include chrome and carbon (both measured in pounds). Since each item varies in its input requirements, the profitabilities of the processes vary. Process one requires 6 lbs of chrome, 4 lbs of carbon, and yields a $30 profit/unit. Process two uses 5 lbs of chrome, 2 lbs of carbon, and yields $23/unit. Process three uses 3 lbs of chrome, 5 lbs of carbon, and yields $29/unit. The manufacturer in deciding on the production schedule is limited by the available amounts of chrome and carbon. There are 26 tons of chrome available and 7 tons of carbon.

(*a*) Formulate a linear programming model to determine the manufacturer's optimal production plan; that is, write the objective function and the constraints.

(*b*) What are the activities associated with the formulation?

5.9. *Paint it Easy*

The president of the "Paint it Easy" paint company is in trouble: People complain that the paint does not last long. Experts now recommend a new formula such that

$$
\begin{aligned}
\text{Boiling point} &\geq 70°C \\
\text{Hardening point} &\leq 4\ hr \\
\text{Plastic} &\leq 70\%\ \text{by volume} \\
\text{Acid} &\geq 15\%\ \text{by volume}
\end{aligned}
$$

Four components, A–D, can be used to produce the paint. Their contribution to each of the preceding characteristics is in proportion to their part in the mixture. The coefficients are:

	A	B	C	D
Boiling point	60	99	15	30
Hardening time (h)	1	4	3	2
% plastic	80	50	2	14
% acid	20	0	0	10
Price per liter ($)	1.0	2.4	1.5	0.8

Write the paint production problem as a cost minimization and explain the decision variables, objective function, and contraints.

5.10. *Commodity Shipment*

Suppose a company has S_1 and S_2 tons of some commodity available at its two storage warehouses, and wishes to transport various amounts to its three retail stores where the demands are for D_1, D_2, and D_3 tons, respectively. Let C_{ij} be the nonnegative unit cost of shipping from the ith warehouse to the jth store.

(a) Write the linear programming formulation, the solution to which satisfies the demands at a minimum cost. What minimum condition is necessary for a feasible solution to exist?

(b) Suppose that $D = D_1 + D_2 + D_3$ tons are available at the factory for shipping to the two warehouses, where it will be stored for a while before being shipped to the retail outlets. Storage costs at the two warehouses are a_1 and a_2 dollars per ton, and their capacities are k_1 and k_2 tons. Ignoring the costs of sending the commodity from the factory to the warehouses, formulate the model that will give the overall shipping plan that will satisfy the retail store demands at minimum total cost.

5.11. *Wheat Shipment*

You own two warehouses, W1 and W2, in which you can store wheat. You can buy your wheat from two sources, A and B. A will sell you up to 400 tons of wheat at $100/ton, B up to 50 tons at $75/ton. You must also pay transportation costs to ship your wheat to your warehouses. The current rate is $0.15/ton-km. The distances from each source to each warehouse are:

$$
\begin{aligned}
&\text{A to W1, 350 km;} \quad \text{to W2, 200 km} \\
&\text{B to W1, 200 km;} \quad \text{to W2, 100 km}
\end{aligned}
$$

(*a*) You are already under contract with A for at least 100 tons of wheat. Assuming that you must supply at least 200 tons to W1 and 150 tons to W2, formulate this problem as a linear programming problem.

(*b*) Source B has become the agent of a third party, who is willing to sell up to 350 tons of wheat for $175/ton. Incorporate this change into your linear program.

5.12. *Heavy Metals Inc.*

HMI sells two rhodium-iridium alloys. The high rhodium blend is 60% rhodium and 40% iridium and the high iridium blend is 20% rhodium, 80% iridium. The two alloys sell for p_r and p_i $/kg.

Two grades of rhodium ore are available. The total cost including processing is C_1 /kg for the higher grade and C_2 for the lower grade, where $C_2 > C_1$. Unfortunately there is only enough of the higher grade to produce L kg of rhodium, whereas there is an abundant supply of the lower grade. Iridium on the other hand is available in any quantity at a uniform cost of C_3/kg including processing.

HMI can afford to spend D dollars in buying and processing the ores. The market will absorb as much of either alloy as HMI can produce. HMI wants to know how much of each alloy to produce and of each ore to purchase. Formulate this as an LP problem, carefully specifying and explaining the decision variables, the objective function, and constraints.

5.13. *Red Cross Relief*

The Red Cross wishes to maximize the amount of relief material it can move from a port to an inland disaster area using the available semi-trailers and vans. The constraints on the situation are

	Semis	Vans
Number available	100	200
Fuel use, gal/day	50	12
Capacity, tons/truck/day	40	15

Additionally, only 4500 gal/day of fuel are available to the relief operations, and the capacity of the ferry that replaces a bridge that has fallen down is 250 vehicles/day.

(*a*) Formulate as an LP problem, specifying and explaining the decision variables, the objective function, and constraints.

(*b*) Graph the activities in the fuel-ferry resource space, and sketch the isoquant for 120 tons of material transported.

(*c*) Can the problem still be formulated as an LP if, when more than 30 semis are used, deterioration of the road will require additional semis to be loaded with only 30 tons/truck/day?

(*d*) Repeat (*c*), but supposing instead that, when more than 60 vans are used, the road will pack down and additional vans can carry 20 tons/truck/day.

5.14. *SMC Factory*

As manager in charge of formulating batches of SMC (sheet molding compound, a plastic composite material used structurally in cars), you need to minimize costs subject to constraints on the properties of the material. SMC can be made by blending the following materials:

	Cost ($/lb)	Tensile (ksi)	Modulus (msi)	Specific gravity
Polyester	0.55	8	0.4	1.10
Vinylester	1.05	10	0.5	1.10
E-glass fiber	1.00	500	10	2.54
Carbon fiber	25.00	300	30	1.70
Kevlar fiber	21.00	400	18	1.44

An order has come in for a batch of SMC meeting the following specification:

$$100 \text{ ksi} < \text{Tensile strength} < 200 \text{ ksi}$$
$$\text{Tensile modulus} > 10 \text{ msi}$$
$$\text{Specific gravity} < 1.9$$
$$\text{Total volume \% of fiber} < 78.5\%$$

Assuming that all material properties combine according to their volume percentage, formulate the design of this SMC as a linear programming problem.

5.15. *Transportation Funding*

A Department of Transportation has asked you to suggest the allocation of the DOT's budget of $500M between highway, rapid rail, bus, and innovative urban systems. Political considerations require that urban populations receive at least $300M in benefits, suburbs at least $200M and rural areas at least $100M.

As a rule of thumb, a $1M investment yields total user benefits of

$1.25M for $1M spent on highways

$1.0M for $1M spent on rapid rail

$1.5M for $1M spent on bus

$.8M for $1M spent on innovative systems

Your research also indicates that the distribution of benefits for each transportation mode is

	Urban	Suburban	Rural
Highway	20%	40%	40%
Rapid rail	30%	50%	10%
Bus	30%	40%	30%
Innovative urban systems	60%	40%	—

(*a*) Formulate an LP problem to maximize total user benefits subject to the Department's constraints.

(*b*) Reformulate the problem to reflect the limited number of "good" sites available for rapid rail development; if more than $75M is spent on rapid rail, additional rapid rail funds are spent at "bad" sites, producing only $.7M benefits for a $1M investment.

5.16. *Beans and Corn*

A farmer is planning to produce beans and corn. The unit profit on a pound of beans is $0.50 for the first 1000 lbs. After this the unit profit is $0.35. Corn profits are divided into three categories. The unit profit for the first 800 lbs is $0.75. The next 400 lbs yield $0.40/lb. Any additional lbs of corn will yield $0.25.

The farmer has a limited storage capacity and thus can produce no more than 5000 lbs of produce, in any combination of beans and corn.

The amount of land available is also a restriction on the output. The farmer has 10 acres of workable land for any combination of the two crops. He has determined that every 2000 lbs of beans requires 4 acres. Every 2000 lbs of corn requires 5 acres of land.

The farmer must use a cooperative machine to harvest these crops. He will have access to this machine for 20 hr. He can use it to harvest 200 lbs of beans/hr or 250 lbs of corn/hr.

Formulate an LP to determine the optimal quantity of each crop the farmer should plant, being sure to define your variables.

5.17. *Chemical Company*

A company makes two chemicals, 1 and 2. These chemicals can be manufactured by three different processes using two different raw materials and a fuel. Production data are given below. Formulate an LP model to estimate the time required to run each process in order to maximize the total amount of chemicals manufactured.

Process	Requirements per unit time			Output per unit time	
	Raw material 1	Raw material 2	Fuel	Chemical 1	Chemical 2
1	9	5	50	9	6
2	6	8	75	7	10
3	4	11	100	10	6
Amount Available	200	400	1850		

5.18. *Irrigation Problem*

A fertile but arid area in Southern California is to be cleared, leveled, fertilized, irrigated, and turned into prime farmland. Dealing specifically with the irrigation problem, a linear program is written to select, from a large number of possible canal and pipeline routes, the cheapest set of irrigation links that will provide adequate water to the entire area.

Given the characteristics of LP, explain how each of the following four considerations can be included in the LP, or why it cannot be included.

(a) It is futile to construct feeder line #2 with a greater capacity than link #1, which connects link #2 to the main supply line.

(b) The cost of a pipeline is a nonlinear function of its capacity.

(c) As bulldozer-hours/week increase, the cost of a bulldozer-hour increases.

(d) Water demand is a function of weather and therefore varies from year to year.

CHAPTER
6

SENSITIVITY
ANALYSIS

6.1 CONCEPT

Sensitivity analysis is the process of investigating the dependence of an optimal solution to changes in the way a problem is formulated. Doing a sensitivity analysis is a key part of the design process, equal in importance to the optimization process itself.

The significance of sensitivity analysis stems from the fact that the mathematical problem we solve in any optimization is only an approximation of the real problem. The exact solution we obtain and use to represent reality is thus not an exact solution to the real problem of design. At best, the optimization process provides a good approximation to the best design of a real system.

None of our mathematical models will ever represent systems exactly. All these representations are approximations in some way. They each differ from reality in any or all of the following three ways:

- Structurally, because the overall nature of the equations does not correspond precisely to the actual situation.
- Parametrically, as we are not able to determine all coefficients precisely.
- Probabilistically, in that we typically assume that the situation is deterministic when it is generally variable.

Structural differences arise as a matter of course in the modeling process. The way we typically construct a mathematical model of a system is to imagine some form we believe is appropriate or useful, and then to match the real situation to this structure. This is the process by which most production functions are made: starting from a Cobb-Douglas or translog formula, we estimate coefficients (see Section 2.3). Similarly, when we wish to attack a problem with linear programming, we deliberately construct a set of linear approximations to the reality. These approximations are useful, informative, and efficient. The point is, however, that they are indeed approximations.

Parametric differences between a model and reality reflect our ultimate inability to measure every aspect of a system absolutely accurately. On the one hand we simply never have enough time or money to measure everything we might want to. On the other, we will frequently run into difficulties knowing how precisely to define a quantity so that we can measure it (see Chapter 14 for an extended presentation of that point).

Finally, most of our models assume that the real situation is deterministic, that it can be described by fixed quantities for any particular situation. Most real problems, however, are highly probabilistic; their performance or characteristics can be best described by a probability distribution of some sort. For example, the thermal efficiency of an electric power plant may be 40% on average but varies over a range depending on the variations in the fuels used, the level of maintenance, and the day to day performance of the operations. As Chapter 15 presents in detail, there is always uncertainty in our estimates and descriptions.

Because the real situation never corresponds exactly to the mathematical model, we cannot be satisfied when we have merely obtained the optimum answer for the mathematical problem. We must consider what the answer or design would be if the model were changed to represent what the system might actually be. We must do this both to understand how sensitive or vulnerable our design might be, and so that we can effectively respond when we do perceive changes. This is the concept behind sensitivity analysis.

This chapter presents sensitivity analysis principally in the context of linear programming. This is because the solutions to linear programming problems automatically include most of the sensitivity information a designer could wish for, and thus the linear programs constitute the predominant basis for sensitivity analysis. Additionally, the linearity of linear programming makes it easier to explain key concepts, which the student can then extend to other forms of optimization.

Most of this chapter is devoted to the two most important aspects of sensitivity analysis, the concept and use of

- shadow prices (Section 6.2)
- opportunity costs (Section 6.3)

Sections 6.4 and 6.5 illustrate their use and explain their relationship to each other. Additionally, the chapter describes

- break-even analysis (Section 6.6)

as a practical means of dealing with a special kind of problem.

6.2   SHADOW PRICES

A shadow price is the rate of change of the objective function with respect to a particular constraint. As indicated in Section 3.3, it is essentially equivalent to the Lagrangean multiplier.

> **Semantic caution:** The shadow price has no necessary connection with money, despite its name. Its units are those of the objective function divided by the constraint. For example, in producing electric power subject to environmental constraints, the shadow price might be in terms of kilowatts per gram of pollutant. The shadow price is expressed in dollars only when the objective function is also, say dollars of profit.

Use of shadow prices. Knowledge of the shadow prices is important because, by indicating the quantitative effects of changes in the constraints, they enable the designer to

- *identify* which constraints might most beneficially be changed, and to *initiate* these changes as a fundamental means to improve the design.
- *react* appropriately when external circumstances create opportunities or threats to change the constraints.

Designers working under constraints—such as a budget, an environmental standard, or the percent of a constituent in an alloy—should identify the shadow prices on these constraints to the extent possible. They then can determine which constraints have the greatest effect on their ability to optimize the design and, from this information, initiate proposals to change these standards to the extent desirable (see box on following page).

Knowledge of shadow prices also helps designers react to possible changes to constraints that may be generated externally. It often happens that customers or clients of a system propose that the specifications of the design be changed: Is this a good idea? Alternatively the legislative or administrative process may propose to change the rules: Will this degrade performance significantly? See box (page 109) for examples.

The use of shadow prices to examine the validity of the constraints is sometimes referred to as *specification sensitivity analysis*, because many of the constraints can be interpreted as specifications. This is a useful way to think of the process: rather than simply accept the rules as given, the designer should question these rules and get them changed when it seems best.

Sign of shadow prices. A key practical question with regard to shadow prices is: What is the sign of the shadow price? In which direction should one change a constraint to improve a design?

The right answer to this question is not obvious. The answer that immediately seems logical to many people is in fact wrong: A positive change in the constraint does not necessarily imply a positive shadow price. As it turns out,

Using Shadow Prices to Initiate Changes of Constraints

Consider again the problem of designing the water supply system for New York City. Suppose the problem had been formulated as

Minimize: Total cost of systems

Subject to (among others): Water pressure at curb ≥ 40 psi

Suppose further that we found that

Shadow price on pressure constraint = $78 million/psi

This means that there is the potential for great improvements in design—savings in cost in this case—if we were to change the constraint. We could then ask:

- Is this constraint absolute, determined by some law of nature, or was it set for convenience at some time?
- If the latter, is the constraint still justified? Can it be changed?
- Is the shadow price sufficiently large to make it worthwhile to go to the trouble of getting the constraint changed?

For New York City in particular, the standard was set rather arbitrarily (at 40 as a round number rather than 38, say), years ago when buildings were different. There is thus a reasonable basis for changing the standard if the improvements in design justify it. In our analyses at the time we worked on the problem, it appeared that it would indeed have been worthwhile to alter the constraint at least a few psi, because of the huge savings in cost.

---

there is no evident connection between the change in constraint and the sign of the shadow price.

To understand the relationship between the sign of the shadow price and the constraints, it is useful to divide them into

- *upper bounds*, which place a maximum constraint on a feasible region, for example: $\sum_i a_{ji} X_i \leq b_j$.
- *lower bounds*, which place a minimum constraint on a feasible region, such as $\sum_i a_{ki} X_i \geq b_k$ (see Section 3.4).

A helpful mental image here is that the feasible region is the space inside the constraints. The upper and lower bounds then constitute the roof and the floor of this space.

Secondly, the concept of relaxation needs to be understood. *A constraint is relaxed* if it is changed so as to increase the size of the feasible region, that is,

Using Shadow Prices to React to Changes in Constraints

Suppose that, as the analyst for a refinery, you have determined that your shadow price on the percent of sulfur in the fuel oil is

Shadow Price = $3.81 a barrel/% sulfur

If a prospective customer who does not care about the sulfur content offers to take a lower grade of fuel oil with 1% more sulfur if you will give a $5 a barrel discount in price, do you accept? No: the change in the constraint would only save you $3.81 and you would lose money (3.81 − 5.00) if you accepted the offer. You might respond by offering a $3 a barrel discount, which would leave you ahead by $0.81.

Alternatively, if the local authorities proposed to force you to take out more sulfur, say 2% more, you could respond by indicating this requirement would raise your price by $7.62 (= 2 × 3.81) a barrel and—let us say—make it impossible to produce profitably. Knowledge of the shadow price thus gives you specific grounds for reacting to proposed changes in specifications.

---

if an upper bound is increased or a lower bound is decreased. The idea here is that the constraints place pressures on the designer and that moving them away, making the feasible region larger, relaxes these pressures.

The relationship between the nature of the shadow prices and the changes in constraints is that

- Relaxing the constraints leads to improvements in the optimum, either increasing a maximum or decreasing a minimum.

Visualizing the feasible region as a space, this rule can be stated colloquially as

- Changes in constraints that "raise the roof" or "lower the floor" will tend to improve the optimum.

The logic behind this rule is simple. When one relaxes a constraint, the feasible region expands—it is the previous region plus an increment. Thus, one can do at least as well after the relaxation as before—never worse. On the other hand, there can be better solutions in the expanded region. The optimum solution after the relaxation of a constraint must necessarily be equal or better.

Conversely, if a constraint is tightened, thus reducing the feasible region, this may exclude the previous optimum solution. Therefore, the optimum solution after a constraint is tightened is necessarily worse if not equal.

It is important to notice that there is absolutely no simple relationship between the sign of the change in constraint and the sign of the shadow price. This is because an increase in the constraint can either relax or tighten a constraint,

Lack of Evident Relationship Between the Signs of Changes in Constraints and the Objective

Consider the problem:

Maximize: X_2

Subject to: $X_1 - 2X_2 \geq 0$

$X_1 \leq 2$

$X_1, \quad X_2 \geq 0$

The feasible region for this problem appears in Figure 6.1, interior to the shadowed lines, that is, the triangle between the origin and point A. The optimum, the highest feasible value of X_2, is obviously at $A(X_1 = 2, X_2 = 1)$.

Suppose one now relaxes the first constraint by 1. Since it is a lower bound, this means we decrease the constraint and have

$$X_1 - 2X_2 \geq -1$$

This expands the feasible region, allowing the optimum to raise to point B $(X_1 = 2, X_2 = 1.5)$. We have a positive change in the objective function associated with a negative change in the constraint.

Relaxing the second constraint by 1 means increasing this upper bound to

$$X_2 \leq 3$$

Again the feasible region is expanded, and the optimum is at $C(X_1 = 3, X_2 = 1.5)$. Here a positive change in the objective is associated with a positive change in constraint.

---

depending on whether it is an upper or lower bound and if one is maximizing or minimizing. The preceding box illustrates the phenomenon graphically.

Because there is no simple sign convention relating to shadow prices, they are often reported in absolute values. (See box on page 112.) This places the responsibility on the analyst to determine what kind of change improves the optimum. The minimum value of the shadow price is thus typically taken to be zero.

> **Semantic caution:** There may be a difference between the formal definition of an upper or lower bound, and what you may visualize. Consider Figure 6.1; the constraint $X_1 - 2X_2 \geq 0$ is a lower bound, but it effectively looks like a bound on the maximum or uppermost value of the objective function.

Range of shadow prices. The concept of the range of a shadow price applies only, in practice, to linear programming. In general, the shadow price is the instantaneous change in the objective function with respect to a specific constraint, $\partial Y / \partial b_j$, as defined in Section 3.2. This rate can vary with the decision variables, and normally will when the constraints are nonlinear, as the application in Section 3.4 illustrates.

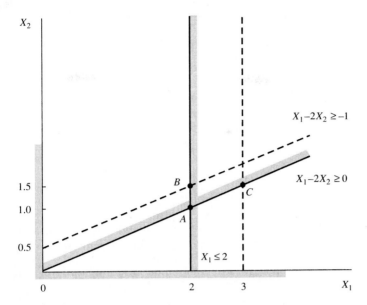

FIGURE 6.1
Illustration for demonstration of lack of evident relationship between signs of changes in constraints and objective.

The peculiarity of linear programming in this regard is that the shadow prices are constant over a range, rather than varying continuously. The output of a linear program correspondingly consists not only of the value of the shadow price but also defines the range of the change in the constraint over which the given value holds.

The existence of a range of constancy for the shadow price is, generally, an artifact of the way we have formulated the problem as a linear program. In reality, one can assume that the linear equations are approximations and that, if we really described the problem accurately with the appropriate nonlinear equations, the shadow prices could usually vary instantaneously. Even though the range of constancy of the shadow prices is thus an artificial result, the concept is most useful in practice.

The range of constancy of shadow prices is useful because it further indicates how sensitive the optimum solution is to the constraint. Indeed, if the range is narrow, we know that even small changes in the constraint could lead to quite different shadow prices, thus that the shadow prices may change rapidly. If, on the contrary, the range is large, we can infer that the shadow prices vary slowly.

The constancy of any shadow price over a range results from the nature of the optimum solution in linear programming. The optimum is at a corner point of the feasible region, defined by the intersection of linear equations of constraints; as one of these equations is changed by a constant amount, so is the intersection and so is the value of the objective function since it is also linear. This constancy goes on indefinitely until something fundamental changes.

Range of Shadow Prices

Consider the same problem as before, augmented by a third constraint as shown in Figure 6.2:

Maximize: X_2

Subject to:
$$X_1 - 2X_2 \geq 0$$
$$X_1 \leq 2$$
$$X_1 + X_2 \leq 4$$
$$X_1, \quad X_2 \geq 0$$

As shown in the previous box, the shadow price on the first constraint is $\frac{1}{2}$; when the feasible region is expanded by lowering this lower bound by 1 (to $X_1 - 2X_2 \geq -1$), the optimum increases by $\frac{1}{2}$.

This shadow price will prevail until the first constraint has reached the intersection of constraints at D(at $X_1 - 2X_2 \geq -2$). Further relaxation of the first constraint then still leads to increases in the optimum, but these will be at a different rate. The optimum corner point will no longer be defined along the second constraint ($X_1 \leq 2$) but along the third ($X_1 + X_2 \leq 4$). The rate of change of the objective function will then be different.

In general, there are upper and lower limits to the range. In this case, the limit in the range in the other direction is point E(at $X_1 - 2X_2 \geq 2$). At that point the feasible region disappears. Further increases in the constraint are then meaningless since there is no solution, let alone an optimum.

The range on the shadow price on the first constraint is therefore from -2 to $+2$.

The range of the shadow price is defined by the intersections of constraints adjacent to the one that defines the optimum of the linear program. Ultimately, as a constraint varies, it intersects with other constraints. The equations defining the optimum corner then change, leading to a change in the shadow prices. This occurs at other intersections. (See box above for an example.)

In general there can be a limit to the range of a shadow price for both increases and decreases. It will often be, however, that the range in either direction is unbounded. This occurs typically with constraints that are not binding at the optimum (slack $\neq 0$, so shadow price $= 0$). The constraint then has a zero shadow price indefinitely in the direction moving ever further away from the optimum; in the other direction, the shadow price is zero only until the constraint is binding (slack $= 0$).

Change in the shadow prices. For linear programming, the shadow prices change in a distinctive manner beyond the range of their constancy. The rule is

- the shadow price reduces beyond its range if the constraint is being relaxed.
- the shadow price increases beyond its range if the constraint is being tightened.

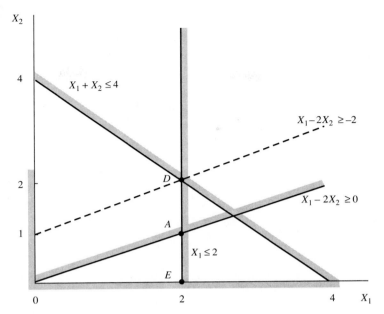

FIGURE 6.2
Illustration for demonstration of range of shadow prices in linear programming.

Because of the way shadow prices are typically reported, in absolute values, shadow prices can only reduce to zero. At that point slack $\neq 0$ and changes in the constraint have no effect. Shadow prices may, on the other hand, increase without limit.

The reason for this rule lies in the convexity of the feasible region and the linearity of the objective function. As we meet up with other constraints, which define a jog in the shape of the feasible region and thus a change in shadow price, the nature of the change in shadow price must be as defined (see box for an example).

Changes in Shadow Prices

Figure 6.3 shows the optimization of Figure 6.2 with the constraint at the end of its range for the shadow price and passing through D. The shadow price from the optimum (at A) to D was equal to $\frac{1}{2}$. What is it beyond the range?

If the constraint is further relaxed by one to $X_1 - 2X_2 \geq -3$, the new optimum will be at F, the intersection of this constraint with $X_1 + X_2 \leq 4$. The coordinates of F are $(\frac{5}{3}, \frac{7}{3})$. The change in X_2, the objective function, associated with the unit change in the constraint and the move from D to F is thus $\frac{1}{3}$. As expected, the shadow price steadily reduces, beyond its range of constancy, in the direction of relaxation.

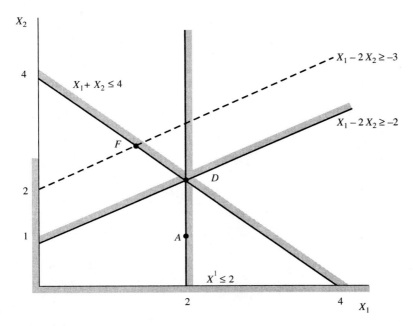

FIGURE 6.3
Illustration for demonstration of nature of change of shadow prices beyond range.

6.3 OPPORTUNITY COSTS

Opportunity costs, in the context of sensitivity analysis, relate to the coefficients of the decision variables in the objective function. In general terms they define the "cost"—in terms of degradation of the optimum, whether the objective function refers to cost, product of some other quantity—of using decision variables that are not part of the optimal design. They have a specialized meaning, which must be carefully understood. This meaning must also be distinguished from a more general one commonly used in economics.

> **Semantic caution:** In economics and management one often refers to "opportunity cost" in the sense of meaning the highest value one could obtain for some resource. Thus the term "opportunity cost of capital" refers to the highest rate of return one could obtain per extra unit available (see Section 12.3). For linear programming and sensitivity analysis, however, where one would be formally maximizing return or profit subject to constraints on the budget, this notion is embodied in the concept of the shadow price of the constraint on available capital. Thus the other usage is particularly confusing because it refers to a totally different sensitivity than the one accepted in optimization.

Definition of opportunity costs. To define opportunity costs formally, we first need to examine the nature of the optimum solution to an optimization. In general, the set of optimal decision variables, $\mathbf{X}^*$, can be divided into two categories. One category consists of all the decision variables that are not used in the optimum design, that is, whose optimal value is zero, $X_i^* = 0$. Generally this category is quite large in any practical problem as there are indeed many possible decisions that we do not take. For example, if we intend to supply New York with fuel oil, we may well use plenty from Venezuela, the Texas Gulf, and elsewhere, but none from Alaska because of poor connections and other opportunities (see box on page 117). The two categories for the optimum set of the decision variables, $\mathbf{X}^*$, are thus the

- *optimal variables*, those with nonzero values at the optimum ($X_i^* \neq 0$). These are said to be "in the solution."
- *nonoptimal variables*, those equal to zero at the optimum ($X_i^* = 0$). These are said to be "not in the solution."

With this distinction in mind, we can now formally define opportunity costs in sensitivity analysis: The *opportunity cost* is the rate of degradation of the optimum per unit use of a nonoptimal variable in the design. The notion of degradation here is important: it refers to the worsening of an optimum. This may either be a decrease—if we are trying to maximize, or an increase—if we are trying to minimize.

It is important to recognize that the use of a nonoptimal variable in the design must make matters worse. If we should ever use a unit of a nonoptimal variable, we would necessarily—due to the constraints—displace some quantities of the optimal variables, thus leading to a worsening. Using again the hypothetical example of the shipment of fuel oil, if we insist on supplying New York from Alaska, we will need less from Venezuela or some other closer place and thus increase costs. Conversely, in the example shown in Figure 6.4, if we used some Activity 3 instead of some combination of Activities 1 and 2, we would reduce production.

Use of opportunity costs. The way the designer should use opportunity costs differs considerably from that of shadow prices. This difference results from the quite distinct functions of the constraints (**B**) and the coefficients of the objective function (**C**) in the optimization process.

The coefficients **C** represent some kind of technical reality of the design which the designer cannot, in general, influence directly. For example, if we are maximizing production, the objective represents the production function and the coefficients **C** each represent the best productivity of each activity or decision variable. Alternatively, if we are minimizing cost, the coefficients **C** are the prices of the items that could be purchased, and these should already be the best available. The constraints, on the other hand, do not represent any best cost or productivity, they are often fairly arbitrary and may be changed.

The result is that the analyst is unlikely to be able to or want to manipulate the coefficients **C**. Thus in general the variation of the optimum with every C_i is not of interest. The only useful variation is in fact that of the optimum with the coefficients of the nonoptimal decision variables, that is, the opportunity costs.

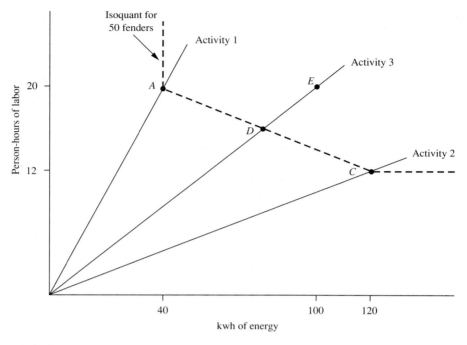

FIGURE 6.4
Illustration for discussion of opportunity cost of Activity 3.

The interest of the opportunity costs lies in the special information we can derive from them in a linear program. The opportunity cost associated with any nonoptimal variable in effect defines the value of the coefficient for that variable when its use would be optimal. This we call the *trigger price* for that variable (using price by analogy to opportunity cost, although the optimum may or may not be expressed in terms of money).

The relationship between an opportunity cost and the trigger price for a variable is direct. Suppose X_k^* is a nonoptimal decision variable for a problem. This means that its contribution to the objective function per unit of X_k, that is C_k, is unattractive. Either C_k is too large if we are minimizing, or it is too small if we are maximizing. In either case, using any unit of X_k in the design worsens the optimum by the opportunity cost, OC_k. It follows that if the coefficient C_k somehow improved (became smaller for a minimization, larger for a maximization), the OC_k would become smaller. As relationships are linear in a linear program, it then follows that if C_k were improved by OC_k, there would no longer be any opportunity price for X_k and it could be used in the optimal design. Therefore:

$$\text{Trigger price} = C_k - OC_k \qquad \text{minimization}$$
$$= C_k + OC_k \qquad \text{maximization}$$

Nonoptimal Decision Variables

Consider the production process described in Section 5.6, Table 5.1, which could use either of two activities. We now add an Activity 3, which requires 100 kwh and 20 person-hours to produce 50 fenders. This is shown on Figure 6.4, which is simply an extension of Figure 5.5.

If one were trying to maximize production subject only to constraints on the resources, one would never use Activity 3. To produce 50 units it requires the resources shown by point E. In fact, that proportion of resources can be used much more efficiently by a combination of Activities 1 and 2, which combine to produce 50 units at point D or 20% more (62.5 units) at E (see previous discussion). Activity 3 is thus a nonoptimal variable in this situation.

Further, if C_k were improved by more than OC_k we would definitely want to use X_k in the optimum design (see box below).

The use of the opportunity costs is thus to define the coefficients of the decision variables which would lead to a change in design. The designer, having defined the optimum design, then continuously monitors the situation to determine when it has changed enough so that a new design ought to be used.

In practice, opportunity costs and trigger prices are most useful in problems of minimizing costs. This is because the prices for goods fluctuate fairly rapidly, as can be verified by following the quotes for commodities in the financial newspapers. Managers of large systems and of plants thus can continually monitor the fluctuations in prices and, by comparing the quotes to their trigger prices, identify possibilities for changing design to maintain optimality for the new circumstances. Alternatively they can define for their purchasing agents and suppliers the price at which they can afford to buy specific goods.

Opportunity Costs

Same problem as above. Activity 3 is nonoptimal. One unit of Activity 3, at E in Figure 6.4, produces 50, whereas the same resources, used in a combination of Activities 1 and 2, can produce 62.5.

These facts can be interpreted as follows:

Productivity per unit X_3: $\qquad C_3 = 50$

Opportunity cost of X_3: $\qquad OC_3 = 62.5 - 50 = 12.5$

Trigger "Price" (here in units of product) for $X_3 = 50 + OC_3 = 62.5$

6.4   ILLUSTRATION

A linear programming procedure normally provides all the sensitivity information previously discussed. The complete output you should expect to get then consists of two parts. First, the optimal answer:

- Optimum objective function, OF^*
- Optimal set of decision variables, $\mathbf{X}^*$
- Slack variables at optimum, $\mathbf{SV}^*$

Secondly, the sensitivity information:

- The set of shadow prices, $\mathbf{SP}^*$
- The ranges of the shadow prices
- The set of opportunity costs, $\mathbf{OC}^*$

These are now all illustrated by an example.

The example is deliberately simple so that the relationships between the different elements of the solution are easy to understand. The problem is sufficiently easy mathematically that it can be solved by inspection, thus avoiding any questions concerning the algorithms for solving linear programming problems. Yet it is complex enough to demonstrate all the interesting conceptual issues.

The problem is:

Minimize: $\text{Cost} = 4X_1 + 12X_2 + 10X_3$

Subject to:
$$2X_1 + X_2 \qquad\quad \geq 2 = b_1$$
$$X_1 + 2X_2 + X_3 \geq 5 = b_2$$
$$X_3 \geq 1 = b_3$$
$$X_1, \qquad X_2, \qquad X_3 \geq 0$$

Physically, this might represent the cost minimization of a product subject to technical constraints. Thus it could be the manufacture of reinforced concrete using cement mix (X_1), special additives (X_2), and reinforcing steel rods (X_3). The constraints would then be interpreted as follows:

- A minimum amount of cement mix and additives is needed to bind everything together.
- The separate contributions of each input add up to at least the desired total.
- A minimum amount of steel is needed for strength.
- The inputs cannot be negative.

The optimal solution to this problem can be determined by inspection. We need to have at least $X_3 = 1$ to meet the third constraint, and then we want to use as much X_1 as possible to meet the other constraints, because it is cheapest to use. (In the first constraint, the effect of using one unit of X_1, which costs 4, is equivalent to using two units of X_2, which cost 24. Similarly, in the second constraint, X_1 is cheapest in meeting a unit's worth of constraint.) The best design is

$$\mathbf{X}^* = (4,\ 0,\ 1)$$

for a minimum objective function

$$OF^* = 26$$

The slack variables, calculated by substituting the optimal decision variables in the constraints, are

$$\mathbf{SV}^* = (6,\ 0,\ 0)$$

Shadow prices. The shadow price on the first constraint is obvious: since there is slack ($=6$), the shadow price on b_1 is zero. This follows both intuitively, from the observation that since we meet the constraint by a wide margin the optimum design is not affected by a unit change in b_1, and formally by the complementary slackness rule ($S\lambda = 0$).

The shadow price on the second constraint is not zero. Its value can be seen fairly directly: a unit increase in b_2 requires a unit change in the decision variables, the cheapest of which is X_1. Thus the shadow price on b_2 is 4.

The shadow price on the third constraint is also not zero. In this case, however, its value results from a fairly complex interplay between the decision variables — as is normally the case, in fact. In general, the values of the shadow prices are not at all obvious and cannot be estimated from any individual equations.

For the third constraint, a unit increase in b_3 implies a unit increase in X_3, which increases cost by 10. The increase in X_3, however, makes it possible to decrease other decision variables: the unit increase in X_3 contributes to meeting the second constraint and thus makes it possible to reduce X_1 by 1, which reduces cost by 4. The net change in the objective function per unit increase in b_3 is, then,

$$SP_3 = +10 - 4 = 6$$

In summary we have:

$$\mathbf{SP}^* = (0,\ 4,\ 6)$$

Note that the zeros of the optimal slack variables correspond to nonzero shadow prices, and vice-versa.

Range of shadow prices. The range of validity for the shadow price of a constraint that is not binding is easy to determine: the shadow price remains equal to zero as long as there is slack. In our problem, the first constraint is not binding when $b_1 = 2$, a point where the slack for the optimum solution is 6. There will continue to be slack for any value of b_1 up to 8 ($=2 +$ slack). Conversely, there would always be slack if b_1 were decreased, so there is no lower bound on the range of the shadow price. The range of validity for $SP_1^* = 0$ is thus: $-\infty \leq b_1 \leq 8$.

The range of validity for a binding constraint is more difficult to determine. One needs to determine when another constraint begins to have an effect. For the second constraint we can lower b_2 (which implies lowering X_1, since X_3 is fixed by the third constraint) until the level of X_1 is restrained by the first constraint, that is until $X_1 = 1$ and $b_2 = 2$. If b_2 were less than 2, the first and third constraints would be binding, the second would not be and its shadow price would then be zero. Therefore the lower bound on the b_2 for $SP_2^* = 4$ is 2. When it comes to raising b_2, however, there is no other constraint that might lead to a change in SP_2^*, so that the range is unbounded. The range of validity for $SP_2^* = 4$ is thus:

$$2 \leq b_2 \leq +\infty$$

Finally, the range of validity for $SP_3^* = 6$ is:

$$0 \leq b_3 \leq 4$$

The shadow price becomes zero if $b_3 = 0$ and X_3 is no longer required. It also changes when b_3 is large enough to create slack in the second constraint and make the first constraint binding. This occurs at $b_3 = 4$: each additional unit beyond that requires an extra unit of X_3 (at a cost of 10) which can no longer be compensated by a decrease in X_1, since the first constraint forces X_1 to be at least 1. So for $b_3 > 4$, $SP_3 = 10$.

Change in the shadow prices. The third constraint provides a good illustration of the way shadow prices vary with constraints. As b_3 is increased, this lower bound constraint is tightened (the "floor is raised") as the shadow price increases. Conversely, as b_3 is lowered (as from $b_3 = 5$ to $b_3 = 3$), the constraint is relaxed (the "floor is lowered") and the shadow price decreases. Figure 6.5 shows the behavior.

Opportunity costs. Opportunity costs exist only for nonoptimal decision variables; they are zero for optimal decision variables by definition. Therefore, since X_1 and X_3 are both part of the optimal design, $OC_1 = OC_3 = 0$.

The opportunity cost of a decision variable that is not in the optimal solution, such as X_2, is determined by *both* the coefficient of that variable in the objective function *and* the nature of constraints. Introducing the nonoptimal variable in the design generally permits one to use less of others.

The use of a unit of nonoptimal X_2 thus leads to an immediate cost of $C_2 = 12$. This is compensated, however, by the possibility of lowering X_1 (not X_3 since its quantity is limited by the third constraint). Specifically, using a unit of X_2 allows us to satisfy the second constraint with two less units of X_1, reducing cost on that account by 8. The net worsening of the objective function due to the use of a unit of the nonoptimal X_2 is thus:

$$OC_2^* = 12 - 8 = 4$$

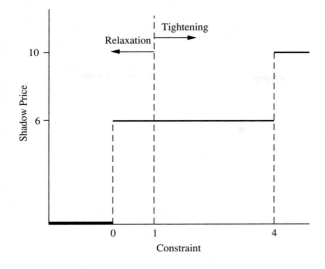

FIGURE 6.5
Shadow prices increase or stay constant as constraints are tightened in a linear program, and vice-versa.

In summary, we have:

$$\mathbf{OC}^* = (0, 4, 0)$$

Note that the zeros of the optimal opportunity costs correspond to the nonzero optimal decision variables, and vice-versa. This effect corresponds to the complementary slackness associated with shadow prices. The reason for this has to do with duality, as explained next.

6.5 PRIMAL-DUAL RELATIONSHIPS

For any given linear programming problem there is a dual—or "mirror image"—problem, which contains all the information of the original or primal problem (see Section 5.10). Particularly important aspects of this relationship are that

* the optimum value of the objective function for the primal problem equals that of the dual.
* the optimal solution to the dual contains all the sensitivity information in that of the primal, coded in different ways.

Specifically, it is true that

* the optimal values of the decision variables in the dual problem are the shadow prices of the primal (and vice-versa).
* the optimal value of the slack variables in the dual problem are the opportunity costs of the primal (and vice-versa).

For this reason, operations research jargon often refers to shadow prices as *dual variables*, and to opportunity costs as *dual slacks*.

For the user, really only interested in the results of the linear program, these relationships between the primal and dual problems are not especially useful. However, since much of the literature on linear programs uses these concepts to describe the results of an analysis, it is important to appreciate this language.

The equivalences stated above can be seen by looking at the example in the previous section. Since the dual to the minimization is

Maximize: $\qquad\qquad\qquad\qquad$ $\mathbf{B}^T\mathbf{W}$

Subject to: $\qquad\qquad\qquad$ $\mathbf{A}^T\mathbf{W} \le C^T \qquad \mathbf{W} \ge 0$

we can write

Maximize: $\qquad\qquad$ $2W_1 + 5W_2 + W_3$

Subject to:
$$
\begin{aligned}
2W_1 + W_2 &\le 4 \\
W_1 + 2W_2 &\le 12 \\
W_2 + W_3 &\le 10 \\
W_1, \quad W_2, \quad W_3 &\ge 0
\end{aligned}
$$

By inspection, as before, we can see that we would like to use as much W_2 as possible, and then W_1 and W_3 as permitted by the constraints. This leads to

$$\mathbf{W}^* = (0, 4, 6)$$

which is equivalent to $\mathbf{SP}^*$ of the primal. We can also see that

$$\mathbf{OF}^* = 26$$

again, as for the primal. Further,

$$\mathbf{SV}^* = (0, 4, 0)$$

which is the $\mathbf{OC}^*$ of the primal.

A more detailed analysis would show that for this dual we would also have

$$\mathbf{SP}^* = (4, 0, 1)$$

the vector of $\mathbf{X}^*$ in the primal, and

$$\mathbf{OC}^* = (6, 0, 0)$$

the slack variables in the primal.

6.6 BREAK-EVEN ANALYSIS

Break-even analysis is an important form of sensitivity analysis. It is much used in practice, particularly in the comparison of alternative technologies for a system.

This method has the advantage of being able to deal with nonconvex feasible regions. It is thus not connected with linear programming, as are the previous methods. In fact, it is not associated with any form of optimization. Break-even analysis is conceptually and mathematically simple.

The essential idea derives from the fact that the creation of any product requires both an initial investment into plant and equipment and then, in production, the cost of labor, power, and supplies. The initial investment is known as the *capital cost*, C_k. The costs of production constitute the *variable cost*, C_v. (Section 14.4 presents these concepts in detail). The variable costs may be nonlinear, particularly as diseconomies of scale arise (see Section 4.5). In practice the variable costs are generally assumed to be linear, as a reasonable approximation when costs are difficult to define precisely. The total cost of production is then

$$\text{Total Cost} = C_k + C_v X$$

The relative size of the fixed and variable costs is a distinctive feature of different technologies. These costs provide the economic basis for choosing between alternative technologies. The typical situation is that one technology costs less to implement than the second, but has higher variable costs:

$$C_{k1} < C_{k2} \qquad \text{but} \qquad C_{v1} > C_{v2}$$

The question is: Which technology should be chosen? Assuming that they perform the same task, this resolves into an economic issue: Which costs less? The answer depends on the level of production: the first technology is cheaper when volume is low, the second will be when volume is high enough. The crucial issue thus concerns the *break-even point*, the level of production where the costs of one equal that of the other, where the economic advantage shifts from the first technology to the second. Break-even analysis defines this the point, which provides the economic basis for technology choice.

Figure 6.6 illustrates the situation. Notice that the feasible region of costs, above the hatched line, is nonconvex. This is typical for questions of technology choice. Switching to a technology that is cheaper at higher volumes of production is a prime reason for economies of scale (see discussion in Section 4.5).

The analysis itself merely consists of solving for the break-even point. As can be seen, this requires finding the volume of production, X, at which both technologies imply the same total cost. For linear costs this is:

$$C_{k1} + C_{v1}X = C_{k2} + C_{v2}X$$

The technologies with lower capital costs and higher variable costs are often low technologies. For example, a high-technology, automated factory costs more to install than an ordinary factory, but is designed to save extensively on the variable costs of labor. Yet important exceptions to this pattern exist: sometimes the higher technology has lower capital costs and higher variable costs. Thus it is for the cost of transport in undeveloped areas. Air transport, which only requires airfields at each destination, often costs less initially than road transport that involves the construction of a highway network. Once roads are built, however, trucks carry goods much more cheaply than aircraft. As part of our work for the U.S. AID and the Government of Colombia, referred to in the applications of Sections 2.6 and 3.4, we did break-even analyses for exactly this situation.

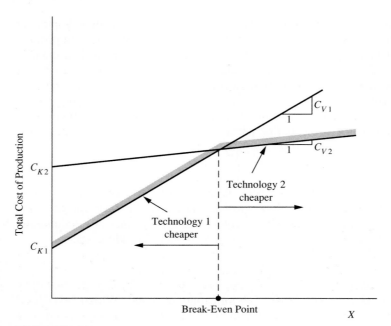

FIGURE 6.6
The break-even point is the volume of production where two technologies lead to the same total cost of production.

6.7 APPLICATION

The collection and disposal of municipal solid waste—garbage—illustrates well the role of sensitivity analyses. This section focuses on how these results were extracted from the optimization and then used in the design of the system. Garbage disposal is an expensive operation, especially in big cities. It requires a lot of transportation and a lot of labor. The amount of trucking required is surprisingly large, especially as existing disposal facilities reach capacity and the expanding cities force new sites to be further and further away. Distances of 10 to 20 miles are common, and some cities have been forced to use dumps 50 to 100 miles away. Garbage collection typically requires many workers to pick up barrels and tip them into the garbage trucks. An efficient system must use its labor and trucks effectively.

Two devices are used in the United States to improve the efficiency of the system. The first is a compactor truck, a vehicle with a mechanism that squeezes the garbage tightly as it is picked up; this permits much more to be loaded into the collection vehicles. The second is the use of transfer stations, at which garbage is unloaded from the compactor trucks for reloading on very large trucks for carting to the ultimate disposal site. The operation of transfer stations is expensive, but they offer two major possibilities for reducing costs:

they permit the use of semi-trailers, which could not be introduced directly in city streets; and they avoid wasting the time of the expensive compactor truck and its crew of garbage collectors on a long haul to a distant dump.

The optimization of a garbage collection system requires careful design of the size, number and location of the transfer points, as well as the corresponding routes for the trucks. The number of possible combinations is very, very large; the constraints on routes, working hours, vehicle capacities, and so on are also enormous. Fortunately it can be formulated and solved by linear programming.

The following illustrations of sensitivity analysis come from an extensive study of Baltimore. It is a good example of the general case of garbage collection, but naturally the specific parameters differ from city to city.

Specification sensitivity analysis played an essential part in the design. The procedure was to optimize the system for one set of specifications, then to vary these constraints, and finally to plot the results to determine the specifications that gave the least expensive results.

The capacity of the transfer point was one specification that was investigated in detail. In any particular analysis this specification was entered as an upper bound constraint on the capacity. Varying this constraint therefore defined the shadow price on the capacity. Figure 6.7 illustrates the results. At the lowest capacities, the size of the transfer point is a binding constraint and its shadow price is nonzero. As the capacity is enlarged, this upper bound constraint is

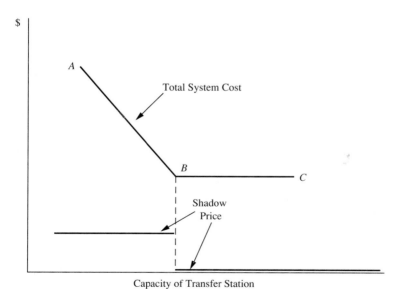

Capacity of Transfer Station

FIGURE 6.7
Changing the upper bound constraint on capacity reduces costs at a constant rate until this constraint is no longer binding.

relaxed, the total cost decreases at the constraint rate defined by the shadow price (as the line *AB* shows). Ultimately, the constraint is no longer binding, there is slack, the shadow price equals zero, and further increases in capacity no longer reduce cost (the line *BC*). (As a second-order effect, the cost actually rises from *B* to *C*, due to the capital cost of a larger transfer station, a factor not included in the minimization of the operating costs by the linear program.)

The number of garbage collections per week was a different kind of specification that was investigated. This was not directly entered into the formulation of the linear program as a constraint; it altered the amount of garbage that had to be picked up in any operation. The range of validity on the shadow price of that constraint did not go as far as the 50% increase implied by going from three collections a week to two, so that shadow prices were useless in this instance. Consequently, the optimization was simply performed twice and the effect noted: collecting three times a week only cost 4% more (assuming people do not create more garbage).

The lack of sensitivity of cost to the number of collections illustrates a point about linear programming and optimization in general: one's intuition about systems is frequently quite wrong. Most people, when asked about the difference in cost between two or three collections a week, immediately think that the better service—with half again as many pickups—should cost about 50% more. The reason this is not so has to do with the way constraints define the solution. In this case, the principal constraint is the volume of the truck, which defines the number of unproductive trips to the dump; if the amount of trash to be collected

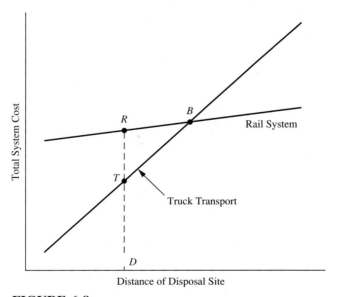

FIGURE 6.8
The relative costs of truck and rail transport define the opportunity costs of the more expensive system and the break-even point.

does not change, the number of unproductive trips stays about the same and so does the total cost. One of the advantages of linear programming is that it helps bring out these counter-intuitive aspects of a system.

Opportunity costs were used in the design to explore the viability of rail as an alternative way to carry the garbage from the transfer station to the disposal site. Figure 6.8 illustrates the approach. The analysis indicated that for the distance (D) involved for Baltimore, truck transport was cheaper (at T) than rail (at R). The opportunity cost of the uneconomic solution was thus the difference in total cost, $(R - T)$, divided by the tonnage involved. This gave the city the guideline it needed in negotiating with the railroad about better prices. If the reduction in the cost of rail did not exceed its opportunity costs, that alternative should not be part of the solution.

A break-even analysis can be derived from the same data. The intersection of the cost functions for rail and truck transport, at B, indicate the distance to the dump that would make rail attractive. This information is useful to planners as they visualize that future disposal sites are indeed going to be further and further from the city.

Overall, the optimization of the garbage collection system was particularly useful to Baltimore because it provided extensive sensitivity analysis. This information enabled the planners and city managers to design the system, to specify its constraints and the mode of operation that would be most economical. The original optimization was, in this case, principally useful as a starting point for the sensitivity analysis.

REFERENCES

de Neufville, R., and Marks, D. H. (1974). *Systems Planning and Design: Case Studies in Modeling, Optimization and Evaluation,* Prentice-Hall, Englewood Cliffs, NJ.

Eppen, G. D., and Gould, F. J. (1985). "Linear Programs: Computer Analysis and Interpreting Sensitivity Output," Ch. 6, *Quantitive Concepts for Management: Decision-Making Without Algorithms*, 2nd ed., Prentice-Hall, Englewood Cliffs, NJ.

Marks, D. H. and Liebman, J. C. (1971), "Location Models: A Solid Waste Collection Example," *ASCE Journal of the Urban Planning and Development Division*, 99, pp. 15–30.

White, J. A., Agee, M. H., Case, K. E. (1984). "Break-Even, Sensitivity and Risk Analysis," Chapter 8, *Principles of Engineering Economic Analysis*, 2nd ed., Wiley, New York.

PROBLEMS

6.1. *Sensitivity Exercise I*
For the linear program

$$\text{Maximize:} \quad Z = X_1 - X_2$$

Subject to:
$$X_2 \geq 5$$
$$3X_1 + 5X_2 \leq 90$$
$$-3X_1 + X_2 \leq 0$$
$$X_1 - X_2 \leq 6$$
$$-X_1 - 3X_2 \leq 6 = b_5$$
$$X_1, \quad X_2 \geq 0$$

(a) Sketch the feasible region.
(b) Determine the optimum solution.
(c) Find the shadow price on the fifth constraint (SP_5) at the optimum solution.
(d) Determine the range of b_5 for which the SP_5 is constant.
(e) Find SP_5 for b_5 above the range on the current value of SP_5; for b_5 below the range.
(f) Plot SP_5 as a function of b_5 for $-\infty < b_5 < \infty$.

6.2. *Sensitivity Exercise II*
Given the linear program

Maximize: $\qquad Z = X_1 + 2X_2 + 5X_3$

Subject to: $\qquad\qquad X_1 + 3X_2 \qquad\qquad \leq 6$
$\qquad\qquad\qquad\qquad\quad 2X_2 + X_3 \leq 3$
$\qquad\qquad\qquad X_1 + \qquad\quad X_3 \leq 15$
$\qquad\qquad\qquad X_1, \quad X_2 \qquad\qquad \geq 0$

Determine by inspection and/or experimentation

(a) the optimal value of the objective function.
(b) the optimal values of the decision variables.
(c) the opportunity costs for any nonoptimal decision variables.
(d) the shadow prices on the constraints.
(e) the value of the slack variable associated with each constraint at the optimum.

6.3. *Sensitivity Exercise III*
Given the linear program

Maximize: $\qquad Z = 6X_1 + 3X_2 + 15X_3$

Subject to: $\qquad\qquad X_1 + X_3 \qquad\qquad \geq 1$
$\qquad\qquad\qquad 3X_1 + 2X_2 \qquad\qquad \geq 2$
$\qquad\qquad\qquad\qquad X_2 + X_3 \geq 5$

answer the same questions as for Problem 6.2.

6.4. *Graphic Analysis*
(a) Graph the following primal linear program and locate its optimal solution.

Maximize: $\qquad Z = 3X_1 + 2X_2$

Subject to: $\qquad\qquad 3X_1 + 4X_2 \leq 12$
$\qquad\qquad\qquad -2X_1 + X_2 \leq 4$
$\qquad\qquad\qquad X_1, \quad X_2 \geq 0$

(b) How much could the objective function be changed without affecting the optimal combination of inputs?
(c) Find the shadow prices on the constraints by evaluating w_i in the vicinity of the primal optimum. What are the opportunity costs of using each of the inputs?

6.5. *Primal-Dual*

For the linear program

$$\text{Minimize:} \qquad Z = 6X_1 + 12X_2 + 6X_3$$

$$\text{Subject to:} \qquad X_1 + \qquad\quad 2X_3 \geq 6$$
$$8X_2 + 3X_3 \geq 2$$
$$X_1 + 3X_2 \qquad \geq 3$$
$$X_i \geq 0$$

determine by inspection and/or experimentation

(*a*) the optimal value of the objective function.
(*b*) the optimal value of the decision variables.
(*c*) the opportunity cost for any nonoptimal decision variables.
(*d*) the shadow prices of the constraints.
(*e*) the value of the slack variable associated with each constraint at the optimum.
(*f*) the dual of the original problem.

For the dual, determine

(*g*) the optimal value of the objective function.
(*h*) the optimal value of the decision variables.
(*i*) the opportunity costs for any nonoptimal decision variables.
(*j*) the shadow prices on the constraints.
(*k*) the value of the slack variable associated with each constraint at the optimum.
(*l*) each of the variables (or set of variables) in parts (*a*) through (*e*) should correspond to one of the variables (or sets) in parts (*g*) through (*k*). Match them up.

6.6. *Iron Alloys*

As manager of an iron foundry, you need to determine the minimum cost charge to a cupola melting furnace producing a cast iron with the following constraints:

	Impurities	Other constraints
	$3.2 \leq$ Carbon $\leq 3.5\%$	Steel scrap #2 $= 30\%$
	$1.4 \leq$ Manganese $\leq 1.6\%$	
	$2.7 \leq$ Silicon $\leq 3.0\%$	
	$0.30 \leq$ Chromium $\leq 0.45\%$	

(All compositions are specified in percent by weight)

Assume you have already formulated a linear programming problem and the computer has determined the following:

Raw material	Value (% in mix)	Opportunity cost ($/ton)	Cost ($/ton)
Pig iron	72.1		58
Silvery pig	3.0		120
Ferrosilicon			
#1	0	12	128
#2	2.9		120
Master alloy			
#1	1.0		200
#2	0	38	260
#3	0	17	238
Silicon carbide	1.0		160
Steel scrap			
#1	0	6.7	39
#2	20.0		30
#3	0	4.2	33

Material	Lower bound (min. constraint) Value (% in mix)	Lower bound (min. constraint) Shadow price ($/ton)	Upper bound (max. constraint) Value (% in mix)	Upper bound (max. constraint) Shadow price ($/ton)	Range (% in mix)
Carbon	3.2	0	3.5	2.4	3.3–3.8
Manganese	1.4	0	1.6	5.0	1.5–1.7
Silica	2.7	0	3.0	3.0	2.9–3.3
Chromium	0.3	0	0.45	6.1	0.35–0.65
Steel scrap #2	—	—	30.0	7.0	22–31

(a) Assuming the costs of the other materials remain constant, at what price should you consider using master alloy #3 in your charge?

(b) The manager of a small factory offers to accept a ton of alloy with 0.2 percent greater carbon content for each 0.1 ton of the steel scrap #1 you are willing to purchase at $38/ton. Will you accept? How much will you profit (or lose) on the deal?

(c) The same factory is using another alloy with less desirable properties than your alloy for $1/ton less. Assuming that the addition of 0.2% greater impurities into your alloy will not greatly affect the mechanical properties, list two ways you might reduce your costs by $1/ton.

6.7. *Gravel Pit*

A company extracts gravel from several sources to satisfy the demand from various clients. A linear program has been run to optimize the distribution of gravel, yielding the following results:

Source	Client	Cost/ton($)	Tons Shipped	Opportunity Cost ($)
1	1	1.80	0	0.25
1	2	1.40	367	0
1	3	3.04	0	1.21
1	4	2.10	535	0
1	5	1.53	0	0
1	6	1.82	0	0.07
2	1	1.60	798	0
2	2	1.25	214	0
2	3	1.90	0	0.10
2	4	2.50	0	0.50
2	5	1.70	0	0.20
2	6	1.40	0	0.17
3	1	2.20	0	0.72
3	2	1.60	0	0.23
3	3	1.97	723	0
3	4	2.30	0	0.18

Source	Tons available	Slack variable	Shadow price ($/ton)	Range
1	1270	368	0	$b > 802$
2	1012	0	0.15	$1379 > b > 798$
3	1570	473	0	$b > 1097$
4	1120	0	0.21	$1309 > b > 1092$
5	2117	516	0	$b > 1601$

Client	Tons contracted	Slack variable	Shadow price ($/ton)	Range
1	798	0	1.75	$1012 > b > 431$
2	881	0	1.40	$1683 > b > 567$
3	1382	0	1.97	$2117 > b > 961$
4	535	0	2.10	$735 > b > 0$
5	2147	0	1.20	$2384 > b > 1602$
6	1346	0	1.31	$1521 > b > 0$

(a) Why are the slack variables for all the client (demand) constraints equal to zero?

(b) Client #6 would like 100 tons of his gravel to be the peculiarly colored stone from source 2. How much extra should you charge him for it, or how large a refund should you give him?

(c) Client #5 finds that she will need 700 tons less than she expected. How large a refund can you afford to give her for reducing the size of her order?

(d) How much would you lose if source #2 had 300 tons less gravel than you expected?

6.8. *Food Distribution*

An island is spanned by a network of railroads. Vegetables, grown in the western hills (nodes 1,2,3,4), must be shipped to the rest of the country. A linear program was written to minimize the transportation cost, subject to

- limited production at each supply node.
- limited capacity of each railroad link.
- demand that must be satisfied at each of the demand nodes.
- continuity that must be maintained at each node.

The computer output produces the following information:

	Link flows at optimum			Link capacity constraints		
Link	Cost/unit (pesos)	Units carried	Opportunity costs	Capacity (maxflow)	Shadow price	Range
$1 \rightarrow 2$	42	0	50	30	0	
$1 \rightarrow 5$	68	63	—	63	12	$59 <$ maxflow < 100
$1 \rightarrow 6$	76	32	—	70	X	$32 <$ maxflow
$2 \rightarrow 1$	42	30	—	30	6	
$2 \rightarrow 3$	107	0	123	21	0	
$2 \rightarrow 5$	143	0	21	27	0	
$2 \rightarrow 6$	113	40	—	60	0	$40 <$ maxflow
$3 \rightarrow 2$	107	0	91	21	0	
$3 \rightarrow 4$	231	0	211	15	0	

	Demand node constraints		
Node	Demand	SP	Range
5	50	143	$41 <$ demand 5 < 57
6	40	113	$38 <$ demand 6 < 45
7	100	201	$93 <$ demand 7 < 117

Note that each link has an actual flow (the variable) and a maximum flow (the constraint).

(a) What is the value of X, the shadow price on the link $1 \rightarrow 6$ constraint?

(b) Improvements on link $2 \rightarrow 5$ will reduce its cost to 120 pesos/unit. Should $2 \rightarrow 5$ be used after the improvements are completed?

(c) How much is it worth paying to increase the capacity of link $1 \rightarrow 5$ by 5 units?

(d) It is possible to satisfy some of the existing demands at node 6 by growing vegetables at that node: one unit can be produced for 100 pesos, *or* four units can be grown for 350 pesos. What does the computer output tell you about these options?

6.9. *Gelderland*

A consultant is using LP to maximize the benefits, in Gelders, of a new port facility for Gelderland. The constraints are:

1. Actual Cost $\leq$ U.S. \$20 M.
2. Probability of an oil spill $\leq 1\%$.
3. Construction time ≤ 5 years.
4. Local workers used in construction ≥ 500.
5. Port capacity ≥ 20 ships at any time.

The output includes the following information:

Constraint	Shadow price	Range
1	15 G/\$	$15 \leq b_1 \leq 22\text{M}$
2	600,000 G/%	$0.8 \leq b_2 \leq 7\%$
3	0 G/year	$3.5 \leq b_3$
4	2000 G/worker	$420 \leq b_4 \leq 700$
5	1M G/ship	$15 \leq b_5 \leq 23$

Also, the following possible features were not part of the optimal design:

Feature	Opportunity cost
deep water tanker berth	15M G
hydrofoil marina	3M G
seaplane facility	2M G

(a) Properly impressing some bank officials will probably increase the size of the loan by \$1M. How many Gelders can the nation afford to spend on a "sales effort" directed at these officials?

(b) An oil spill would cost the tourist industry about 10M Gelders. Would it pay to relax the environmental standards? (Hint: calculate the expected cost of relaxed standards.)

(c) Skilled foreign labor will speed construction of the port, at somewhat greater cost. Is this idea worth pursuing?

(d) It has been suggested that the port be built to accommodate less than 20 ships and that excess ships could be served by barges costing 500,000 G. Should the consultant design for 20 ships? 18 ships? Get more information (what kind)?

6.10. *SMC Factory II*

Having used LP to solve for the optimal design of SMC in Problem 5.14, you have obtained the following sensitivity information:

Raw material	% in mix (volume %)	Opportunity cost ($/lb)	Cost ($/lb)
Polyester	51	—	0.55
Vinylester	0	0.44	1.05
E-glass Fiber	24.5	—	1.00
Carbon Fiber	24.5	—	25.00
Kevlar Fiber	0	8	21.00

Constraint	Shadow price	Range Max	Range Min
Tensile < 200 ksi	0.019	296	103
Tensile > 100 ksi	0	—	—
Modulus > 10 msi	1.012	20	4.1
Specific gravity < 1.9	0	—	—
Fiber volume % < 78.5	0	—	—

(a) By how much must the price of Kevlar fall before it would be incorporated in the SMC formulation?

(b) Your client now needs SMC with a tensile strength not greater than 150 ksi. By how much and in what direction will the cost of this new formulation change (if at all)?

(c) The client is willing to relax the constraint on specific gravity by 10%. How much are you willing to pay for this change?

(d) If the modulus of the mixture must be at least 21 msi, will your production costs increase or fall and by how much?

6.11. *DEBON AIR*

DEBON AIR is looking into expanding into cargo transport from an already secure position in the crop dusting area. With a block of ready cash, DEBON plans to buy a new fleet. A linear program was commissioned to minimize the cost of this purchase, subject to various constraints. A portion of the results follow:

Aircraft type	Number purchased	Number available	SP($)	OC($)	Range
A	2	10	—	—	—
B	0	10	—	5×10^5	—
C	6	6	10^6	—	0–20

Capacity needs	Needed	Purchased	SP($)	Range
Short haul capacity	5×10^5 lbs	8×10^5 lbs	—	—
Long haul capacity	2×10^5 lbs	2×10^5 lbs	70	10^5–10^6

Fleet fuel efficiency requirement (fleet avg.)	Actual	SP($)	Range
10 mpg	10 mpg	10^6	1–15

Use the above information to determine quantitative answers. If a quantitative solution is not possible, state so and explain why.

(a) If one more plane of type C were available, how much less would the new fleet cost?

(b) If DEBON's long haul capacity needs had been 10^5 lbs higher, would the new fleet cost more or less than the current configuration? By how much?

(c) An aircraft manufacturer proposes an aircraft whose technical specifications and price are identical to those of plane A, with one exception—its fuel economy is 10% better. Should DEBON AIR buy this aircraft? Why or why not?

(d) The government circulates proposed regulations that would require future airline fleet expansions to be such that the mean fuel efficiency of the new craft is 12 mpg. In the DEBON protest, the cost of such a regulation to DEBON is detailed. What is its value?

6.12. *Computer Run*

This problem is to be solved using a PC. Formulate and solve the LP to answer the questions.

A small steel company makes specialty alloys to customer specification. One customer requires an alloy involving four metals, and has specified the following composition:

Metal	Requirements
A	No more than 15%
B	At least 25%
C	Between 40% and 50%
D	No more than 8%
Impurities	None

This steel company can acquire its ores from several sources. These ores contain both the required metals and impurities, which should be separated before the production of the alloy. The cost of this separation is the same for all ores and is quite small. The percent composition of these ores is

Ore	Metal A	Metal B	Metal C	Metal D	Impurities
1	20	20	40	0	20
2	15	0	20	5	60
3	0	40	40	0	20
4	15	15	20	0	50
5	20	20	20	20	20
6	5	8	17	10	60

Finally, there are limits to the amount of each ore available to the steelmaker:

Ore	Tons available	$/ton
1	2200	30.00
2	1800	10.00
3	1750	32.00
4	700	20.00
5	900	22.00
6	1700	12.00

(a) The customer wants 4000 tons of alloy. What is the minimum cost per ton of alloy? Which ores will be purchased? What percentage of the total metal requirement will ore 3 represent? What percentage of the total ore requirements?

(b) The customer calls to inform the steelmaker of an error in the specification of the alloy: there must now be no more than 14.5% of metal A in the alloy. What is the minimum penalty that should be charged to keep profits/ton fixed?

(c) The manager of the mine that supplies ore 4 is desperate for business. How much of a kickback must the steelmaker demand to assure the owner that 1% of the metal composing the alloy shipment will come from mine 4?

(d) The manager of the mine that supplies ore 3 proposes to announce a 15% increase in production. How would this change the cost/ton of the special alloy?

(e) The steelmaker feels that it may be possible to cheat on the 0% impurity level. How much could the profit/ton be improved by introducing a 1% impurity? (Assume that the cost of the impurity is zero.)

(f) In the discussion, the customer asks for an estimate on another order of special alloy. This alloy will be subject to the original (not the revised!!) specifications, except that the percentage of metal D must be no higher than 6%. Can you estimate the cost/ton of a 4000 ton order of this alloy?

(g) Suppose that the mine supplying ore 6 has just been struck. The manager of the mine can only supply 1400 tons of ore. How much of a penalty should the steelmaker exact from the mine manager to preserve the profit?

6.13. *Stomp II*

STOMP, Inc., having taken our advice from Problem 5.6, has prospered. Still manufacturing stereo nameplates and bird cage hinges, it has expanded its operations substantially. It now purchases varying grades of metal from several suppliers and has managed to expand the market for nameplates, which is now able to absorb 80 cases of plates a week. Luckily, the demand for bird cage hinges has remained strong and the market easily absorbs all that STOMP can produce. STOMP's only trouble is its union, which still will not allow its members to operate production machinery for more than 40 hours per week.

A new linear program, maximizing weekly profit, has been commissioned. A portion of the output follows.

Metal supplier	Price ($/ton)	Amount bought (ton/wk)	Supply constraint (ton/wk)	Shadow price	Range	Opportunity cost
I	20	1000	1000	1.5	$600 \leq X \leq 1300$	—
II	25	0	2000	—		2.5
III	22	400	1000	—		—
.	.	.	.	.		.
.	.	.	.	.		.
.	.	.	.	.		.

	Price	Amount bought	Supply constraint	Shadow price	Range
Machine Time	$25/hr	40 hr/wk	40 hr/wk	150	$35 \leq X \leq 46$
.	.	.	.	.	.
.	.	.	.	.	.

	Price	Amount sold	Demand constraint	Shadow price	Range
Cases of Nameplates	$200/case	80 cases/wk	80 cases/wk	150	$65 \leq X \leq 90$
.	.	.	.	.	.
.	.	.	.	.	.
.	.	.	.	.	.

(a) Supplier I wanted to cut his weekly deliveries to STOMP by 100 tons/wk. How much can STOMP afford to offer him to get him to maintain his current weekly deliveries?

(b) Supplier II wants to get some business from STOMP. What price should she charge in order to attract the attention of STOMP's metal buyers?

(c) STOMP is offered an overseas franchise in nameplates, which would allow STOMP to sell 15 more cases of nameplates each week. The price of the franchise is $2250/wk. Should STOMP buy the franchise?

6.14. *Gravel Company*

A gravel company has contracts to supply gravel to four construction projects in Massachusetts:

1. A highway in Berkshire county (1500 tons).
2. A shopping mall in Salem (1000 tons).
3. A runway extension at Logan Airport (1700 tons).
4. An urban development project in Worcester (500 tons).

The company owns three gravel pits in New Hampshire, in New York, and in Connecticut. The marginal cost of producing and shipping a ton of gravel from pit to user is about:

	Pit		
Client	NH	NY	CT
1	$2.20	$1.20	$1.70
2	1.60	2.20	1.90
3	2.50	3.10	2.70
4	2.10	2.00	1.80

No more than 40% of any project's gravel may come from the Connecticut pit, which contains a fair amount of silt. Only 800 tons of gravel are currently available at the New York pit. The objective is to minimize cost.

(a) What are the constraint equations?

(b) Indicate what sensitivity output or other data from your LP will answer each of the following questions:

   (i) What is the most we should pay for offshore dredging of gravel for the Logan project?

   (ii) How much more would it cost to require that 50 tons of the New York gravel be used on the Salem project?

   (iii) What is the maximum price at which Connecticut gravel would be used for the Berkshire project?

   (iv) How much of the 800 tons of New York gravel will be unused?

CHAPTER
7

DYNAMIC PROGRAMMING

7.1 CONCEPT

Dynamic programming is a powerful method of optimization which overcomes the three major drawbacks of linear programming. It can be applied to problems that

- are nonlinear.
- have nonconvex feasible regions.
- have discontinuous variables.

These substantial advantages are obtained at a significant price, however. Dynamic programming is limited to dealing with problems with

- relatively few constraints.

Dynamic programming complements linear programming. It works well on the nonlinear, nonconvex problems that are impossible for linear programming, but cannot handle the large number of constraints that linear programming deals with routinely. In practical situations, which may actually involve both nonconvex feasible regions and many constraints, analysts will have to make approximations to fit either the linear or dynamic programming approach. They thus need to be familiar with their relative strengths.

Conceptually, dynamic programming represents a completely different approach to optimization than linear programming. Linear programming is based on the use of optimality conditions. As described in Section 5.3, the consequence of linearity is that we can define in advance the nature of the optimum (it is at a corner point, from which all departures worsen the objective function). Linear programming then consists of an organized search through a set of possible solutions until the optimality criterion is met. Dynamic programming, however, has no optimality criterion we can define in advance.

Dynamic programming is based on the concept of enumeration. The basic idea is simple: we systematically enumerate possible solutions, calculate how well each performs and select the best. Since we enumerate the possible solutions, it does not matter if the feasible region is convex or not—or if it is linear. Enumeration is the principle that gives dynamic programming the power to deal with these nonlinear, nonconvex problems that linear programming cannot.

Dynamic programming carries out this approach in a special way, based on some specific characteristics of the problem that it assumes to hold. These conditions, presented in detail in Section 7.2, are crucial because the enumerative approach to optimization is, for any reasonable problem in practice, computationally impossible if we try to list all the possible solutions.

To appreciate the advantages of dynamic programming it is important to understand that a complete evaluation of all the possible designs of a system is simply unthinkable for the foreseeable future. Even the fastest modern computers would be unable to calculate the performance of all the solutions to a relatively simple system.

The difficulty with a complete enumeration is that the number of possible solutions is an exponential function of the number of possible decisions, the number of values these may have, and the number of periods over which the system is considered. The general rule is

Maximum number of Possible Designs
$$= \left[(\text{Number of Values})^{(\text{Number of Variables})} \right]^{(\text{Number of Periods})}$$

For the design of facilities at particular sites, this formula can be stated more specifically as

$$\text{Possible Designs} = \left[(\text{Sizes})^{(\text{Locations})} \right]^{(\text{Periods})}$$

This number is huge for even relatively small problems, and astronomical for really significant problems such as the design of a regional telephone network; the organization of a distribution system for a major company; et cetera. Even supercomputers would require weeks if not months to evaluate individually each of all the possible configurations of such systems (see box).

The special approach used by dynamic programming is *implicit enumeration*. It is said to be implicit because it considers all possible design

Practical Impossibility of Complete Enumeration

Consider first a simple problem: The design of ten facilities, such as warehouses in a distribution system, each of which could be in any one of ten sizes. The total number of possible combinations is thus 10^{10}: The first variable has 10 possible levels, each of which combines with 10 for the second giving 10×10 combinations for these two, then each of these has ten more for the third variable, giving $10 \times 10 \times 10$, and so on.

Suppose that a computer could identify and list these possible designs at the rate of 100,000 per second, which would be a very good speed. The complete enumeration of all the possible designs would then take

$$\text{Time Required} = 10^5 \text{s} = \text{More than a day!}$$

If we were interested in designing a substantial system, such as the water distribution system for the Salt Lake City area as described in Section 5.11, the problem would be very much larger. It might thus have 30 possible locations at a minimum, at least 5 possible sizes for each, and be concerned with the evolution over 3 periods. The total number of logical combinations is then

$$\text{Possible designs} = \left[(5)^{30}\right]^3 \sim 10^{60}$$

If we had a super super computer of the future, 100,000 times as fast as the preceding one, thus doing 10^{10} evaluations a second, the time required to enumerate all the possible combinations would be on the order of 10^{40} centuries!

---

combinations in principle, but not in fact. Based on certain crucial assumptions about a problem (described in Section 7.2), it systematically eliminates many sets of possible combinations because they can be shown to be inferior. In practice, implicit enumeration carries out the elimination of possible solutions in a series of stages. Implicit enumeration is thus a repetitive process of optimization that identifies and eliminates whole sets of inferior solutions before they have to be considered individually in detail.

The following example illustrates the concept of implicit enumeration. Consider an automobile trip a person might take across the United States, from San Francisco to Washington for example. This is too long to be done in a day, it must be done in stages, let us say 6 days. As the country is wide enough, the traveler can choose many different destinations each day, for example 10. The question is, what is the best route to take?

In general, the answer to this problem is far from obvious. The best route, for example the fastest or the least expensive, depends on distance; difficulties along the way, such as mountains or poor roads; weather conditions, such as snow or heat; congestion, which may reduce speed; administrative or legal restraints,

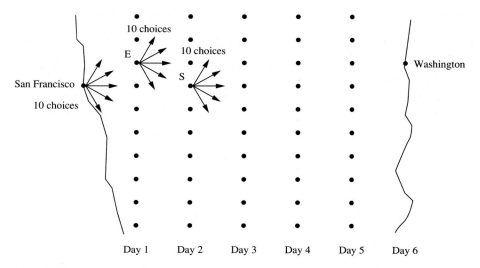

FIGURE 7.1
Example cross-country drive of six days, with 10 possible destinations for each intermediate stage.

such as enforced speed limits; and so on. This example in fact is representative of a large number of practical problems such as those of routing telephone calls or computer messages, or the scheduling of trucks and trains.

Figure 7.1 maps the problem. As shown, the driver has 10 choices each day. There are thus 10^5 possible routes in all: one route to reach any point at the end of the first day, say E (Elko, Nevada); thus 10 ways to reach any point at the end of the second day, say S (Salt Lake City, Utah)—that through E and each of the other nine points for day 1; and so on until Washington.

Implicit enumeration works by doing a partial optimization at each stage. It selects the best way to reach any point at that stage, and discards all the other possibilities. Thus for the second stage of our problem: using implicit enumeration we would look at each of the 10 ways to reach point S, and determine which is best—for instance that passing through point E. All the other possibilities for getting to S (nine in this case) would be dropped. Consequently—and this is where the implicit enumeration arises—so would all the possible routes to Washington whose first two days reach point S other than through E. We would not need to consider those explicitly since we would already know that they could not be optimal. It is important to realize that in this way we have, at point S, not merely discarded 9 possible solutions but $9(10^3)$ since there are 10^3 ways to proceed from S to Washington. Since this reasoning applies to each of the 10 points that we might reach by the end of the second stage, the partial optimization at this stage has eliminated $9(10^4)$ or nearly all the 10^5 possibilities. The effort required to do this has, however, been relatively small: the partial optimization at the second

Practicality of Implicit Enumeration

Consider the water distribution problem for the Salt Lake region, the one that had $[(5)^{30}]^3$ possible solutions.

Using implicit enumeration, we would have to consider approximately $(5)(30)(3) = 450$ different possibilities. This is quite feasible, even with a personal computer.

---

stage actually only considered 10^3 possible paths, 10^2 for each of the 10 points that could be reached at the end of day 2.

Implicit enumeration thus drastically reduces the number of possible solutions that have to be evaluated. Specifically, it transforms the number from the exponential that describes the total number of combinations

$$\text{Maximum Number of Solutions} = (\text{Levels})^{(\text{Stages})}$$

to a simple multiplicative relationship

$$\text{Solutions by Implicit Enumeration} \sim (\text{Levels})(\text{Stages})$$

This is the feature that makes dynamic programming practical (see box).

Dynamic programming can be applied to many different types of problems. Some can be organized into levels and stages in a fairly obvious way, since they describe a process that proceeds sequentially through time or space, as with the preceding example. The way other problems can be formulated in a form suitable for dynamic programming can be fairly subtle, either because they involve complex relationships between different points in time or space or because they do not represent any sequential process. Sections 7.4 and 7.5 present several examples of different kinds of problems on which dynamic programming can be applied.

> **Semantic caution:** There is nothing inherently "dynamic" about dynamic programming. The term originated because this method was originally applied to problems in which time was an essential factor, specifically the launching of missiles or interceptor fighters, which had to reach a critical altitude and speed in a minimum time. As Sections 7.4 and 7.5 demonstrate, dynamic programming applies equally well to many problems that are quite static.

7.2 ASSUMPTIONS

The assumptions necessary for dynamic programming are those that enable us to perform valid partial optimizations along the way. These operations are the means by which dynamic programming cuts the number of evaluations to a feasible size, and they are absolutely crucial to the method.

Independence of Return Functions

Consider the transcontinental trip discussed as an example in Section 7.1. Independence of the return functions would mean that the value of anything we might do on the first day does not depend on what we might do the second or any other day. Concretely, independence implies for example that the cost of going from San Francisco to Elko does not depend on what we do after Salt Lake City, and vice-versa.

In this case, it would seem fairly obvious that the return functions are independent. But this is not necessarily so. For example, the cost of the trip beyond Salt Lake might well depend on how we got there: if we had stayed on the interstate highways and our car were still in good condition, these onward costs might be low; if, however, we had gone cross-country through the desert, we might have severely damaged our engine, making all further segments much more expensive. The return functions would then not be independent.

Consider another case, where the $g_i(X_i)$ represent the value of investments in projects X_i. These return functions might be totally independent, representing, for example, loans by the World Bank to different countries for quite different purposes. They might also be quite dependent, however. This would be the case if two or more facilities competed for the same market. The return from an investment in any one might be quite high, as a monopoly, but could be very much lower if investments are made in any of the competitive projects.

Formally, the assumptions permit us first of all to *decompose* the objective function $G(\mathbf{X})$, that is to break it up into a number of individual functions, $g_i(X_i)$, associated with each variable. Thus we want to be able to write:

$$G(\mathbf{X}) = [g_1(X_1), \ldots , g_n(X_n)]$$

Two conditions are sufficient to permit the decomposition of the objective function, separability and monotonicity. These are the assumptions we must make about a problem if we wish to use dynamic programming to optimize it.

The objective function is *separable* if each of the individual functions $g_i(X_i)$ are *independent* of the values of the other $g_j(X_j)$, $j \neq i$. This means the values of each $g_i(X_i)$ depend uniquely on X_i and are totally unaffected by what has or may happen elsewhere in the system. The separability condition is met quite commonly in practice, but there are many counterexamples and the analyst must be particularly careful about this assumption (see above box).

In the jargon associated with dynamic programming, the $g_i(X_i)$ are said to be *return functions*. They show the return, that is the contribution towards the objective function, associated with each X_i.

Monotonicity of Multiplicative Functions

Consider the multiplicative objective function

$$G(\mathbf{X}) = [g_1(X_1)][g_2(X_2)]$$

If both return functions are positive and real, then it is fairly obvious that increases in either will increase $G(\mathbf{X})$. Thus, if

$$g_1(X_1') = 5 \qquad g_1(X_1'') = 4$$

$$g_2(X_2) = 8$$

we have

$$g_1(X_1') > g_1(X_1'')$$

and

$$[g_1(X_1')][g'(\mathbf{X})] = 5g_2(X_2) = 40$$
$$> [g_1(X_1'')][g'(\mathbf{X})] = 4g_2(X_2) = 32$$

However, if we allow the return functions to be negative or imaginary, we can easily find situations for which the objective function is not monotonic. Thus, if

$$g_1(X_1') = +5 \qquad g_1(X_1'') = -1$$

$$g_2(X_2) = -3$$

we have

$$g_1(X_1') = 5 > g_1(X_1'') = -1$$

but

$$[g_1(X_1')][g'(\mathbf{X})] = (5)(-3) = -15$$
$$< [g_1(X_1'')][g'(\mathbf{X})] = (-1)(-3) = +3$$

The objective function is *monotonic* if improvements in each $g_i(X_i)$ lead to improvements in the objective function. To define this idea formally, consider the objective function separated into two parts, $g_i(X_i)$ and $G'(\mathbf{X})$:

$$G(\mathbf{X}) = [g_i(X_i), G'(\mathbf{X})]$$

The objective function is monotonic if, for all cases where $g_i(X_i') \geq g_i(X_i'')$ for the different levels X_i' and X_i'',

$$[g_i(X_i'), G'(\mathbf{X})] \geq [g_i(X_i''), G'(\mathbf{X})]$$

Additive objective functions:

$$G(\mathbf{X}) = \sum g_i(X_i)$$

are always monotonic. Increases in any $g_i(X_i)$ necessarily make $G(\mathbf{X})$ larger.
  Multiplicative objective functions:

$$G(\mathbf{X}) = \prod g_i(X_i)$$

are monotonic only if the return functions are both nonnegative and real (see box on p. 145 for examples). In systems design this restriction never seems to present a practical difficulty.

7.3 SOLUTION STRATEGY

To optimize a system using dynamic programming, we need to deal with four elements:

• The *Organization* of the problem
• The *Formula* to be used in the partial optimizations
• The *Constraints*
• The *Solution* itself

This section discusses each in turn.

  It is important to note that dynamic programming is not based on a standard formulation, as linear programming is. Dynamic programming is more an approach or a concept rather than a formula. The analyst wishing to use dynamic programming will often have to use imagination and skill to organize a problem so that it can be solved efficiently. To illustrate how this can be done, Section 7.5 gives examples of different kinds of formulations.

  The fact that dynamic programming problems can differ from each other substantially leads to a great practical difficulty: good computer programs for dynamic programming are hard to find. Those that may be available to you may not suit your particular problem. Likewise, companies that develop software are naturally interested in large markets to pay their costs, and have thus not provided a range of dynamic programming programs to meet the various needs.

Organization. The first and essential part of the solution is to organize the problem into levels and stages. Then one must define the corresponding return functions. It is often not obvious how one can do this. Much of the interesting work in dynamic programming has in fact been in the development of new formulations that divide different systems problems into suitable levels and stages.

  The stages are generally easier to imagine. The simplest case is when the program we have is *sequential*, that is, it represents a process that has a natural order through time or space. The example problem used in Section 7.1, concerning the transcontinental trip from San Francisco to Washington, was sequential: it embodied a natural progression from west to east. Possible stages in a sequential problem are fairly obvious; they represent some division of the time or space. For example, each stage in a sequential problem might represent:

- *A division of time*—days, hours, seconds, and so on—as for the example problem in Section 7.1
- *A division of space*—such as blocks of 500 miles in the example problem—which would not correspond to the division of time since it might take more or less than a day to cover the distance, depending on the route chosen
- *A sequence of choices*—as in a game of chess or the sequence of midcourse corrections that can be given to a missile—which may have no intrinsic implication for the amount of space or time required.

The stages of a nonsequential problem are often simply the several parts of a system. For instance:

- The different possible investments in a portfolio of loans or shares in companies
- The various redundant components or machines in a system

For nonsequential problems the order we assign to the different stages will be absolutely arbitrary and, for all practical purposes, have no consequences for how fast or well the solution is obtained.

Defining the levels to be used in dynamic programming can be difficult. The simplest case is when the stage represents an investment in a particular project: the level is then the degree of commitment to that project. Thus, if Stage i represents the construction of an electric plant at a specific site, X_i will be the level of investment in that plant.

The "levels" may also be nominal: they may represent situations or names rather than degrees or levels of anything. In the example of the transcontinental trip of Section 7.1, the levels were cities along the way (Elko, Salt Lake City) that did not need to have a particular relation to each other latitudinally or otherwise.

In general, it is more accurate to refer to the *states* of a system at each stage rather than "levels." The state is the description of situation attained as the result of a transition from one stage to another. For instance, a state might be:

- The speed and altitude of a missile as a result of the number of stages of its guidance systems
- The position on the chess board
- The wealth of a gambler resulting from the probabilistic outcomes of a roulette wheel

The examples in the next two sections illustrate this concept.

In defining the levels or states of each stage, the analyst cannot use continuous functions. This is because the cost of a dynamic program is a direct proportion to the number of levels considered, and a continuous function implies an infinite number of levels—and infinite costs. The analyst must define the levels in steps, as a discontinuous function.

This necessity is generally an advantage. Dynamic programming deals easily with situations that are naturally discontinuous—as linear programming does not. For example, if we are determining the optimal number of aircraft in a fleet, we recognize that the number of aircraft must be an integer. We may have 52 or 53, for example, but not 52.4. In linear programming, which uses continuous functions, it is difficult or expensive to restrict the number of aircraft to integer values; we may have to solve a problem and then round out the result somehow. Dynamic programming, however, can define its feasible levels in any convenient way, specifically by using integer numbers. It can therefore determine an accurate answer where linear programming cannot.

The analyst must consequently be careful in defining the specific levels. The levels should preferably relate to discrete levels to the extent these are part of the actual problem. Their number should also represent a compromise between the desire for greater precision and the need for keeping computational costs down.

Finally, the definition of the return functions for each stage, $g_i(X_i)$, can be most complex. The simplest case again occurs when each stage is nonsequential and represents an investment of level X_i in a particular project, for example the construction of an electric plant. The return function $g_i(X_i)$ could then represent the profits or the amount of energy obtained from this investment. This kind of return function can typically be expressed as a simple formula or curve.

The return function for a sequential problem represents the change in state from one stage to the next. It can sometimes be expressed as a formula. Just as commonly it will be defined by a table providing each $g_i(X_i)$ in terms of states in the previous stage, $i-1$, and the state X_i of stage i. Thus, in the transcontinental problem: the return function for stage 2 is the 10 by 10 matrix giving the cost (or mileage or travel time) from each city in stage 1 to each city in stage 2. The cost from Elko to Salt Lake City would be one entry in this matrix.

When return functions have to be described by tables rather than formulas, all subsequent calculations become more cumbersome. Additionally, it will take much more time to describe a problem. On the other hand, if certain transitions between stages are not feasible, they may simply be omitted from the $g_i(X_i)$ matrix. This possibility makes it easy to describe restrictions that would otherwise be very difficult to define with constraints, as required by linear programming.

Formula. The solution itself consists of two parts:

- Partial optimization at each stage.
- Repetition of this process through all stages.

The object of the partial optimization is to define the best result that can be obtained at any level or state at the end of a specific number of stages. This quantity is given by the *cumulative return function*, by analogy with the return function that relates to only one stage. The cumulative return function is denoted

Cumulative Return Function

Again consider the transcontinental automobile trip. Suppose that the traveler wishes to minimize cost.

The return functions for each stage would be the cost of getting to each city in that stage from the previous stage. Thus $g_1(X_1)$ would give the costs from the starting point, San Francisco, to each city in stage 1, such as Elko. Also, $g_2(X_2)$ would give the costs that could be incurred in the second day's trip, including that from Elko to Salt Lake City.

The cumulative return function, however, indicates the best result over previous stages. Thus:

$$f_2(\text{Salt Lake City})$$

is the least cost of getting to Salt Lake City in the first two stages. It is the cost of the San Francisco-Elko-Salt Lake City route, if that is best.

---

by $f_s(K)$, which designates the effect of being in state K, having passed through or examined the first s stages (see box).

The cumulative return function is built up iteratively, from stage to stage. It is defined in terms of the return function of the current stage and the cumulative return function for previous stages:

$$f_i(K) = [g_i(X_i), f_{i-1}(K)]$$

Sometimes the cumulative return function can be defined by a closed-form equation. Its formula is then known as a *recurrence function*, so called because it repeats the definition of the function for each stage. Often, however, the cumulative return function will simply be defined by examination of the various possibilities as entered in a table (on paper or in computer memory). The examples in the next two sections illustrate how this can be done.

Special conditions exist for the first stage. The cumulative return function, $f_1(K)$, is then equal to the return function for that stage, $g_1(X_1)$. This follows from the fact that $f_0(K)$, the best that can be done over no stages, has no meaning.

Constraints. Constraints in dynamic programming are dealt with quite differently than they are in linear programming. They are almost never written as equations. Indeed, a dynamic programming problem may not be described in terms of equations.

Most constraints in dynamic programming are embedded directly in the organization of the problem. For example, if there is a restriction on the maximum number of levels or states for any stage, only that number is provided. For our transcontinental drive for instance, if a snowstorm blocked five cities in stage 2, these could simply be dropped from the description of the problem. Similarly, if certain transitions between stages are not feasible, they are simply not entered into the description of the problem. Thus, if the route from Elko to Salt Lake City is closed for repairs, that route is either dropped from the description of the $g_2(X_2)$—or given an infinite cost, which eliminates it from consideration.

Constraints that limit several X_i at once are difficult to enter into the program. Here again, what is easy for linear programming is difficult for dynamic programming. The general rule is that only one such constraint can in practice be incorporated with dynamic programming. This is done by means of the recurrence formula, as the example in Section 7.4 shows.

Solution. The optimal solution is provided by the cumulative return function over all the stages. This function is constructed so as to define the best solution over the preceding s stages and so must, when we have considered all stages, define the best value of the objective function.

In addition we need to know $\mathbf{X}^*$, the optimal value of the X_i variables. In the language associated with dynamic programming, the optimal set of X_i is known as the *optimal policy*. To obtain the optimal policy we must determine how we reached the optimal solution. This is in fact quite easy since the cumulative return function is always defined in terms of the return function for the last stage:

$$f_i(K) = [g_i(X_i), f_{i-1}(K)]$$

Knowing the optimal solution, we then know the transition from the previous stage that brought us to that point; from the cumulative return function for the previous stage we can trace back one more stage, and so on. In practice, since we do not know which path eventually leads to the optimum, the dynamic program must keep track of the optimal path to each level of each stage.

Dynamic programming provides a limited amount of sensitivity information as part of the solution. We are pretty much limited to asking how the optimal solution would change if we wished to end up at a different state at the end of all stages. This is most useful when we have a budget on investments and wish to define the shadow price on that constraint. The example in Section 7.4 illustrates this point.

7.4 EXAMPLE

Suppose we wish to maximize the hydroelectric power produced by building dams on three different river basins, subject to a budget of $3 million.

The problem is suitable for dynamic programming provided the return on each investment, that is, the hydroelectric power from each dam, is independent of the others. As a practical matter these projects will be independent so long as the river basins do not interconnect. If they did, a dam on one river might change the water available to another dam and thus change its return function.

The problem is nonsequential since there is no necessary order in which investments have to be made. We may eventually decide to build the facilities in some order, but we are free to do so as we wish.

Organization. The stages are the individual projects. Since there is no necessary order, we can label any project we want as stage 1, another as stage 2, and the third as stage 3.

The levels are the amounts we can invest in each project. For simplicity, suppose these are 0, 1, 2, or 3 million dollars. We could have more levels if we wish, to obtain greater accuracy. The method would not change, however. Note that the increments between each level are the same. Organizing the problem this way makes it much easier to write the recurrence formula and to execute the program. It is not absolutely necessary, but strongly recommended if at all possible.

The return functions, $g_i(X_i)$, are the amounts of power produced by each dam at stage i (that is, site i) for an investment of level X_i at that site. Table 7.1 defines the return functions for this problem. As can be seen from their plots in Figure 7.2, the feasible region is both nonconvex, due to $g_2(X_2)$, and nonlinear. The objective function is additive since it represents the sum of the power produced:

$$\text{Power} = \sum g_i(X_i)$$

Constraints. The budget constraint implies that

$$\sum X_i \leq 3$$

This restriction will be embedded into the organization of the problem by limiting the number of levels at each stage. These investments can in no case be greater than the budget. (They can, however, be less.) Additionally, the investments cannot be negative, $X_i \geq 0$. This constraint will be embedded in the detailed description of the problem, as shown by the subsection on network representation that follows.

Recurrence formula. The recurrence formula for additive objective functions such as this one is

$$f_i(K) = \text{Max}[g_i(X_i) + f_{i-1}(K - X_i)]$$

This equation is to be understood as the maximum return that can be obtained by

TABLE 7.1
Return functions for the investment problem

Level of investment, X_i	Return function, $g_i(X_i)$		
	$i = 1$	$i = 2$	$i = 3$
0	0	0	0
1	2	1	3
2	4	5	5
3	6	6	6

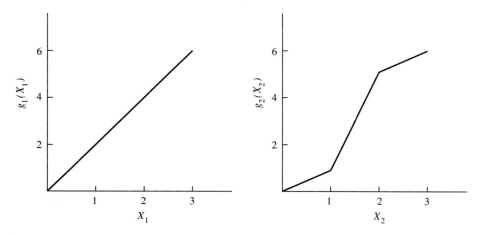

FIGURE 7.2
Return functions $g_i(X_i)$, showing the value of one, two, or three units of investment in a dam for each river basin site of the example problem.

investing some level of money K over s stages is equal to the maximum of all the combinations of investing X_i in stage i and the balance, $(K - X_i)$ in the previous stages. [Note: Max[x, y] is to be read as the maximum of all the combinations of x and y, related by addition or multiplication as defined within the brackets.]

Network representation. The problem can be represented by a network similar to the one for the illustrative situation in Section 7.1. Figure 7.3 does this.

By analogy to the transcontinental drive, we can express the investment problem as starting from point A (no investments in any project) to point M (a budget of 3 invested over 3 projects). We want to find the optimal path to do this, that is, the best transition from stage to stage. These transitions represent the investments in the next stage, $g_i(X_i)$, as labeled in Figure 7.3.

This network differs from the map of the transcontinental drive in two respects. First of all, the paths from left to right are all level or downward sloping: this is because all the investments in any project are greater or equal to zero, $X_i \geq 0$. This means that the number of combinations in a complete enumeration in this case is less than the maximum given in Section 7.1. The network also illustrates how infeasible transitions are dropped from the network of logical possibilities.

The second difference is that we have included several endpoints for this network, points J, K, and L in addition to M. These points define the maximum return we could obtain for lesser amounts than the budget. They are thus useful in sensitivity analysis.

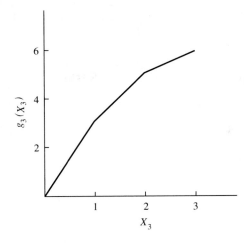

FIGURE 7.2 (*continued*)
Return functions $g_i(X_i)$, showing the value of one, two, or three units of investment in a dam for each river basin site of the example problem.

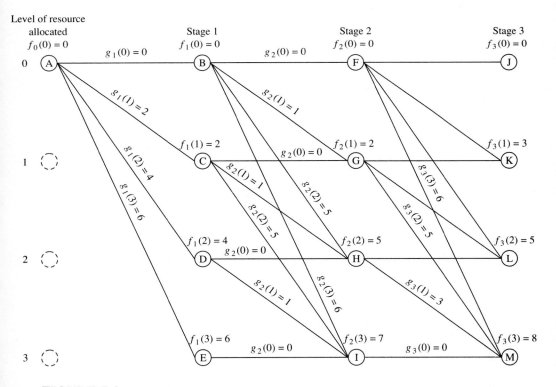

FIGURE 7.3
Nodal representation of example problem illustrating the many ways in which the four levels of investment (for zero, one, two, or three units) can be spent on three projects or stages.

Solution. We want to find the best way to spend the budget ($3 million) over all 3 projects: $f_3(\$3M)$. We build this cumulative return function from $f_1(K)$, using the recurrence formula.

The cumulative return function for the first stage is equal to the return function of that stage, as indicated in Section 7.3. Thus:

$$f_1(K) = g_1(K)$$

$$f_1(0) = 0 \qquad f_1(1) = 2 \qquad f_1(2) = 4 \qquad f_1(3) = 6$$

To determine the cumulative return function for the second stage we must consider all the combinations for investing 0, 1, 2, and 3 million dollars over two stages, as defined by

$$f_2(K) = \text{Max}[g_2(X_2) + f_1(K - X2)]$$

To find $f_2(0)$ is easy. There is only one way to do this, by spending nothing on both projects 1 and 2:

$$f_2(0) = \text{Max}[g_2(0) + f_1(0)] = 0$$

To find $f_2(1)$ becomes more complicated. There are now two ways to invest; either $X_1 = 1$ or $X_2 = 1$. Thus:

$$f_2(1) = \text{Max}\{[g_2(1) \quad + f_1(0)] \text{ or } [g_2(0) + f_1(1)]\}$$
$$= \text{Max}[(1 + 0) \text{ or } (0 + 2)] = 2$$

Similarly, $f_2(2)$ requires three combinations, and $f_2(3)$, four. We find for each:

$$f_2(2) = 5 \qquad f_2(3) = 7$$

as Figure 7.3 indicates.

Finally, for the third stage we proceed just as previously. If we are only interested in the optimum, we need only calculate:

$$f_3(3) = \text{Max}[g_3(X_3) + f_2(3 - X_3)]$$
$$= \text{Max}[(0+7) \text{ or } (3+5) \text{ or } (5+2) \text{ or } (6+0)] = 8$$

The optimum policy is determined by looking at how we obtained the optimum. In this case we can see that

$$f_3(3) = 8 = g_3(1) + f_2(2)$$

So to obtain this optimum we must set $X_3 = 1$ and invest $2 million on the previous two projects. Looking further we find that

$$f_2(2) = 5 = g_2(2) + f_1(0)$$

which implies $X_2 = 2$ and $X_1 = 0$. The optimal policy is thus

$$\mathbf{X}^* = (0, 2, 1)$$

This is path *ABHM* in the network in Figure 7.3.

Sensitivity analysis. The sensitivity to changes in the budget constraint can be obtained simply by calculating $f_3(K)$ where K is less than the budget. We can thus find $f_3(2) = 5$ as shown by point L in Figure 7.3. The shadow price on the budget for the first $1 million decrease (from 3 to 2 million dollars) is thus 3.

Note that, because the feasible region is not convex in this case, the shadow price does not change monotonically as the constraint tightens, as we would expect for linear programming. Thus, for the second $1 million decrease in budget (from 2 to 1 million dollars) the shadow price is

$$f_3(2) - f_3(1) = 5 - 3 = 2$$

Yet the shadow prices for the third $1 million decrease in budget (from 1 million dollars to zero) is

$$f_3(1) - f_3(0) = 3 - 0 = 3$$

In this case the shadow price both increases and decreases as we tighten the constraint from a budget of $3 million.

Comparison with marginal analysis. If one attempted to apply marginal analysis to this problem, one would not get to the right answer. This is because, by marginal analysis, we would invest each increment of money where it immediately seemed most productive, and we would miss opportunities for increasing returns to scale.

Referring to either Table 7.1 or Figure 7.2, we can see that, by marginal analysis, the best way to invest our first million dollars is in project 3, to obtain $g_3(1) = 3$. The best way to invest our second and third million is project 1 or 3. Thus by marginal analysis our apparent—but erroneous—best policy is (2, 0, 1) or (1, 0, 2) for a total of 7. By looking myopically at the marginal returns, project 2 consistently looks unattractive although it eventually has the highest returns and should be part of the optimal policy. The example demonstrates the usefulness of dynamic programming for situations involving nonconvex feasible regions.

Tree representation. Another way to look at the proliferation of possible designs when we do complete enumeration is by means of a "tree." This shows the possible choices at any stage and, by the time we reach the last stage, all the possible combinations. The "tree" for our problem appears in Figure 7.4. It is an extensive form of the network of Figure 7.3.

The advantage of the tree representation is that it provides a convenient way of showing how the partial optimization of each stage eliminates classes of possible designs. In the operations research jargon associated with these trees, we say that we "prune" the tree at each stage. (Keeping with the botanical allusion, we also say that, as the number of possible combinations proliferates, the tree becomes a "messy bush.")

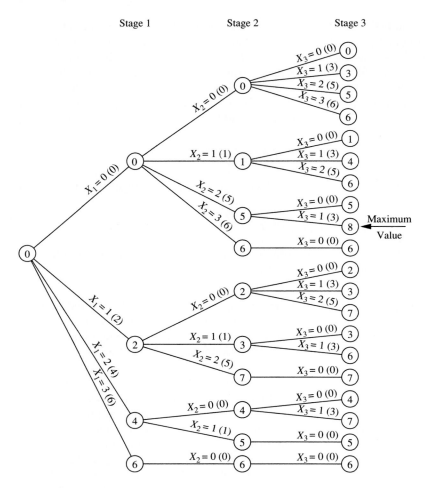

FIGURE 7.4
The "tree" of all combinations of three units or less over three projects in
the example problem, showing the value of each combination of allocations.
Note: Read $X_1 = 1(2)$ as the return associated with setting the first decision
variable X_1 at 1 is 2. The number in the circle gives the total value or return
of all preceding allocations.

Consider the number of ways of allocating $1 million over the first two
projects. The two possibilities appear in Figure 7.5a. One of them is worse and
is pruned—along with its three possibilities for stage 3 shown in Figure 7.4.
Similarly, when we consider how to allocate $2 million over two projects, we drop
some more possibilities, together with their sequels (Figure 7.5b). Altogether,
when we have finished with the partial optimization at the second stage, we are
left with only four alternatives—one for each level (Figure 7.6).

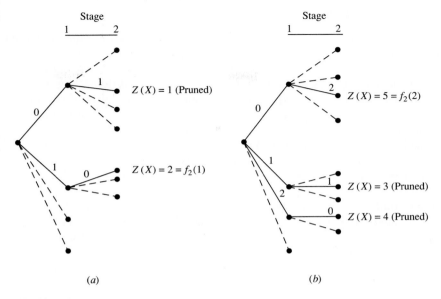

FIGURE 7.5
Pruning of suboptimal combinations at the second stage of the example
problem, shown as a schematic from Fig. 5.5. (*a*) One unit over
two stages; (*b*) two units over two stages.

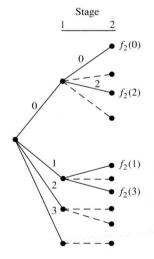

FIGURE 7.6
Optimal combinations at each level for the example
problem, shown as a schematic of Fig. 7.4. All but
four combinations, one for each level, are pruned
away at each stage.

7.5   FURTHER FORMULATIONS

This section shows how dynamic programming can be applied to three important classes of problems: inventory planning, replacement scheduling, and reliability analysis. The optimization of inventories over time is a sequential problem, similar to the introductory example in Section 7.3. The difference is that the development is through time rather than over space. The question of scheduling the replacement or renovation of equipment is another kind of sequential problem. The reliability analysis is a nonsequential problem like the example in Section 7.4. The reliability analysis requires a multiplicative recurrence function, moreover. These three examples thus cover the range of situations for which dynamic programming is most useful.

Inventory analysis. The purpose of an inventory is to keep a supply on hand to meet demands when needed. If one runs out of inventory, and cannot meet a requirement, one generally incurs a loss: this might be the profit foregone on a sale that was not made, or the cost of halting production until the item needed is available.

Maintaining an inventory is expensive. One must both buy the supply in advance (perhaps borrowing money to do so), and pay for its storage, maintenance, and security. This encourages one to keep inventory as low as possible.

There are two reasons to keep an inventory fairly large, however. The bigger it is, the less likely one is to run out due to sudden surges in demand. Further, by ordering in large lots, one may be able to benefit from volume discounts and economies of scale. Optimizing an inventory requires a careful balance between the advantages and disadvantages of size. The objective is to determine the least expensive size of inventory in any period, that is, in any stage.

The typical inventory problem involves the following elements:

- The *beginning inventory*, I_0, the amount on hand for the beginning or first period of the analysis
- The *ending inventory*, I_N, the amount desired for the last period of the analysis
- The *requirement* or use, R_i, for each period
- The *production*, Y_i, or amount of resupply for each period
- The *costs* of both holding inventory in any period, C, and of obtaining the resupply, $C(Y)$

The optimal policy will specify the amount to be produced in each period. The Y_i are the decision variables; all the other parameters are considered set or beyond the control of the analyst. The ultimate objective is to find the least cost, over all N periods, of achieving the desired final inventory: $f_N(I_N)$. The return function $g_i(X_i)$ for each period represents the financial implications of producing Y_i. This involves both the cost of production itself and of holding the inventory this production leads to. This is the inventory of the previous period, plus production, minus use:

$$I_i = I_{i-1} + Y_i - R_i$$

Store Inventory

Consider a store with a starting inventory of 2 in October, monthly demands of 3 through December, and a desire to end up with no inventory in January:

$$I_0 = 2 \qquad R_i = 3 \qquad I_4 = 0$$

Assume that costs of holding inventory are 10 per unit per period and that the costs of production of supply has economies of scale up to 5 units/month:

Y_i:	1	2	3	4	5
$C(Y_i)$:	80	140	180	200	210

Observe that, since demand is 3, the most we can have on hand in December is 3 if we are to eliminate stock by January. Note also that the largest increase in inventory from one period to the next is 2, since this is the maximum supply less demand.

Table 7.2 presents the results. The optimal costs for November, stage 1, are simply the $g_i(Y_i)$. Thus the cost of having an inventory of 2 is the cost of producing 3 units, to meet the demand, plus the cost of holding the inventory:

$$f_1(2) = C(Y_i = 3) + C(2 + 3 - 3) = 180 + 20 = 200$$

The optimal values for December, stage 2, derive from the recursion formula. Thus to have zero inventory, one can start with zero in November and produce 3, start with 1 and produce 2, et cetera. So:

$$f_2(0) = \text{Min}[(80 + 180) \text{ or } (150 + 140) \text{ or } (200 + 80) \text{ or } (230 + 0)]$$
$$= 230$$

TABLE 7.2
Analysis of inventory problem with optimal cost, $f_i(X_i)$, and optimal path for each point

Inventory Level	Oct.	Nov.	Dec.	Jan.
0		*80	*230	*390
1		*150	*260	
2	*0	*200	*310	
3		*230	*390	
4		*250		

(Month spans the Oct., Nov., Dec., Jan. columns)

Therefore:

$$g_i(Y_i) = C(Y_i) + C(I_{i-1} + Y_i - R_i)$$

The recursion formula for the cumulative return function seeks the minimum of the additional costs and the previous inventory:

$$f_i(I_i) = \text{Min}[g_i(Y_i) + f_{i-1}(I_i - Y_i + R_i)]$$

Note that, to be in state I_i in period i, we had to be in state $I_{i-1} = (I_i - Y_i + R_i)$ in period $i - 1$. See box (page 159) for an example of this analysis.

Replacement scheduling. The components of a system normally degrade over time and have to be replaced. When this should happen is rarely obvious. Any machine can usually be maintained, and it is generally cheaper to pay the maintenance bill in any period than to buy a new machine. Yet the replacement should cut maintenance costs for many years. When should one take advantage of this possibility? For example, when should you trade in a car for a newer one?

Dynamic programming is an effective way to determine an optimal replacement policy. To do so, one needs to have the costs or benefits of buying the possible range of newer components, ones that will last for one or more periods. In this kind of problem, the stages are conveniently the beginning of each period, and the states describe the useful life of the equipment. The analysis seeks to find the least cost policy of buying and maintaining equipment over a given total number of periods. See box for example.

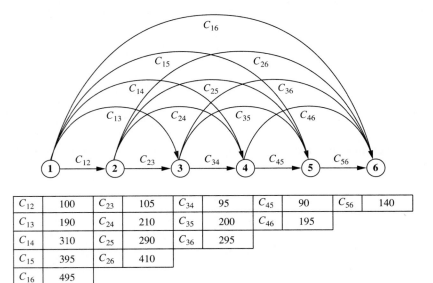

C_{12}	100	C_{23}	105	C_{34}	95	C_{45}	90	C_{56}	140
C_{13}	190	C_{24}	210	C_{35}	200	C_{46}	195		
C_{14}	310	C_{25}	290	C_{36}	295				
C_{15}	395	C_{26}	410						
C_{16}	495								

FIGURE 7.7
Replacement schedule data.

Replacement Schedule

A company has a contract to produce insulated pipe for the construction of an Arctic pipeline over five years . It must thus acquire and maintain a machine to wrap tubes over this total period.

The company could equip itself in many ways. For example, it could buy a new machine every year, selling the old one for scrap or reuse elsewhere. It could also buy a single machine for the whole five years. Figure 7.7 illustrates the various transitions that could occur from stage 1, the start of year 1, to stage 6, the end of the fifth year, that is the start of year 6.

The table in Figure 7.7 indicates the costs C_{ij} of acquiring in stage i a machine that will be replaced in stage j. Thus, $C_{12} = 100$ means that buying a machine at the beginning of the first year that will only serve until the beginning of year 2 costs 100. These costs are the $g_i(X_i)$.

Table 7.3 presents the results. The cumulative return function for the beginning of the first year, $f_i(X_i)$, is just the $g_i(X_i)$. The optimal cost for having a machine that will be replaced at the beginning of year 3, that is, one that will be replaced one year from stage 2, is

$$f_2(1) = \text{Min}\left[C_{13} \text{ or } (C_{12} + C_{23})\right]$$
$$= \text{Min}\left[190 \text{ or } (100 + 105)\right] = 190$$

Ultimately we want, at the end of the fifth year which is the beginning of year 6, to have zero life in our equipment. For this problem, the optimal result is: $f_6 = 480$. The optimal policy is first to buy a machine for two years, then for one year, and finally for 2 years again.

TABLE 7.3
Analysis of replacement schedule with optimal cost and optimal path for each point

Years of Machine-Life	1	2	Beginning of Year 3	4	5	6
0						
1	100	190	285	375	480	
2	190	310	390	480		
3	310	390	485			
4	395	495				
5	495					

Reliability analysis. A system can be made more reliable in two ways: by increasing the reliability of any component, and by providing additional, redundant components. These components, placed in parallel with others, increase reliability because they can function when the others fail.

The object of a reliability analysis is to determine how to maximize the probability that a system will function. The idea is to allocate resources optimally to the possible components. In this regard the analysis is identical to the investment example in Section 7.4.

Reliability analysis can only be done by dynamic programming if the probability of failure of each component is independent of that of the others. This is a basic requirement for dynamic programming (see Section 7.2). The method cannot be used when the failure of the parts is all due to a common cause, such as a fire that affects all parts concurrently.

The dynamic programming version of reliability analysis differs from the investment problem in that its cumulative return function is multiplicative. This is because the probability that several independent components function simultaneously is a factor of the probabilities of individual components. The point of this example is to show how to deal with such multiplicative functions.

In practice the analysis focuses on minimizing the probability of failure of a system. Of course, this achieves the same result as maximizing success since the two are complementary:

$$P \text{ (Success)} + P \text{ (Failure)} = 1.0$$

The reason for focusing on the failure of the system is that its probability is much easier to calculate. Given the assumption of independence, it is the multiplication of the probability that all parallel components fail simultaneously:

$$P \text{ (Failure of System)} = \prod {}_i P \text{ (Failure of Each Component)}$$

The probability of success is much more complicated to calculate: it is the sum of all the combinations of ways in which the system could operate.

The first step of the analysis is thus to convert all the data on the probability of success of components into their complementary probability of failure. The step is necessary because, for understandable psychological reasons, manufacturers like to accentuate the positive high performance of their parts, rather than draw attention to the fact that these may also fail.

As with the investment problem, the return functions $g_i(X_i)$ for greater investment X_i in any part is simply the capability achieved, that is, the probability of failure of a part. Note that this is a decreasing function: more expense should reduce the probability of failure. The recursion function is similar to that for the investment, except that it is a minimization and a multiplication:

$$f_i(X_i) = \text{Min } \{[g_i(X_i)][f_{i-1}(K - X_i)]\}$$

See box for an example of reliability analysis.

Reliability Analysis

Consider a system that can have up to three parallel components to provide redundancy. The probability of failure or nonperformance of each depends in the investment made in the part, as indicated in Table 7.4. The question is: how should the system be designed to maximize the reliability, that is, to minimize the probability of failure?

The results of the analysis appear in Table 7.5, organized as Table 7.2. As usual, the optimal performance for the first stage is simply $g_1(X_1)$. The optimal values for the next two stages derive from the recursion formula. The best way to spend 2 units on the first two components, for example, is the minimum of the probability of failure achieved by no investment in the first part and 2 units in the second, $\{f_1(0)\}\{g_2(2)\}$, 1 unit of investment in each, and so on:

$$f_2(2) = \text{Min } [(1.0)(0.4) \text{ or } (0.4)(0.5) \text{ or } (0.3)(1.0)] = 0.20$$

The optimal design in this case is triple redundancy, achieved by placing one unit of investment in each part:

$$f_3(3) = (0.4)(0.5)(0.6) = 0.12$$

This solution is not intuitively obvious. Indeed, part 1 is far superior to the other two for any level of investment; as Table 7.4 shows. Yet this kind of diversified solution is characteristic of reliability problems: because probabilities for parallel components multiply, better performance is often achieved by redundancy than single superior components.

TABLE 7.4
Return functions for reliability analysis

Investment level, X_i	Return function $g_i(X_i)$		
	$L = 1$	$L = 2$	$L = 3$
0	1.0	1.0	1.0
1	0.4	0.5	0.6
2	0.3	0.4	0.5
3	0.2	0.3	0.4

TABLE 7.5
Analysis of reliability problem with optimal cost, $f_i(X_i)$, and optimal path to each point

Investment	Component		
Level	1	2	3
0		*1.0 —— *1.0	
1		*0.4 ← *0.4	
2		*0.3 \ *0.2	
3		*0.2 \ *0.15	*0.12

REFERENCES

Wagner, H. M., (1975). "Introduction to Dynamic Optimization Models," Chapter 8 *Principles of Operations Research*, 2nd ed., Prentice-Hall, Englewood Cliffs, NJ.
Winston, W. L., (1987). "Deterministic Dynamic Programming," Chapter 18, *Operations Research: Applications and Algorithms*, PWS Publishers, New York.

PROBLEMS

7.1. *Engulf and Devour*

The safety engineer for Engulf and Devour's Lakeside factory has estimated the number of employee disabilities (measured in sick days/year) that can be avoided by various measures: covering dangerous machinery (CDM), providing protective clothing (PPC), improving ventilation (IV), and/or lowering noise levels (LNL). The information is summarized in the following table.

	Measures			
Investment (10^3\$)	CDM	PPC	IV	LNL
0	0	0	0	0
10	5	15	2	5
20	10	22	12	7
30	15	25	15	15
40	20	25	17	25
50	22	30	25	26

(a) Use dynamic programming to determine how a \$70,000 budget could be most effectively employed to reduce disabilities.

(b) How much of a difference would it make if management cut back the safety budget to \$60,000? How much money would be saved for each additional sick day the budget cut would cause?

(c) Could this problem be solved by linear programming? Why or why not?

7.2. *Stereo*

Felicia has decided to subscribe to a service, offered by Bob's Stereo Outlet, that will optimize her stereo system purchase. Having decided to buy a tape deck, a turntable, a pair of speakers, and a receiver, Felicia fills out the following form, indicating the value to her of each component:

Model	Price($)	Tape	Turntable	Speakers	Receiver
A	200	0.1	0.2	0.1	0.3
B	400	0.3	0.3	0.2	0.4
C	600	0.5	0.5	0.5	0.5
D	800	0.9	0.8	0.9	0.8
E	1000	0.9	0.9	1.0	0.9

What would the BSO recommend Felicia buy for $1000? For $2000?

7.3. *Exam Cram*

Howie McKim has a maximum of six hours of study time before the Systems Analysis midterm. He knows what material will be covered on the test, how well prepared he is in each area, and how much an additional hour of study will help him in each area:

Hours of study	MA	LP	SA	DP
0	5	15	2	5
1	10	22	12	7
2	15	25	15	15
3	20	25	17	25
4	22	25	25	25

MA = Marginal Analysis
LP = Linear Programming
SA = Sensitivity Analysis
DP = Dynamic Programming

(*a*) Use dynamic programming to allocate Howie's study time to maximize his point grade on the midterm.
(*b*) How many fewer points will he get if he takes an hour off to work for the presidential candidate of his preference?
(*c*) Could this problem be solved by linear programming? Why or why not?

7.4. *Fire House*

City planners must determine the "optimal" allocation of fire stations to three districts. Zero to three stations may be located in a district. The table below shows the relationship between the number of stations and the annual expected property damage due to fires, based on statistical data. Differences among districts are due to population, construction materials, and so on. A budget constraint restricts the total number of stations to five.

District	Number of stations per district			
	0	1	2	3
1	2.0	0.9	0.3	0.2
2	0.5	0.3	0.2	0.1
3	1.5	1.0	0.7	0.3

(a) Determine the optimal allocation by dynamic programming.
(b) Could the problem be solved by linear programming? Why or why not?
(c) Write an equation for the recurrence formula.

7.5. *Rat Patrol*

A Boston rat crawls out of its hole at Beacon and Arlington Streets and decides to raid its favorite garbage can behind a store at Newbury and Exeter Streets. Based on previous experience with cats, traffic, and lighting conditions, the rat estimates travel time (in minutes) for each block as shown:

Newbury St.		5		3		1		4	
	2		3		2		5		4
Commonwealth Ave.		6		2		2		2	
	2		2		3		6		2
Marlboro St.		8		3		3		2	
	3		2		2		4		1
Beacon St.		5		2		2		3	

Arlington St. Berkeley St. Clarendon St. Dartmouth St. Exeter St.

(a) Find the rat's minimum route to the garbage can.
(b) How long will the trip take by the shortest path?
(c) If, instead, the rat decided to chew on a telephone pole at Marlboro & Dartmouth, how long would that trip take from its hole?

7.6. *Winter Inventory*

A company manufacturing large industrial equipment projects sales of 3 units/month in January, February, and March. Beginning inventory in January (ending inventory in December) is 2 units. The company desires that ending inventory in March also be 2 units. Demand for any month may be satisfied from beginning inventory or that month's production. Ending inventory in any month is limited to 5 units, and production during any month is limited to 5 units. There is a $10,000 holding cost for any unit left in inventory at the end of a month. Production cost depends on the number of units manufactured in a month as follows:

Units/Month	0	1	2	3	4	5
Cost ($000)	0	80	100	120	130	140

(a) Define the objective, decision variables, objective function, constraints, and the return functions for each stage.

(b) Determine the optimal production schedule for January, February, and March.

7.7. *Ad Campaign*

Muncho wants to start a TV ad campaign for its new line of desserts. Market studies tell it how many potential customers may be attracted by ads on the three major TV networks (see following table). Suppose advertising time costs the same on all networks and that Muncho's budget limits the ad campaign to five hours.

Millions of customers who will see the ad on different networks:

Number of hours	Network		
	ABC	CBS	NBC
1	3	1	2
2	5	2	4
3	6	5	6
4	6	6	6

(a) How should Muncho buy ad time to attract the most customers?

(b) Write the recursion formula for the problem.

(c) Could Muncho use linear programming to solve this problem? Why or why not?

7.8. *Cheryl Consultant*

Cheryl Consultant has an opportunity to invest in one or more of four proposal writing projects A, B, C, or D. Any investment in a project must be made in $1000 increments. Moreover, there are limits to the amounts Cheryl might invest effectively in any one project: $7000 for A; $5000 for B and D; and $6000 for C. Cheryl is also willing not to invest at all in a project if her money might be invested more profitably in the other projects. Cheryl estimates her returns for investments as follows:

Project	Level of investment (in $1000)						
	1	2	3	4	5	6	7
A	5	10	15	25	35	50	55
B	3	6	12	18	30	30	30
C	20	35	45	55	60	65	65
D	9	16	29	37	45	45	45

(a) If Cheryl has $8000, what is her optimal strategy?

(b) What will her returns from this strategy be?

(c) Suppose Cheryl's friend Jill offers her an extra $1000 if Cheryl agrees to repay Jill $3000. Should Cheryl accept the offer? Explain your answer.

(d) If Cheryl only has $7000, how should her investment plan change?

7.9. *Unit Fund*
The Unit Fund wants to assign 10 volunteers to solicit contributions from the companies in four office buildings. The director estimates the contributions (in kilo bucks) as follows:

Building	Number of volunteers							
	0	1	2	3	4	5	6	7
1	0	5	10	15	25	35	50	55
2	0	3	6	12	18	30		
3	0	20	35	45	55	60	65	
4	0	9	16	29	37	45		

No additional pledges would be received by sending more than seven volunteers to building 1, more than five to building 2, more than six to building 3, and five to building 4.
(*a*) How should volunteers be assigned, and how much will they collect?
(*b*) How does the solution change if there are nine volunteers?

7.10. *V. Erner Brawn*
Colonel V. Erner Brawn, coordinator for the Advanced Space Shuttle, has to determine the allocation of NASA R&D funds that will maximize the probability that three technological breakthroughs (A, B, & C) will take place in time to incorporate them into the advanced shuttle. Specialists estimate that the probability that any breakthrough will occur in time is a function of project funding as follows:

Project	Funding (in 10^7 dollars)			
	0	2	4	6
A	0.1	0.2	0.3	0.4
B	0.1	0.3	0.4	0.6
C	0.1	0.1	0.2	0.5

Assuming that the above probabilities are independent, the likelihood that all three occur in time is the product of the individual probabilities.
(*a*) If NASA funding is $100,000,000 [10 times 10^7], what probability of success should Colonel Brawn report to her superiors?
(*b*) How should she allocate her funds?
(*c*) How much money is needed to triple the probability of success?
(*d*) How should funds then be allocated?

7.11. *Stagecoach*
When Mark Off decides to seek his fortune in San Francisco, the stagecoach is the only real means of transportation from the East, where he lives, to the West.

The entire trip requires four stops, regardless of routing. Worried about the dangers involved in such a trip, Mark reasons that the insurance premiums between stops measures the inherent danger of each link.

					Insurance premiums ($ × 10^3)					
From stop	**To stop:**	**2**	**3**	**4**	**5**	**6**	**7**	**8**	**9**	**SF**
1		3	3	6						
2					7	4	8			
3					4	4	5			
4					6	3	3			
5								6	9	
6								7	7	
7								8	5	
8										5
9										4

(a) State Mark's objective function for going by the safest route.
(b) How is his problem characterized and analyzed in terms of stages?
(c) What route should he take to go to San Francisco?
(d) Mark's father, Pop Off, lives in stop 8. Find an optimal routing from the East to the West that goes through stop 8.

7.12. *Mark Off Again*

Mark Off receives an urgent request from the Tsar to find a route to Rostov from Vladivostok. The expenses associated with each leg of the journey are for protection against attacks by Cossacks and local tribesmen. Find an optimal routing.

						Expenses (rubles × 10^3)						
From stop	**To stop:**	**2**	**3**	**4**	**5**	**6**	**7**	**8**	**9**	**10**	**11**	**12**	**R**
V		5	6										
2				4	7	11							
3				8	6	9							
4							9	12	13	14			
5							8	15	12	8			
6							10	9	8	7			
7											12	11	
8											9	8	
9											7	5	
10											9	9	
11													2
12													3

7.13. *Truck Loading*

Consider a truck whose maximum loading capacity is 20 tons. Suppose that there are four different items, various quantities of which are to make up a load to be carried to a remote geographical area. Suppose we wish to maximize the value of what the truck carries to the inhabitants, given the following weights and values of the four items.

Item	Weight (tons)	Value
1	3	5
2	4	7
3	5	8
4	6	10

(a) Find the optimal solution by dynamic programming.
(b) Write the recurrence formula for this problem.
(c) Define the assumptions of dynamic programming.

7.14. *Amplifier*

Consider a three-stage amplifier, where the gain in each stage is a function of the expenditure on that stage, and the total gain equals the product of the gains of the three stages.

	Stage		
Cost ($)	1	2	3
0	1	1	1
1	2	1.5	2.5
2	3	2	3
3	4	5	6

For $0, you can put in wire. Spending more than $3 per stage produces no additional gain. Determine the maximum gain attainable for $0, $1, $3, $4, $5. How would each maximum be achieved?

7.15. *Burn Out*

Three independent systems can be used to detect overheating of a large and expensive machine. The probability that any one of these systems tends to operate is inversely related to its quality and cost.

Cost ($, 10^3)	Probability of failure of system		
	A	B	C
0	1	1	1
1	0.9	0.8	0.9
2	0.8	0.7	0.7
3	0.6	0.6	0.6
4	0.5	0.5	0.5

(a) Use DP to select the best design(s), given a $4,000 budget.
(b) Write a recursion formula for this problem.

7.16. *B, D, and M*

Two companies, B and D, and university M are independently trying to solve a robotics problem by different methods. Their probability of success is 0.6, 0.4, and 0.2, respectively. A consultant has determined that these probabilities would improve if more money were invested in the projects according to the following schedule. The government, wishing to maximize the probability that the problem will be solved, is prepared to support the research with $6 million.

Support (10^6)	Company B	Company D	Univ. M
None	0.60	0.40	0.20
1	0.75	0.55	0.40
2	0.85	0.65	0.55
3	0.90	0.75	0.65
4	0.93	0.82	0.73
5	0.95	0.87	0.80
6	0.96	0.91	0.86

(a) How should the government allocate its money? Assume that, with respect to this research, the government does not think in units of less than $1 million.
(b) How does the solution obtained by dynamic programming compare with the strategy of backing the most advanced company completely? Are you prepared to justify backing anyone else?

7.17. *Circuit Reliability*

An electronic circuit consists of four parts connected in series as shown:

$$\text{Input} - \text{Part 1} - \text{Part 2} - \text{Part 3} - \text{Part 4} - \text{Output}$$

The circuit functions properly only if *all four* parts function properly. Each part of the circuit is built by connecting a number of identical components in parallel. Each component in each part functions or fails independently of other components in the circuit. A given circuit part functions properly if *at least one* of the components in this part functions properly.

For convenience, we define

P_i = probability that a particular component in part i will function
C_i = unit cost of each component in part i

Suppose that we are given:

Part	P_i	$C_i(\$)$
1	0.9	2
2	0.8	4
3	0.7	3
4	0.6	1

To calculate the reliability of the circuit, we note:

(a) P(Circuit functions) $= \prod_i$ P (part i functions)

(b) P(Part i functions) $= 1 - $ P (part i fails)
    $= 1 - $ P (all components in i fail)
    $= 1 - $ [P(one component in i fails)$]^n$
    $= 1 - [1 - P_i]^n$

Assume a budget of \$16 and use dynamic programming to design the most reliable circuit.

CHAPTER
8

MULTIOBJECTIVE
OPTIMIZATION

8.1 THE PROBLEM

Most systems either produce several different outputs or serve a variety of purposes at once. A factory almost always makes distinct products: an automobile
factory may make cars and trucks; a refinery can turn crude petroleum into a
range of distillates. Service facilities likewise typically accomplish several goals:
schools, for instance, both teach children and provide custodial care so parents
can work outside the home; a dam on a river may both control floods and provide
some recreational benefits associated with its reservoir.

The preceding chapters have all dealt with optimization over only one
objective, benefit or cost, in contrast to the reality of the multiple outputs for any
system. This focus is based on two reasons. The first is that it is often realistic
to assume that multiple outputs can all be translated into a single overriding
objective. The managers of a factory producing cars and trucks may, for example,
really be concerned with profits rather than types of vehicles; they may thus be
quite prepared to express each different output in terms of its profitability. The
second reason for the focus on single objective optimization is that it is virtually
impossible to achieve an optimum over many objectives at once.

The essential difficulty with multiobjective optimization is that the meaning
of the optimum is not defined so long as we deal with multiple objectives that
are truly different. For example, suppose that we are trying to determine the best
design of a system of dams on a river, with the objectives of promoting "national
income," reducing "deaths by flooding," and increasing "employment." Some
designs will be more profitable, but less effective at reducing deaths. How can
we state which is better when the objectives are so different, and measured in such

different terms? How can one state with any accuracy what the relative value of a life is in terms of national income? If one resolved that question, then how would one determine the relative value of new jobs and other objectives? The answer is, with extreme difficulty. The attempts to set values on these objectives are, in fact, most controversial.

To obtain a single global optimum over all objectives requires that we either establish or impose some means of specifying the value of each of the different objectives. If all objectives can indeed be valued on a common basis, the optimization can be stated in terms of that single value. The multiobjective problem has then disappeared and the optimization proceeds relatively smoothly in terms of a single objective.

In practice it is frequently awkward if not indefensible to give every objective a relative value. The relative worth of profits, lives lost, the environment, and other such objectives are unlikely to be established easily by anyone, or to be accepted by all concerned. One then cannot hope to be able to determine an acceptable optimum analytically.

The focus of multiobjective optimization in practice is to sort out the mass of clearly inferior solutions, rather than determine the single best design. The result is the identification of the small subset of the feasible solutions that are worthy of further consideration. Formally, this result is known as the set of noninferior solutions.

8.2 NONINFERIOR SOLUTIONS

To understand the concept of noninferior solutions, it is necessary to look closely at the multiobjective problem. Formally, it consists of several objectives:

$$\mathbf{Y} = (Y_1, \ldots, Y_k)$$

each of which is a different function of the inputs, $\mathbf{X}$

$$Y_k = g_k(\mathbf{X})$$

The problem of multiobjective optimization is thus:

Optimize: $\qquad \mathbf{Y} = g_1(\mathbf{X}), \ldots, g_k(\mathbf{X})$

Subject to: $\qquad$ constraints on $\mathbf{X}$

The essential feature of the multiobjective problem is that the feasible region of production of the solutions is much more complex than for a single objective. In single objective optimization, any set of inputs $\mathbf{X}$ produces a set of results Y that could be represented by a straight line going from bad (typically zero output) to best; the production function is then simply defined as locus of these best or technically efficient solutions (refer back to Figure 2.1). In a multiobjective problem, any set of inputs $\mathbf{X}$ defines a multidimensional space of feasible solutions, as Figure 8.1 indicates. There is then no exact equivalent of a technically efficient solution.

The *noninferior solutions* are the conceptual equivalents, in multiobjective problems, of a technically efficient solution in a single objective problem.

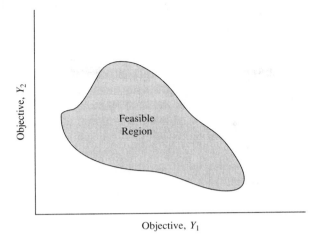

**FIGURE 8.1
Feasible region of
multidimensional
production for a specific
set of inputs X.**

Formally, a noninferior solution $\mathbf{Y}^*$ for a given set of $\mathbf{X}$ is one such that no other feasible solution for the same $\mathbf{X}$ is better on all objectives $\mathbf{Y}_k$. If some other feasible solution improves on some objectives, it must degrade on others. Figure 8.2 illustrates the concept with respect to the status quo, $\mathbf{Y}_0$, that exists without the project defined by the inputs $\mathbf{X}$. Graphically, the noninferior solutions are the outer shell of the feasible solutions for any set of inputs $\mathbf{X}$, in the direction of improving the objectives.

> **Semantic caution:** The noninferior solutions are sometimes referred to by other names: dominant solutions, Pareto optimal solutions, and the production feasibility frontier. The term "noninferior solutions" lacks elegance but seems preferable to the alternatives in that it is both descriptive and accurate. The term "dominant solutions" is misleading and should be avoided: no solution in the noninferior set dominates any other in the set.

The preferred design for any problem should be one of the noninferior solutions. So long as all objectives worth taking into account have been considered, no design that is not among the noninferior solutions is worthwhile: it is dominated by some designs that are preferable on all accounts. This is the reason multiobjective optimization focuses on the determination of the noninferior solutions.

It is often useful to group the noninferior solutions into major categories. The purpose of this exercise is to facilitate discussions about which solution to select. Indeed, to the extent that it is not possible to specify acceptable relative values for the objectives, and thus impossible to define the best design analytically, it is necessary for the choice of the design to rest on judgement. As individuals find it difficult to consider a large number of possibilities, it is helpful to focus attention on major categories.

The noninferior solutions are best divided into two types of categories: the major alternatives and the compromises. *A major alternative group* of noninferior solutions represents the best performance on some major objective. As Figure 8.3

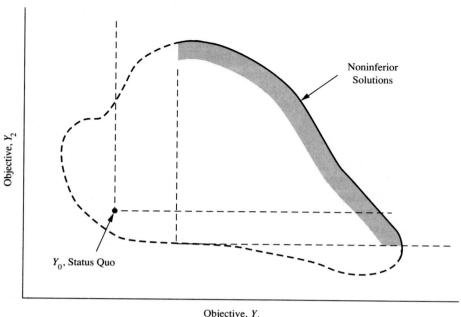

FIGURE 8.2
The noninferior solutions as the outer shell of the feasible region in the direction of improving the objectives.

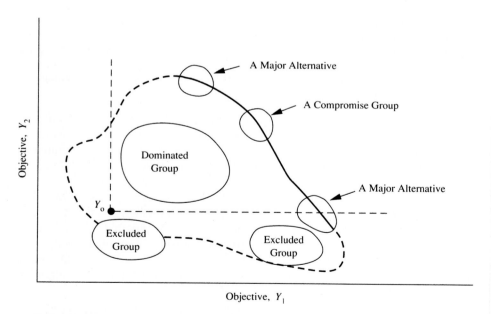

FIGURE 8.3
Groups associated with noninferior and other feasible solutions.

176

indicates, the major alternatives represent polar extremes. A *compromise group* lies somewhere in between the major alternatives.

The remainder of the feasible region of solutions is likewise usefully categorized into dominated and excluded solutions. *Dominated* solutions are those that are inferior in all essential aspects to other solutions. They can thus be set aside from further consideration. *Excluded* solutions are those that perform so badly on one or more dimensions that they lie beneath the threshold of acceptability. They thus may be dropped from further consideration.

The concepts of noninferior solutions and of major categories are often highly useful in a practical sense. They organize the feasible designs into a small number of manageable ideas and draw attention to the choices that must be made. These ideas can be applied even when the feasible region is not defined analytically. See the box for an example.

Use of Categories in Multiobjective Optimization

The choice of a site for a second major airport for Sydney, Australia was definitely a multiobjective problem. As with most projects centering on the location of a major facility, it involved many distinct issues. Major concerns for an airport are, in general: cost, accessibility, safety, and environmental impact.

The feasible solutions for Sydney were highly constrained by mountains, the city, and the sea. At the time of the study we did in 1984, only 11 distinct locations seemed worth considering, 10 new ones and the existing airport. Their total costs were all roughly comparable, and all were deemed to meet the required threshold of safe operation. Our analysis consequently paid attention to the two remaining major objectives of maximizing accessibility and environmental compatibility.

Close examination of the 11 feasible solutions indicated that they could be placed into each of the groups illustrated in Figure 8.3. Three sites fell into excluded groups: Goulbourn turned out to be too inaccessible, another had unsafe wind considerations, and a third was prohibitively expensive and hazardous since it involved clearing a vast expanse littered with unexploded artillery shells. Five other locations were fairly clearly dominated by other sites. The three remaining locations could then be viewed as two major alternatives and a possible compromise: Wilton represented the most environmentally compatible feasible solution, in great part because it is so far from people whom it might disturb; and Badgery's Creek, somewhere in between, represented a possible compromise. See Figure 8.4.

The division of the possible sites into these categories had the practical benefit of helping the Australian government decide between the different sites, each with their distinct advantages and disadvantages in detail. Based on this analysis the Minister for Aviation selected Badgery's Creek and Wilton for detailed analysis. The existing airport was excluded as being environmentally inappropriate for a major long-term expansion involving many additional runways.

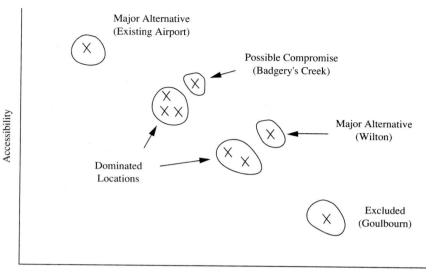

FIGURE 8.4
Application of categories to the feasible locations for a Second Sydney Airport.

8.3 CONSTRAINT METHOD

This and the next section describe the two major ways of defining the noninferior solutions: the constraint and the weighting methods. Both have a common kind of approach to the task. They transform the multidimensional problem, which cannot be solved explicitly, into a series of one-dimensional problems for which solutions can be obtained. The basic difference between the two methods lies in how they make this transformation to one-dimensional problems.

The choice between the constraint and the weighting method is a question of convenience rather than one of principle. Each has distinct operational advantages and disadvantages. Which should be used depends on the specifics of the problem. Guidelines for selecting between the methods occur at the end of the next section.

The *constraint method* generates a systematic exploration of the noninferior solutions. It can define these as precisely and in as much detail as desired, however complex the surface of noninferior solutions may be. The major disadvantage of the constraint method is that it can be tedious and expensive.

The essential idea of the constraint method is to optimize one objective while representing all the other objectives as constraints. This process defines a noninferior solution, if any solution is feasible. Systematic repetition of this process, with different constraints on the objectives, generates the entire set of noninferior solutions.

The representation of objectives as constraints is an explicit expression of what is often done implicitly in practice. In designing a water supply system, for example, there are at least two major objectives: level of cost and level of quality. In practice, the quality objective has generally been expressed as a set of minimal constraints on purity and water pressure. This reduces the design to the single objective problem of minimizing cost (refer to Section 3.1). The constraint method extends this idea by varying the constraints and, thereby, making evident the relationship between the several objectives.

The way the constraint method generates the noninferior solutions is best shown graphically. For this purpose consider the situation with two objectives, Y_1 and Y_2, illustrated by Figure 8.5. If we maximize either objective without placing any restraint on the other, we obtain a noninferior solution. Point A, for example, represents the design with the greatest possible Y_2 and some level of Y_1. Suppose we now set a minimum constraint on the level of objective Y_1, such as $Y_{1B} > Y_{1A}$. If we now maximize Y_2 again, but subject to this minimum constraint on the other objective, we obtain another noninferior solution, Point B. We can repeat this process as often as we care or can afford to and thereby get more and more noninferior solutions. There is no theoretical limit to the precision with which we can define the noninferior solutions by the constraint method.

The constraint method has a noticeable disadvantage when there are three or more objectives. The difficulty is then that as the analysis systematically imposes combinations of constraints on the objectives, many of these combinations lead to infeasible solutions. Figure 8.6 indicates how this may occur. Much computational effort may thus be wasted using the constraint method. Whether this is important depends on its cost.

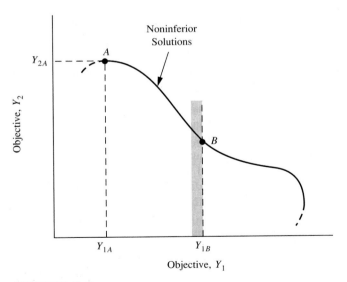

FIGURE 8.5
The constraint method defines the entire set of noninferior solutions by systematically varying the constraints on the objectives.

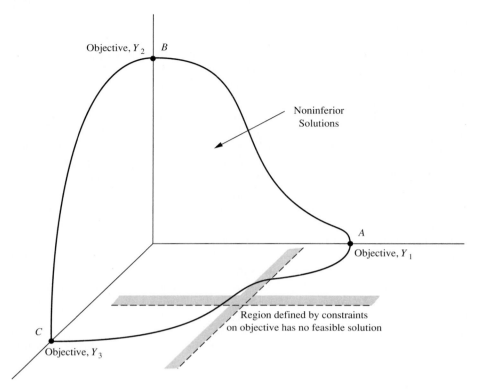

FIGURE 8.6
The constraint method often leads to infeasible solutions when there are three or more objectives.

A practical, step-by-step procedure for applying the constraint method is as follows:

1. Optimize for each objective by itself, without any constraints on the objectives. These results define limits on the range of noninferior solutions as points A, B, and C do in Figure 8.6.
2. Optimize on one objective, placing constraints on only one other objective. Iteratively change this constraint until you reach the end of the maximum feasible value of this objective. Repeat for other objectives. This process traces out noninferior solutions such as those shown by AB, BC and AC in Figure 8.6.
3. Optimize now with two constraints, and proceed similarly to above. This traces out noninferior points in three dimensions.
4. Proceed as before for as many dimensions as desirable or necessary.

The constraint method works both when the solutions can be defined mathematically, or are only defined individually, as was the case for the design of the

Second Sydney Airport (see box in Section 8.2). The method implicitly assumes that linear programming will be used in any mathematical analysis, as it is the only method that can readily deal with multiple constraints.

8.4 WEIGHTING METHOD

The *weighting method* also generates a systematic definition of noninferior solutions. It accomplishes this somewhat faster than the constraints method. Its major disadvantage is that it may miss or misrepresent some portion of the set of noninferior solutions, in ways that the constraint method avoids.

The essential idea of the weighting method is to transform the multiobjective problem (see Section 8.2):

Optimize: $\qquad\qquad$ $\mathbf{Y} = g_1(\mathbf{X}), \ldots, g_k(\mathbf{X})$

Subject to: $\qquad\qquad$ constraints on $\mathbf{X}$

into a single objective problem. This is done by introducing a set of weights, w_k, for each objective. One then proceeds to optimize the weighted sum of the objectives:

Optimize: $\qquad\qquad$ $\sum \mathbf{w}\mathbf{Y} = \sum w_k g_k(\mathbf{X})$

Subject to: $\qquad\qquad$ constraints on $\mathbf{X}$

Solving this problem defines a noninferior solution. Systematic repetition of the process for different sets of weights defines most of the noninferior solutions — although not all.

The various sets of weights used in the weighting method do not have to be given a meaningful interpretation. Most basically, the sets of weights can simply be thought of as absolutely arbitrary numbers that serve the purpose of generating the set of noninferior solutions.

The weights can also be interpreted as the relative values of each objective. If one really did believe that each unit of achievement of objective Y_k were exactly worth w_k, then maximizing the weighted sum of the objectives, $\sum w_k Y_k$, would maximize total value. Thus, for the automobile factory producing cars and trucks with known degrees of profitability, the multiobjective problem of determining what is the best mix of these objectives can be put as the single objective problem of maximizing profits.

In practice, one generally does not know what the values of different objectives should be. It is also unlikely that these should be constant over the entire range of achievement of these objectives. These facts imply that one should not be particularly concerned about — nor attach much significance to — the numbers used as weights. One need not worry if the numbers do not appear realistic, nor spend effort in the exercise of determining what the weights ought to be; they are simply means that help define the noninferior set.

Kuhn and Tucker demonstrated that the solution to the weighted optimization $\sum w_k Y_k$ defines a noninferior solution to the multiobjective problem, provided some minimal sign conventions were respected. (This result is an extension of their optimality conditions, see Section 3.3). The only limitation is that increasing quantities of each objective Y_k should be desirable, and each weight should correspondingly be positive, $w_k \geq 0$. The point of these conventions is to insure that increases in the weighted sum $\sum w_k Y_k$ always correspond to an increase in desirability. In practice, this limitation poses no difficulty since any objective can be interpreted so that increases are more desirable; for example, if we were concerned with minimizing lives lost through some catastrophe such as an earthquake, one could redefine the objective as maximizing the number of lives saved through protective means (see discussion in Section 5.2).

The way the weighting method generates the noninferior solution is also conveniently shown graphically. Again, consider a situation with two objectives Y_1 and Y_2. As Figure 8.7 shows, isoquants of the quantity to be maximized by the weighting method, that is, the weighted sum $(w_1 Y_1 + w_2 Y_2)$, are simply straight lines. The desired maximum is the feasible design that reaches the highest isoquant, as point E does in Figure 8.7. This design must be a noninferior solution, as can be seen. Repetition of this process for different sets of weights defines additional noninferior solutions.

The weighting method has a couple of computational advantages over the constraint method. Its calculations are somewhat simpler since the constraint method increases the number of constraints, which is a basic determinant of the difficulty of the calculations (see Section 5.4). The weighting method also does not waste calculations since there will always be a feasible solution, whatever the weights used. The constraints method, on the other hand, may cycle through sets of constraints for which there is no feasible solution (see Section 8.3).

The major disadvantage of the weighting method is that it may not provide the analyst with a complete description of the noninferior solutions. Most obviously, this method may miss potentially significant features. As Figure 8.8

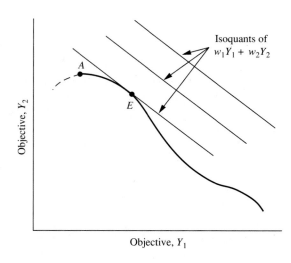

FIGURE 8.7
The weighting method defines a set of noninferior solutions by systematically varying weights on the objective.

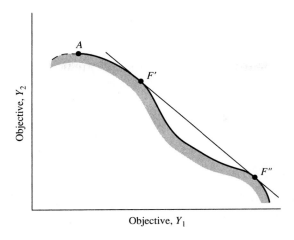

FIGURE 8.8
The weighting method has the disadvantage of skipping over reentrant portions of the feasible region, such as that between F' and F''.

illustrates, the weighting method can simply skip over reentrant portions of the feasible region. It may thus portray the set of noninferior solution as a convex region even if it is not, and may suggest feasible solutions where none exist.

A secondary disadvantage of the weighting method is that it makes it difficult for the analyst to define the noninferior solutions with equal coverage throughout the feasible region. The analyst cannot determine the spacing of the points defined on surface, as can be most easily done with the constraint method. Constant incremental changes in the weights used do not translate into an equal grid across the space of noninferior solutions, as Figure 8.9 suggests.

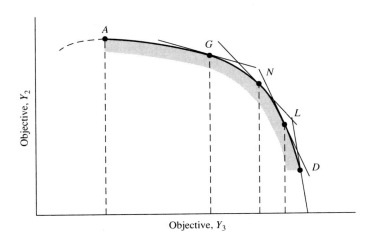

FIGURE 8.9
The weighting method makes it difficult for the analyst to control the spacing with which the noninferior solutions are defined.

The step-by-step procedure for applying weighting method is generally similar to that for the constraint method. In detail:

1. Optimize for each constraint by itself, to determine the range of noninferior solutions. This is conveniently done by solving the weighted sum of the objectives with all except one w_k equal to zero.
2. Optimize over two constraints, with two w_k not equal to zero. This defines the edges of the space of noninferior points.
3. Proceed as above, using successively more w_k not equal to zero, for as many dimensions as desirable or necessary.

Throughout this process it is useful to recognize that it is the relative values of w_k that count, not their absolute size. In two dimensions, for example, the weighted sum $(3Y_1 + 2Y_2)$ defines the same noninferior solutions as $(30Y_1 + 20Y_2)$; graphically the slopes of the isoquants in Figure 8.7 would be the same. This fact means that the analyst can simply vary the w_k between 0 and 1.

The weighting method is particularly easy to apply when the alternative solutions are defined individually, as in the case for the design of the Second Sydney Airport (see box in Section 8.2). This is because the characteristics of the different feasible designs can easily be placed in the spread-sheet programs now commonly available in business computers, and it is then easy to assign relative weights and define the corresponding noninferior solutions. Special programs are also available for this task.

The choice between the weighting and the constraint method depends on the specifics of the system being designed. In general, the constraint method is preferable because it gives a more reliable description of the noninferior solutions. When the computational costs are a big burden, however, the weighting method may be preferred. It may also be selected when a spread-sheet analysis is possible. Whenever a weighting function is chosen, its results should be examined carefully to determine if, within the range of designs that may be chosen, the weighting method has misrepresented the feasible region.

8.5 DISPLAY MECHANISMS

The identification of the noninferior solutions is a crucial element of the analysis of a multiobjective problem. This is so because it focuses attention on the small set of possible designs that are worth considering.

The question is, what does the analyst do with the results? How can they be used to lead to the final selection of the preferred design? How can they be discussed? How should we present the results of a multiobjective analysis? The answers depend on whether the analyst is dealing with two, three, or more objectives.

For the two-objective problems, the most effective presentation is a simple graph of the kind used throughout this chapter. Clients usually have little difficulty understanding such figures. They also typically appreciate the fact that these

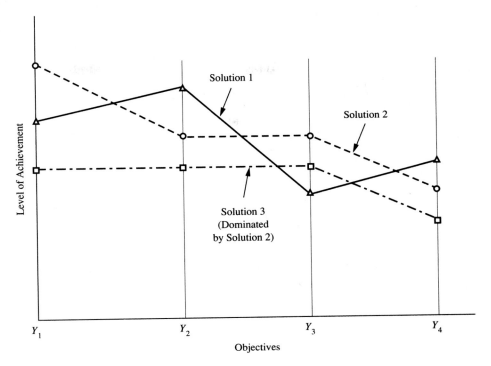

FIGURE 8.10
A profile easily displays the performance of designs on many objectives.

presentations allow them to see what they would have to give up on one objective to obtain an improvement on the other. These trade-offs help people select the final design.

For many dimensions, a simple graph is no longer possible and an entirely different mechanism must be used. The one that appears easiest to understand is the *profile*. This is a simple device in which the level of attainment of each objective is scaled vertically along distinct points on the horizontal axis. This may be done either as points on a line or as a bar chart. The performance of any specific noninferior solution then appears as a wavy horizontal line as Figure 8.10 indicates. Dominated solutions will have lines completely under some other solution; these may be discarded, unless they need to be specifically included for comparison. This kind of figure becomes confusing as more solutions are displayed simultaneously. This presentation is thus most effective when it compares only a few of the possible choices.

For three dimensions, one can either use profiles or an extension of the two-dimensional graph. The graph is best suited to technical audiences, used to this medium. The graph represents a series of slices through the three-dimensional space of possibilities, parallel to the plane of two objectives, and orthogonal to the third. Figure 8.11 illustrates the idea.

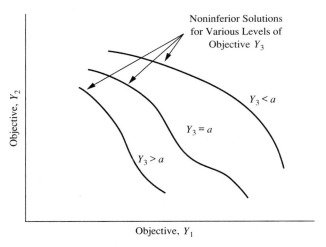

FIGURE 8.11
A graphical representation of three-dimensional, noninferior solutions.

8.6   APPLICATION

The optimal design may in some cases become obvious once the noninferior solutions are defined. This section explains this possibility and illustrates it by an application of multiobjective optimization to the design of a large system.

The application concerns the development of an important river basin in Argentina, the Rio Colorado. This river flows east from the Andes all the way across the country, passing through four distinct regions. The plans for the river involve the whole range of projects conceivable for a river basin: flood-control dams, hydroelectric projects, agricultural diversion canals, and industrial uses. Colleagues at MIT worked on this project in the early 1970s as part of their research into the practice of multiobjective optimization.

Two objectives were central to the discussion. Each had its special constituency and advocates. On the one hand, both the international agencies lending money for the project and the national government wanted to make sure the investments were profitable: they wanted to maximize the contribution to national income. The regional authorities in the river basin were, on the other hand, concerned with fairness in the distribution of the water and its benefits. They were unwilling to let any province have either an excessive or an inadequate share of the water even if that allocation did not maximize national income.

The two objectives could be represented mathematically fairly directly. The contribution to national income was simply the difference between the benefits and costs (with due allowance for interest and similar expenses, see Chapter 11). Fairness, in this context, could be represented by the relative allocation of water to each province: the fairest case being when each province received an equal amount.

The analysis itself centered around a large linear program where the allocations of water to projects, and thus to each province, were the principal decision variables. In this context the constraint method of multiobjective optimization was the better choice. In detail, the analysis maximized contributions to national income with progressively more stringent constraints on the fairness of the water distribution to the provinces.

The noninferior solutions defined by the analysis appear in Figure 8.12. The result was a curve with a distinct *"knee,"* a salient portion of the feasible region of designs. This phenomenon is actually quite common. It is particularly interesting because it represents a special situation in which the noninferior solutions by themselves define the optimal design.

When the noninferior solutions have a "knee," the optimal design is almost always around this region. This is because all concerned will recognize that they can each get most of what they want. They will also recognize that they can achieve significant gains on one objective at little cost in terms of the others. Individuals can thus feel comfortable with this choice even when they would not feel happy about having to decide on the relative value of different objectives. Groups with a variety of different interests, and relative preference for the objectives, can likewise agree that solutions around the knee are satisfactory, even when they cannot agree among themselves on the relative importance of the several objectives. Thus it was for the plans for the Rio Colorado: as a result of the multiobjective optimization, the regional, federal, and international authorities agreed on a design represented by the knee of the noninferior solutions.

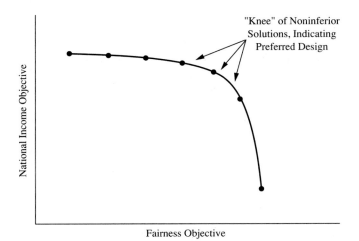

FIGURE 8.12
Noninferior solutions for the development of water resources in the Rio Colorado basin in Argentina.

REFERENCES

Giocoechea, A., Hansen, D. R., and Duckstein, L. (1982). *Multiobjective Decision Analysis with Engineering and Business Applications*, Wiley, New York.

Ignizio, J. P. (1982). "Multiobjective Linear Programming," Part 4, *Linear Programming in Single and Multiple-Objective Systems*, Prentice-Hall, Englewood Cliffs, NJ.

PROBLEMS

8.1. *Personal Objectives*

Imagine that you are in the market for a car. Consult the automobiles for sale section of a major newspaper. Select a popular model for which many offers are available. Plot these alternatives in terms of their mileage and cost. In terms of these objectives alone, which are the dominated, excluded, extreme, and compromise solutions?

8.2. *The Curve*

NIS Consultants has evaluated proposed sites for a municipal sewage facility along two objectives: entire fecal fumigation (EFF) and environmental quality improvement (EQUI). The optimal performance of each site is given by the following (EFF, EQUI) pairs:

A	(20, 135)	B	(75, 120)	C	(90, 100)	D	(35, 1050)
E	(82, 250)	F	(60, −50)	G	(60, 550)	H	(78, 500)
I	(70, 620)	J	(10, 500)	K	(40, 350)	L	(30, 800)
M	(95, −200)	N	(55, 220)	O	(40, −80)	P	(30, 500)
Q	(30, 900)	R	(60, 950)	S	(80, −150)	T	(45, 550)
U	(25, 1080)	V	(70, 800)	W	(63, 450)		

(a) Identify the dominated, excluded, and noninferior solutions.

(b) Which do you classify as extreme and compromise solutions? Discuss your answer.

8.3. *Optimizing*

Identify the noninferior solutions of Problem 8.2 by

(a) Maximizing EFF subject to EQUI $\geq b$ where b = 200, 400, 600, 800, and 1000 in turn.

(b) The weighting method, assigning relative values to (EFF, EQUI) of (20, 8), (40, 6), (60, 4), and (80, 2).

8.4. *Another Computer Run*

See Problem 6.12. Assume that the customer really thinks in terms of two objectives, minimization not only of cost, but also of impurities. Trace the noninferior solutions for these two objectives by

(a) The constraint method.

(b) The weighting method.

8.5. *Analysis*

Assuming that the set of noninferior solutions for the objectives X and Y can be described by the function: $Y = 50 - X^2$; describe the noninferior solutions by

(a) Maximizing Y subject to $X \geq 1, 2, 3, 4$, and 5

(b) Maximizing $Z = w_x X + w_y Y$

CHAPTER
9

SYSTEMS
OPTIMIZATION
PROCEDURE

9.1   THE PROBLEM

No single procedure can deal completely with all aspects of a system. Any single method must, in order to perform, make some assumptions about the real problem, must simplify it to some degree. It is thus likely to leave out some considerations that may be important overall.

As systems analysts, having the responsibility for a careful investigation of the entire situation, we must incorporate all the important elements. The question is, how can this be done efficiently? This chapter presents a procedure for using all the elements of optimization to achieve a best design.

9.2   DESIGN PROCEDURE

The recommended procedure for systems design consists of four main steps. These are each explained in detail in what follows. They are:

1. *Screening* of the feasible solutions to obtain a small set of noninferior solutions.
2. *Sensitivity Analysis* of these best solutions, to determine their performance in realistic situations.
3. *Dynamic Analysis* to establish the optimal pattern of development over time.
4. *Presentation*, the organization of the final result in a way that makes sense to the client.

Screening. Efficiency, economy of effort, must be the first consideration in organizing the overall analysis. The total number of feasible solutions to any realistic problem may be astronomical (see Section 7.1). It is essential to reduce this set as rapidly as possible to a manageable number.

The reduction of the alternatives to a small number is called *screening*, by analogy to sorting things with a sieve. The methods used to do this are commonly called *screening models*. These are usually linear programs, since these are ideally suited for handling very large problems, with thousands of variables and constraints—once the proper simplifying assumptions have been made.

The result of the screening process is one or more "optimum" or noninferior solutions (see Section 8.2). Any of these is optimal only in the sense that it optimizes the simplified mathematical description of the problem used for the optimization. Being solutions to approximations, they are at best approximations themselves.

The screening process in effect defines *regions of optimality*. The results are best interpreted as first-order estimates of the nature of the actual best designs for a system. These regions need to be examined in detail.

Sensitivity analysis. This explores the region of optimality in two ways. The first is by the organized methods described in Chapter 6. The second is by detailed engineering analysis of the system.

In the formal process, a specification sensitivity analysis (see Section 6.2) should be conducted to determine how the optimum would change if the problem were formulated differently. Similarly, the opportunity costs (see Section 6.3) should be examined to see if the optimum design is likely to change, given the known or anticipated changes in the parameters of the objective function.

Detailed engineering analysis is equally important. These should examine the problem in all its complexity, without the assumptions (such as linearity) which are the basis of the screening models. These may be entirely analytic, as through production functions (see Section 2.6); may be computer simulations; or may use complex physical models. In any event, this kind of full analysis is, of course, both time-consuming and expensive: only a few of them can be done.

With regard to the detailed engineering analysis, the screening process in effect provides an experimental design. It provides a sound basis for deciding what kind of detailed analysis to perform. It is an analytic substitute for the intuitive processes that otherwise lead designers to explore alternatives.

Overall, the sensitivity analyses generally reveal many ways in which the "optimum" answers of the screening process can be improved. They can demonstrate that some designs perform better over a wide range of the likely conditions. They may also indicate the importance of factors otherwise assumed away.

Dynamic analysis. The factor that is most typically assumed away in the initial analyses concerns staging of development over time. Typically, the screening models and engineering analyses look at a situation, a pattern of loads for a single period. The reason for this is simple: when the number of combinations is exponential in the number of periods (see Section 7.1) it is impractical to look at all combinations in the feasible region over many periods. The optimal pattern of development of time should eventually be incorporated.

This dynamic analysis can be done reasonably easily after the screening and sensitivity analyses. The number of plausible designs has by then been reduced to a handful for any period.

Dynamic programming is typically best suited for this analysis. As illustrated in Section 7.4, it deals effectively with nonconvex feasible regions such as those generated by exponential growth and economies of scale.

Presentation. A system design will only be implemented if it is approved by the clients. A major system must be endorsed by a company, a governmental agency, or a political process. With few exceptions, these executives, company directors, or politicians are not systems analysts. These individuals must be persuaded of the benefits of the design, if the systems analysis is to come to a successful conclusion.

Every effort should thus be made to ensure that the results can be understood. It is not enough to be right, one must be seen to be right. The client needs to see why the proposed plan is preferable to alternatives, to appreciate that the trade-offs between objectives are reasonable. Simple yet clear ways to present results, such as those illustrated in Section 8.5, become most valuable. In practice, the success of many of the most important projects has depended on the clarity and apparent reasonableness of the final presentation to the clients and the public. The site selection for the Second Sydney Airport (see Section 16.9) is a good example of this fact.

9.3 APPLICATION

The systems analysis for the development of the Delaware River Basin provides an excellent example of the recommended design procedure. It both illustrates the process well and clearly demonstrates its value.

The Delaware River Basin is a large, complex system of tributaries, facilities, and governmental boundaries and interests. It contains over 25 million people and a major segment of U.S. industry. It also supplies water to about 15 million more people around New York City. For most countries, it is at a national scale.

The issue of how best to channel and use the river has been carefully studied for many years. For the better part of the century, the U.S. Army Corps of Engineers developed plans for additional projects in the river. Their mathematical analyses were backed by large physical models of the basin which could be exercised to explore alternatives and validate the numerical studies. Their work represented the forefront of detailed engineering studies.

The systems analysis looked at a series of projects that included 35 reservoirs, 21 hydroelectric plants, and 4 major cities that require water. Assuming only two possible sizes for each facility, and ignoring the constraints on water quality and capacity of the facilities, there were over 500 million alternatives. Only a few thousand of them could, at very best, be examined in any detail by engineering studies.

Screening. The analysis team selected linear programming for the preliminary screening, primarily because of its efficiency compared to alternatives. Nonlinear functions were made piecewise linear. Nonconvex feasible regions were linearized as a preliminary approximation.

The program was formulated very much like that for Salt Lake City (see Section 5.11). The difference was that the analysts paid more attention to the detailed operating characteristics of the system. For example, they incorporated the monthly variations in stream flows. The reference by Jacoby and Loucks gives details.

The screening process resulted in a range of optimal designs. This is because the analysts recognized that there are wide variations in rainfall, and thus in patterns of water supply. They ran the linear program with a variety of flows and amounts of water in the reservoir, thus obtaining a range of optimal designs. This kind of solution is typical.

Sensitivity analysis. Each of these solutions was subjected to sensitivity analyses. They also defined starting points for detailed engineering analyses, which would modify the more approximate solutions of the linear program, and would look for others that would perform better.

Dynamic analysis. Once the static screening and detailed engineering simulation analyses were complete, the optimal scheduling of the projects could be determined by a relatively simple model.

The analysis divided the period from 1980 to 2010 in five-year stages. It was assumed that any project was either operational or nonexistent at that time. Further, it was also assumed that the benefits of each project were independent of each other; although this would not normally be true for a river, it was a reasonable assumption here since the projects were separated by existing, older facilities. These assumptions made it possible to create a recurrence formula and execute dynamic programming.

Presentation. To gain acceptance of their final results, the analysts were careful to validate each of the plans generated by the screening process with standard engineering simulations. They were always prepared to show their clients that their results were equivalent in every major detail to those that were known to be at the forefront of the field. Their analyses were thus credible.

Secondly, the analysis led to a design that was very significantly better than the previous best solutions. The linear program led the designers to locate design concepts that had escaped the intuitions of even the most experienced engineers responsible for the project systems analysis. This was, of course, most convincing.

Note that the detailed engineering analyses were not absolutely necessary to develop the design that emerged from the systems analysis. Yet if the engineering simulations had not been performed, the results would have been suspect, and the systems analysis might not have been accepted. When validated by the detailed analyses, however, the proposed design was absolutely convincing.

9.4 RESULTS

Systems analyses typically lead to major improvements in design, at very little cost compared to the benefits. For the Delaware River Basin, for example, the net benefits of the plan developed by systems analysis were 37% better than those estimated for the best design generated by usual procedures. The annual benefits alone were several times greater than the cost of the analyses; the total benefits were thus about 100 times the costs. Similarly, the analysis of the Third Water Tunnel for New York City (see Section 4.6) cost only $50,000 but led to savings of hundreds of millions of dollars.

These kinds of excellent results, obtained at modest cost, are the main motivation and real justification for applied systems analysis. Naturally these results are not guaranteed, but the opportunities are there.

REFERENCES

de Neufville, R., and Marks, D. H. (1974). *Systems Planning and Design: Case Studies in Modeling, Optimization and Evaluation*, Prentice-Hall, Englewood Cliffs, NJ.

Jacoby, H. D., and Loucks, D. P. (1972, 1974). Chapter 17 in de Neufville and Marks (1974). Also "The Combined Use of Optimization and Simulation Models in River Basin Planning," *Water Resources Research*, 8, pp. 1401–1414.

SYSTEM
EVALUATION

CHAPTER
10

INTRODUCTION

10.1 PURPOSE

This introduction describes the overall features of evaluation. The objective is to put into context the specific approaches and techniques presented in subsequent chapters.

This chapter is unique compared with other discussions of evaluation. The basic argument is that different methods are suitable for different circumstances. It compares the various approaches to evaluation and suggests when each might be most suitable. This presentation is unique because other texts focus on particular approaches, such as engineering economy or decision analysis, and ignore the basic issue the analyst continually faces: what is the best approach to use for a specific problem?

This chapter sets the tone for the entire section on evaluation. The techniques are presented in relation to the issues they deal with rather than their disciplinary source. The idea is to provide the systems analyst with a synthesis of the methods that relates directly to the problems.

The chapter begins by defining the purpose of evaluation and the fundamental problem this creates for the analyst: the choice of the appropriate method. It next identifies and describes the major assumptions that can be made about a particular situation or investment that is to be evaluated. Finally, it matches the different evaluation techniques with the circumstances they deal with most effectively. This organization provides the analyst with useful guidelines for choosing which approach to use in any particular situation.

10.2   NATURE OF PROBLEM

The purpose of evaluation is to help decisionmakers choose among projects and strategies. It does this by estimating how much any choice may be worth.

Operationally, the task of evaluation consists of identifying the potential advantages and disadvantages of any action and comparing them in some specific way. Generally speaking, evaluation leads to either of two results:

1. The identification of worthwhile choices, in which the advantages are greater than the disadvantages.
2. The ranking of choices by some index of merit, which indicates the relative value of each project and thus, within the limits of its precision, also identifies the best choices.

Decisionmakers naturally would prefer evaluations that define the best choices clearly. But they must also have confidence that these rankings are a valid indication of the relative merit of the possible choices. These two criteria create a fundamental dilemma for the analyst. The problem lies in the fact that precision in the evaluation depends on the assumptions one makes about the situation. As a rule, precision is increased by making more simplifying assumptions. Conversely, however, more simplifying assumptions make the evaluation less realistic and the results less acceptable.

To illustrate the relationship between simplification, precision, and reality, consider an evaluation you might personally face. Suppose that you have savings you want to invest. You would have several possible choices, for example, a savings account from which you can withdraw at any time, fixed placements for a specified period, and investments in some business. In general, the evaluation of these choices can be seen as a complicated problem: the returns from any investment may be risky; you may also have several objectives, for example to make a profit, to protect your savings, and to maintain flexibility in their use. If you consider all the complications, the evaluation can be difficult and the results unclear. How, for instance, does one measure security or flexibility in the use of one's assets, and how does one balance these considerations against profits? If you simplify the question by focussing on monetary returns, then one can carry out a probabilistic analysis that is quite exact, even though the overlapping distributions of the returns from the different projects may not lead to an unambiguous ranking. Further simplifying the problem by assuming that the returns from the investments can be predicted does allow one to establish a single, clear ranking of the investments—but eliminating risk may seem too unrealistic and make the result unacceptable.

The primary objective of the analyst is to achieve the most useful evaluation possible, the one that ranks the choices most clearly, while maintaining sufficient realism. The difficulty in achieving this objective is that no one approach or technique of evaluation is best for all occasions. The techniques depend on the nature of the assumptions made, and the legitimacy of the assumptions depends in turn on the context of the evaluation.

The first problem for the evaluator is, thus, to choose the method of evaluation suitable for the occasion. This requires the analyst to begin by thinking about the situation and which assumptions are realistic.

10.3   POSSIBLE ASSUMPTIONS

The assumptions that can legitimately be made about any situation depend on the context of the evaluation. They are defined by the nature of both the decision-makers and the projects.

The range of assumptions can be broadly divided into two categories of

1. Comparability between the elements of any evaluation
2. Degree of uncertainty in the possible choices

Comparability is the greater issue as it enters into all aspects of the evaluation. It concerns the possibility of comparing

1. Objects over time
2. Quantities of objects at any single time
3. Different objects
4. The preferences of different decisionmakers

The consequences of any choice may be valued differently depending on when they occur. A given amount of money, for example, is generally more valuable now than in the future because we can invest it and make it grow into a larger amount. It is consequently not appropriate to compare monetary benefits and costs that occur at different times directly; they should be transformed to a comparable basis (See Chapters 11 and 12). Other consequences may be assumed to be comparable over time. A life saved through a safety program might be equally valuable to society whenever it occurs.

It may or may not be reasonable to assume that each unit of benefit or cost is equally valuable. A starving person would presumably value the first plate of food much higher than the second or third. But in other situations the decisionmaker may indeed value consequences linearly with quantity. For example, a manufacturer may consider each unit of production equally valuable, when they all sell for the same price (See Chapter 14).

Only in special situations may we realistically assume that different kinds of consequences of a choice are directly comparable. The value of investments in safety, health, and economy are not comparable in any obvious way. Think for example of how you would establish the value of a life, and then think whether any individual would accept this price as realistic. Or think of trying to evaluate different materials for constructing an automobile: On what basis can we compare ductility, strength and ease of fabrication? The consequences are most directly comparable when all of them have immediate economic implications in that they produce profits and losses (See Chapters 18, 19, and 20).

Different decisionmakers or different parts of a community may, finally, have quite different tastes. When should we assume that it is reasonable to perform an evaluation with only one set of preferences? Clearly when we are concerned with a single decisionmaker. Possibly when we are working with a company or agency whose members are agreed on common goals. At other times it would be unreasonable to assume we can directly compare the preferences of various groups concerned with a decision. This topic is covered in more advanced texts (See Chapter 21).

The question of uncertainty cuts across these issues of comparability. The essential issue here is whether the evaluation assumes that the consequences of any choice can be predicted sufficiently accurately in advance. If yes, the analyst can work with a limited description of each choice. But if not, as is often the case (See Chapter 15), the consequences of each choice should be described by probability distributions, and the calculations become much more extensive. This extra effort limits—due to constraints on budget and time— the depth of analysis that may be devoted to other issues. It also changes the nature of the evaluation.

Taken as a whole, the set of assumptions that can be made about a situation defines the complexity and nature of the evaluation. It also defines the approach that should be taken.

10.4   HIERARCHY OF METHODS

The available methods for evaluation are based in three different disciplines: engineering, economics, and operations research. Each of these traditions focuses on a separate set of issues. Each is therefore appropriate for different kinds of problems.

The most basic approaches to evaluation are those of engineering economy. The essential issue here is how to compare money over time. The techniques consist of simple formulas, presented in Chapter 11. The pivotal parameter in this approach is the discount rate, which is the means of establishing the comparisons over time. Chapter 12 discusses the choice of this quantity. Engineering economy leads to a variety of related criteria of evaluation, such as the benefit-cost ratio, and these are presented in Chapter 13. This entire body of methods assumes that all parties to the evaluation agree on a single objective, that its valuation is linear with quantity, and that the consequences can be predicted. Generally these consequences are valued in terms of money, but sometimes, when the possible choices are all directed toward a single objective, for example the number of lives saved by different safety programs, the benefits may be numbered in terms of that objective. Engineering economy is most obviously suitable for situations in which the various projects have predominantly financial effects. Among these would be investments that either reduce costs or produce marketable goods, such as factories, transportation, energy conservation and production, et cetera.

Recently, operations research has led to the development of decision analysis. This method focuses on the existence of uncertainty about the descriptions of the consequences of any choice. Since the planning and design of engineering systems inherently involves considerable uncertainty about both costs and effects, as Chapters 14 and 15 indicate, decision analysis is a most useful technique. It provides an effective means to represent the choices and the risk, to calculate the preferred choice at any time (see Chapter 16), and to define optimal strategies over time (Chapter 17). Decision analysis is the only approach to evaluation that is really suitable when uncertainty is a major factor.

Operations research has also led to a parallel development of practical methods of dealing with the lack of comparability between different quantities of any item, that is, the nonlinearity of their values. These methods are developed for both single and multiple attributes in the three chapters on utility functions, Chapters 18, 19, and 20. Utility functions are often presented integrally with decision analysis in theoretical texts, but as these techniques address quite different issues, applicable in different circumstances, they are developed separately here.

Welfare economics also deals with nonlinear valuations of consequences. The principal method here is that of "social cost-benefit analysis," an extension of ordinary benefit-cost analysis. (The term cost-benefit is due to the fact that the techniques were first put into practice in Britain!) The calculations are direct, once the preferences of a group are defined. The particular contribution of this approach is that it exploits the characteristics of the nonlinear functions to define optimal policies analytically, and that these solutions provide quite practical guidelines. This is a most useful result and makes this the procedure of choice when values are nonlinear and uncertainty is not an issue. For situations involving multiple parties with different preferences, finally, there are no operational techniques. The problem is too complicated to permit satisfactory analytic solutions except in simple textbook examples. Work in economics and operations research, however, has led to some guidelines that are useful to the analyst. These two topics are covered in more advanced texts (See Chapter 21).

The relative position of the different approaches to evaluation are summarized in Table 10.1. They form a hierarchy from the simplest techniques of engineering economy, which are only legitimate if strict conditions can be accepted, to the most general concepts of welfare economics.

Each of the major approaches and issues in evaluation are presented in detail in the following chapters:

Engineering Economy: 11 to 14
Decision Analysis: 15 to 17
Nonlinear Valuation: 18 to 21

TABLE 10.1
Hierarchy of evaluation techniques

Approach		Assumptions made				Operational characteristics
Disciplinary basis	Evaluation method	Time value	Uncertain consequences	Nonlinear values	Multiple decisionmakers	
Engineering economy	Benefit-cost, etc.	X				Easy formulas
Operations research	Decision analysis	X	X			Probabilities inaccurate Computations easy
Operations research	Decision analysis with utility	X	X	X		Utilities approximate
Economics	Social cost-benefit analysis	X		X		Value data difficult to obtain
Economics	Welfare economics	X		X	X	Only general guidelines available

Because the presentation aims to develop a synthesis between the several techniques of evaluation, the organization does not divide the detailed material into conventional bundles. For example, texts in both economics and decision analysis discuss nonlinear valuation of preferences using their own approaches and little, if any, reference to the alternative. Here both possibilities are presented together so that the analyst can see the relative strengths of each and choose between them as the occasion warrants. The chapters on decision analysis focus on methods of dealing with uncertainty. This differs from a conventional treatment in that it incorporates methods of assessing the uncertainty, but leaves the methods for obtaining the nonlinear values to the subsequent section.

CHAPTER
11

COMPARISON
OVER
TIME

11.1 THE PROBLEM

Many projects, particularly large systems, evolve over a long time. Costs incurred in one period generate benefits for many years. The evaluation of whether these projects are worthwhile must therefore compare benefits and costs that occur at quite different times.

The essential problem in evaluating projects over time comes from the fact that money has a time value. A dollar now is not the same as a dollar later. The money represents the same nominal quantity, to be sure, but a dollar later does not have the same usefulness or real value as a dollar now.

The problem is one of comparability. Since a dollar now and a dollar later are not the same, we cannot estimate total benefits (or costs) simply by adding up the benefits (or costs) that occur at different times. That would be like adding apples and oranges. To make a valid evaluation, we need to translate all costs and benefits into comparable amounts.

From a formal mathematical point of view the solution to this problem is simple. It consists of a handful of formulas that depend on only two parameters. The formulas can easily be estimated by hand calculator and are routinely embedded in spreadsheet programs available on personal computers. Their results have also traditionally been displayed in extensive tables, which are standard features of engineering handbooks. This chapter presents and explains these essential formulas.

From a practical point of view the solution is delicate, however. The values generated by the formulas are quite sensitive to their two parameters, the duration or "life" of the project, N, and—most particularly—the discount rate, r. Furthermore, these factors cannot be known precisely. They are therefore somewhat arbitrary. This reality transforms the problem of evaluating projects over time into something of an art. Chapter 12 presents methods for estimating the discount rate, and Chapter 13 presents the various ways the results of the simple formulas can actually be used in evaluations of projects.

11.2 DISCOUNT RATE

A dollar now is worth more than a dollar in the future because it can, in general, be used productively between now and then. At a personal level, for example, you can place money in a savings account and get a larger amount back after a while. In the economy at large, businesses and governments can use money to build things, grow food, educate people, and do other worthwhile activities.

Additionally, any given amount of money now is typically worth more than the same amount in the future because of inflation. As prices go up due to inflation, the money you have now will buy less and less. The $100 you have now will, so long as there is inflation, buy more food and clothing than $100 a year or more from now.

The *discount rate* represents the way money now is worth more than money later. It determines by how much any future amount is discounted, that is, reduced, to make it correspond to an equivalent amount today. The discount rate is thus the key factor in the evaluation of projects over time. It is the parameter that permits us to compare costs and benefits incurred at different times.

The discount rate is generally specified as a rate, given as some percent per year. Normally this rate is assumed to be constant for any particular evaluation. Because we usually have no reason to believe it would change in any known way, we take it to be constant over time when looking at any project. It may, however, be quite different for various individuals, companies, or governments, and may also vary from any person or group as circumstances change. Chapter 12 indicates how to choose the appropriate discount rate.

The discount rate is similar to an interest rate, but is actually quite a different concept. It is similar in that both can be stated in percent per period, and both can indicate a connection between money now and money later. The difference is that the discount rate represents real change in value to a person or group, as determined by their possibilities for productive use of the money and the effects of inflation; the interest rate narrowly defines a contractual arrangement between a borrower and a lender. This distinction implies a general rule:

$$\text{discount rate} > \text{interest rate}$$

Indeed, if people were not getting more value from the money they borrow than the interest they pay for it, they would be silly to go to the effort and nuisance of incurring the debt. Chapter 12 on the choice of discount rate goes into this issue in detail. For the moment it is sufficient to recognize that the discount rate is mathematically similar to an interest rate.

11.3 FORMULAS

Four formulas cover the basic range of situations an analyst should know in order to compare money at different times. Each corresponds to one of the four situations defined by whether one is dealing with a unique amount of money or a series of constant periodic revenues or costs. Table 11.1 defines the position of these four formulas.

Only two formulas need to be remembered in practice. This is because the formulas for going from the present to the future are the inverse of those going from the future to the present. This becomes evident below, as each formula is defined.

The notation for the formulas is defined by Figure 11.1 and the following:

- *The Present Amount*, P, is either money spent or received now, or the value now of future sums.
- *The Future Amount*, F, is some amount in the future N periods from now.
- *The Series of Equal Amounts*, R, is a constant stream of equal amounts received at the end of each of N periods.
- *The Period* is the fixed interval of time for which the discount rate is defined. It is typically, but not necessarily, a year.

Compound amount formula. This defines the future value of a given amount at present after N periods:

$$F = P(1 + r)^N$$

where r is given as a decimal (for example, $r = 10\%$ is stated as $r = 0.10$). This is also the formula used to calculate the way interest compounds, as in a bank account. It is simply a direct extension of the way money changes in value over time: after the first year P is worth r percent more, for a total value of $P(1 + r)$; after the second year this grows by another r percent to $P(1 + r)^2$, and so on.

The *compound amount factor* is simply the quantity that defines the equation: $(1 + r)^N$. Table 11.2 provides a few interesting values of this factor, along with those of other factors defined as follows.

TABLE 11.1
Role of the four formulas for the evaluation over time

Moment in time	Types of amounts	
	Unique	Constant series
Present to future	Compound amount	Capital recovery
Future to present	Present value	Series present value

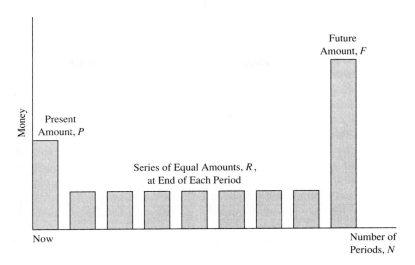

FIGURE 11.1
Illustration of terms used in formulas for comparing money over time.

TABLE 11.2
Summary tables of factors used in evaluations over time for various periods and discount rates

Number of periods	Compound amount at			Capital recovery at		
	5%	10%	15%	5%	10%	15%
5	1.28	1.61	2.01	0.231	0.264	0.298
10	1.63	2.59	4.06	0.130	0.163	0.199
15	2.08	4.18	8.14	0.0963	0.131	0.171
20	2.65	6.72	16.4	0.0802	0.117	0.160
50	11.5	117	1084	0.0548	0.101	0.150

Number of periods	Present value at			Series present value at		
	5%	10%	15%	5%	10%	15%
5	0.783	0.621	0.497	4.33	3.79	3.35
10	0.614	0.386	0.247	7.72	6.14	5.02
15	0.481	0.239	0.123	10.4	7.61	5.85
20	0.377	0.149	0.0611	12.5	8.51	6.26
50	0.087	0.0085	0.0009	18.3	9.91	6.66

Present value formula. This defines the present value of a future sum at N years. It is simply the inverse of the compound amount formula:

$$P = F(1 + r)^{-N}$$

The *present value factor* is the quantity that defines this formula:

$$(1 + r)^{-N} = (\text{compound amount factor})^{-1}$$

(See box for application of the above two formulas.)

Capital recovery formula. This defines the stream of N constant payments R that are equivalent to a present sum P. It might, for example, be an annuity one could buy.

This formula is a bit tricky to derive, but ends up quite simply. It is easiest to determine first the value of the future sum that is equivalent to the series. This is:

$$S = \sum R(1 + r)^i = \frac{R[(1 + r)^N - 1]}{r}$$

where the far right hand expression is the formula for the sum of a geometric series, as given by any mathematical handbook. The equivalent present value is obtained by dividing by $(1 + r)^N$. After rearranging the terms, this results in

$$R = \frac{P[r(1 + r)^N]}{[(1 + r)^N - 1]}$$

The *capital recovery factor*, *crf*, is the complicated expression of r and N above. Thus:

$$R = P(crf)$$

Compound Amount and Present Value

Suppose you buy $100 worth of Government Savings Bonds that pay 5% a year for your sister's new baby. What will this child be able to cash them in for in 20 years, when it is time to go to college? Using the compound amount formula we get from Table 11.2

$$\text{Future Amount} = \text{Present Amount} (1 + 0.05)^{20}$$
$$= 100(2.65) = \$265$$

Conversely, suppose you propose to buy a "zero" bond, a certificate that simply promises to pay its face value at maturity. What would be the proper value now for a $1000 "zero" bond in 20 years, using a discount rate of 10%?

$$\text{Present Amount} = \text{Future Amount} (1 + 0.1)^{-20}$$
$$= 1000(0.149) = \$149$$

Note that the capital recovery factor converges to r for long periods. As N is large, $(1 + r)^N >> 1$, and then

$$crf \sim r \qquad \text{for large } N$$

This is evident in Table 11.2; looking across at 50 periods, one sees that the capital recovery factor approximates the discount rate.

Series present value formula. This defines the present value of a constant series of payments R. It is simply the inverse of the preceding. Thus

$$P = R \left(\frac{1}{crf} \right)$$

The *series present value factor*, the multiplier of R to obtain P, is thus the inverse of the capital recovery factor, as the formula states. (See box for application of these last two formulas.)

As the reader can now appreciate, the only two formulas that need to be remembered in practice are the compound amount factor and the capital recovery factor. They summarize the essence of establishing comparability between money at different times.

Capital Recovery and Series Present Value

Suppose you are considering the idea of paying $5000 to increase the insulation of the house in which you plan to live the next 50 years. If your personal discount rate is 15%, how much should the annual energy savings be to justify the investment?

$$\text{Annual Savings Necessary} = \text{Present Cost } (crf)$$
$$= 5000(0.15) = \$750$$

from Table 11.2.

Conversely, suppose someone wishes to buy your business on the installment plan, paying you $100,000 in 10 yearly payments of $10,000. If your discount rate is still 15%, how does this offer compare with someone else's bid of $60,000 right now?

$$\text{Present Value of Installments} = \text{Annual Amount} \left(\frac{1}{crf} \right)$$

$$= 10,000(5.02) = \$50,200$$

from Table 11.2.

The $60,000 offer is far superior, even though the installment plan offers a larger nominal amount.

11.4 APPROXIMATIONS

Two approximations of the formulas are useful. They permit the analyst to determine the relative importance of present and future amounts, without reference to tables or computers. They help determine which elements of a project are critical, and which can be neglected.

Exponential approximation. This formula exploits the fact that the compound amount factor tends toward the exponential as the size of the periods becomes smaller, the compounding period becomes smaller, and the compounding becomes continuous rather than periodic:

$$(1 + r)^N \sim e^{rN}$$

Use of Rule of 72

This approximation is useful when reasonable estimates have to be made on the spot. Such was the case when the author was participating in a discussion of the Board of Directors for the Massachusetts Port Authority. The topic, in 1986, was the future size of the major Boston airport. The current traffic was about 24 million passengers a year, and some consultants had just argued that it was reasonable to expect that the traffic in the year 2010 would be 40 million.

The Chairman of the Board turned to me as an independent expert and asked first if I considered the forecast reasonable. My thinking was as follows:

The forecast is for 24 years hence. If the current traffic doubled in that time, to 48 million passengers, the compound rate of growth would be $\frac{72}{24} = 3\%$. But as the forecast was for significantly fewer than 48 million passengers, the implied rate of growth is less than 3%, probably about $2\frac{1}{2}\%$ (it is actually about $2\frac{1}{4}\%$). My answer on the spot was this: that "the implied rate of growth was far less than half the historical average, and thus probably unreasonable."

The Chairman then asked when I thought the 40 million forecast could be reached. Reversing gears, I reasoned:

The historical rates of growth in traffic have been about 7% a year, and sometimes as high as 10%. Traffic could then double in $\frac{72}{7} \sim 10$ years or possibly as soon as $\frac{72}{10} \sim 7$ years. Since we are concerned with a traffic level less than double, a couple years off either estimate would be appropriate. So I answered "In about 8 years or so," and, rounding off to a nice figure such as planners like to use, continued "that is, quite possibly around 1995."

The exponential approximation is always somewhat of an overestimate. The continuous compounding implied by the exponential both continually builds up the present value and builds on the increments. The overestimate is typically quite small, however. Over 20 years at $r = 5\%$, for example, the overestimate using the continuous approximation is only about $2\frac{1}{2}\%$. The exponential approximation is thus quite satisfactory for most preliminary evaluations of projects.

Rule of 72 (or 70). The rule of 72 (or 70) derives directly from the exponential approximation. It is based on the fact that

$$e^{0.693} = 2.0$$

This means that, using continuous compounding, a present sum doubles for any combination of $rN = 0.693$. To a first approximation, this doubling rule is taken as $rN = 70$, where r is now thought of as a percent rather than a decimal.

This characteristic is generally ascribed to $rN = 72$. The logical excuse is that the exponential approximation is an overestimate and that, to compensate for this fact, it is desirable to increase the exponent necessary for doubling. The real reason appears to be that 72 can be more easily divided by more numbers than 70, and is thus more convenient (see box).

11.5 SENSITIVITY TO DISCOUNT RATE

The formulas for comparing the value of money at different times are quite sensitive to their two parameters, the discount rate, r, and the life of the project, N. They are especially sensitive to the discount rate.

The value of either of these two parameters is never defined precisely, unfortunately. They are both a matter of judgment. Even if the analyst is required by law or some outside constraint to use particular values of these parameters, they have still been somewhat arbitrarily defined by someone. Professional responsibility therefore implies that the analyst be aware of the sensitivity of the evaluation to both of these parameters.

The present value of future sums decreases rapidly for any reasonable discount rate. (This can safely be assumed to be within 5 to 15% in constant dollar terms, as Chapter 12 discusses in detail.) As Figure 11.2 shows, the dropoff in value is quite steep. The value of $100 ten years from now is easily worth half that, $50 or less, depending on the discount rate selected.

The phenomenon has a significant implication for any evaluation. It means that the analyst can almost totally discount both long-term future benefits and costs in any evaluation. As Table 11.2 and Figure 11.2 indicate, the present worth factor becomes less than 1% as soon as about 30 years or so. Unless long-term future benefits or costs are absolutely stupendous in comparison to those of the present, they can really be neglected in the evaluation.

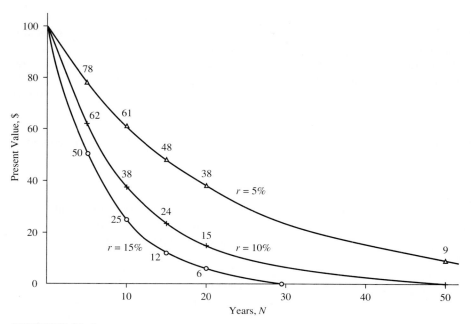

FIGURE 11.2
Present value of $100, N years from now at discount rates of 5, 10, and 15%
per year.

The present value of future sums is also very sensitive to the discount rate that is selected. Choosing a discount rate of 10% instead of 5%, or of 15% instead of 10%, virtually cuts the present value in half.

This fact means that the overall desirability of any project can be very sensitive to the discount rate selected. As can be imagined, and as is discussed in Chapter 12, the consequence is that the selection of discount rates frequently becomes highly politicized. Advocates of particular kinds of projects will fight to define the discount rate to favor their enterprise.

11.6   SENSITIVITY TO PROJECT LIFE

The value of a project is also sensitive to the number of years, N, it provides benefits. Normally, the useful life of an investment can only be estimated if it has a relatively short life, which has been observed frequently. Such is generally the case with machine tools and other mechanical parts. The useful life of large, unique projects, such as power plants or refineries, is quite uncertain. Often the useful life of a project is defined arbitrarily.

In practice, the overall value of a project is not especially sensitive to the length of life selected for it. This is because the evaluation is already particularly sensitive to the discount rate. Normally, the longer the useful life of a project,

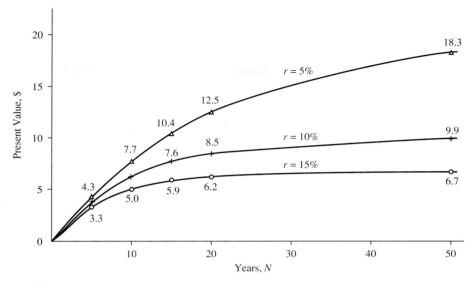

FIGURE 11.3
**Present value of a series of $1 per year for N years, at discount rates of 5,
10, and 15% per year.**

the more benefits are included in an evaluation and the better the project. The
overall increase is generally relatively small, however.

The relative insensitivity to project life is illustrated by Figure 11.3, which
plots the cumulative present value of a constant stream of money for N years,
as given in Table 11.2. As can be seen, the rate of increase is essentially flat
beyond 20 years, for discount rates of 10% and more. The net increase in value
obtained by increasing the project life from 20 to 50 years is only about 15%
This is not enough to alter the desirability of a project enormously.

The length of a project's life is only really important when the discount rate
is low. Thus when $r = 5\%$, the increase in present value by increasing the project
life from 20 to 50 years is about 50%. This is significant. This sensitivity is due,
as can be seen by looking at Figure 11.2, to the fact that the value of future
money does not drop off to zero for 5%. This is another reason that people fight
for a low discount rate—it makes long-lasting projects, such as railroad lines or
dams, look more attractive.

11.7 APPLICATION

To illustrate the formulas presented in Section 11.3, and the sensitivity to discount
rate and project life, consider the example portrayed in Figure 11.4. This graph
shows the *cash flow* of revenues and costs for a project, that is, the sequence
through time of the flow of money into and out of an organization.

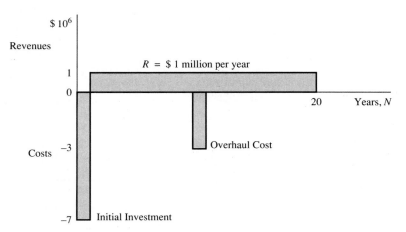

FIGURE 11.4
Cash flow of revenues and costs for example project.

This project is fairly typical. It involves a substantial initial investment to produce a stream of benefits for some time. It also involves some substantial future cost, as for a complete overhaul of the system. This might be, for instance, the acquisition of a ship.

The revenues and costs of the project are as shown in Figure 11.4: revenues of $1 million a year for 20 years, totalling $20 million; costs of $7 million initially and $3 million in 10 years, totalling $10 million.

If we were, wrongly, just to look at the nominal or stated revenues and costs, the project looks good. The nominal revenues are twice the nominal costs and this could be interpreted as a 100% profit. The difficulty is that since money has a time value, comparing money at different times on an equal footing is invalid. The future costs and benefits should be properly discounted.

For the example, we use a discount rate of 10%, which is a reasonable value to use if all future revenues and costs are stated in constant dollars (see Chapter 12 for a detailed discussion).

To place all future sums on the same footing, regardless of when received, we discount them to the present. In doing so we are calculating the present value of all future cash flows, which business people refer to as the *discounted cash flow* of the project.

The present value of the costs is the sum of the initial investment, undiscounted since it occurs now, and of the future cost of overhaul, discounted using the present value factor for 10% and 10 years, given in Table 11.2:

$$\text{Present Value Costs} = 7 + 3(0.386) = \$8.158 \text{ million}$$

The present value of the series of uniform revenues is given by the series value factor for 20 years at 10%:

$$\text{Present Value Revenues} = 1(8.51) = \$8.51 \text{ million}$$

Given these two results we see that the revenues are slightly larger than the costs, when all costs and revenues are placed on a comparable basis. The difference between these two values, the benefits minus the costs, is the *net present value* or NPV:

$$\text{Net Present Value} = 8.51 - 8.158 = \$0.352 \text{ million}$$

Since the NPV is positive, the project is marginally worthwhile, at least when a discount rate of 10% is used.

This result is quite sensitive to the discount rate, as can be seen by redoing the sums with a discount rate of 15%. We then have

$$\text{Present Value Costs} = 7 + 3(0.247) = \$7.741 \text{ million}$$

and

$$\text{Present Value Revenues} = 1(6.26) = \$6.26 \text{ million}$$

Therefore

$$\text{Net Present Value} = 6.26 - 7.741 = -\$1.481 \text{ million}$$

The project now does not appear worthwhile since NPV is negative. On the basis of present values, costs now exceed revenues. The higher discount rate, which makes all future money less significant, particularly affects the revenues.

Finally, the result is not especially sensitive to the life of the project. Suppose that the revenues of the project proceed for 50 years, with no further overhaul or other cost. We then obtain, using a discount rate of 15% again,

$$\text{Present Value Revenues} = 1(6.66) = \$6.66 \text{ million}$$

Although we have increased the life of the project by 150%, and added $30 million in nominal revenues, the present value of the revenues has only increased by $0.4 million, or a mere 6%.

11.8 OPTIMAL PROJECT SIZE

The fact that money has a time value has important implications for the optimal size of a project. This section explains the phenomenon and provides guidelines for determining the optimal size of a project.

The direct implication of the time value of money is that investments should be deferred until needed. There is no sense in sinking capital into a project—and thus paying interest on a loan or losing out on the profits this money would otherwise provide—unless there are substantial benefits that compensate for the time cost of the money. Thus, in general, designers should look for ways to build up a system incrementally, providing extra facilities just in time, when actually needed.

The incentive to defer projects can be counterbalanced by many factors, of course. Some facilities can only be provided in specific chunks, and must be built large if at all. Runways for an airport generally fall into this category, for example. At other times the systems designers may face a unique opportunity to proceed and cannot afford to waste it. Having received permission to build a power plant say, planners have a strong incentive to proceed, to avoid the possibility that future politics might change the rules.

Economies of scale (see Sections 2.4 and 4.5) provide the major incentive to build larger projects and to build them in anticipation of need. The existence of economies of scale means that it is cheaper, per unit of addition, to build large rather than small. This incentive is directly opposite to that of the time value of money, which is to build small increments only as needed.

The effects of economies of scale and the time value of money balance each other to define an optimal size of a project for any situation. This calculation naturally depends on the specifics of a particular case, but it is possible to derive general guidelines. The procedure is to define a general expression for the total present value cost of a system, and to minimize it as a function of the size of the project.

To illustrate the way to define the optimal size of a project, consider a basic case. Assume that a system needs to have a constant increase in capacity each year, G. The designers can provide this in small amounts, or in bigger additions that would satisfy N years of the requirement. From Section 4.5, the general cost function for GN units of capacity is: $C(GN) = A_0(GN)^a$. The present value of the total costs of all the additions built to infinity in N year chunks, PV_N, can usefully be stated as the cost of the first increment plus the present value of all future additions starting with the next one built N years hence:

$$PV_N = A_0(GN)^a + e^{-rN}PV_N$$

The advantage of this way of stating the present value is that it reduces simply to

$$PV_N = \frac{A_0(GN)^a}{(1 - e^{-rN})}$$

The optimal size of the project is defined by the value of N that minimizes the present value of all costs.

The optimal project size, defined by the optimal interval, N^*, can be derived as above. For our particular case, it is given implicitly by the formula:

$$\frac{rN^*}{(e^{rN^*} - 1)} = a$$

This can be understood by looking at Figure 11.5. This shows the way the effects of economies of scale and the discount rate balance each other. For higher discount rates, the optimal interval and project size decreases. Conversely, when economies of scale are more important (lower a), the optimal project size increases. Note that for typical values of the discount rate around 10% (see

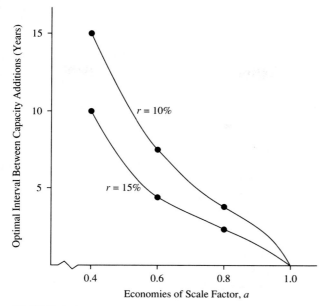

FIGURE 11.5
The optimal project size as defined by a balance between the discount rate, *r*, and the economies of scale.

Sections 12.4 and 12.5), the economically optimal project size should cover only about 5 to 10 years of growth even for large economies of scale.

REFERENCE

ATT Company, (1977). "Economic Study Techniques," Chapter 12, *Engineering Economy*, (3rd ed.), McGraw-Hill, New York.

PROBLEMS

11.1. *Asphalt and Concrete Pavements*

A local government faces the classic dilemma of choosing between a design with high first cost and longer life and one with a lower first cost but shorter life: concrete versus asphalt pavements for an access road. The projected first cost per square yard of roadway is $21.00 for the concrete pavement and $17.80 for the asphalt.

Either pavement would have to be resurfaced eventually with asphalt, but at different times. The best information is that the concrete base was to be resurfaced every 27 years, and the asphalt base every 17 years. Annual maintenance costs for either roadway will be $8000.

(*a*) Assuming a 10% real discount rate, how much cheaper would the more expensive material have to become to be competitive on this job?

(*b*) At what rate or interest are the two costs equal?

(*c*) Which solution would you recommend if (1) the national government pays 50% of the initial costs but none of the maintenance or replacement costs (a typical kind of subsidy) or (2) the local government sells municipal bonds that, because of tax advantages, only have to pay 6% real interest?

11.2. *New Car*

A salesperson is shopping for a new automobile and is comparing the benefits and costs of various models that he or she is considering. One such model has the following costs and benefits that are approximated to occur at the end of the year. The salesperson's policy is to get a new car every three years.

Year	Cost ($)	Benefits ($)
0	10,600	
1	1600	6000
2	2000	5600
3	2400	7000

Using $r = 5\%$, what is the present value of benefits? Of costs?

11.3. *Patent Sale*

An inventor contracted to give a corporation the exclusive right to use a patent. The corporation agreed to pay the owner $1000 a year at the end of each of the first 4 years while developing a market for the invention; $5000 at the end of each year for the next 8 years; and $2000 at the end of each year for the final 5 years of the 17-year life of the patent. After two years, the corporation wishes to buy the patent outright: what is the maximum the corporation could afford to pay the owner at this time if it requires a 16% rate of return on investments before income taxes?

11.4. *Trust Fund*

Reed Ekasch was born on July 1, 1967. On July 1, 1968, an aunt started a trust. She then paid $1000 each July 1 up to and including 1979—a total outlay of $12,000 by the aunt. One purpose of the trust was to help finance Reed's college education: it was provided that $2500 should be withdrawn for this purpose each year for four years, starting with the boy's 18th birthday, July 1, 1985—a total withdrawal of $10,000. The remainder of the trust is to accumulate until Reed is 30 years old on July 1, 1997, to help him finance the purchase of a home. If the trust earns 6% compounded annually after taxes, how much will Reed receive on his 30th birthday?

11.5. *Ace Woodworking, Ltd.*

AWL is thinking of computerizing its order processing system. It currently spends $2.5 million/year doing it by hand. For the 10-year life cycle of the system, the two bids are analyzed as follows:

	Costs (in current $, 10^6)			
System	**Initial**	**Repair**	**Maintenance**	**Operating**
IBM	16	included 2	included	included
HAL	4.5	(five years from now)	1/year	0.5/year

Which system should the company choose if its real annual discount rate is: 5%? 10%? 15%?

11.6. *XYZ Corporation*

The production department of XYZ Corporation is thinking of buying one of two numerically controlled zipper machines. Either would last 10 years. Additionally, the costs, in $\$ \times 10^3$, are:

	Machine X	Machine Y
Initial Investment	20	30
Salvage Value	5	7
Annual Operating Cost	12	6
Annual Maintenance Cost	2	4

Assume that the annual costs are paid at the end of each year and the salvage value at the end of the tenth year. Using a discount rate of 15%:
(*a*) What is the present worth of the cash flow for machine X? Machine Y?
(*b*) Which machine should be purchased?

11.7. *Ren O'Vait*

The famous architect, Ren O'Vait, has bought a dilapidated Victorian mansion. In addition to various structural and cosmetic defects, the heating system needs replacement. Ms. O'Vait must choose between a conventional gas-fired furnace and a solar heating system with a small backup gas heater. Based on her preliminary designs, she estimates the following costs:

	Gas	Solar/gas
Initial cost	$5000	$15,000
Annual nonfuel	100	300
Annual fuel costs	1400	200

(*a*) Assuming a 20-year design life for both systems, and a discount rate of 8%, which system is cheaper?
(*b*) Which system would be preferred if the discount rate were 5%? 10%?
(*c*) Which system will be favored if, with a discount rate of 8%, the time horizon is reduced to 15 years? Extended to 25 years?

(*d*) How much would the price of gas have to change to make the two options equally attractive?

(*e*) If the costs of home improvements are deductible from taxable income, which system will be favored?

11.8. *Snowbird High*

On December 1, the superintendent of schools finds out that the heating plant in Snowbird High will not last through the season. The boiler and firebox must either be repaired extensively or replaced during the December holidays. There are three choices:

- The present coal-fired system can be completely overhauled at a cost of $40,000. It should then last another 20 years, 5 years beyond the time when the building is to be torn down and replaced. Annual heating cost with this system will be about $5000.

- A new gas-fired boiler can be installed. It is a prefabricated unit with an estimated useful life of 10 years. It costs only $20,000 to install but $6000 per year to operate.

- A residual oil unit could heat for only $3500 per year. The unit would last at least 30 years and would cost $65,000.

None of the above units could be salvaged if the building is abandoned.
What is the best solution for a discount rate of 7%? 10%?

11.9. *Hi-Tacky PC's*

You have been working hard in graduate school and decide you should purchase your own personal computer. Two types are available:

- Brand PC costs $2500, will last for 9 years, and comes with a yearly maintenance fee of $100.

- Hi-Tacky PC costs $1600, has no maintenance fee, but its hard disk must be replaced every 3 years at a cost of $1000.

Over 9 years and using a 10% discount rate in your calculations, which PC should you purchase based on Net Present Value?

11.10. *Balloon Payment*

Normally, the Ready-Tech company sells its blood analysis machines to labs on long term "Regular" leases: $10,000/year for 10 years. The sales manager suggests an "Easy Start" program of $6000/year for the first 5 years followed by "balloon payments" of $18,000/year for the next 5. "We'll take in $20,000 more!" he says, "We may even double our net profit!"

(*a*) If Ready-Tech's discount rate is 20%, is "Easy Start" better than "Regular" for the company?

(*b*) How would the situation change if the initial payments under "Easy Start" were $7000/year?

11.11. *Size That Project!*

(*a*) The airport authority needs to process 1000 more passengers an hour at the peak periods, each year. It estimates that this requires an extra $1000\,m^2$

annually. What size project is most economical if its discount rate is 10% and it realizes moderate economies of scale in construction, $C(Y) = A_0 Y^{0.7}$?

(b) The municipal water board needs to add 50 acre-feet of reservoir capacity each year, on average. It has strong economies of scale in constructing the tanks, $C(Y) = A_0 Y^{0.5}$; and has a low discount rate since it raises money through low yield municipal bonds, $r = 6\%$. How big should it build the next reservoir?

(c) Same as (b), but for a private company that must get money from its banks, $r = 12\%$.

(d) A trucking company must acquire 50,000 m^2 of warehouse space a year. Its discount rate is 15% and it hardly sees any economies of scale, $C(Y) = A_0 Y^{0.9}$. How many years in advance should it build?

CHAPTER
12

CHOICE OF DISCOUNT RATE

12.1 THE ISSUES

The choice of the discount rate is the single most critical element in any evaluation of benefits and cost over time. This is true for two reasons. The most obvious one is that the present values of future benefits and costs are intrinsically very sensitive to the discount rate, as Section 11.5 describes in detail. Relatively small changes in the discount rate can make a significant difference in whether a project appears desirable or not. The general rule is that higher discount rates make projects look less attractive. (Note, however, that exceptional counterexamples to this rule can be constructed, in which higher discount rates sometimes make a project more attractive. See Section 13.3 and especially Figure 13.2.)

The second reason the choice of the discount rate is often crucial is because it is a prime determinant of the choice of technology. Indeed, because higher discount rates minimize long-term benefits, they are therefore unfavorable to *capital intensive* projects—those investments such as steel mills, nuclear power plants, or concrete highways, whose large initial investment is repaid over many years. The choice of a lower discount rate is thus often a choice for such projects, as compared to their less capital-intensive alternatives—such as the manufacture of plastics, fossil fuel electricity, or asphalt highways.

The connection between the choice of discount rate and the choice of technology is quite subtle. Most designers are actually unaware of the phenomenon, and certainly few like to think that their expertise takes second place to a simple financial parameter. Yet it is so, as Section 12.2 discusses in detail.

222

The logic of what the discount rate should be is actually quite straightforward, as Section 12.3 indicates. In any textbook case, it is easy to determine the proper discount rate. The difficulty is that, in real situations, there is no method that clearly gives the right answer with good precision. As a practical matter, the choice of the discount rate is thus imprecise and rather arbitrary in the end.

The twin facts that the choice of the discount rate is a matter of judgment and can have rather enormous economic and technical implications make this selection highly controversial. Powerful political and economic interests will almost always be affected by the choice and ever ready to argue against it. Section 12.6 deals with their major counterarguments.

The final issues concern the ever-bothersome questions of how to treat risk and inflation. Sections 12.7 and 12.8 cover these questions, and Section 12.9 gives a variety of examples illustrating how one should think about the choice of discount rate.

12.2 A DETERMINANT OF TECHNOLOGY

Designers and managers are constantly having to face a fundamental kind of choice as they consider projects. Over and over the issue is: should they select the alternative which costs less initially but more to operate? or should they invest more at the beginning, to save money on operations and maintenance? On a personal level, for example, you may have to choose between regular tires and radials if you own a car. A builder might have to choose between a wood or a brick house, a city between paving its streets with asphalt or concrete, and a company between obtaining power from fossil fuels or by investing in hydroelectric or nuclear power. As these examples suggest, this choice between saving money now or later is, as a general rule, a choice between technologies.

This choice between technologies is often determined by the discount rate. As the parameter which establishes comparability between present and future sums of money, it settles the question of whether future savings justify extra expense at the beginning. Specifically, it determines if the net present value is positive or not.

Consider two technologies, A and B. Each implies some initial costs, C_{kA} and C_{kB}, and future recurring costs of operation and maintenance, C_{rA} and C_{rB}. The only interesting situation is if one technology has lower initial costs but higher operating costs, say:

$$C_{kA} < C_{kB}$$

$$C_{rA} > C_{rB}$$

(If one technology is always cheaper, the choice is trivial, of course.) The choice as to whether A is more economical than B is thus simply whether the extra initial cost of B, $C_{kB} - C_{kA}$, justifies the future savings it generates, $C_{rA} - C_{rB}$. This issue can be viewed as a distinct evaluation, with the time stream of costs shown in Figure 12.1.

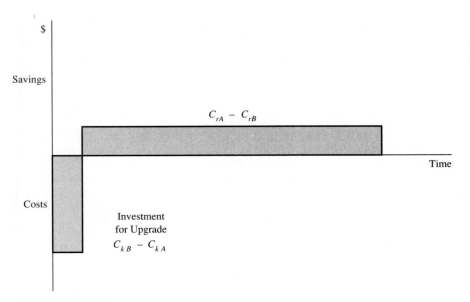

FIGURE 12.1
The cash flow of costs and savings associated with the choice between a "low capital–high recurring cost" technology (A) and "higher capital–lower recurring cost" technology (B).

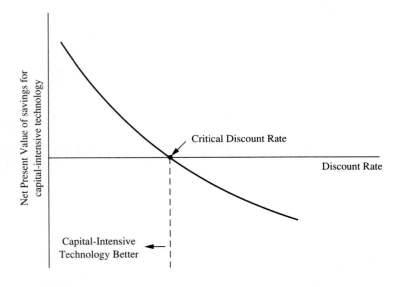

FIGURE 12.2
Lower discount rates make capital intensive technologies appear better in comparison to less capital intensive technologies.

The extent to which the discounted savings exceed the present costs depends directly on the discount rate. These net savings, the net present value of the savings minus the present costs, decrease with increases in the discount rate. The relationship is generally as in Figure 12.2. For discount rates below the *critical discount rate*, at which the net present value of the savings is zero, the technology that requires more initial capital is better; for higher discount rates, the less capital-intensive technology is more economical (see box).

The choice of the discount rate therefore can determine which technology appears best. The temptation to manipulate this selection for particular advantage can thus be great. Powerful economic and political interests allied with one technology or another will encourage this. When the U.S. Federal Highway

---

Dependence of Net Present Value on Discount Rate

Suppose your organization has the choice between two air conditioning systems, the regular and the "power-miser." The regular costs $10,000 to install and $3000 a year to operate. The "power-miser" has an initial cost of $18,000 but uses only $1800 of power a year. Both would last 10 years.

The choice between the two systems is a question of whether the benefits of the annual savings (3000 − 1800 = $1200 a year) justify the additional initial cost of $8000. Is the net present value of the upgrade to the more expensive system positive?

If the discount rate were zero, such that future benefits were not discounted, the upgrade is clearly worthwhile.

$$\text{NPV } (r = 0) = 1200(10 \text{ years}) - 8000 = \$4000$$

Conversely, if the discount rate were extremely large, future benefits would be discounted, totally in fact, for infinite r:

$$\text{NPV } (r = \infty) = 1200(0) - 8000 = \$ - 8000$$

The project is not worthwhile.

The variation of net present value with the discount rate can be obtained from Table 11.2. For example, for $r = 5\%$:

$$\text{NPV } (r = 5) = 1200(7.72) - 8000 = \$1264$$

The range of results is summarized as follows:

$r\%$	:	0	5	10	15	infinity
NPV ($)	:	4000	1264	−632	−1976	−8000

The critical discount rate, below which the more capital-intensive system is preferred, is around $8\frac{1}{2}\%$ by interpolation.

The overall dependence of net present value on discount rate for this evaluation of the upgrade plots is as in Figure 12.2.

Administration promulgated a regulation, some 20 years ago, that the discount rate for federally funded highways would be zero, this was widely interpreted as a victory for the cement industry over the asphalt interests. (Roads made of concrete cost significantly more than asphalt roads, but require less maintenance and less frequent replacement.)

Other financial arrangements can also influence the choice of technology, as is evident by how we can shift the curve of net savings in Figure 12.2. For example, the rules in the United States whereby the federal government pays the states up to 90% of the initial costs of highways, but none of the later operating and maintenance costs, systematically shifts the curve upward for the states, by the reduction in the differential initial costs. This shifts the critical discount rate to the right, and favors concrete as the more capital-intensive technology for building highways (see box). Similarly, the peculiarities of the tax system in the United States allow states and cities to obtain money at very low rates for public purposes, such as highways. This lowers their discount rates and also favors capital-intensive technologies such as concrete highways. Is there any wonder that the U.S. interstate highway system is almost entirely built of concrete? Yet other highways, built without federal funds—such as

---

Raising Critical Discount Rate by Capital Subsidies

You are reevaluating the alternative air conditioning systems: there now is a subsidy on the initial investment. (These arrangements are quite common: businesses may benefit from "investment tax credits" that lower the net cost of new investments; local governments may receive grants from the central government.) Specifically suppose that the subsidy amounts to 20% of the initial cost.

The initial cost of the upgrade to the more expensive system is correspondingly reduced by 20%. The cost of the upgrade is now

$$18,000(0.8) - 10,000(0.8) = \$6400$$

implying a 20% savings compared to the previous cost:

$$8000 - 6400 = \$1600$$

The net present value of the upgrade thus systematically increases by $1600 for all values of r, since the operating costs do not change. The new range of results is

$r\%$	:	0	5	10	15	infinity
NPV ($)	:	5600	2864	968	–376	–6400

The new critical discount rate is $13\frac{1}{2}\%$ by interpolation. The 20% subsidy on capital costs has, in this case, raised the critical discount rate by 5% and made the capital-intensive technology far more attractive.

---

the Massachusetts Turnpike—are built of the less capital-intensive alternative, asphalt. This illustrates the potentially powerful effect of the choice of discount rate on the choice of technology.

12.3 LOGICAL BASIS

The discount rate is the mathematical means for establishing whether a project is worthwhile, as indicated by a positive net present value. The discount rate must therefore be chosen so that the set of worthwhile projects it defines matches what is really acceptable to a person or organization.

Anybody's set of worthwhile projects consists of all those with the greatest returns on investment that fit into their budget. The other opportunities, which offer lower returns, are not worthwhile to a person: to include them within a budget, better projects would have to be dropped and the person would suffer a loss. The discount rate should thus be set so that all the best projects that fit within a budget are included, and all the rest excluded.

At any time, every individual or group has a wide range of investment opportunities. These will naturally never be the same at all times for all persons; opportunities arise and disappear. Acting rationally, the investor first places money in the most rewarding opportunity, then the one with next highest returns on investment and so on. The matter of investing sequentially into the projects with the greatest returns generates the kind of curve shown in Figure 12.3.

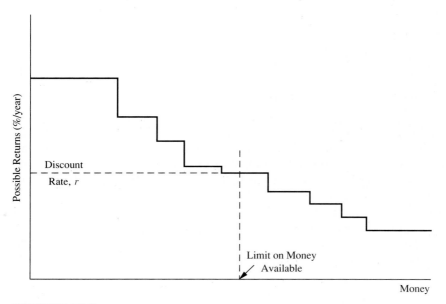

FIGURE 12.3
Representative pattern of possible returns on investment for a particular individual or company.

Ultimately it becomes asymptotic with the return available from the essentially unlimited opportunities to place money in banks or government bonds at their prevailing rate of interest. In practice, companies or individuals run out of capital well before these lowest opportunities. This limit on money available varies for each investor, of course; it depends on how much money one starts with, on how much banks might be willing to lend, and on legal limits that may exist on how much one can borrow. The intersection of this limit with the curve of returns on investment defines the discount rate for the investor (see box).

Pattern of Returns on Investment

Imagine yourself just after the holiday shopping. You have a $500 debt on your credit card on which you pay 18% annually, have borrowed $1000 from your local bank at 12%, and have a savings account paying 6% — with, unfortunately, no money in it.

Your pattern of returns on investment, if these are your only opportunities, is as follows. You presumably could put as much money in the bank as you wished.

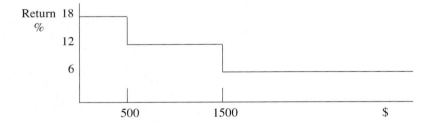

Your discount rate depends on how much cash you have to spend on the investment — on the unspent total of what you received as holiday presents, for example. If this is between $500 and $1500, your discount rate should be 12%: only alternatives offering returns at least this high are worthwhile to you. If you have less that $500, your discount rate should be 18%.

Finally, if you were considering a project whose cost exceeds the steps of the graph, your discount rate would be a weighted average of the above rates. If the proposed project cost $750, say, and that was all the cash you had, your opportunity cost would be 18% on the $500 and 12% on $250, for an average of:

$$\frac{[18(500) + 12(250)]}{750} = 16\%$$

The discount rate should thus represent the productivity of the last increment of money available to a person, company, or government, the marginal productivity of capital to that agency. It simultaneously should be the

- lowest acceptable rate to any investor.
- highest rate among the remaining opportunities if more capital were available.

The beauty of the discount rate can now be explained. It provides an immediate indication of whether any project falls within the economic range of acceptability for an investor. Suppose the return on investment of a project, r_p, just equals the discount rate; $r_p = r$. Then the project has a net present value of zero, when discounted at the rate of $r\%$. Similarly, a project that returns at a higher rate, $r_p > r$, has a positive net present value. Conversely, if the project returns at some lower rate, $r_p < r$, it has a negative net present value. In short, by using the proper discount rate, we can immediately tell if a project is economically acceptable simply by looking at the sign of its net present value.

The discount rate can also simply be viewed as the shadow price on the budget. It is indeed the increase in return an investor could obtain for each extra dollar available.

> **Semantic caution:** The discount rate is frequently in practice referred to as the *"opportunity cost" of capital.* This is confusing because, as indicated in the discussion of shadow prices and opportunity costs in Chapter 6, these concepts are quite different. The reason the discount rate is called the opportunity cost is because, if investors want to obtain money for a new project without borrowing more money, they have to give up the opportunity to do some other project. Acting rationally, this would be one with the lowest return on investment of all they have invested in, that is, one with a return equal to the discount rate.

The difference between the discount rate and the interest rate should now also come into focus. The discount rate for any investor acting rationally should be substantially above the interest rate on any loans. Investors borrow money because they see that by doing so they can make a profit, the difference between their discount rate and the interest they pay. Conversely, if the interest rate were higher than the discount rate, rational investors would pay off their loans. Finally, the discount rate generally exceeds the interest rate by a fair margin because bankers and other lenders like to see a comfortable cushion to protect their loans, and never seem to lend as much as the borrower might want.

12.4 RATE FOR PRIVATE SECTOR

The productivity of money in commerce and industry is typically well over 10% a year, and frequently closer to 15 or 20%. These numbers are difficult to pin down precisely, because they vary significantly between types of industry, individual companies, and with the general state of the economy.

In general, the rates of return are lower in industries regulated by the government than for companies that are not. The reason is that they are allowed less profit, in exchange for the lower risk associated with a regulated industry. Electric power companies in the United States commonly have rates of return on the order of 10%, and banks of about 12% or so. Manufacturing companies often appear to have returns of 15% or more.

Calculating the rate of return for any company requires a detailed, sophisticated analysis of its accounts, together with an understanding of the applicable tax laws. Individual companies rarely go through this kind of exercise. In practice they typically set a corporate standard, which they believe to approximate their reality. Sometimes they do this indirectly, as by setting a minimum criterion of acceptability, particularly of the payback period (see Section 13.3). The discount rates used in industry, either explicitly or implied, typically appear to be 15 or 20%.

In the United States, various investment banks and stock brokers attempt to calculate the rates of return of companies whose stock is traded publicly. They do this by statistical analysis of the past performance of any company in comparison to other similar companies. The results derived from these analyses have the appearance of being quite accurate, since they are given to several decimal points. But appearances are deceiving. These results depend crucially on dubious assumptions, most particularly that the future will be similar to the past 20 years or so, which is always a doubtful proposition. In any case the figures generated by these analyses are comparable to those given above.

12.5 RATE FOR PUBLIC SECTOR

Most of the controversy surrounding the choice of the discount rate concerns the rate the government should use. This is because governments are, generally, run by politicians more sensitive to political pressures than economic realities.

Despite the political controversy, the rational economic rule is simple: the discount rate for government and public sector projects ought to approximate the discount rate for business and industry. The reasoning is that

- the money the government raises comes from taxes on the private sector.
- the money thus taken from companies and individuals restricts their opportunities to invest in productive facilities or to pay off debts, as for mortgages.
- the private sector discount rate represents the loss of productivity to society, the opportunities foregone because of taxes.
- the government should, therefore, use this rate when evaluating its own projects to make sure that society as a whole is not a loser—as it would be if money were diverted from projects with higher productivity to ones with lower productivity.

The best economic minds are now agreed on this general reasoning.

In practice, the discount rate for government is often taken to be lower than the average rate of returns in private industry, somewhat closer to those in regulated industries. The rationale is that government activities involve less risk. A 10% discount rate is now widely used: in the United States, this is the rate required by the federal Office of Management and Budget for the evaluation of national projects; the World Bank uses 10% in its feasibility studies; the British Airports Authority has been using 14%; and so on.

12.6   ALTERNATIVE ARGUMENTS

The alternative arguments concerning the selection of the discount rate are directed toward establishing a lower rate, closer to 3 or 5%. The proponents of these arguments are interested in justifying capital-intensive projects with long lives, the kind of project that is not favored by high discount rates. The arguments are particularly directed toward government, to justify massive public works such as highway or waterway construction in the United States, railroads in some countries, steel mills in others. They are not aimed at private enterprise, which simply could not survive economically if it adopted the arguments proposed.

Even though these arguments do not seem at all appropriate, it is important for any analyst to be aware of them and prepared to deal with them. This is the reason they are summarized here.

The first major argument is that the government's discount rate ought to equal the interest rate it pays on its bonds, particularly the long term bonds. This principle is not right. As pointed out in Section 12.3, nobody's discount rate should equal their interest rate, unless they have unlimited money available. In general, as Figure 12.3 illustrates, there is a wide gap between the two. As even governments have to operate eventually within the constraints of their budgets, their discount rate should certainly be above the rates they pay on their bonds.

This argument used to be popular in public works agencies in the United States some years ago. At that time, the average interest rate paid by the United States on its bonds—many of which had been issued during the Depression and World War II—was quite low, almost 3%. Now that the average interest rate paid by the United States on its bonds is closer to 8%, and that economic rationality has been imposed by the U.S. Office of Management and Budget, this "interest rate" argument is on the way to disappearing in the United States.

The second line of argument is emotional. It runs along the lines of "look at all the worthwhile projects we could not build if we evaluated them with a high discount rate." The key word here is "worthwhile." The argument presumes that certain people, such as government officials or technocrats, already know what is best, what is worthwhile, independent of any evaluation or careful analysis.

This argument often gets quite emotional, because the discussion over any one project quickly gets transformed into whether one is for or against some acknowledged social good. For example, controversy over a project to irrigate lands and create new farmland can get translated into an argument as to whether or not one is really against agriculture and poor farmers, when really—in this case—the issue is that reclaiming desert land at a cost many times the value of good farmland elsewhere is simply a waste of money that no rational person would contemplate, if it were not to be paid for by the government.

The use of reasonable discount rates, of about 10%, in no way prevents us from spending money on any social concerns a government and its people choose: health, education, welfare, or whatever. If the public values these services highly, and is willing to pay for them, they will be provided. Use of a high discount rate ensures that the government provide its goods and services rationally, with the right scale and the right technology. Use of a high discount rate does not prevent us from spending on highways, for example, but it does impel us to choose the type of construction that makes economic sense.

12.7   TREATMENT OF RISK

In the private market, projects that are riskier than others are forced to pay higher interest rates to attract capital. A speculative new company will have to pay the banks several percentage points more for its borrowings than established, prime customers. Private companies, which always run the risk of bankruptcy, have to pay more than the government. This extra amount of interest is known as the *risk premium*. The question is, should this amount somehow be included in the discount rate?

As a practical matter, the risk premium already is included in the discount rates described in the previous two sections. The speculative new company, borrowing at a rate several points above the prime rate of interest, should have a discount rate above this higher interest rate. The regulated electric utility, typically an established company whose continued existence is guaranteed by the government, will be able to borrow money more cheaply, will invest in projects whose marginal productivity is correspondingly lower, and should have a lower discount rate.

When a particular project is especially risky, the evaluation ought to account for risk directly. As the discussion on evaluation methods in Chapter 10 indicates, decision analysis (described in Chapters 16 and 17) is the preferred way to appraise projects with a high component of risk.

12.8   TREATMENT OF INFLATION

Inflation is the loss in value of money over time. It is the phenomenon represented by observations that money now does not buy what it used to. Inflation is typically measured by *price indexes*, which indicate how much money is required, at any time, to buy a standardized collection of items. The usual way to express inflation is in terms of percent per year, just as the discount rate.

The question always is: how should we deal with inflation in an evaluation? Should it be included in the discount rate? Should future benefits and costs be adjusted? Should it be ignored, or what?

The answer is that we should do what is necessary to establish comparability between money now and money later. This is the central idea of the evaluation of projects over time, and the role of the discount rate.

The general rule is that if future revenues and costs are measured in future dollars, the ones that are inflated, then we must include this effect in the evaluation. This can be done by either of two equivalent procedures:

• Deflating all future revenues and costs by the rate of inflation
• Increasing the discount rate by the rate of inflation

Both procedures lead to exactly the same result: money later is discounted for both the time value of money and for inflation (see box).

Conversely, if future revenues and costs are measured in *current dollars*, at prices unchanged due to future inflation, then there is no need to account for inflation in the evaluation. The next section provides examples of these situations.

To apply these rules we also need to know whether the inflation rate is already included in the discount rate, as may be the case for private companies. Indeed, to the extent that a company estimates its productivity by looking at

---

Alternatives for Dealing with Inflation

Imagine that you are buying a house and can choose between two kinds of 20-year mortages offered by the bank. One requires you to pay $10,000 more now than the other, but saves you $2000 a year in payments.

Suppose that your personal discount rate is 10% in current dollars and that you estimate inflation to be 5% a year. Which mortgage is better for you?

Mathematically, the question is whether the extra $10,000 payment has a positive net present value. You can calculate this two ways.

Recognizing that the future payments will be in inflated money, you can increase the discount rate by the rate of inflation and proceed accordingly. Using Table 11.2, you then find

$$NPV = 2000(\text{series present worth at } 15\%) - 10,000$$
$$= 20,000(6.26) - 10,000 = \$2520$$

Alternatively, you can first deflate the annual payments by the 5% inflation to obtain equivalent amounts in current dollars, and then discount these amounts using the corresponding 10% discount rate. The effect is most easily seen using the exponential form of the compound amount factor (see Section 11.4):

$$(1 + r)^N = e^{rN}$$

The annual savings expressed in current dollars are then $2000(e^{0.05N})$. The present value of each annual payment is then $[2000(e^{0.05N})]e^{0.10N}$. This is equivalent to $2000(e^{0.15N})$ which leads to the same result as before.

Which of the alternatives is easier to use depends on the situation. No general rule applies.

---

its annual return on its investment, it incorporates the inflation rate. This is because its investment was years ago, and its returns are now, in inflated money. This situation makes the evaluation process as simple as possible: measure future revenues and costs in the amounts you expected to see, that is, inflated, and apply the standard discount rate for the company, which accounts for the inflation. For government, whose discount rate is approximated as a low round number, it is generally safe to assume that the discount rate does not include the effect of inflation.

What the future inflation rate may be is always a question. It is both quite variable and dependent on the situation. Recent experience in the United States well illustrates the potential variability over time: in the 1970s the annual rate of inflation routinely exceeded 10% per year, in the 1980s it fell to around 4 to 5%. As this indicates, the inflation rate can be controlled by government policy, and thus varies enormously between countries. Some, like Switzerland, seem consistently to have very low rates of inflation, a few percent or so; others, like Argentina, Brazil, and Israel, have suffered from chronic hyperinflation on the order of 100% a year.

The rate of inflation also depends on the industry. At any time, different sectors of the economy undergo changes and experience quite different rates of price changes. Recently in the United States, for example, the inflation in the costs of healthcare was two or more times the national rate. To track these different inflation rates, industrial associations and government agencies routinely publish specialized price indexes such as the Wholesale Price Index, the Consumer Price Index, and the Construction Price Index. Always in the spirit of establishing comparability in an evaluation, the rule is to use the inflation rate suitable to the situation.

12.9   EXAMPLES

This section provides a series of samples illustrating the principles of selecting a discount rate for a variety of situations.

Example 1: An individual has $200 to buy new tires. She has $1000 outstanding on her credit card, for which she is paying 18% a year, and unlimited opportunities to put money into a 6% savings account. Question: at what discount rate should she evaluate her two alternatives for buying tires, the long-lasting radials or the cheaper belted tires that will have to be replaced sooner? Answer: 18%. Any extra investment in tires should provide at least this return or she would be better off paying off some of her credit card bill. Note that this rate includes both inflation and replacement tires, since she pays for both with future money. Her discount rate free of inflation is (18% − inflation rate).

Example 2: The same person has to choose between an ordinary refrigerator and an energy-efficient model that is expected to save 500 kwh/yr. The electricity now costs $0.10 per kilowatt-hour. Question: Should she adjust for inflation in doing the evaluation? Answer: With this information, no. The savings are given in current dollars, unaffected by inflation, so they are directly comparable to current costs once the discount rate free of inflation has been applied.

Example 3: She now finds out that, as a result of a regulatory decision, the cost of electricity will increase by 15% a year over the lifetime of the refrigerator. Question: Now how should she deal with inflation in her evaluation? Answer: Since she is dealing with future costs, she should either deflate them by the expected rate of inflation, or evaluate them with the discount rate including inflation (in her case 18%).

Example 4: A city plans to expand a toll bridge to accommodate more cars. The toll is now $1.00 a trip. Question: Should this be adjusted for inflation in the evaluation? Answer: Almost certainly yes. This case differs from that of Example 2 in that prices for tolls tend to stay constant whereas other prices adjust for inflation. So here the current price can be assumed to be the future price, and should be adjusted downward to account for inflation.

REFERENCES

ATT Company, (1977). "Return and Income Taxes," Chapter 8, *Engineering Economy*, 3rd ed., McGraw-Hill, New York.
Baumol, W. J., (1968). "On The Social Rate of Discount," *American Economic Review*, Sept., Vol. 57, No. 4, pp. 778–802. See also comments in Vol. 60, No. 5, pp. 909–930, 1969.

PROBLEMS

12.1. *Personal Discount Rates*

Some effort has been made to sell small cars and certain other goods on the basis of reduced energy and maintenance costs. However, most consumer purchases are based on the purchase price and performance. For appliances and machinery whose operating costs are large compared to the initial cash outlay, such naïve approaches may result in choices that are more expensive than necessary.

(a) Consider a refrigerator which costs $300, uses 1600 kwh of electricity per year, and requires an annual one-hour service call. If service costs $10/hr, electricity costs 3 cents/kilowatt-hour, the purchaser's discount rate is 10%, and the refrigerator lasts 10 years, what is the life cycle cost of the refrigerator (total discounted cost)? What is the equivalent annual cost? Which measure (life cycle or annual cost) would you find most useful in choosing a refrigerator?

(b) An improved refrigerator is introduced. Better insulated and more efficient than the standard, it costs $700, uses only 600 kwh per year, and is otherwise identical. Which refrigerator is the better choice for a purchaser in Plainville, where electricity is 3 cents/kwh and service $10/hr? In New York City, where electricity is 7.6 cents/kwh and service is $15/hr? Assume both buyers have a 10% discount rate.

(c) Consider two different New Yorkers. Connie Ross, a junior executive, lives in a posh Manhattan apartment building. She finds her salary barely adequate to maintain her lifestyle and has considered getting a loan from her credit union (at 12% interest). However, she still has $1500 in the bank, drawing 10% interest.

Ralph White works overtime as an electronics assembler to support his family. He has never been able to save more than a minimum down payment for any major purchase; eligible only for dealer financing and being in a high-risk category, he pays about 20% interest on the remainder of the purchase price.

Which refrigerator is a better investment for Connie? For Ralph?

12.2. *Student Finances*

You are a student with a monthly income of only $600, and in some difficulty.

- You owe the student store $200, on which you pay an 18%/yr interest rate, calculated monthly, on unpaid balances.
- Your bicycle was just stolen and you want to buy one that regularly sells for $220, but is selling for $200, this week only, for cash.
- Your room and board is prepaid and you need $100 in expense money for the month.
- You have a $100 Savings Bond that earns 5%/yr, and $200 in the local savings bank that earns 6%/yr.
- You have $300 in a checking account. This money earns no interest and requires a $1.50 service charge for any month in which the balance is less than $200.

(*a*) How should you change your investments, if at all?
(*b*) What is your opportunity cost of another $100 this month?
(*c*) If you buy the bike this week, rather than next month at $220, what is its true cost?
(*d*) What is your discount rate?

12.3. *Inheritance*

Assume you receive $5000 to invest for your future. Your available alternatives for this money are:

- Use up to $2500 of it to pay a tuition loan, on which you pay 12% interest on unpaid balances.
- Put as much as you want of the $5000 in a savings bank to earn 5% per year.
- Buy a discounted bond for $5000 (the smallest denomination), that is redeemable only after 3 years for $8500. You can then reinvest this money in more of the same type of bonds.

(*a*) What is the opportunity cost, in percent, of the $5000?
(*b*) What discount rate should you use for evaluating an investment opportunity for the entire $5000 in some other business? for only $2500 of the $5000?

12.4. *Money Store*

The Money Corporation is considering a new product line. Its present financial situation is as follows:

- It can borrow money at the prime interest rate of 9%.
- The average annual inflation rate is 5%.
- The interest on tax-free government bonds is 7%.
- Its marginal after-tax return on other investments is 10%.
- It pays corporate taxes at the rate of 40%.

What discount rate should the company use in evaluating its expansion proposals, given that its benefits and costs for these projects (but not for the other investments) are in terms of current dollars? For example, benefits accrued in 2000 are in terms of today's dollars. (What counts here is your explanation of the right answer.)

12.5. *DR Review*
  (a) What is the meaning of the government's discount rate?
  (b) When should it be used?
  (c) How might it be determined?
  (d) What might be an appropriate rate for the United States?

12.6. *Port Authority*
The Port Authority is evaluating alternatives to repair or replace its bulldozers. Some have high initial cost but lower future costs, while other alternatives defer costs to the future. What discount rate should be used under the following set of conditions? Why?

  • Savings certificates from the local bank pay 5%.

  • The lowest or prime rate available to local borrowers is 9%.

  • Public Facilities construction bonds sold several years ago pay 8%; more could be sold at $8\frac{1}{2}\%$.

  • The funds for the repair of trucks must come from a reserve in the current operating budget. At the end of the year money left in the reserve can be carried forward to reduce the following year's operating budget or it can be used to retire bonds ahead of schedule.

12.7. *Park Hue*
Park commutes 10 miles by train and subway at a cost of $6/day. Having just received a promotion that entails a free parking space, Park is trying to decide whether to buy a second car (the first being used by the family) to drive directly to work. This would save 10 min.
  (a) Define the time streams of the relevant costs and benefits. What do you estimate the opportunity costs of Park's time to be?
  (b) Define and justify your choice of discount rate for the evaluation. Then calculate the net present values of the alternatives.
  (c) How does your evaluation change if Park had no family and no first car?

12.8. *Snowbird High Again*
Refer to Problem 11.8. Suppose that all repair and replacement costs will have to be covered by a contingency fund that has a current balance of $80,000. Contingency fund money not committed by January 1 will revert to the city's general fund and be allocated in whatever manner the city council sees fit.
    The current financial market is approximately as follows: an average annual inflation rate of 3% has driven the interest rate paid by local banks to 8%; high-grade corporation bonds pay 9%; and school board bonds which are tax exempt pay 7%.
  (a) What solution makes the most sense if you are the superintendant?
  (b) If you are the school board and have to raise money for the project?
  (c) If you are a member of the city council, and anticipate a tax rebate to citizens?

12.9. *Hi-Tacky Corporation*

The Hi-Tacky Corporation is considering a new energy efficient heating system that will provide savings in current dollars of $5000/yr. Based on the following information:

- Taxes are paid at the rate of 50%.
- Inflation has an annual rate of 8%.
- The prime interest rate is 7%.
- After-tax return on other long-term investments is 12%.
- Savings certificates from the local bank pay 5%.

What discount rate should it use when evaluating the heating system?

12.10. *Start-Up*

Your friend the entrepreneur has just started a new business. Your advice is needed on the discount rate to be used to evaluate new opportunities. Looking through the financial records, you find that your friend could already

- insulate the building for $40,000, which would save 5600 gal/yr of fuel, currently valued at $1/gal.
- pay off $80,000 borrowed at a rate of 12% on the balance.
- pay $20,000 for an annuity paying $3200/yr for 30 years.
- lend to another entrepreneur who guarantees to double a $30,000 investment in 5 years.

Your friend has $60,000 in cash for investment. Estimating inflation at 4% a year, what is your friend's minimum discount rate for a $20,000 investment? a $60,000 investment?

12.11. *Government Procurement*

The local government has several options for its $200,000 project fund:
  (i) Establish an in-house desk-top publishing office, to get annual savings estimated at $28,000 in today's money.
  (ii) Exercise an option to buy the land under their parking area, on which they now have a 30-year lease at $38,000/yr.
  (iii) Buy the computer equipment they now lease for $70,000/yr. This will have to be junked in 5 years.

Estimating inflation at 6% annually, rank the above projects.

CHAPTER
13

ECONOMIC EVALUATION

The purpose of an economic evaluation is to determine whether any project or investment is financially desirable. Specifically, an evaluation addresses two sorts of questions:

- Is any individual project worthwhile? That is, does it meet our minimum standards?
- Which is the best project in a list of possibilities? What is the ranking of projects on this list?

This chapter shows how both these questions should be answered.

Economic evaluations are difficult to do correctly in practice. This is in great part because this work is done by middle-level managers or staff who necessarily, by the fact that they see only part of their company's or agency's activities, cannot realistically take all the appropriate factors into account. The result is that most evaluations are done on the basis of assumptions often out-of-date or otherwise inaccurate for the situation at hand.

Conceptual difficulties are another source of error and confusion in economic evaluation. A number of the standard criteria for evaluation contain biases which make them inappropriate and even quite wrong for particular kinds of situations. This chapter focuses on these issues so that the practitioner will be able—to the extent possible within the requirements of employers or clients—to select the most suitable criteria of economic evaluation.

The core of this chapter is the presentation of the variety of possible criteria for evaluation, in Section 13.3. These include net present value, benefit-cost ratios, internal rate of return, cost-effectiveness ratio, and payback periods. Each method is discussed in detail and then compared to the others in Section 13.4. The chapter concludes with an application illustrating the way an economic evaluation can be done.

13.1   BASIC METHODOLOGY

The essence of all economic evaluation is a discounted cash flow analysis. The first step in every situation is to lay out the estimated cash flow, the sequence of benefits and costs over time. These cash flows are then discounted back to the present, using the methods shown in Chapter 11, either directly or indirectly in the case of the rate of return and payback period methods. The basic analysis can in all cases be simply done by the spreadsheet programs routinely available for personal computers.

The evaluation then assesses the merit of projects by comparing the discounted cash flows of benefits and costs. The project appears to be worthwhile if the benefits exceed the costs. The relative ranking of the projects is then determined by one of the several evaluation criteria—discussed in Section 13.3—that manipulate the discounted cash flow in various ways.

The methods of evaluation differ from each other principally in the way they handle the results of the discounted cash flow analysis. The present value method focuses on the difference between the discounted benefits and costs, the benefit cost and other ratio methods involve various comparisons of these qualities, and the rate of return method tries to equalize them. The question of what one does with the results of the discounted cash flows is the central problem of economic evaluation.

Most methods presume that the discount rate to be used in the cash flow analysis is known. This is often a reasonable assumption, since many companies or agencies require that a specific rate be used for all their economic evaluations. In many instances, however, the discount rate must be determined; this may be done as shown in Chapter 12.

It will be essential to remember, in carrying out an evaluation, that the correct selection of the discount rate may be crucial. The choice of the rate can easily change the ranking of projects, making one or another appear best depending on the rate used. This is because lower rates make long-term projects, with benefits in the distant future, appear much more attractive—relative to short-term projects with immediate benefits—than they would be if a higher rate were used (see Section 11.4). This phenomenon is discussed and illustrated in Section 13.3, which presents the different criteria of evaluation.

13.2   MINIMUM STANDARDS

Every evaluation deals with two distinct sets of projects or alternatives: the explicit and implicit possibilities. The explicit set consists of the opportunities that are to be considered in detail; they are the focus of the analysis. The implicit set, which can only be defined imprecisely, is important because it provides the terms of reference for the evaluation and defines the minimum standards.

Explicit set of alternatives. This is a limited list of the potential projects that could actually be chosen. The list is usually defined by some manager concerned with a particular topic, for example:

- An official of the department of highways, responsible for maintenance and construction of roads
- A manager of a computer center, proposing to acquire new equipment
- An investment officer for a bank, presenting a menu of opportunities for loans to construction projects

The lists of projects suggested by each of the preceding situations illustrate two characteristics typical of the explicit choices considered by an evaluation. The explicit set is

- limited in scope, in that it only includes a portion of the projects in front of the organization as a whole. Thus the manager of the computer center is only competent in, and only considers various ways to improve the information systems; whether money should be spent on developing a new product or replacing the central heating is literally not his or her department.
- limited in number, being only a fraction of all the projects that could be defined over the next several years. Usually, the explicit list deals only with the immediate choices, not the ones that could occur during the next budget or decision period.

The fact that the sets of projects we consider explicitly are limited poses a basic problem for any organization. The difficulty is that any procedure that analyzes separate sets of projects independently can quite easily lead to a list of recommended choices that are not the best ones for the group. By optimizing for each subset of the entire range of alternatives that exist over time, over the departments of an organization, and over its regions, we are likely to suboptimize for the organization as a whole. For example, consider a company with a computer department, a research laboratory, and a producing plant: if we evaluate the projects proposed by each group we can determine the best computer, the best instrument, and the best machine tool to buy. But this plan may not be in the best interests of the company; it is quite possible that the second best machine tool is a better investment than the best instrument, or that none of the computers is worthwhile financially.

The issue is: How does an organization insure that the projects selected by its components are best for the organization as a whole? In addressing this question we must recognize that the obvious answer, of considering all possible projects simultaneously, is neither practical nor even possible. A large number of analyses could be done, but the level of computation is not the real obstacle.

An analysis of all alternatives at once is not practical because it would be extremely difficult for any group in an organization to be sufficiently knowledgeable both to generate the possible projects for all departments, and to estimate their benefits and costs; they simply would not have sufficient knowledge of the topic, region, or clients. Further, the analysis of all alternatives at once is not even conceptually feasible because we are unable to predict what options will be available in the future. We can therefore never be sure that the projects we select from a current list, however comprehensive it may be, will include all the opportunities that will occur over the life of the projects, and that might otherwise be selected. Some degree of suboptimization cannot be avoided.

To lessen the possibility for suboptimization it is necessary to create some means to make the evaluation of any set of explicit alternatives less dependent on other evaluations. This can be done by creating a substitute for the whole list of innumerable possible alternatives. This is the role of the implicit alternatives.

Implicit set of alternatives. This set generally represents all the projects that have been available previously and that might be available in the reasonable future. Since it refers in part to unknown prospects, it can never be described in detail. It thus indicates, with inherent imprecision, what could be done instead of the immediate, explicit alternatives.

The implicit set of alternatives is of interest because it establishes the minimum standards for deciding if any explicit project is worthwhile. To illustrate this, consider the situation in which a person has been making investments and has consistently been able to choose possibilities that provide yearly profits of 12% or more, and has rejected all others with lesser returns. Faced now with the problem of evaluating an explicit set of specific proposals, this person will naturally turn to past experience for guidance. If the investment possibilities have not fundamentally changed, the person may assume that there are continued possibilities—the implicit set of alternatives—for earning 12% or more as before and should correctly conclude that any explicit choice can only be worthwhile if its profitability equals or exceeds the 12% implicitly available elsewhere.

The minimum standards suggested by the implicit alternatives can be stated in several ways. An obvious and common way is to stipulate a minimum acceptable annual rate of return. Minimum standards of profitability can also be expressed quite differently, however. In business, they are typically stated in terms of the highest number of periods that will be required for the benefits to equal the initial investment (the maximum payback period, see Section 13.3). Minimum standards can also be defined in terms of minimum ratios of benefits to costs.

Organizations use minimum standards for the economic acceptability of projects as the way to reduce the possibility of suboptimization. These standards force each separate department or group to take into account the other opportunities available to the organization: they cannot, for example, choose projects unless they are at least as good as others available elsewhere to the organization.

13.3 EVALUATION CRITERIA

This section defines the several criteria for economic desirability used in evaluation. These fall naturally into two groups. The first consist of a variety of ways of using the discounted cash flow of benefits and of costs associated with any project. These are the net present value, the benefit-cost ratios, and the internal rate of return. The second group includes two variants that provide a way around some of the operational difficulties associated with the other criteria: these are the cost-effectiveness ratio and the payback period.

The definition of each method is followed by a discussion of its major advantages, disadvantages, and uses. The next section, 13.4, summarizes this information for reference. Throughout this discussion, all references to benefits, B, and costs, C, are taken to be given in present values as calculated by the formulas of Section 11.3.

Net present value. The net present value of a project (NPV) is simply the difference between the discounted benefits, B, and costs, C, associated with the project:

$$NPV = B - C$$

Naturally, analysts should maximize NPV. In practice, projects would be ranked by this quantity.

Some academics assert that the net present value criterion should be used in all economic analyses. This prescription should be resisted. NPV only provides a good comparison between projects when they are strictly comparable in terms of level of investment or total budget. This condition is rarely met in the real world, as indicated below. The practical consequence is that net present values are primarily used for the analysis of investments, particularly of specific sums of money, rather than for the evaluation of projects, which come in many different sizes.

The advantage of the net present value criterion is that it focuses attention on quantity of money, which is what the evaluation is ultimately concerned with. NPV differs in this respect from the other criteria of evaluation, which rank projects by ratios and which thus do not directly address the bottom line question of maximizing profit.

One disadvantage of NPV is that its precise meaning is difficult to explain; practical-minded people such as businesspersons thus tend to avoid the concept. NPV suggests profit, but in fact is not profit in any usual sense of the term. In ordinary language, profit is the difference between what we receive and what we pay out. As an example, consider an investment now for a lump sum of revenue later. This is, crudely,

$$\text{Profit} = \text{Money Received} - \text{Money Invested}$$

More precisely, if we had to borrow money to make the original investment, the profit would be net of interest paid:

$$\text{Profit} = \text{Money Received} - (\text{Money Invested})(1 + i)^N$$

where i is the interest rate. This profit can also be placed in present value terms, using the appropriate discount rate for the group concerned:

$$\text{Present value of profit} =$$
$$(\text{Money Received})(1 + r)^{-N} - (\text{Money Invested})(1 + i)^N(1 + r)^{-N}$$

The important aspect to notice is that

$$\text{NPV} \neq \text{Present value of profit}$$

This is because the discount rate is not, in general, equal to the interest rate. As Chapter 12 indicates, the discount rate already reflects some degree of profitability. Thus, even when the net present value equals zero, the project may be profitable, as understood in common language. A project with NPV = 0 is simply not advantageous as compared to other alternatives the group has. Net Present Value thus indicates "extra profitability" beyond the minimum. As a reader, you probably found it difficult to grasp this subtlety; this demonstrates the point that NPV is a difficult measure to use.

Another difficulty with the net present value criterion is that it gives no indication of the scale of effort required to achieve the result. To see this, consider the problem of evaluating the two projects defined in Table 13.1. If one considers only net value, Project S appears best. Most investors would consider that an absurd choice, however, because of the difference in scale between the projects. Taking scale into account, T presumably gives a much better return than S: the money saved by investing in T rather than S can be invested either in other explicit projects or ones that will eventually be available and that will offer more net present value than S. In any case, net present value by itself is not a good criterion for ranking projects.

Formally, the essential conditions for net present value to be an appropriate criterion of the evaluation and ranking of projects are that

- we have a fixed budget to invest.
- projects require the same investment.

These conditions rarely hold. On the contrary, it is most generally the case that the list of projects consists of a variety of possibilities of different costs. Often a central problem in the evaluation and choice of systems is to define which size of system to build and how much to spend. Analysis of net present value is not particularly helpful in those contexts.

Benefit-cost (or cost-benefit) ratio. The benefit-cost ratio is the quotient of the monetary value of benefits of a project divided by its costs:

$$\text{Benefit/Cost} = B/C$$

TABLE 13.1
Evaluation of projects S and T, illustrating how net present value criterion masks scale of effort required

Project	Benefit ($)	Cost ($)	Net value ($)	NPV as % of cost
S	2,002,000	2,000,000	2000	0.1
T	2000	1000	1000	100

It is nondimensional by definition. The presumption is that projects with a benefit-cost greater than 1.0 are desirable, because benefits exceed costs. It is also assumed that projects with higher benefit-cost ratios are more desirable.

> **Semantic caution:** Professionals sometimes refer to cost-benefit analysis when evaluating projects using benefit-cost ratios. This analysis is exactly the same, the only perceptible difference is in language. Cost-benefit analysis is the term used in Britain, many countries of the British Commonwealth, and thus sometimes in international organizations. For particular definitions of benefits that attach value to benefits different from economic prices (see Section 21.3), the British also refer to Social Cost-Benefit Analysis.

The benefit-cost ratio is principally used in the evaluation of large-scale public projects. For these kinds of investments it is clearly the evaluation criterion preferred by many professionals. However, because this criterion has an inherent bias toward projects requiring heavy capital investments and against projects with high recurring costs due to sales or operations, as explained in what follows, the benefit-cost is not used by groups responsible for these kinds of projects. Benefit-cost ratios are thus typically associated with government proposals to build dams and canals in the United States, and airports and public transport railroads in Britain. Benefit-cost analysis is avoided by agencies dealing with irrigation, healthcare, education, or similar activities with recurring annual costs, and is apparently never used by business.

The advantages of the benefit-cost ratio are that

- it compares projects on a common scale.
- it directly provides an indication of whether a project is worthwhile (does the ratio exceed 1.0?).
- it provides an easy means to rank projects in order of relative merit.

The benefit-cost ratio is, therefore, much more useful in practice than NPV, since it permits us to deal easily with projects of different size.

Conversely, however, an immediate disadvantage of this criterion is that it requires that all benefits be assigned a monetary value. For a typical flood control project in the United States, for example, the benefit-cost evaluation requires prices for such items as human life and days of aquatic recreation, prices that are highly speculative at best. Benefit-cost analyses consequently give little weight to, and are biased against, objectives that are desirable but not easily measured by economics such as education, health, and environmental quality.

The major analytic weakness of the benefit-cost ratio lies with the ambiguity of the treatment of recurring costs and the consequent bias in favor of capital-intensive projects. As indicated in Sections 12.2 and 11.7, any project involves two quite different kinds of costs, which can be broadly classified as either capital or recurring. The capital costs, C_k, are the immediate, generally quite sizeable, investments. They are characteristically recuperated gradually over the life of the project, which may easily be many years and even up to 20 or more for public works. The recurring costs, C_r, on the other hand, are relatively small at any time and are spread out fairly smoothly over the life of the project. They consist of continuous costs of operation, maintenance, and administration of a project. They are typically paid out of current revenues. The essential difference between capital and recurring costs is thus their distribution over time and their relationship to the stream of benefits of a project. Figure 13.1 illustrates the situation.

The ambiguity for calculating the benefit-cost ratios arises in the following way. The normal rule for calculating benefit-cost ratios is to compare benefits to *all* costs:

$$\frac{\text{All Benefits}}{\text{All Costs}} = \frac{B}{(C_k + C_r)}$$

Alternatively, however, one can argue that costs repaid almost immediately are not really costs to the project and are not really relevant to the ultimate issue, which is whether the net revenues or benefits from any period justify the initial investment. In this second case the appropriate criterion is

$$\frac{\text{Net Benefits}}{\text{Investment}} = \frac{(B - C_r)}{C_k}$$

These two benefit-cost ratios are far from equivalent. The Net Benefit ratio is necessarily greater:

$$\frac{\text{Net Benefit}}{\text{Cost}} > \frac{\text{Benefit}}{\text{All Cost}}$$

It can easily be the case that a project that appears undesirable when total benefits are compared to costs is actually quite profitable when the focus is on net benefits (see box). Businesses, which typically have high costs of sales each year, are quite aware of this fact and never use benefit-cost ratios.

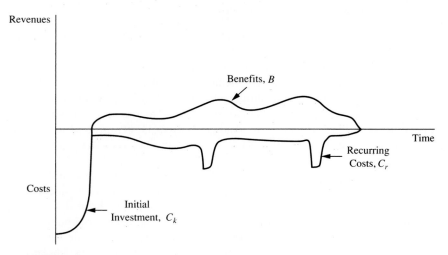

FIGURE 13.1
The relationship of benefits to capital and recurring costs.

Bias of Benefit-Cost Analysis Toward Capital Projects

Consider the two projects shown in Table 13.2, both with the same initial investment of $C_k = \$1,000,000$, and having a useful life of 10 years. They differ as to the stream of benefits and costs over time. Figuring all benefits and costs on a present value basis, Project K has low recurring costs of only $50,000 per year, with annual benefits of $200,000. It is representative of capital-intensive projects such as hydroelectric facilities, communications satellites, and so on. Project R, however, has high annual costs of $500,000 as well as big annual benefits of $700,000. It is typical of the large class of projects with high recurring costs either due to operations, such as irrigation of crops by pumping, or due to the rapid turnover of stock, as in a supermarket or retail stores more generally.

For an accountant looking at the results each year, the meaningful difference is that Project R earns $50,000 more annually, and ends up netting twice as much as Project K. On that basis Project R is clearly to be preferred. But the benefit-cost analysis would have us prefer Project K to R as indicated in the table!

The fact is that the benefit-cost ratio counts the recurring costs, which are covered immediately by the benefits, on the same basis as the capital investment, which is sunk for a long time. This leads to a bias against projects with high recurring costs and toward those with large investments. This is why the benefit-cost ratio is favored by agencies interested in capital-intensive public works.

TABLE 13.2
A comparison of a capital intensive and operations project
(all costs and benefits in present values)

Project	K		R
Investment, C_k	$1,000,000		$1,000,000
Annual costs, C_r	$ 50,000		$ 500,000
Annual benefits	$ 200,000		$ 700,000
Annual net return	$ 150,000		$ 200,000
Useful life	10 Years		10 Years
Total benefits	$2,000,000		$7,000,000
Total costs, $C_k + C_r$	$1,500,000		$6,000,000
Benefit/cost ratio	1.34	better than	1.17
Annual return	15%	worse than	20%
Net present value	$ 500,000	worse than	$1,000,000

There is no satisfactory way around the bias of the benefit-cost ratio against projects with high operating costs. This is because the broad classification of costs into two types is not sufficiently precise for any real situation. Since projects rapidly appear more desirable as more costs are subtracted from the divisor, there would be great temptation to manipulate the ratio. It would thus be difficult to be confident in the meaning and comparability of benefit-cost ratios computed on the basis of net benefits. Government agencies and other users of benefit-cost ratios have thus strenuously resisted attempts to use any ratio other than that of benefits to total costs.

The bias of the benefit-cost ratio against projects with high operating costs is a main reason why many specialists recommend the use of the net present value criterion. The difficulties with that criterion, however, do not make the choice clear.

Another disadvantage of the benefit-cost criterion is that the relative rank it gives to projects depends on the discount rate used. This is because, as indicated in Section 11.5, lower discount rates favor projects with longer-term benefits. Thus these can appear better than projects with benefits accruing sooner if a lower rate is used in the analysis. Table 13.3 illustrates this phenomenon: Project A, with the more immediate benefits, appears better than Project B for a discount rate of 10%; the ranking is reversed for a discount rate of 3%. This again underlines the importance of selecting the proper discount rate.

Internal rate of return. The internal rate of return (IRR) is the discount rate for which the net present value of a project is zero. That is,

$$\text{Internal Rate of Return} = r_{irr}$$

such that

$$\text{NPV (project)} = 0$$

The concept is that the internal rate of return indicates the real return of any project, what we called r_p in Section 12.3. It is a precise way of expressing the common notion of "return on investment." For evaluation, the idea is that projects should thus be ranked from the highest internal rate of return on down.

TABLE 13.3
Example of how ranking of projects by benefit-cost criterion can depend on discount rate used

Project	Investment C_k ($)	Annual benefit R ($)	Project life N years	Benefit-cost at discount rate of 3%	Benefit-cost at discount rate of 10%
A	1000	200	10	1.71	1.23 (best)
B	1000	125	20	1.86 (best)	1.06

The internal rate of return is now increasingly used by sophisticated analysts in business. For many, however, the complexity of its use has overwhelmed its conceptual advantage. As the internal rate of return becomes easier to calculate with the wider use of personal computers, it may be more widely used.

The advantage of the internal rate of return criterion is that it overcomes two difficulties inherent in the calculation of both net present value and of benefit-cost ratios. These are that

* it eliminates the need to determine, indeed to argue about, the appropriate discount rate.
* its rankings cannot be manipulated by the choice of a discount rate.

It also focuses attention directly on the rate of return of each project, a feature that cannot be understood from either the net present value or the benefit-cost ratio.

The obvious disadvantage of the internal rate of return criterion is that it is generally difficult to calculate. A direct solution for the internal rate of return is available only for projects with a stream of constant benefits, R, over a period: The internal rate of return can then be found from handbook tables as the discount rate for which the capital recovery factor equals R/C_k. Usually, the internal rate of return must be found by trial and error (see box). These calculations have been a real burden in the past, but can now be done relatively easily with standard spreadsheet programs available on personal computers.

Calculation of Internal Rate of Return by Trial and Error

To find the internal rate of return, we first pick two trial discount rates to calculate the net present value of a project. From these answers we guess the approximate location of the IRR, and calculate a new net present value. This procedure goes on until the answer is obtained to the accuracy desired. This can be done automatically by a spreadsheet program of a personal computer.

Consider the project Q in Table 13.4. First try discount rates of 10 and 20%:

$$r = 10\% \;\rightarrow\; \text{NPV} = +4.09$$

$$r = 20\% \;\rightarrow\; \text{NPV} = -4.76$$

The internal rate of return seems to lie in between. Try

$$r = 15\% \;\rightarrow\; \text{NPV} = +1.19$$

The internal rate of return is thus somewhat larger. Try

$$r = 16\% \;\rightarrow\; \text{NPV} = +0.19$$

The actual solution for internal rate of return here, to the author's satisfaction, is:

$$\text{IRR} = 16.18\%$$

TABLE 13.4
Examples of projects that can lead to ambiguous solutions for the internal rate of return

Project	Investment ($)	Annual benefit ($)	Project life (years)	Closure cost, year $N + 1$ ($)
P	C_k	R	N	$C_c > RN - C_k$
Q	200	100	5	310

Another disadvantage of the internal rate of return criterion is that it can be ambiguous. The solution of the condition that NPV = 0 can lead to two or more solutions; one then really cannot tell what the internal rate of return is. This ambiguity can occur whenever a project involve some final costs of closing the project, C_c. These could occur through the requirement to clean up a site on completion, as required in the United States for strip mines, to pay pensions or severance pay to workers, or to settle claims. The ambiguity can arise whenever the closure costs exceed the total undiscounted benefits less the investment:

$$\text{Condition for Possible Ambiguity: } C_c > RN - C_k$$

In this situation, shown in Table 13.4, the net present value is clearly negative for two discount rates:

$$r = 0 \rightarrow \text{NPV} = RN - C_k - C_c < 0$$
$$r = \infty \rightarrow \text{NPV} = -C_k < 0$$

If there is any discount rate for which NPV is positive, there must be two solutions that make NPV = 0 (see box and Figure 13.2).

Finally, the internal rate of return also leads to different rankings than those produced by the benefit-cost ratio. Table 13.5 makes the point.

Example of Ambiguity in Calculation of Internal Rate of Return

Consider Project Q in Table 13.4. One solution (see previous box) is

$$\text{IRR}_1 = 16.18\%$$

The other is lower since for a zero discount rate the net present value is negative. Thus

$$r = 0\% \rightarrow \text{NPV} = -10$$

The second solution is in fact:

$$\text{IRR}_2 = 3.89\%$$

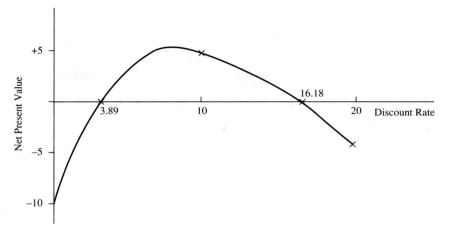

FIGURE 13.2
Net present value as a function of discount rate for Project Q, illustrating its ambiguous values of 3.89% and 16.18% for the internal rate of return.

Cost-effectiveness ratio. The cost-effectiveness ratio is similar to the benefit-cost ratio. The main conceptual difference is that benefits are measured by their physical quantity rather than in monetary units. This quantity is considered the effectiveness of a project. The ratio is thus

$$\text{Cost-Effectiveness} = \frac{\text{(Units of Benefit)}}{\text{Cost}}$$

For example, one might evaluate safety projects in terms of "lives saved from accident per thousand dollars." Naturally, we wish to maximize cost-effectiveness.

It is sometimes useful to invert the cost-effectiveness ratio, so that one has the average cost per unit of effectiveness. This can be useful when one tries to estimate suitable prices for services.

Cost-effectiveness is widely used in government agencies, particularly those that produce services that do not have a market price, or for which it seems

TABLE 13.5
Example of how ranking of projects by internal rate of return and benefit-cost ratio can differ

Project	Investment C_k ($)	Annual benefit R ($)	Project life N years	Benefit-cost $r = 3\%$	Internal rate of return (%)
A	1000	200	10	1.71	15.10 (best)
B	1000	125	20	1.86 (best)	10.93

unsuitable to charge a price. These services include public goods such as environmental protection, defense, public health, and police. The criterion is only suitable when the benefits do not have a monetary value: it would be appropriate for the Environmental Protection Agency to do a cost-effectiveness analysis to find the best way to reduce a carcinogenic pollutant, but not to evaluate a new heating system that would reduce the energy bills of its headquarters.

The principal peculiar advantage of the cost-effectiveness ratio is indeed that it avoids the awkward issue of trying to assign monetary values to benefits such as "lives saved." These estimates are extremely controversial both as regards the actual value and the ethical basis. There are, for example, many ways used in practice to value life; the courts, for example, do this routinely when awarding death benefits. These amounts vary widely, however, and there is no good average value. Furthermore, there is also considerable argument about the proper ethical basis for assigning a price to life: should all life be valued equally? or should the family be compensated more for the loss of the breadwinner than for a dependent grandparent? Any monetary value assigned to such benefits is therefore not likely to be widely acceptable, so that neither is a benefit-cost analysis based on such figures. It is therefore preferable, for these cases, to sidestep this difficulty and to focus on getting the greatest benefit for the public's money. This is an objective that all can support.

Our analysis of the primary water supply system for New York City provides a good example of the use of cost-effectiveness analysis. In this case, a main objective of the investment in City Tunnel Number 3 was to raise the minimum pressure of the water as delivered. Designs with different diameters and layouts were more or less effective as shown by Figure 13.3 (a reproduction of Figure 4.10). In this case we were able to indicate that the original design was not particularly cost-effective, and that much more value for money could be obtained with a less expensive design using a smaller diameter. This is the project that was chosen.

A major disadvantage of the cost-effectiveness ratio is that it does not define any minimum standard. Since it does not place effectiveness on the same scale as cost, it provides no way to know whether the improvements offered by a project are worthwhile in all. Thus in Figure 13.3, we can identify the best design for a project if we are going to do it, but cannot use the analysis to justify the project itself. What if there is no need for the "benefit" provided by the project and if it is therefore essentially worthless?

Payback period. The payback period is the number of periods, usually measured in years, it takes for the net *undiscounted* benefits of each period to equal (to pay back) the initial investment. The method assumes that these benefits are equal in each future year. The formula is then:

$$\text{Payback Period} = \frac{\text{Initial Investment}}{\text{Annual Net Undiscounted Benefits}}$$

The concept of the payback period is distinct from the other evaluation criteria in that it explicitly recognizes some of the time aspects of a project.

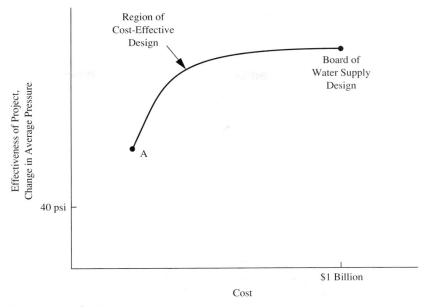

FIGURE 13.3
Cost-effectiveness curve for the Third City Water Tunnel for New York City, the envelope of best performance for the cost of hundreds of designs simulated by computer. The most cost-effective designs are at the knee of the curve.

The nature of the payback period can be appreciated by considering its formula in detail. Given that a project provides an annual net benefit of R each period for N periods, the payback period is

$$\text{Payback Period} = \frac{C_k}{R}$$

This can be restated in terms of a benefit-cost ratio by recalling (see Section 11.3) that

$$\text{Present Value of Benefits} = \frac{R}{(\text{Capital Recovery Factor})}$$

We then have

$$\text{Payback Period} = \left[\frac{\text{Benefit}}{\text{Cost}}\right]^{-1} (\text{Capital Recovery Factor})^{-1}$$

That is, the payback period varies inversely with the benefit-cost ratio: the shorter the payback period, the higher the benefit-cost.

The relationship between the payback period and the benefit-cost ratio is more obvious when we consider the limiting case for long term projects for which the capital recovery factor approximately equals r (see Section 11.3). Then

$$\left[\frac{\text{Benefit}}{\text{Cost}} \right] = [r(\text{Payback Period})]^{-1}$$

As a project will only be acceptable if [Benefit/Cost] $\geq$ 1.0, the minimally acceptable payback period must be smaller than $1/r$. Thus for a discount rate of 20%, the minimum payback period is less than five years. In practice, companies often insist on payback periods of as little as two to three years.

The great advantage of the payback period is that it is simple and can be applied by anyone. It is thus an excellent mechanism for allowing middle managers and technical staff to choose among proposals without going through a detailed analysis, or to sort through many possibilities before using another criterion.

Situations suitable for the use of the payback period are often found in industry. These are projects in which some constant benefit is expected to accrue for an extended period as a result of a particular investment. A typical case would be the purchase of a new machine that would save some quantity of operating expenses each year, or some insulation or control that would regularly save on energy costs.

The disadvantage of the payback period criterion is that it is crude; it does not clearly distinguish between projects with different useful lives. For any projects with identical useful lives, for which the capital recovery factor will be identical, the payback period gives as good a measure of economic desirability as the benefit-cost ratio. When the useful lives of projects are different, the capital recovery factors are not identical and the payback period criterion can give a poor indication of the desirability of a project.

Table 13.6 provides an example of this. Project V has a shorter payback period than Project W, and would appear better by this criterion. Yet Project W is in fact more economically desirable for a wide range of discount rates. This is because W provides substantial benefits over a much longer period. Thus over a six year cycle, Project V would have to be repeated twice for a total cost of $4000 and benefits of $6000, whereas Project W would only cost $2000 and yield benefits of $4800, greater net benefits and a higher benefit-cost ratio for a range of suitable discount rates.

TABLE 13.6
Evaluation of Projects V and W, illustrating limitation of payback criterion

Project	Investment C_k ($)	Benefits by year ($)						Payback period, years	NPV at 10%	IRR (%)
		1	2	3	4	5	6			
V	2000	1000	1000	1000				2	487	23.4
W	2000	800	800	800	800	800	800	2.5	1484	32.7

13.4 COMPARISON OF CRITERIA

Table 13.7 summarizes the major features of the criteria of economic evaluation. The essential message is that no one criterion is best for all purposes. Each has its own place and role.

Businesses will generally use the internal rate of return or payback period criteria, depending on who they have doing the analysis. Senior managers and others examining major investments for the company should use the internal rate of return for its precision, despite its difficulties. Middle managers and technical staff primarily responsible for operations will find the payback criterion most effective, given its simplicity and the fact that its inaccuracy as a method may be no worse than the inaccuracy of the data.

Government agencies and international development organizations will prefer to use the benefit-cost ratio for evaluating major capital-intensive and public works. For them the general ranking of projects is an important consideration. The fact that this criterion is not perfect theoretically, since it has a bias toward capital-intensive projects and does not indicate scale, is not especially significant in a political environment, where many decisions are made for noneconomic reasons and it is mostly important to make choices that are financially worthwhile, if not optimal.

Government agencies responsible for the delivery of services which effectively do not have market prices — such as defense, fire protection, public health, and education — should use cost-effectiveness analyses to evaluate alternatives for improving these services. Because attempts to assign monetary values to such items as lives saved, cancers avoided, and years of education are so controversial — both regarding the numbers and on fundamental ethical grounds — it is most reasonable to avoid such issues. Cost-effectiveness analysis serves this purpose well.

Academics, particularly those who have not had to deal with real problems, tend to prefer the net present value criterion for its theoretical clarity. In practice, it is difficult both to apply to the important task of ranking projects of different size, and to explain to others. Surveys of business and government practice indicate that neither group ever really uses this criterion.

The differences between the net present value, benefit-cost ratio, and the internal rate of return can be illustrated graphically. Consider a situation in which we have to decide on the size of a project, for example, the height of a hydroelectric dam or the production capacity of a factory. For any given level of investment, C_k, and discount rate, r, we can calculate the net present value of the project. Each solid line in Figure 13.4 shows a possible locus of these answers for a project for which there are sizable initial fixed costs, followed by decreasing marginal returns. This graph permits us to see how the different evaluation criteria can lead to a different conclusion about the optimal size of the project.

The optimal size according to the net present value criterion using the discount rate r, is A, since this investment maximizes net present value. The optimal size according to the benefit-cost ratio is B, however, since this design

TABLE 13.7
Summary comparison of criteria for economic evaluation

Criterion	Characteristics				Advantages	Disadvantages
	Reflects scale	Ranks easily	Non $ benefits	Ease of use		
Net Present Value, NPV	NO	NO	NO	OK	Focus on value	Not Good for Ranking, Difficult Concept
Benefit/ Cost, B/C	YES	YES	NO	OK	Ranks Easily	Bias vs. Operations
Internal Rate of Return, IRR	NO	YES	NO	LOW	Approximates Rate of Return	Ambiguous Solutions
Cost/ Effectiveness, C/E	YES	YES	YES	GOOD	Handles Non-monetary Benefits	Projects May Not Compare
Payback Period	YES	YES	NO	HIGH	Simplicity	Inaccuracy

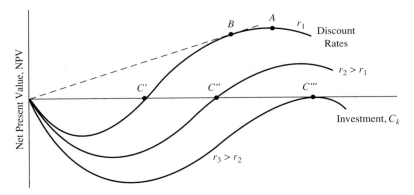

FIGURE 13.4
Illustration for showing how net present value, benefit-cost, and internal rate of return criteria lead to different prescriptions (see text).

maximizes that ratio. The solution obtained by the use of the internal rate of return is quite different: there is a different IRR for a wide range of sizes of projects, as indicated by C' and C'', and the project with the highest internal rate of return will be farthest to the right, at C'''.

13.5 RECOMMENDED PROCEDURE

How should the analyst proceed? Given the many criteria available, which should be used? The question appears complex but generally is not difficult to answer.

The first issue to resolve, in any situation, is whether the analyst really has a choice. Frequently there is no freedom: the client, agency or company has a set way of evaluating projects. In those majority of cases, the analyst will simply have to make the most of the established criterion.

How should the analyst cope when the standard evaluation criterion used by the client is inappropriate? The responsible approach is to explain carefully, as an addition to the evaluation, why the client should make adjustments in this particular case. For example, suppose a company is using the payback period criterion to evaluate machines with quite different lives: as illustrated by Table 13.6, this approach can be quite misleading. The way the author would cope with this situation is (1) to carry out the payback period analysis so that the company's managers would have an immediate point of comparison in their usual form, (2) to point out the perversity of the criterion in this specific case, so as (3) to end up with an alternative analysis that, exceptionally, seems more suitable.

When the organization routinely uses a couple of different criteria, the choice should be made according to two rules:

- Match the effort involved in the analysis with the importance of the issue.
- Use the method most suited to the peculiar nature of the problem.

The first rule leads companies to choose the payback criterion for "small" projects (which can be as large as $10 million) and the more complicated internal rate of return for larger projects. The second rule is that one should use cost-effectiveness analysis if the benefits are not monetary and, as indicated in Chapter 10 (particularly Section 10.4), decision analysis when there is considerable risk involved.

REFERENCES

Au, T., and Au, T. P., (1983). "Benefit-Cost Ratio Method," Chapter 7, and "Internal Rate of Return Method," Chapter 8, *Engineering Economics for Capital Investment Analysis*, Allyn and Bacon, Boston.

ATT Company, (1977). "Mathematics of Money," Chapter 5, and "Inflation and the Cost of Money," Chapter 10, *Engineering Economy*, 3rd ed., McGraw-Hill, New York.

PROBLEMS

13.1. *New Product Line*

An entrepreneur is considering three possibilities for investment but only has the time and management resources to do one. The initial investment and benefits of each choice are given below. Each investment is expected to last eight years.

	Financial aspects of product ($ \times 10^3$)		
	A	B	C
Initial investment	35	50	90
Annual net benefits	10	13	20
Liquidation value at end	0	2	5

(*a*) Rank the choices by net present value and benefit-cost ratio using an 8% discount rate, and by internal rate of return.

(*b*) Which product should be chosen?

13.2. *Envelope Machines*

The Eastern Stationery Co. has narrowed its choice to two alternatives for a new machine that makes envelopes from precut pieces of paper. The Ace Envelope Machine costs $20,000 and has an expected useful life of seven years. The Acme Heavy-Duty Envelope Former costs $26,000 and has an expected life span of ten years. Both machines have operating and maintenance costs of $9000 per year, can handle Eastern's demand, which is stable, and should have scrap values of $1000 at the end of their lives.

(*a*) It is clear that the Ace machine is the less expensive one of the two choices. Should Eastern buy it?

(*b*) What method of evaluation would you recommend?

(*c*) Using a discount rate of 12%, determine which machine Eastern should purchase.

13.3. *Energy-Saving Devices*

The owner of a small business wants to buy one of three energy-saving devices for his store. The costs and benefits are given in the following table. Each device has a five-year life.

	Financial aspects of device ($ \times 10^3$)		
	A	**B**	**C**
Device cost	2000	3000	3500
Annual energy savings	600	875	900
Salvage value	0	0	500

(a) Rank the devices by payback period, net present value, and benefit-cost ratio using a 10% discount rate.

(b) Rank them by payback period, net present value, and benefit-cost ratio using a 12% discount rate.

(c) Which device is better? Discuss and defend your choice.

(d) Sketch net present value vs. discount rate for devices A and B on a single graph by plotting NPV at 0, 10, 12, and 15%.

(e) Indicate on the graph the range of discount rates for which device A would be favored to B, and for which B would be favored to A.

(f) Discuss the importance of selecting a discount rate.

13.4. *Venture Banking*

A venture banking firm is comparing two ventures that are competing for an available $1 million in start-up cash. After this initial investment, the following operating costs and revenues (in $ \times 10^3$) are expected during the next eight years.

	A Operating		B Operating	
Year	Cost	Revenue	Cost	Revenue
1	100	370	300	0
2	100	370	300	0
3	100	370	300	0
4	100	370	300	1170
5	100	370	300	1170
6	100	370	300	1170
7	100	370	300	1170
8	100	370	300	1170

(a) Using a discount rate of 15%, calculate net present value, benefit-cost ratio, and net benefit-cost ratio for both A and B. Which venture should be undertaken?

(b) Same as (a), but with 20% discount rate.

13.5. *Machine Purchase*

The manager of a production plant has space for one new machine. The possible choices, with estimates of costs and benefits, are shown below. Each machine is assumed to have a five-year life.

Benefits and cost items	Values of machine ($ \times 10^3$)			
	A	**B**	**C**	**D**
Initial cost	72	25	189	26.8
Annual net benefits	20	7.45	50	8
Salvage value at end of life	0	0	15	0

(*a*) For each machine, using a discount rate of 8%, calculate the net present value, the benefit-cost ratio, and the payback period.

(*b*) Which machine should be chosen? Why?

13.6. *Mine Road*

A mining company wishes to build a road to a new quarry which, according to best estimates, will be productive for ten years. The benefits of the road will be $2M a year for ten years, after which it will be abandoned. The company has to decide among a macadam, an asphalt, or a concrete road.

Type of cost	Cost of pavement type ($M)		
	Concrete	**Asphalt**	**Macadam**
Initial, K	7	5.8	3
Annual maintenance, A	0.2	0.45	1

Using 8 and 15% discount rates, rank the alternatives by the two types of benefit-cost ratios, $(B - A)/K$ and $B/(K + A)$, and by net present value. Which road should the company choose?

$$P = \frac{R}{crf} \qquad \frac{1}{crf} \text{ for } 8\% = 8.56 \qquad \frac{1}{crf} \text{ for } 15\% = 5.85$$

13.7. *Null Alternative*

A company, whose discount rate is 5%, may choose to invest in one of the three projects described below:

Characteristic	Project		
	A	**B**	**C**
Initial cost, $M	31	26	37
Annual benefits, $M	5	5	10
Project life, years	10	8	5

(*a*) Rank the projects by benefit-cost ratio, net present value, and internal rate of return. Which project do you recommend?

(*b*) Sketch the stream of benefits the company may expect to receive on its $40M current capital over the next ten years for each project, including the null alternative. Now which project will you recommend?

13.8. *Strip Mine*
A strip mine, which eventually will have to be reconverted to a forest, is expected to have the following costs and benefits ($M):

Year	Cost	Benefit
0	10	
1		5
2		10
3		15
4–14		(breaks even)
15	25	(clean up)

(*a*) For each of the following discount rates, evaluate the project by net present value and determine whether it ought to be implemented: $r = 0\%$; $= 100\%$; $= 10\%$

(*b*) Calculate the internal rate of return. Does this mean the project is worthwhile?

13.9. *Alternatives*
Compare the following investments on the basis of the net present value, benefit-cost, net benefit-cost, and internal rate of return:

Investment	Item	Benefits and costs by year ($M)					
		0	1	2	3	4	5
1	Benefits	0	30	75	111	0	0
	Costs	90	10	25	37	0	0
2	Benefits	0	34	34	34	34	34
	Costs	75	9	9	9	9	9

Which alternative would you recommend to maximize profits, assuming an 8% opportunity cost of money?

13.10. *New Car (Again)*
See Problem 11.2. Having calculated the present value of benefits and costs,
(*a*) Evaluate this model by net present value, benefit-cost ratio, and the internal rate of return.
(*b*) Is the car a good buy? Discuss your answer.

13.11. *Transit System*
Suppose you are hired by the mayor to evaluate two sets of designs for improving the local transit system. Their costs and benefits are, in $ \times 10^3$:

Plan	Initial cost	Annual benefit
A	200	30
B	600	75

The mayor tells you to assume a 20-year life for the systems and to use a discount rate of 8%.

(a) Calculate the net present value and benefit-cost ratio for each of these designs.

(b) Do you think 8% could correctly reflect the discount rate? Why or why not?

(c) Assuming 8% is the correct opportunity cost, which design should the mayor choose? Discuss the basis for this selection.

13.12. *Criteria Review*

What are the advantages and disadvantages of each of the following criteria:

(a) benefit-cost ratio

(b) net benefit-cost ratio

(c) internal rate of return

(d) net present value

13.13. *Easy Start*

Ready-Tech's sales manager (see Problem 11.10) approaches a lab that uses the two-year payback method of evaluating commitments to new equipment. The lab would have to spend $8000 on space changes to accommodate the machine. They would then save $12,000/yr in labor costs, which, under the $10,000/yr "Regular" lease would give them a net savings of $2000/yr. The lab discount rate may be assumed to be 20%.

(a) What is the lab's payback period under the "Regular" lease? Under the "Easy Start" lease with initial payments of $7000?

(b) Should the lab acquire the machine under "Easy Start?" Discuss your evaluation.

CHAPTER
14

COST ESTIMATION

14.1 THE PROBLEM

Costs are a crucial element in systems analysis. As stressed in Chapter 1, optimal design requires a full consideration of values on a par with the technical aspects. It is meaningless to talk of a best design if one has not factored in costs: as defined by the production function (Chapter 2), there are a multitude of technically efficient combinations that may produce a desired result. Costs or relative values are the means to identify the truly best designs from the many technical candidates. The optimality conditions of Section 4.2 make this point clear: the optimum is defined by an equal weighting of Marginal Products and Marginal Costs.

Despite the importance of costs, engineers and designers tend to minimize their role in systems analysis. This is a natural psychological problem: we all normally focus on the areas we know and disregard the others. Thus it is usual for engineers to imagine simplistically that costs are something you can "look up" or "get from the accountants." This is a fundamental mistake that can have profound consequences.

The fact is that it is difficult to determine the costs to use in a systems analysis. The most obvious figures are likely to be wrong; if they are used the design is almost certainly going to be poor. The problem is to determine the appropriate costs. To do so, a systems analyst must deal with several issues, each discussed in turn in this chapter. These concern:

- *Estimation*, the measurement of the concept
- *Concepts*, the correct idea about what is to be estimated
- *Dynamics*, the variation in costs over time
- *Technological Choice*, the further variation in costs due to fundamental changes in the structure of costs

14.2 ESTIMATION

The answer to the question: "what is the cost of X?" would seem straightforward, even trivial. In everyday life, we are accustomed to determining and comparing the prices of things we want. We typically do not find this difficult; we check the price tags in different stores, read ads in the papers, and so on. It is natural to think that we could easily extend this process to the determination of the costs of steel, computers, trucks, labor, and all the other inputs X to a production process. Unfortunately, this is not the case.

The estimation of costs is complex because they are routinely misstated—from the point of view of a systems analysis. Published costs, either in trade journals or an organization's books of account, suffer systematically from errors of omission and commission. Some elements of costs are normally left out, and others are routinely distorted.

The root cause of these difficulties lies with the accounting system, the formal procedures for keeping track of money in any organization. This system has been constructed for distinct purposes, which it usually accomplishes well. Its goals are, however, quite different from those of systems analysts. This is what makes measurements of costs difficult.

Accounting systems have been designed to keep managers and employees honest. One basic motivation is to account for all receipts and expenses. Accounts are thus meticulous tabulations of all monies received and spent. To facilitate this purpose, accounts use conventional categories of types of expenses—such as payroll, transport, insurance, and so on. This fact is a primary source of the errors of omission—from a system analyst's point of view.

Accounting systems are also designed to present financial situations conservatively. The idea is to counterbalance the managers' tendency to over-state their performance and profits. Accounting systems thus deliberately avoid using subjective appraisals of value. They have, for example, typically excluded inflationary effects and recorded the value of an asset as the price originally paid for it rather than try to represent what it is really worth in the market. In the same vein, accounting systems routinely assume that assets lose value over time. This depreciation is set by standard formulas which easily do not reflect reality. These conventions are the sources of systematic distortions in our estimates of costs for systems analysis.

Errors of omission. Suppose a company pays $500 per ton to a supplier for some material. Superficially, it might appear that this cost per unit must be the marginal cost of that material, the figure that is needed for an optimization. But is it really? Does it include all the factors that represent the cost to the system of acquiring and using a unit of that material?

Normally, the cost entered into the accounts of a company omits many of the elements that constitute the true cost of an item. What about transportation, for instance? If a company's employees pick the material up, the cost of their time, their vehicle, and its fuel should be part of the marginal cost of the item.

So should its insurance and packaging. The difference between the amount that is paid for and what is usable after breakage and theft should also be factored in. Every transaction in an organization must also be serviced by a broad range of people such as purchasing agents and accountants. Their services are part of the cost of an item, as are even their medical expenses and pension rights. All these elements are some part of the marginal cost of an item. The accounting system will deal with them in a variety of categories, quite distinct from that in which the price paid to the supplier is entered. This price simply does not reflect the true marginal cost.

The omissions do not always increase costs. The stated price may not reflect subsequent rebates or discounts for prompt payment. It may not include associated services or other benefits. The true cost of any input depends on all the surcharges and discounts that are an effective part of the price paid to obtain it, but which are buried in the accounting system.

Errors of commission. Consider an agency that acquired property in a city 25 years ago or more. Conventionally, the value of the land in the accounting books will be stated as the amount actually paid; no increase due to inflation would have been incorporated. Thus, even if the increase in real estate prices had been moderate, the true value of the property would be several times its original cost. With only 6% average annual increases in value, the true cost would be over four times higher after 25 years (see the "rule of 72," Section 11.4).

Depreciation as practiced in accounting introduces a comparable form of distortion. The value of buildings and equipment is routinely reduced by formula each year independent of what actually happens to the value of the property (unless it is actually destroyed). Established companies thus usually have substantial assets whose nominal costs are close to zero.

The conclusion to be drawn from this discussion is that systems analysts cannot simply "look up" the costs of the inputs; they cannot rely on the massive data generated by the accounting system to provide them directly with good estimates of the costs they require for optimization. A most careful effort is necessary in order to obtain good estimates of the costs that should be used in the analysis.

14.3 CONCEPTS

Marginal costs are at the heart of a systems analysis, as Chapter 4 indicates. We need to know the incremental effects on total costs of any decision to use resources in a design. This is the key concept in estimating costs.

Determining marginal costs can be confusing. First, one must of course distinguish between historic costs and the future costs that would actually apply to the system being designed. Secondly, it is important to refer to the "opportunity cost" of any use of a resource. This is its total effect on the system and may be quite different from its price. Finally, one has to deal with the complexity of allocating *joint costs*, those that are shared by many items.

Future versus past costs. Future costs are the only ones relevant to future decisions. They are not easy to determine. They can be presumed to be different from the historic costs tabulated in the accounting system. Even after the accounting data have been carefully analyzed to determine the true cost of an item (see Section 14.2), these *"actual costs"* are not immediately relevant; they need to be adjusted to future conditions.

To get estimates of future costs, one must first adjust present or historic costs for inflation and whatever other factors that may occur over time. These forecasts are quite difficult to make accurately, as the example in Section 15.1 emphasizes. Reasonable estimates of current trends in the costs of materials and labor are available, however, in specialized trade publications. The *Engineering News-Record* compiles these estimates for civil engineers, for example. Their series has the merit of projecting unit costs by regions, so that estimators can adapt to the specific local situations that may apply.

Future costs also differ from current costs because we learn to do things better, to avoid past mistakes. The rule of thumb, reflected by the empirical learning curve, is that we may hope for a 10% to 30% reduction in unit costs as the cumulative number of units produced doubles, as indicated in Section 4.5. Naturally, this general phenomenon needs to be validated for any company and any activity. Past trends can be plotted into the learning curve for that activity, and extrapolated into the future.

Opportunity cost versus expense. The "opportunity cost" of an item is its value in the best available alternative. It is the maximum value that must be given up if the resource is used in the project under consideration. Used in this sense, which is traditional, the concept is the same as that used when referring to the "opportunity cost" of capital (see Section 12.3). By definition, the "opportunity cost" of a resource is its true marginal cost, and should be used in the analysis.

> **Semantic caution:** As indicated in Section 12.3, the "opportunity cost" as used in economics does not have the same meaning as in linear programming; it really is the shadow price of that resource (see Sections 6.2 and 6.3).

The opportunity cost of an item is often much higher than its price or the expense of getting it. This is a source of confusion in estimating the true marginal cost: an analyst may focus on the price and neglect the real value.

As an example of the potential difference between the opportunity cost and the price of something, consider a person who wishes to build a home on a piece of land that would sell for L. The marginal cost of the land is clearly L if the person has to buy it. But what if the person already has it, perhaps because it was an inheritance? The expense of using it is nothing; there is no outlay of capital for it. But the opportunity cost—and the marginal cost to be used in the analysis—is still L: if the land is not used for a home, it could be sold for L and the person using it still gives up L by devoting the land to construction.

In general, the "opportunity costs" of items often differ substantially from the money paid for them because these prices fail to adjust to actual values. For example, suppose that a particular resource is an especially ingenious designer who is good at reducing manufacturing costs. The opportunity cost of using this designer on some project is the maximum net amount this person would save if used on alternative projects—this could be millions. Theoretically, if really worth this much, a talented designer could negotiate an equivalent salary (perhaps through a capable agent and with free agent status). In practice, the designer's salary is likely to be limited by industry standards and will not reflect true opportunity cost. Operationally, the marginal cost of using the designer on a project is not just that person's salary, it is also the loss of savings to the best alternative project.

Joint costs. Costs that are incurred for the benefit of many different activities are *joint costs*. For example, a university has a president, central staff, and libraries that are concerned with all its activities: education and research in many fields. By definition these costs are not uniquely associated with any one activity.

True marginal costs are difficult to determine whenever there are significant joint costs. There is no clear way to allocate joint costs. How, for instance, should one divide up the cost of operating a university library? Would it be right to do so according to the number of students? Or would this be unfair to the undergraduates who require less of the expensive research journals? Should it be according to the number of books borrowed, regardless of their cost? And so on.

Accounting systems routinely allocate joint costs to activities on the basis of formulas which, although perhaps quite satisfactory for accounting, may be inappropriate for a systems analysis. For example, a common procedure is to allocate joint costs in proportion to revenues.

Thus at MIT the library expenses are largely prorated to the research contracts according to their size; the use by students is minimized. This is a pleasant way to get research contracts to pay for the libraries. But this perspective does not give what the systems analyst needs to know in thinking about increasing student enrollment. The accounting formula does not indicate the true cost on the library systems of additional students. This marginal cost of an action is what is required and is the concept to keep in mind.

14.4 DYNAMICS

The marginal costs of an activity depend on the period under consideration, on whether we are concerned with the short run or the long run. As a general rule, the short run costs do not equal the long run costs.

For many purposes it is sufficient to divide costs into capital costs, C_k, and variable costs, C_v, as was done in Sections 6.6, 13.3, and 13.4. More precisely, costs can be thought of as being fixed, C_f, and variable. The *fixed costs* are all those that cannot be changed at any time. They obviously include the capital costs invested in the plant, but also the other fixed commitments that cannot be immediately changed, such as leases on equipment and contracts with staff.

The exact content of the fixed costs depends on the period under consideration; the longer the period, the more that can be changed. Leases that must be paid in the short run do not have to be renewed in the longer run, for example. A variety of expenses can thus pass from fixed to variable costs, and this changes the marginal costs over the different periods.

Similarly, the variable costs differ between the short run and the long run. In the short run, production is normally limited by the facilities already in place. This means that it will be difficult, that is expensive, to expand production in the short run. Given a plant of particular size, for example, one can exceed normal production capacity by going to overtime and paying the work force more. The shadow price on the short-term constraints is generally high (see discussion in Sections 3.2 and 6.2). In the long run, however, one would have the opportunity to build extra capacity, to reduce overtime and other costs of congestion, and thus to lower the variable costs.

The effects of the differences in the fixed and variable costs over time typically follow a systematic pattern. This is shown in Figure 14.1: the average cost of making a unit of Y normally rises relatively rapidly either above or below the level of production for which a system is designed. In the longer run, however, the system can be tailored to a higher or lower level of output, and needless expenses can be dropped by closing facilities, or an extra plant can be added to avoid congestion or overtime.

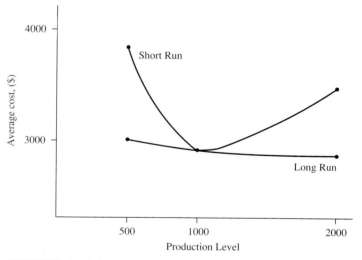

FIGURE 14.1
Typical relation between short- and long-run average costs, as illustrated by example situation.

Long- and Short-Run Costs

Consider a manufacturing system producing units of Y. At any time it has fixed costs of $100,000 for its central staff (president, supervisors, and so on) and $200,000 per warehouse. In its most efficient configuration, it has one warehouse for every 250 units produced. Its variable costs are $2000 per unit of Y up to its design capacity, beyond which they double, due to overtime payments to the workers and other costs of congestion.

To calculate short-run average costs, we have to start from the current situation. Suppose the system is now configured to produce 1000 Y. Its total costs in $\$ \times 10^3$ are then:

$$C(Y) = 100 + 4(200) + Y(2) + Y'(2)$$

where Y' is the extra production beyond the design level of 1000. The average cost can be calculated by dividing by Y. Doing this for three levels of production we obtain:

	Production level		
	500	**1000**	**2000**
Short run Average cost, ($)	3800	2900	3450

To calculate long-run average costs we have to deal with the state of the system when configured for the appropriate level of production. If this were less than 1000, warehouses would be closed; if it were more, additional ones would be opened and overtime reduced. For example, the total cost for a long-run production of 500 would be:

$$C(Y)_{500} = 100 + 2(200) + Y(2)$$

For 2000 it would be:

$$C(Y)_{2000} = 100 + 8(200) + Y(2)$$

We then have:

	Production level		
	500	**1000**	**2000**
Long run Average cost, ($)	3000	2900	2850

Figure 14.1 compares the above results.

The precise relationship between the short- and long-run costs depends on the specifics of any situation, and must be calculated accordingly. See the box on page 269 for an example.

14.5   TECHNOLOGICAL CHANGE

Long-run, future costs may also differ from either the short-run or historical costs because of technological change. In estimating the cost of a new system we must recognize that we may be dealing with a different production function than we currently face. This naturally leads to a different cost function (see Sections 4.4 and 4.5).

Most obviously, new discoveries will lead to greater efficiencies. Thus, jets replaced piston engines in aircraft, computers replaced mechanical calculators, and fiber optics replace metallic telephone lines.

More subtly, the change in technology will occur because a change in scale will make one technology cheaper on average than another. Typically, as indicated in the discussion of break-even analysis in Section 6.6, higher levels of production will lead to technologies with higher capital cost but lower variable costs. As the amount transported in a region increases, for instance, it may be cheaper to use railroads than highways: the greater traffic compensates for the extra capital cost.

This second kind of difference between long-run and current costs does not require any new technology; it may even revert to an old one, as when subways are built in cities to replace automobile transport. For this reason this kind of technological change may be forgotten by systems designers, when it should not be.

14.6   SUMMARY

Costs, critical parameters of systems analyses, are difficult to estimate. The required figures are not obvious; they are typically buried in accounting data and must be carefully constructed.

There is no simple set of procedures that will yield the correct numbers. To obtain valid estimates one must focus on the essential issue: what is the incremental effect of the proposed changes to the system?

Since systems design is mainly concerned with future projects, analysts should keep in mind the ways costs change over time. In the long run costs are typically more flexible than in the short run as current constraints change. In addition, technological change may alter the possibilities radically.

REFERENCES

ATT Company, (1977). "The Nature of Costs," Chapter 6, *Engineering Economy*, 3rd ed., McGraw-Hill, New York.

Pindyck, R. S., and Rubinfeld, D. L., (1989). "The Cost of Production," Chapter 7, *Microeconomics*, Macmillan, New York.

PROBLEMS

14.1. *Cost Analysis*
Define the fixed, variable, marginal, and average costs for the cost functions:
(a) Cost $= 100 + 24X^2$
(b) Cost $= 100 + 12X + 0.7X^2$

14.2. *Airport Expansion*
An airport authority is expanding its facilities to reduce waiting time for takeoffs and landings, and generally to improve its service. The work costs $20M of which 20% will be for flight takeoff and landing, 15% for improved passenger flow, 30% for improved freight handling, and 35% for general maintenance and appearance. The airport is used by three airlines whose number of flights, passengers, and tons of freight last year were:

Airline	Flights	Passengers	Freight, tons
A	5000	250,000	600
B	3000	200,000	250
C	2000	50,000	150

What costs would you suggest be charged to each of the airlines for expansion and improvement of the airfield? Justify your answer and explain any assumptions that you have made.

14.3. *Costs of Seasonal Service*
This is an example of a general problem, faced by all producers that face seasonal variations. For specificity we consider an electric power system with the following simplified pattern of use: in 9 months of the year 100 MW of capacity are required; in the remaining 3 months, 150 MW are needed.

Suppose the annual capital cost of building units of capacity is $5M/year for each 50 MW plant (i.e., $0.1M per MW); the operating cost is $0.01M/MW-month; and the annual overhead on the system is $3M/yr.
(a) What is the average cost per MW-month produced?
(b) What is the average cost per MW-month of producing the base load, that is, the steady use of 100 MW each month?
(c) What is the average cost per MW-month of providing for the peak load of 50 extra MW for each of three summer months?
(d) Suppose that the base use in the off peak period were to increase by 10 MW, while the peak use did not rise. What is the marginal cost to the system of providing these extra 90 MW-months of power?
(e) Suppose the system has to supply 90 MW-months more power evenly during the three peak months, thus requiring 30 MW more capacity. Suppose further that this new capacity will—because of new technology and safety regulations—have a capital cost of $0.4M/MW annually. How does this affect the cost to the consumer? Discuss.
(f) The situations represented in (d) and (e) are reasonably typical. Discuss the implications for efforts designed to get customers to shift their pattern of use from peak to off-peak.

CHAPTER
15

RISK
ASSESSMENT

15.1 THE ISSUE

Most of engineering planning and design assumes that we know the strength, cost, and performance of our materials, that we can determine what the loads on a system will be and how it will respond. This assumption is convenient because

- It enormously simplifies the complexity of design—we can deal with only one situation instead of the many combinations of possibilities that would occur if different parameters took on different values.
- It allows designers to bypass the mathematical difficulties of probability and statistics—never popular subjects.

Unfortunately, this convenient assumption is generally false. Nothing is really certain in this world (except death and taxes, as the saying goes, and these are even uncertain as to time and amount). The fact is that our environment is not deterministic; it is probabilistic.

Experienced designers are well aware of the inconvenient reality of risk. They know that the stated strength of materials is a crude approximation; that, for example, tests of bars of steel with a nominal strength of 40 ksi will actually yield values mostly distributed above that value but with some below. They know that the costs of a project are extremely difficult to estimate accurately. They also know that forecasts of traffic, of growth, of demand for a product are notoriously unreliable. Numerous retrospective analyses have demonstrated the truism that "The forecast is always wrong."

Costs specifically are difficult to estimate, even in the simplest situation. Cost overruns are not a peculiarity of military spending; who has not found out that the cost of repairing a car or television set is quite different from the estimate? Figure 15.1 documents a specific case of this phenomenon. It concerns the cost of resurfacing airport runways, which is one of the very simplest projects to estimate. A resurfacing project requires one to roll asphalt over a relatively flat and smooth surface of clearly specified dimensions. It is a low-technology job, involving known quantities and no hidden elements. And yet, as Figure 15.1 shows, professional engineers have great difficulty in making correct estimates of the cost of this simple project. Weather is a factor, the performance of management or labor is variable, there may or may not be competition to lower the cost of the job. It turns out that the real costs are not only higher than the estimates on average (an understandable bias) but, most importantly, are broadly distributed!

Forecasts of future loads on a system are especially subject to large error. This is because it is people who ultimately place demands on the system — by choosing to use electricity, to call their friends, or to buy a product — and people's psychology and reasons for choice are almost beyond comprehension. This phenomenon is nicely illustrated by the analysis of the forecasts of the

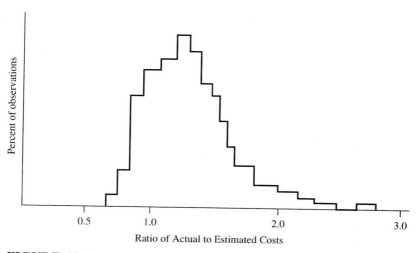

FIGURE 15.1
Probability distribution of ratio of real to estimated costs for routine airport projects (data in constant dollars for Western United States).

TABLE 15.1
Unreliability of forecasts as illustrated by large median error (source: U.S. FAA six-year forecasts)

Forecast passengers	Forecast error (median, %)
U.S. Domestic	> 15.8
U.S. International	> 20.4

U.S. Federal Aviation Administration. This agency employs the most competent professionals, using the most careful procedures, to publish annual forecasts of airline traffic. They have been doing this for about 30 years, which allows us to estimate their reliability with confidence. Table 15.1 shows the result of one of many analyses of the FAA data: their median error in forecast in just six years is about 20%! This example helps make the point: Forecasts are unreliable.

What difference does this make? One might well ask. Is it not equally likely that the actual numbers are above as below the forecast? That the errors cancel out over the long run? That we do just as well by sticking to the deterministic forecast? The answer is no and again no. The distributions do matter.

Most immediately, the distributions affect evaluation because they often involve ratios, such as for benefit-cost. The average value of such ratios is simply not the ratio of the averages of the numerator and denominators. Specifically,

$$EV\left(\frac{B}{C}\right) \neq \frac{EV(B)}{EV(C)}$$

where $EV(\cdot)$ is a standard notation to indicate expected value. Evaluations based on deterministic or average forecasts can thus easily be incorrect. (See box for concrete examples.)

Additionally, it is normal for people to feel quite differently about relative departures from the average. Typically, a catastrophic loss is much more significant to a person than a spectacular gain. In general, as developed fully in Chapters 18 to 20, people value relative gains and losses in a highly nonlinear manner. This phenomenon makes it even more inappropriate to focus on linear averages.

The bottom line is both that there is considerable uncertainty in the benefits and costs of a system, and that it matters. Neglecting the uncertainty is valid only as a first approximation, when the consequences are not especially important nor the situation especially risky. In general, however, the system designer must deal with risk, and must first of all assess it.

Average Benefit/Cost versus Ratios of Average Benefits and Costs

Consider a simple example where the benefits and costs are symmetrically distributed around their respective averages. The benefits are either 2 or 10, $EV(B) = 6$; the costs are 2 or 4, $EV(C) = 3$. The ratio of average benefits to costs is thus:

$$\frac{EV(B)}{EV(C)} = \frac{6}{3} = 2$$

Now consider two possible cases. The average benefit/cost ratio for each is significantly different from the above ratio of averages.

Case 1: Benefits and Costs Are Independent

These parameters may easily vary quite independently of each other. The benefits might fluctuate according to the whims of the public or the success of marketing, neither of which may bear any relation to the relative success in controlling costs. In this case there are four possible combinations:

Result	Benefit	Cost	B/C
Wild success	10	2	5
Success	10	4	2.5
Breakdown	2	2	1.0
Loss	2	4	0.5
Average			2.25

Case 2: Benefits and Costs Are Correlated

Both factors may also sometimes be correlated. Good management will successfully control costs and market the project and bad management will not. In this case there are only two possibilities:

Result	Benefit	Cost	B/C
Wild success	10	2	5
Loss	2	4	0.5
Average			2.75

15.2 METHODS

Estimates of probability and risk can be made by one of four basic methods. In order of increasing judgment and difficulty, these are:

- Logic
- Frequency
- Statistical Models
- Judgment

These are presented in turn.

This discussion is primarily directed toward the explicit estimate of probability distributions. It also applies to estimates of specific levels of any item of interest, such as the cost of a new facility. Indeed, once we recognize that no parameter can be known with absolute certainty, every estimate must—whether we like it or not—be considered part of a probability distribution. An estimate of the level of any parameter must realistically be considered a most likely or modal value, which could vary over some range—whether that is expressed or not.

Logic. In some cases probabilities can be deduced by logical argument. This occurs when the number of possibilities is finite and can be defined in advance, and when the mechanism that creates the outcomes is clearly specified. These cases are extremely rare in practice.

Logic is most easily applied to problems involving card games, the rolling of dice, roulette wheels, and the like. For example, we may calculate the probability of obtaining a queen from a deck of cards as $\frac{1}{13}$—assuming that the pack is a complete, standard set without any jokers and has been thoroughly shuffled.

This method permits exact calculations of the probability of many complicated situations. For example, you could use logic to estimate the probability of getting a pair of aces when your opponent has two kings, and other items of similar interest. It therefore occupies an important place in textbooks on probability. Unfortunately, real problems in systems design do not generally meet the narrow conditions necessary to make this method practical.

Frequency. Many probability distributions can easily be estimated simply by observing the frequency with which events have occurred in the past. Observing these frequencies is the same as observing the past probability distribution. This approach thus applies when we can reasonably assume that the probability of future events has not been altered by any process that has occurred between the time of observation and the moment of interest.

The frequency method is therefore routinely applied to natural phenomena such as earthquakes and patterns of rainfall. It should not be applied unquestionably to these problems, however. Just because an event is produced by nature does not mean that it is unchanged by anything we do. The number of earth-quakes, for example, routinely increases when we build a major water reservoir in a region: the heavy load of the water can cause abrupt settlements. Likewise, patterns of rainfall can vary when human settlement eliminates forests and discharges warm particulate matter to the atmosphere.

This method can also be applied to many aspects of engineered systems, especially those where reason or experience indicates that the probability distributions are reasonably constant. For example, the probability distribution of the length of telephone calls, a pattern needed to design efficient telephone systems, has been traditionally estimated by the past frequency of calls of specified length. (See box for another example.)

In applying the method we must always be on the lookout for reasons why the process has changed and past frequencies are no longer good estimates of the probability distribution. This typically occurs when technology changes. The length of telephone calls in many cities, for example, has been noticeably changed by the way people use personal computers to access mainframes over the telephone network.

Probability of Failure of Dams

Until recently, the major U.S. agencies in charge of the construction of dams assumed that their probability of failure was zero. The line was that "well-built dams" (to be understood as ours) "do not fail." This is a good example of the overconfidence discussed in Section 15.5. It is also an argument difficult to maintain in the face of the failure of a major dam such as the Teton Dam in Idaho.

Colleagues and I estimated the probability of failure of major dams on behalf of the U.S. Water Resources Council. We did this by frequency analysis.

Our first step was to identify a period over which the frequency of failure could reasonably be considered stable. We took this to be the period backward toward the last major change in the technology of construction of dams, specifically the development of the methods to build large concrete dams safely.

We then turned to the catalogs listing the major dams worldwide to identify both their number in any year and the cases of failure. We could thus calculate the accumulated experience with major dams, which we measured in "dam-years," and compare it to the observed number of failures.

The probability of failure of major dams thus turns out to be

$$P(\text{Failure of Dam}) = 10^{-4} \text{ per dam-year}$$

Specifically, a major dam that operates for 100 years has an estimated probability of failure of

$$P(\text{Failure of Dam}) = 1\% \text{ over life of dam}$$

Statistical models. Statistical models for the estimation of parameters combine the main elements of both the frequency method and the judgment method, which is described below. A statistical model is essentially one or more equations describing a relationship between some parameter, y, and other quantities, x_i:

$$y = f(x_i)$$

These models are derived by statistical analysis of past data on y and x_i, as described in specialized texts.

Because these models rely on past data, they incorporate the assumption of the frequency method that the situation in the past can legitimately be extrapolated to the present or future. Additionally, these methods incorporate judgment, which is involved in specifying the exact form of the function $f(x_i)$. Even if theory suggests the general ingredients of the function, much judgment is required to specify its exact form. Economic theory indicates, for example, that the quantity of an item that will be bought depends on its price and quality. The actual form of the equation combining price and quantity, whether additive or multiplicative, and the precise way these quantities should be measured is not uniquely specified by theory. Much judgment is thus involved in using statistical models.

Statistical models tend to be deceptive. This is because they typically appear to be very technical and sophisticated. From a strictly mathematical point of view, these models may indeed be very precise. This fact does not, however, preclude the other reality that the sophisticated analysis is based on judgments that are open to question. The result is that, despite the appearance of precision, statistical models are generally about as inaccurate as methods based on judgment alone. A chain is as strong as its weakest link. Table 15.1 made the point, as does Figure 15.3 subsequently.

Judgment. Many estimates must, finally, be based on judgment. Systems designers may, for example, be required to estimate the cost or performance of a new space shuttle, computer, or material. Managers may have to estimate the public's acceptance of a new product or operation as against other alternatives. In general analysts often have to deal with situations for which there is no exact precedent. Unique situations preclude the use of frequency or statistical means to provide estimates. The analyst may, of course, use previous experience to guide the estimate but will, at the end, have to rely on judgment.

The estimates derived from judgment are known as *subjective probabilities*, subjective in that they emerge from individual feelings about a situation rather than purely from objective measures. Subjective probabilities are often highly debatable, even if they are derived from expert opinion. Individual experts are often quite positive about their estimates, an overconfidence discussed in Section 15.5, but groups of experts are quite likely to disagree.

While subjective estimates are often questionable, they will often be all the analyst has and must, therefore, be used as a start. Because these estimates are dubious it is important to revise them as soon as possible with additional information about the situation. The proper revision of estimates is a key ingredient to any risk assessment in practice.

15.3 REVISION OF ESTIMATES

A frequent problem in risk assessment is that of revising preliminary estimates of probability on the basis of new information. To appreciate the range of situations in which it is necessary to know how to revise previous estimates of probability, consider these examples:

- Exploration: Teams are sent out to prospect for desirable properties, such as geologists looking for conditions favorable to oil.
- Experimentation: Prototypes are built and tested before full-scale production is begun.
- Diagnosis: Routine tests are applied to a population to see which members warrant special attention, as for a disease.
- Market studies: New products are distributed in specific areas to see how customers will respond.

A most important feature of the problem is that, in general, the acquisition of new information does not remove all uncertainty about a situation. New information only changes our perception of the probabilities of various outcomes. When exploratory geologists find a salt dome, for example, they have not proven that oil is present; they have found a condition which makes oil more likely. Even when drillers actually tap oil, they have not removed all uncertainty about its extent or volume. Likewise, an experiment cannot prove or disprove that a full-scale process will work. The experiment may have been faulty; there may be difficulties extrapolating from the experiment to the larger reality.

There is also always uncertainty in the relation between the information acquired and the phenomenon of interest. Formally, there is always the possibility of "false positives" and "false negatives." "False positives" are the erroneous indications that a situation exists when it actually does not. For example, a person reacts positively to a tuberculosis test when not infected. A "false negative" is the opposite; it is the false indication that a situation does not exist. For example, a person passes the tuberculosis test when actually infected. (See Section 17.3 for a detailed discussion.)

These are two formal methods for revising preliminary probabilities on the basis of new information: Bayes' Theorem and Likelihood Ratios. Bayes' Theorem is the standard formula, and is best used when there is only one piece of information to be incorporated in the revision of an estimated probability. Likelihood ratios are best when there are many pieces of information.

The possibility that the new information is either incomplete or misleading means that we must be careful how we interpret it. This is especially important because, as Section 15.5 indicates, the intuitive methods people use are notoriously influenced by subjective, psychological biases.

Bayes' Theorem. Bayes' Theorem is a simple process for revising estimates of probabilities. The difficulty in understanding it lies in the elements of the formula. These are simple enough too, but generally are puzzling when first seen.

There are four elements to Bayes' Theorem. They are defined as follows.

1. The *Prior Probability*, $P(E)$, of an event E. This is the preliminary estimate of probabilities that you have before new information is acquired.
2. The *Posterior Probability*, $P(E/O)$, of the event E after some information has been acquired in the form of a specific observation O. This is the revised estimate of probability. The notation E/O is to be read "E given that (or conditional on) O having been observed." It indicates that this piece of information has been included in the estimate.
3. The *Conditional Probability*, $P(O/E)$, of the observation and the event E. This is the frequency with which an observation is associated with the existence of E, for example, that salt domes (O) are present when there is oil (E). It is important to note here that the relationship between O and E is not symmetric. For example, the probability of observing that a person is male given that the person is a king is: $P(\text{male/king}) = 1.0$, since by definition kings are men. On the other hand, since there are only a few kings on earth, the probability that any male is a king is about one in a billion: $P(\text{king/male}) \sim 10^{-9}$. In general, $P(O/E) \neq P(E/O)$.

Example for the Definition of Probabilities

Consider a factory with two kinds of staff: line workers, L, and staff, S. There are 600 line workers and 150 staff. The ratio of the sexes in each category is different: Men constitute 60% of the line workers and 10% of the staff.

Suppose that we were interested in the probability that a factory worker we meet belongs to the staff:

1. The prior probability is the frequency of staff workers. They are 150 out of a total of 750, so $P(\text{Staff}) = 0.2$.
2. The posterior probability after having made an observation, that he is male for example, is $P(\text{Staff/Male})$. This is not obvious from the data and must be calculated by Bayes' Theorem (after the observation of the worker's sex is made).
3. The conditional probabilities in this case are the frequency of male staff members: $P(\text{Male/Staff}) = 0.1$; $P(\text{Male/Line}) = 0.6$.
4. The probability of the observation of a male is their frequency among the total number of factory workers

$$P(\text{Male}) = P(\text{Male/Staff})\, P(\text{Staff}) + P(\text{Male/Line})\, P(\text{Line}) = 0.5$$

This may also be viewed as the total number of men divided by the number of factory workers.

---

4. The *Probability of the Observation*, $P(O)$. This is the probability of making the observation, O, considering all the ways it may occur. (Note, this is for a specific observation that has been made, not for a distribution over all possible values that could be made.) The observation may indeed be associated with outcome E_1, and all the other possible outcomes E_i. The probability of observing O is then

$$P(O) = \sum P(O/E_i) \, P(E_i)$$

These definitions are illustrated by the example in the preceding box.

Bayes' Theorem is a straightforward use of the above elements:

$$P(E/O) = P(E) \left\{ \frac{P(O/E)}{P(O)} \right\}$$

The revised estimate of probability is simply the preliminary, prior estimate multiplied by a factor for revision, based upon an observation. Applying Bayes' Theorem is direct, once the elements have been defined (see box).

The strength of the factor of revision of the estimate, that is, the ratio of the prior and posterior estimates of the probability, depends on two considerations.

Use of Bayes' Theorem

We are at the same factory used to illustrate the definition of the different kinds of probabilities. Being just about to meet a male worker, you want to estimate the probability that he is on the staff.

You thus calculate:

$$P(\text{Staff/Male}) = P(\text{Staff}) \left\{ \frac{P(\text{Male/Staff})}{P(\text{Male})} \right\}$$

$$= 0.2 \left\{ \frac{0.1}{0.5} \right\} = 0.04$$

It is thus apparent that the revision is quite strong, due to the disassociation of the observation with the event of interest: few staff members are male, $P(\text{Male/Staff}) = 0.1$. The prior probability is divided by five.

Conversely, if you wanted to use the observation that the member is a man to revise the prior estimate that he is a line worker, you would calculate:

$$P(\text{Line/Male}) = 0.8 \left\{ \frac{0.6}{0.5} \right\} = 0.96$$

The revision here is not particularly strong (ratio $= 1.2$) since the frequency of male line workers is about equal to that in the factory as a whole.

These can be seen directly from the formula for the factor: $\{P(O/E)/P(O)\}$. The revision is stronger when the observations are rare: the factor is greater when the denominator $P(O)$ is small. Conversely, the revision is stronger when the observation is either closely associated with or quite disassociated from the event of concern: the factor is greater when the numerator $P(O/E)$ is near either extreme, 0 or 1.0. It follows that strongest revisions to initial estimates of probability will be due to rare observations uniquely associated with the event of interest.

Likelihood ratios. Likelihood ratios provide a rapid means to revise prior estimates of probability when one obtains a sequence of independent observations bearing on some event. They enable us to bypass repeated applications of Bayes' Theorem. This is convenient because it is quite tedious to apply Bayes' Theorem over and over. In addition to having to use the formula once for each observation, one also has to recalculate $P(O)$ at each iteration because it changes with each new estimation of $P(E)$. The likelihood ratio permits us to collapse all this effort into a single formula that never requires any recalculations.

The use of the likelihood ratio involves the concept of complementary probability. The *complementary probability* of an event E is the probability that event E does not occur, that is, that some other event or events, non-E, occur instead. Since an event either occurs or not, $P(E)$ and the complementary probability, $P(\text{non-E})$ sum to one:

$$P(E) + P(\text{non-E}) = 1.0$$

For example, if $P(E)$ is the probability that a person you meet in the street is male, $P(\text{non-E})$ is the complementary probability that the person is female.

> **Notation:** In discussing probabilities, the use of a horizontal line over a symbol often indicates the nonexistence of that variable. This use can be confusing because the same notation is sometimes used to denote average values of a variable. To avoid difficulty, we will consistently refer to nonexistence of a variable X as "non-X."

A *likelihood ratio*, LR, is simply the ratio of the probability of event E and the probability of all complementary events, non-E:

$$\text{LR} = \frac{P(E)}{P(\text{non-E})}$$

The likelihood ratio thus implicitly defines the probability of event E. Since $P(\text{non-E}) = 1 - P(E)$, we can express the formula for LR in terms of $P(E)$ only. Solving for $P(E)$ we get

$$P(E) = \frac{\text{LR}}{(1 + \text{LR})}$$

The likelihood ratio is similar to the odds sometimes used in betting. In horse racing, for example, it is usual to give odds in the form $X{:}Y$ to win. Thus, if a horse is 3:2 to win, it means that the estimate is that it has 3 chances to lose for 2 to win. The likelihood ratio on losing is $\frac{3}{2}$ = 1.5. The estimated probability of losing is then

$$P(\text{Lose}) = \frac{1.5}{2.5} = 0.60$$

To explain the use of the likelihood ratio, consider first the simplest situation, in which we have one observation. We have a prior estimate of probability $P(E)$, have made the observation, O_j, and wish to obtain the posterior probability $P(E/O_j)$. Defining LR_i as the likelihood ratio after i observations, we have by definition

$$LR_1 \equiv \frac{\{P(E/O_j)\}}{\{P(\text{non-}E/O_j)\}}$$

This can be restated by applying Bayes' Theorem to both the top and bottom of the ratio. We thus obtain

$$LR_1 = \left\{ \frac{P(E)\left\{\dfrac{P(O_j/E)}{P(O_j)}\right\}}{P(\text{non-}E)\left\{\dfrac{P(O_j/\text{non-}E)}{P(O_j)}\right\}} \right\}$$

This expression can be simplified by cancellation of the factor that is common to both top and bottom of the ratio, $P(O_j)$. This elimination explains why $P(O_j)$ does not have to be calculated when using likelihood ratios instead of Bayes' Theorem. The result is

$$LR_1 = LR_0 \left\{ \frac{P(O_j/E)}{P(O_j/\text{non-}E)} \right\}$$

That is, the revised likelihood ratio after one observation is the original likelihood ratio times a factor uniquely associated with the observation. The posterior probability, $P(E/O_j)$ can then be found as:

$$P(E/O_j) = \frac{LR_1}{(1 + LR_1)}$$

The likelihood ratio after some observation is conveniently restated using the concept of the conditional likelihood ratio. The *Conditional Likelihood Ratio*, CLR_j, for any observation O_j, is defined as

$$CLR_j \equiv \left\{ \frac{P(O_j/E)}{P(O_j/\text{non-}E)} \right\}$$

Using this concept the revised likelihood ratio after a single observation O_j is then simply

$$LR_1 = LR_0(CLR_j)$$

Note that the conditional likelihood ratio can be determined in advance regardless of the number of observations. It does not depend on the actual estimate of the probability of E. Use of this concept provides the way to define a single formula to determine, in advance, the probability of E after a specified number of observations.

The general formulation using likelihood ratios is an extension of the result for a single observation. Each time an observation of type j is observed, one

---

Use of Likelihood Ratios

Consider a bottle-making factory. Suppose that its machines can either be OK or, 10% of the time, defective:

$$P(D) = 0.1 \qquad P(OK) = 0.9$$

The bottles sometimes come out cracked due to heat stresses. The frequency of cracking depends on the state of the machine. Assume that this frequency is

$$P(C/D) = 0.2 \qquad P(C/OK) = 0.05$$

If we sample 5 bottles produced by a particular machine and observe that 2 are cracked, and 3 are uncracked, what is the probability that the machine is defective? That is, $P(D/[2C, 3U]) = ?$

To calculate this by likelihood ratios we need

$$LR_0 = \frac{P(D)}{P(OK)} = \frac{0.1}{0.9} = \frac{1}{9}$$

together with the conditional likelihood ratios for each type of observation:

$$CLR_C = \frac{0.2}{0.05} = 4$$

$$CLR_U = \frac{0.8}{0.95} = \frac{16}{19}$$

We can then get the likelihood ratio after the five observations:

$$LR_5 = LR_0 \, (CLR_C)^2 \, (CLR_U)^3 = \left(\frac{1}{9}\right)(4)^2 \left(\frac{16}{19}\right)^3 = 1.062$$

Therefore:

$$P(D/[2C, 3U]) = \frac{LR_5}{(1 + LR_5)} = 0.515$$

updates the likelihood ratio by the appropriate conditional likelihood ratio. Thus

$$LR_N \equiv LR_0 \prod (CLR_j)^{N_j}$$

where N is the total number of observations, N_j is the number of observations of type j, and $N = \sum N_j$. Note carefully that the revision only depends on the number of observations of each type, not on the order in which they are presented. This general formulation is useful because it enables one to calculate directly the effect of many different observations.

In practice, the use of the general likelihood ratio is simple:

1. Calculate LR_0 and the conditional likelihood ratio CLR_j for each type of observation O_j.
2. Count the number of observations of each type j.
3. Calculate LR_N by formula.
4. Recover the revised estimate of the probability of event E.

Use of the likelihood ratio to revise estimates of probability assumes that we have conditional probabilities for any of the observations O_j that may be made. This means that we have the frequencies $P(O_j/E)$ and $P(O_j/\text{non-E})$. (See box.)

15.4 CONTINUOUS PROBABILITY DISTRIBUTIONS

Conceptually, the revision of estimates of probability when the distribution is continuous is the same as when the probabilities are discrete. In practice, however, the calculations are much more complicated. This section outlines these difficulties, leaving the full treatment to specialized texts.

Dealing with continuous distributions involves a complex of related issues:

- Integrations must be used instead of summations.
- The information itself tends to come in distributions, rather than in discrete pieces of data.
- The use of Bayes' Theorem may become nearly impossible, when dissimilar distributions have to be considered jointly.

By itself, the problem of integration is the simplest concern. For example, in estimating the probability of an event, given all the ways it can occur, we simply substitute the integration for the summation to obtain

$$P(O) = \int \text{pdf}\,(O/E)\,d\text{E}$$

where pdf($\cdot$) denotes the probability distribution of a quantity.

The real difficulty arises when we consider the nature of the information we receive. When dealing with continuous distributions, the new information itself tends to occur as a distribution. A typical situation is that engineers have a prior estimate of the measurement of a quantity (such as the strength of a material, the speed of an aircraft on the radar, the distance of a satellite) and then obtain a second series of measurements, also as a probability distribution. The problem then becomes one of incorporating a probability distribution, instead of a single piece of data, into Bayes' Theorem.

The melding of the two probability distributions, those of the prior estimate and of the new data, is generally problematical. It is only relatively easy if the two distributions are "conjugate distributions," that is, if they have specific convenient properties. When they do, Bayes' Theorem can be applied quite directly (see box). This is not always the case, however, and the calculations can become extremely complicated.

Bayes' Theorem for Continuous Probability

Colleagues at Stanford University undertook a study to determine how the estimates of the compressibility of soil foundations were changed by the information derived from soil samples. Focusing on the soil along the San Francisco Bay, they obtained the a priori estimates of experienced soils engineers, the results of soils tests, and calculated revised estimates of the strength. All data were in the form of probability distributions.

The distributions used were those of the t-statistic, partly because it is the proper distribution for a normal distribution when both statistics are unknown, partly because t-distributions are "conjugate functions" that permit the relatively easy application of Bayes' Theorem.

The expression for the revised estimates, using these convenient assumptions, was given by

pdf(true mean/m, k, d)

$$= d^{d/2}\{d + k(\text{true mean} - m)^2\}^{-(d+1)/2}(k)^{1/2}\{b(1/2, d/2)\}$$

where

$$m = \text{pooled mean}$$
$$k = (\text{sample variance})^{-1}$$
$$d = \text{degrees of freedom}$$
$$b(\cdot) = \text{beta function}$$

The expression makes the point: a "simple" result for continuous probability distributions is actually quite complex and tedious to calculate. Advanced texts provide the details.

15.5 BIASES IN ESTIMATION

Professionals must often estimate probabilities according to their best informed judgment. Although we might wish for objective measures, the reality must be estimated subjectively, as Section 15.2 describes.

A key difficulty here is that people are biased estimators. As repeated experiments demonstrate, both individuals and groups systematically provide skewed estimates of the probability of events. This section describes the major kinds of biases. The idea is to alert readers to their effects so that they can compensate for them in practice.

Overconfidence is arguably the root cause of the common types of biases. A general phenomenon is that all persons act as if they know much more about a situation than they actually do. Even when they know they are quite ignorant about a topic they typically endow their estimates with unwarranted precision. Psychological theory offers many other reasonable explanations of why people bias their estimates. However, the best guidance that can be offered to compensate for the biases is: restrain your confidence; be modest.

Three most obvious manifestations of bias in the estimate of probabilities are

- Overly narrow range of estimates
- Inadequate response to new information
- Hedging of estimates

These are each discussed below.

Narrow range of estimates. This is the prime case of overconfidence: people regularly will estimate a quantity very precisely, within a narrow range, even when they have little justification for such confidence. They are willing to say, in effect, that there is a very high probability that the value is what they say it is, and low probability that it is anything else. In this they are generally wrong.

In practice, this bias is manifest in two kinds of situations: the estimate of different values and the forecast of future states. It is, of course, most immediately evident when they deal with current values that can be checked. This is easily shown in a classroom or for any group by asking simple questions whose answers can be found in some reference work (the box on the following page provides an example of these "almanac questions").

The overconfidence that we can easily demonstrate using almanac questions also routinely occurs in professional practice. The only difference is that we rarely get a chance to observe it positively. We often do see that an expert's estimate turned out to be wrong. But since we rarely can see how often the expert's estimates are wrong, we cannot usually demonstrate the overconfidence.

A symposium held at MIT did demonstrate this overconfidence rather neatly, however. In preparation for a speciality conference on soil mechanics, 10 world

Length of River Nile

This is an example of the "almanac questions" that can be used to demonstrate people's overconfidence in their estimates. To conduct the experiment you need to have a willing group of participants (a class or a group of colleagues), and some specific physical facts that can be looked up in an encyclopedia or almanac. These facts could be items such as the distance to the moon, the amount of rainfall in July, or the population of Peru. The author's favorite has been the length of the River Nile.

The organizer of the experiment asks each participant to estimate the value of the fact selected, and to provide the plus or minus range for this value such that there is a 50:50 chance that it includes the true value. Note that it is easy to provide a range that must include the true value; it presumably is minus to plus infinity. This is also a uselessly broad estimate. In effect the organizer requests each member to provide a best estimate with 50% confidence limits.

If the estimates were accurate, one should find that, on average, half of the estimates actually did include the true value. This is not what happens. Typically, only 10 to 20% of the estimates include the true value. The rest have excluded it because they set their range much too narrowly: they were overconfident.

Test yourself: what do you estimate the length of the River Nile to be, with plus or minus 50% confidence limits?

When the author asks this question in class he routinely gets answers such as 500 ± 200 miles, 1800 ± 400 miles, and so on. The true value, hidden so your eye did not catch the answer before you addressed the question, is slightly more than twice the current year, in miles.

---

class experts were requested to estimate the strength of an embankment, with 50% confidence limits. They were given a full set of data on the soil and the state of the embankment. On one of the field trips associated with the conference, the embankment was loaded until it failed, thus creating an almost unique opportunity to demonstrate overconfidence among professionals.

The overconfidence was painfully obvious, as Figure 15.2 shows. In this case not one of the experts included the true value in their 50% confidence limits. Based on both psychological experiments and professional experience, this kind of result appears quite standard. The lesson is: do not be overconfident in your own estimates or those of others—allow generously for the possibility of being wrong.

Similarly, overconfidence in forecasting becomes evident when one compares forecasts with what actually occurs. This is most easily done when forecasters have provided high and low estimates, as they sometimes do. Figure 15.3 is a typical example of the comparison; the narrow range clearly excludes the reality, and demonstrates overconfidence. Similar comparisons can be made for all kinds of statistically based forecasts, because they normally provide confidence limits on their parameters.

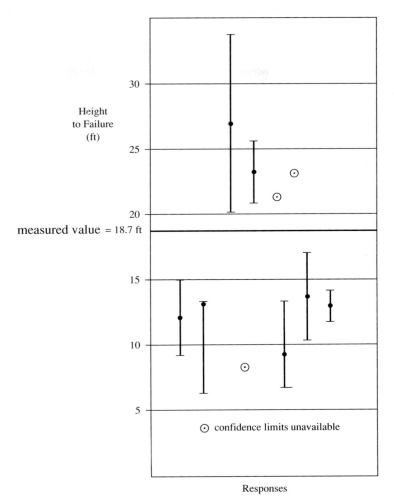

FIGURE 15.2
Demonstration of overconfidence: The true value of the strength of the embankment, as measured by the height of the load, was outside all of the experts' 50% confidence limits.

Inadequate response to new information. As another form of overconfidence, people typically fail to adjust their estimates adequately to new information. They are usually conservative, in that they tend to stick close to their initial estimates. They indicate, in effect, that they know better and do not really need to be influenced by new information.

The relative importance of the new information compared to the initial estimate becomes evident by looking at the general formula for the likelihood ratio:

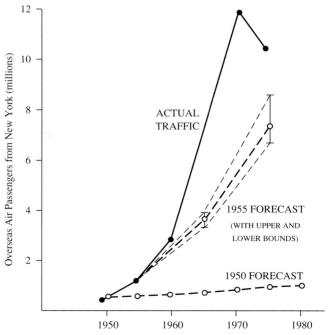

FIGURE 15.3
Overconfidence as demonstrated by the comparison of actual results and the narrow range forecast by experts.

$$LR_N = LR_0 \prod (CLR_j)^{N_j}$$

The driving factor in this equation is the multiplication of powered conditional likelihood ratios. After only a few observations the effect of LR_0 and the initial estimates have been dissipated. The previous box illustrating the use of likelihood ratios demonstrates this effect. We may thus conclude that, in general, analysts should not be confident in their initial estimates; they should rather rely on the evidence of multiple observations.

This phenomenon has been repeatedly demonstrated in carefully controlled psychological measurements. It can also be informally demonstrated with colleagues (see box).

Hedging of estimates. People are said to "hedge" when they act so as to avoid extremes and ensure that the outcomes of a situation are close to the averages. The term is generally used in connection with investments, specifically when investors buy insurance against the fluctuations of the market.

Demonstrating Inadequate Response to Information

The organizer of the demonstration prepares by setting up a simple situation and calculating possible results in advance. This person then asks a colleague or members of a group to provide estimates of a quantity according to the information provided. The comparison of the individuals' estimates with the proper estimate generated by Bayes' Theorem demonstrates the overconfidence. Typically, the individuals' estimates change slowly when they should change much more dramatically.

For example, consider an electronic assembly, with a 10% a priori probability of being faulty:

$$P(\text{Faulty}) = 0.10$$

Suppose that if the assembly is faulty it has a 50% probability of generating an error signal:

$$P(\text{Signal/Faulty}) = 0.5$$

while a good assembly can also generate error signals, but at a lower rate:

$$P(\text{Signal/Nonfaulty}) = 0.1$$

The questions to ask are then, for example, what is the probability that a part is faulty if repeated tests generate one error signal? One error and one OK? 2 error signals? And so on.

The correct answers are conveniently found by the likelihood ratios. For this case,

$$\text{LR}_0 = \frac{P(\text{Faulty})}{P(\text{OK})} = \frac{1}{9}$$

$$\text{CLR}_{\text{signal}} = 5$$

$$\text{CLR}_{\text{OK}} = \frac{5}{9}$$

so that, after n tests:

$$\text{LR}_n = \left(\frac{1}{9}\right) (5)^{\text{errors}} \left(\frac{5}{9}\right)^{\text{oks}}$$

For example, what would you estimate the probability of being faulty to be after two error signals? Write down your answer and compare it with the correct solution, calculated as

$$\text{LR}_2 = \left(\frac{1}{9}\right) (5)^2 \left(\frac{5}{9}\right)^0 = \frac{25}{9}$$

so that

$$P(\text{Faulty/2 Error Signals}) \sim 70\%$$

People likewise hedge their estimates of a quantity when they provide responses that avoid extreme values. They then act as if they are unwilling to accept that the actual value of this quantity may be quite different from the average. This bias is thus similar to the overconfidence previously discussed: people avoid wide ranges.

The classic demonstration of hedging consists of asking individuals to estimate the frequency of letters in a language, for example, in English. Their answers will tend to cluster around the average value of $\frac{1}{26}$ = 4%, and they will systematically underestimate the actual high frequency of common letters such as "e," and overestimate the frequency of improbable letters such as "q" and "z." (Their usual frequency is, in fact, 13% for "e" and 0.25% each for "q" and "z.")

15.6   APPLICATIONS

This section provides a sequence of examples to illustrate the application of the methods discussed.

Frequency estimates. The probability, the risk of many kinds of events, is commonly deduced from careful examinations of the historical record. The estimate of the probability of failure of large dams discussed in Section 15.2 is a good example of the process.

The same approach can also be used to estimate probability distributions. This is commonly done for earthquakes, floods, and other natural events. It can also be applied to recurrent human situations, such as the estimate of costs discussed in Section 15.1. The method is suitable whenever the underlying causes of the event of interest have not changed significantly from the past.

Statistical models. These are most commonly found in situations thought to be well described by some theory, particularly economics. They are thus routinely used to estimate future demand for the services of a system, such as traffic on a communications network, passengers in aviation, and so on. They are equally used to estimate future prices (since price is the complement to quantity demanded in standard economics) as for oil and other commodities.

Statistical models, ultimately based on judgment for their form and thus results, nicely illustrate the pervasive problem of overconfidence. The analyses typically lead to narrow confidence limits on the values of the parameters—and thus on the results. But as the discussion of the aviation forecasts in Section 15.1, and as Figure 15.3 shows, it is quite possible to be confident and wrong.

In fields that have been extensively analyzed it is furthermore possible to obtain probability distributions on the parameters of statistical models using the frequency approach. Figure 15.4 illustrates the result. It simply shows the distribution of a key parameter of demand models, individual responsiveness to

FIGURE 15.4
Probability distribution of price elasticity, for North Atlantic Business Travel by air, based on 59 statistical studies.

price, based on many independent studies of the same situation. Note that this distribution spans a broad range ($-3 <$ price elasticity < 0) and contradicts the typically overconfident claims made by individual studies that this parameter can be determined with 95% confidence limits of ± 0.1 or less.

Judgment. This is most obviously called for in situations for which there is no appropriate experience or statistics. This is common whenever one is dealing with new technology, for example. The best if not the only estimates of the performance of new aircraft, the demand for new computers, or the efficiency of robots will come from experts. Judgment is also the standard approach used to estimate risk in unique, individual situations concerning, for instance, the likelihood of being a victim of or winning a lawsuit.

Computer-based expert systems, which build on expert judgments, also naturally use Bayes' Theorem extensively. In a typical application, an expert system for finding oil (or making a medical diagnosis) will use the formula to revise prior probabilities based on new information such as the response to a probe. If the system is normally subjected to repeated measurements, as in the quality control of a production line or the warm-up testing of a computer, likelihood ratios may be used.

REFERENCES

Ascher, W., (1978). *Forecasting: An Appraisal for Policy-Makers and Planners*, Johns Hopkins University Press, Baltimore, MD.
de Neufville, R., and Marks, D. H., (1976). *Systems Planning and Design, Case Studies in Modeling Optimization and Evaluation*, Prentice-Hall, Englewood Cliffs, NJ.
Fischhoff, B., Lichtenstein, S., Slovic, P., Derby, S. L., and Keeney, R. L., (1981). *Acceptable Risk*, Cambridge University Press, Cambridge, England.

Folayen, J. I., Hoeg, K., and Benjamin, J. R., (1970, 1976). Chapter 23 in de Neufville and Marks (1976), also "Decision Theory Applied to Settlement Predictions" *ASCE Journal of Soil Mechanics and Foundations*, Vol. 96, July 1970, pp. 1127–1141.

PROBLEMS

15.1. *Money Bags*

You are a contestant on the "Money Bags" TV game program. Monty, the MC, has placed two bags of cash in front of you and told you that you may take one of them. One bag contains 60 $10 bills and 40 $1 bills while the other holds 20 $10 bills and 80 $1 bills. You do not know which bag has the $640, but you would very much like to choose that one.

(*a*) Monty will let you draw a bill from one of the bags before you decide which bag to choose. If you pull out a $10 bill from one of the bags, should you choose that bag?

(*b*) If Monty lets you draw three bills from one of the bags, replacing each bill before drawing the next, and you pull out one $10 bill and two $1 bills, which bag should you take?

(*c*) If Monty tells you to draw one more bill from the same bag before making your decision, and you pull out a $10 bill (total sample: 2 $10 bills and 2 $1 bills), which bag should you choose? Explain the significance of drawing this last $10 bill.

15.2. *Diskette Drives*

Suppose that you are the programming supervisor for a group developing software for a new personal computer. Among your duties, you must select the number of retries your programmers must attempt when their programs retrieve information from the diskette drives.

Within this PC, you know that during an attempt to retrieve data from the diskette drives, one of two things will occur: either the data is successfully collected or the program receives a signal that the data cannot be retrieved. Thus, you know that any program must take the following steps:

1. Request information from the diskette drive.
2. Check for the error signal.
3. If there is no signal, the data was collected successfully—continue to the next step.
4. If there is a signal, try step 1 again.
5. If the signal is detected N times in a row, abort the program.

You know that this error signal is generated whenever there is a diskette problem; it also can occur even though there is nothing wrong with the diskette. According to the device specifications, if there is a diskette problem, this signal is generated 100% of the time. Alternatively, if there is no diskette problem, this signal is generated 30% of the time. The probability that there is a diskette problem is 20%.

How many attempts to read diskette data should be made if company policy is that software should abort only if there is a 99% certainty that there is a diskette problem?

15.3. *Lie Detector*
A lie detector has a hitting rate of 80% and a false alarm rate of 50%. That is, the probability of the machine giving a positive result (indicating "LIE!") is 0.80 if the subject is lying, but 0.50 if the subject is telling the truth.

Suppose a subject is known a priori to have a 20% chance of lying on any particular test.
(*a*) What is the probability that this subject is actually lying if the machine says "LIE"?
(*b*) If the machine was improved by raising its hitting rate to 99%, how would your answer to part (*a*) be modified? Is that a significant improvement?
(*c*) Suppose you now have a subject who you think will lie four times out of five, on any trial. What is the new answer to part (*a*)? Does the lie detector improve your prior belief?

15.4. *VLSI Chips*
A manufacturing line produces VLSI chips of which 25% do not meet specifications. An automatic testing device is used to run four different independent tests on the chips. If a chip does not meet specifications, it has an 80% chance of failing any one of the tests. A chip that does meet specifications will also fail the tests 40% of the time.
(*a*) If a certain chip passes three of the tests but fails one, what is the probability that the chip meets specifications?
(*b*) If one of the tests produces independent results when repeated a number of times on a given chip, what is the minimum number of tests that must be run to achieve 90% probabilty that the chip does not meet specifications?

15.5. *Oil Drilling*
In a certain oil-rich region, there is prior probability of $\frac{2}{3}$ that any field will produce a profitable oil well. Test drillings are made to determine whether or not a well in a given field would be profitable. There is a 75% chance that the test drilling would be positive if in fact a field would support a profitable well. There is a 50% chance of a negative test if a field would not support a profitable well.
(*a*) Assuming two test drillings, one positive and one negative, are made in a field, find the revised probability of producing a profitable well in the field by (1) successive applications of Bayes' Theorem; (2) likelihood ratios.
(*b*) If five tests are made, three positive and two negative, what is the revised probability of producing a profitable well?
(*c*) When should likelihood ratios be used instead of Bayes' Theorem? What advantage do they have?

15.6. *Sonny Reyes*
Sonny Reyes, the famous photovoltaic (PV) manufacturer, is testing a new PV panel. If a panel does not meet specifications it has a 80% chance of failing the test. A panel that does meet specifications has a 20% chance of failing the test. Overall, four in five panels meet specifications.
(*a*) Define the formula for the prior likelihood ratio for this problem.
(*b*) Define the conditional likelihood ratios for this problem.
(*c*) Write the formula for the posterior likelihood ratio, if a panel first fails and then passes a second test.
(*d*) Solve for the posterior probability of a panel meeting specifications.

15.7. *SIDA Testing*
The incidence of SIDA, a deadly disease, among a certain population is 0.01%. Individuals, randomly selected from this population, are submitted to a SIDA test whose accuracy is 99% both ways. That is to say, the proportion of positive results among people known to be SIDA affected is 99%. Likewise, testing people that are not suffering from the disease yields 99% of negative results. The test gives independent results when repeated.
    An individual tests positive.
(a) What is the probability that this person is actually affected? (Use both Bayes' Theorem and likelihood ratios.)
(b) Discuss the above result as regards the interpretation of the positive result.
(c) The test is then repeated twice. What is the probability that the person has SIDA if all three tests are positive? If the two subsequent tests are negative?

15.8. *Weather Expert*
The radio predicts a 60% chance of freezing weather. Your meteorological friend, May Vin, tells you she knows better: it is sure to freeze. From experience you know that she only gets it right 80% of the time.
(a) What should your estimate of freezing weather be?
(b) What would it be if May had predicted "no freezing weather"?

15.9. *Summer Goods*
Of the summer goods, some are bad. Two percent are defective. Visual inspection is cheap, but only correct half the time. A detailed examination, however, gives a correct diagnosis 90% of the time. Normal procedure is to look the goods over and then to examine in detail the ones that seem defective visually. Goods that fail both tests are rejected.
(a) What percent of the goods that pass visual inspection are in fact defective?
(b) What percent of defectives are not detected by the total examination process?
(c) If the detailed examination were applied to all goods, what percent of defectives would pass? Discuss whether you think this policy would make sense.

15.10. *Championship Playoff*
Before the infinite series, it looks as if either team A or B is equally likely to win the series. Past frequency indicates that "champions" win 70% of their games.
(a) If team A wins the first game, what is the probability that it is a "champion"?
(b) Use Bayes' Theorem to calculate how many times in a row team A should win so that the probability that it is a "champion" is greater than 90%. Then validate this by likelihood ratios.
(c) What is the probability that any team is a "champion" if it wins 2 out of 3 games? 3 out of 5? 4 out of 7?

CHAPTER
16

DECISION
ANALYSIS

16.1   OBJECTIVE

This chapter presents the concept and methods of decision analysis, a fundamentally important method of evaluation. This is the approach that should be used whenever the outcomes of potential projects are highly uncertain. Since the planning and design of systems typically must deal with massive uncertainty about the future, as the previous chapter shows, decision analysis is a most valuable tool.

Formally, *decision analysis* is a method of evaluation that leads to three results:

1. It *structures* the problem, which otherwise appears very confusing to most people due to the complexities introduced by uncertainty (Sections 16.3 and 16.4).
2. It *defines optimal choices* for any period, based on a joint consideration of the probabilities and the nature of any outcome of a choice, specifically by calculation of an expected value (Sections 16.5 to 16.7).
3. It *identifies an optimal strategy* over many periods (Sections 16.8 and 16.9).

Decision analysis rests on the simple proposition that a planner or designer should use all the important information available about a problem, specifically the fact that the performance of any system is uncertain. This premise makes decision analysis very different from the traditional economic evaluations, which focus only on the typical or most likely outcome of a situation.

Recognizing the risk of a situation has two important consequences for an evaluation. Mechanically, it makes any evaluation far more complex and requires many more calculations. This fact has inhibited the development of decision analysis, which is only now—with the diffusion of computers—becoming an integral part of systems analysis.

Most importantly, the perception of risk fundamentally changes the nature of the optimal choice over time for any system. Once we acknowledge that we do not know how the future will evolve, we must also accept that it would be presumptuous to define the single best development over time. We must instead determine a *strategy* of choice, a range of possible choices whose final selection will depend on how events occur.

The concept of *insurance* is the equally important corollary to that of a strategy. Since uncertainty prevents us from knowing exactly which series of choices will be best over time, our selection at the first stage of any sequence must provide us with the flexibility to develop as needed later on. It must both position us to take advantage of good opportunities as they arrive, and give us the capability to avoid disaster. This flexibility must be paid for, however. Buying the ability to respond easily to future events is the insurance we must build into an optimal strategy.

16.2   PRIMITIVE MODELS

It is important to understand that decision analysis offers substantial advantages over the other methods for dealing with risk that are now used in practice. Decision analysis is not just a refinement, a more complex version of the primitive approaches that have been used, it represents a real change. The primitive models are not simplistic versions that could be used for first-order approximations; unfortunately, they are wrong.

Perversely, the primitive models of decision analysis are increasingly pervasive. The use of a spreadsheet program on a personal computer makes it easy to lay a problem out for this kind of analysis. As the primitive models seem to be reasonable, if one is not familiar with their fatal flaws, they are also seductive. These two characteristics of ease of use and superficial appeal make the primitive models popular. But they can be completely misleading. That is the reason this section discusses these approaches in detail: it is necessary to warn the reader against error and to motivate the use of the more appropriate decision analysis.

The general problem considered by both decision analysis and the primitive models has three features:

- A set of *possible decisions*, D_i, that the decisionmaker might take
- A set of *uncertain events*, E_j, that may occur
- The *outcomes*, O_{ij}, that result from having chosen D_i and being subjected to E_j

The risky events E_j are often referred to formally as *states of nature*. In practice decision analysis typically makes an important assumption, which should be carefully noted. The premise is that the probability of any outcome of a choice depends only on passive forces of nature. This excludes the probability of competitors, friends, or enemies who would actively try to influence the outcome of any choices we might make. Game theory deals with this possibility, and is discussed in more advanced texts.

To illustrate the above definitions, consider a typical problem of deciding whether or not to wear a raincoat as you go out. The decisions may be either "wear a raincoat" or "do not wear a raincoat"; the possible events correspond to the weather (fair, misty, rain, downpour, and so on) and the outcomes could be how wet you might become.

The primitive models all differ from decision analysis in that they assume that the probabilities of possible outcomes are not known, indeed cannot be known. They rest on the idea that all that can be assumed is that different outcomes might happen, depending on the situation. Decision analysis assumes that at least some assessment of the probability of events is possible and should be used.

> **Semantic caution:** The primitive models are sometimes said to represent procedures for "decisionmaking under uncertainty," where uncertainty is complete absence of knowledge about the probability outcomes. This is not the meaning used in this text. The view here is that there is never either complete ignorance or knowledge of probabilities. There are only varying degrees of impression about them, that is, uncertainty in the sense of ordinary language.

The primitive models generally describe the problem by a payoff matrix. A *payoff matrix* is a table representing possible outcomes of the available decisions. The decisions are typically arrayed along the vertical axis. The horizontal axis represents the several possible states of nature. The cells in the payoff matrix then each represent the outcome associated with the intersecting decision and state of nature. This is the kind of information an analyst can easily tabulate using a spreadsheet program on a personal computer.

An example situation is depicted by the payoff matrix shown in Table 16.1.

TABLE 16.1
Payoff matrix for example problem

Possible computer system	Annual Profits ($ \times 10^3$) if jobs require		
	Linear programming	Dynamic programming	Engineering economy
Mainframe	90	40	35
Minis	60	80	10
PCs	0	0	120

This represents the hypothetical outcomes for a consulting firm faced with the choice between three different types of computer systems: a large mainframe, some minicomputers, and individual personal computers (PCs). The states of nature in this case represent the typical kind of analysis needed by their clients over the next several years, a set of requirements presumed to be determined by the vagaries of the general economy. The outcomes are then a measure of net benefits to the company.

This example problem will illustrate the operation and inherent weakness of each of the four traditional primitive models. These are those associated with the Laplace, the Maximin, the Maximax, and the Regret criteria. Recently another primitive approach has become popular, largely due to the use of computers and spreadsheet programs. This is the Weighted Index criterion. It will be illustrated by a different example. Each of the five methods is discussed in turn.

Laplace criterion. The Laplace model proposes that since the probabilities of the states of nature are not known, they should be assumed equal. This simple notion, possibly attributed unjustly to the great French mathematician, has a fair amount of intuitive appeal. Experience shows, for example, that there always are some members of a class of students who spontaneously suggest this model when confronted with an example problem such as that of Table 16.1.

The Laplace model defines a simple criterion for choice: select the system with the most desirable expected value. According to this procedure, the preferred choice in the example problem should be the Mainframe computer since the expected value of this option gives the greatest net benefits:

$$E \text{ (Mainframe)} = \tfrac{1}{3}(165) = 55 \quad \text{"Best"}$$

$$E \text{ (Minis)} = \tfrac{1}{3}(150) = 50$$

$$E \text{ (PCs)} = \tfrac{1}{3}(120) = 40$$

TABLE 16.2
Altered payoff matrix to illustrate the peculiar weakness of the Laplace criterion, its sensitivity to irrelevant states of nature

Possible computer system	Annual profits ($ $\times 10^3$) if jobs require			
	Linear programming	Dynamic programming	Benefit cost	Present value
Mainframe	90	40	35	35
Minis	60	80	10	10
PCs	0	0	120	120

The peculiar flaw of the Laplace model is that it is sensitive to the description of the states of nature, and that its selection can be altered by the introduction of trivial or irrelevant possibilities. To appreciate this phenomenon, consider the payoff matrix in Table 16.2: it is the same as that of Table 16.1 except that the engineering economy jobs have been divided into two components, benefit-cost and present value analysis. This modification to the payoff matrix evidently does not reflect any real change in the actual problem. Yet because of this trivial change the Laplace model identifies a completely different choice as optimal: it now recommends personal computers! Thus:

$$E \text{ (Mainframe)} = \tfrac{1}{4}(200) = 50$$

$$E \text{ (Minis)} \quad\;\; = \tfrac{1}{4}(160) = 40$$

$$E \text{ (PCs)} \qquad = \tfrac{1}{4}(240) = 60 \qquad \text{``Best''}$$

The Laplace criterion assigns probabilities without regard to the real facts. Thus in the example problem it ascribes a probability to engineering economy problems of $\tfrac{1}{3}$ in one case and $\tfrac{1}{2}$ in the other, even though the problem has not changed. This is evidently absurd, and it is surely better to assign probabilities with some reflection, even if these subjective estimates cannot be precise.

Maximin criterion. The maximin criterion indicates that the decisionmaker should choose the option that maximizes the minimum benefit obtainable. This notion also has some intuitive appeal; many people do like the idea of knowing that they have protected themselves against some worst case. For the example problem in Table 16.1, this model thus recommends the Mainframe as the best choice: its minimum profit is 35, greater than 10 or 0 for the other two options.

The difficulty with the maximin criterion is that it totally disregards most of the information we have about the problem. In the example, the procedure ignores five out of the nine entries in the payoff matrix—it only looks at the minima for each possible decision, in this case four cells. Furthermore, it gives absolutely no consideration to whether the different states of nature that lead to the minimum returns are likely or not. This model should therefore not be used; it cannot be wise to disregard relevant information systematically.

Maximax criterion. The maximax criterion is the converse of the maximin: it proposes that the decisionmaker maximize the maximum return available. Logically, it makes as much sense as the maximin: it simply would appeal more to the optimist rather than the pessimist. For the example problem, this model recommends PCs as the best choice since it offers the possibility of the absolute maximum return in the payoff matrix: 120.

This criterion compounds the deficiencies of the maximin criterion. It discards all but one entry in the payoff matrix, focusing only on the highest value. Furthermore, since most individuals do care a great deal about the worst cases that might happen, as Chapters 18 and 19 describe, this model has little appeal.

Regret criterion. The regret criterion is a combination of a criterion similar to the maximin and of the concept of regret. *Regret* is defined, for any option and a specific state of nature, as the difference between the benefit actually received and the maximum benefit that could have been obtained if the appropriate choice had been made. Thus, with reference to Table 16.1, if one had chosen Mainframes and Linear Programming jobs were received, the regret would be zero since one had made the best choice for the state of nature. The regret for the same choice would be 40 if Dynamic Programming jobs were received, since one could have had that much more if one had chosen Minis (i.e., 80 − 40), and the regret would be 85 (i.e., 120 − 35) if one received Engineering Economy jobs. Regret associated with a choice is thus defined with respect to the best outcomes for the states of nature, rather than in comparison with any specific other choice.

The notion of regret has considerable intuitive appeal. Many people define their success relative to others rather than in absolute terms. The concept is reflected by efforts to "keep up with the neighbors" or, conversely, by the "I don't care if I'm mediocre just so long as I'm above class average" attitude. The regret criterion has in fact been used quite considerably in the design of engineering systems, particularly in the development of water resources.

The criterion for selection in dealing with regret is similar to the maximin criterion on benefits. The difference is that one wishes to minimize regret, and specifically to minimize the maximum regret. This is then the *minimax criterion*. It is the inverse of the maximin criterion, and has all its weaknesses and specifically that of ignoring most of the information available about the problem.

In practice, the regret model involves two steps:

1. Transformation of the payoff matrix into a matrix showing "regret"
2. Application of the minimax criterion to this regret matrix

For the example problem, the appropriate regret matrix appears in Table 16.3.

TABLE 16.3
Regret matrix for the example problem of Table 16.1

Possible computer system	Annual "Regret" ($ × 10³) if jobs require		
	Linear programming	Dynamic programming	Engineering economy
Mainframe	0	40	85
Minis	30	0	110
PCs	90	80	0

The recommended choice is the Mainframe computer since this selection has the smallest maximum regret (85, compared to 110 for Minis and 90 for PCs).

The regret procedure has an additional, serious, peculiar flaw: the ranking of the choices can depend on the type of choices specified. This is because the regret associated with any choice is not an intrinsic property, but is a property defined relative to other possibilities. The consequence is that the ranking of the choices can be biased by the set of choices compared, as well as by irrelevant alternatives, as shown further under the discussion of the weighted index criterion.

The regret procedure can also be intransitive. This phenomenon, a reflection of the sensitivity of the procedure to the set of choices compared, is demonstrated by paired comparisons of the possible decisions in the example problem. The regret matrices associated with each of these three possible combinations appear in Table 16.4. Comparing the Mainframe and Minis choices, the regret criterion indicates that Minis should be preferred:

$$Minis > Mainframe$$

Considering Minis and PCs, the latter appear best:

$$PCs > Minis$$

When comparing PCs and the Mainframe choices, however, what seemed like the worst choice now appears best:

$$Mainframe > PCs$$

This kind of problem should be sufficient reason to reject the regret criterion forever.

TABLE 16.4
Regret matrices for paired comparisons of the options in the example problem

| Possible computer system | Annual "Regret" ($ $\times 10^3$) if jobs require | | |
	Linear programming	Dynamic programming	Engineering economy
Mainframe	0	40	0
Minis	30	0	25
Minis	0	0	110
PCs	60	80	0
Mainframe	0	0	85
PCs	90	40	0

Notation: The symbol $>$ similar to the greater than symbol but with curved legs, should be read as "is preferred to." Facing the other direction, $<$, it means "is preferred by."

Weighted index criterion. The weighted index method has great intuitive appeal and is widely used. In some contexts it has even been the standard approach. This is notably the case in materials engineering, where the issue is to select the material that is best for some application.

The method operates on a table of consequences similar to but different from the payoff matrix previously defined. The difference is that the columns of the table represent known characteristics of each choice rather than possible outcomes associated with different events (see box). In this respect the weighted index method is not strictly comparable to the other criteria. It is discussed here because it is both a primitive method of choice and shares the same kinds of difficulties as the other criteria.

The general concept of the weighted index criterion is that the optimum choice is the one that provides the best weighted average of all the characteristics of the problem. These may be weighted equally or in any ratio that the designer chooses. Thus, for the example shown in the box, it is desirable to keep both the cost and the density of the part down, so that the material with the lowest weighted average of these characteristics will be best.

The first difficulty of the weighted index method lies in the selection of weights. In this regard it has the same drawback of the Laplace criterion in that it is sensitive to the way the columns are defined.

The greater difficulty of this method is associated with the normalization of the characteristics. All the components of the weighted index must indeed be

---

Table for Weighted Index Method

Consider the problem of choosing a material for some component of an automobile. In this application, both cost and density (or weight) are important characteristics, the latter because greater weight reduces the fuel economy of the vehicle.

The problem is conveniently described by a table, as generated from a spreadsheet program on a personal computer. For some four materials, it could be as follows:

Material	Cost	Density
A	50	11
B	60	9
C	80	7
D	120	10

normalized to avoid the dominance of characteristics that happen to be measured in small units. This normalization can be done with respect to a variety of constants such as the extreme values of the characteristics, or average values, or all the values associated with one of the alternatives (see box).

The difficulty is that the ranking of the choices derived from different normalizing constants may easily not be the same. In fact, they can generally be quite different. Table 16.5 shows the dependence of the weighted index on the normalizing constraints for the four materials discussed in the boxes. As Table 16.6 shows, the resulting rankings are dramatically different. In this case, specifically, whether A, B, or C appears best depends on which provides the basis for the normalizing constants. Alternatively, whether C is first, second, or third in the ranking depends on whether one normalizes on the largest, average, or smallest costs.

Further, the weighted index criterion is sensitive to irrelevant alternatives. If one eliminates material D from the analysis, because it is constantly unattractive and really irrelevant, then the ranking of the remaining materials may be quite turned upside down: C progresses from worst to best! It is not possible to state which (if any!) of these rankings is meaningful or correct. A method so capricious certainly should not form the basis for serious decisions.

Normalization of Characteristics

The normalization defines the values of each characteristic with respect to the reference value. To achieve this, we divide each value of a characteristic for a choice by the reference value for the characteristic.

Refer now to the example choice of materials with the characteristics shown in the previous box. Suppose we wish to normalize all entries in the table of characteristics with respect to material A. The reference value for cost will thus be the cost associated with material A, 50. The normalized cost for material A is thus 1.00 $(= \frac{50}{50})$, for material B it is 1.20 $(= \frac{60}{50})$; and so on. Likewise, the reference value for density is also material A in this case, and the normalized density for A is again 1.00 $(= \frac{11}{11})$; for material B it is 0.8182 $(= \frac{9}{11})$; and so on.

If we normalized by extreme values, the procedure would be the same but the divisor different. For cost it would either be 50 or 120, depending on whether we selected the upper or lower extreme. For density it would be 7 or 11. Note that these reference points need not be connected with the same material.

In fact, the reference point need not be connected with any material. If we normalized on averages, the reference value for cost would be the average cost, 77.5 $(= \frac{310}{4})$, which is not the cost of any material. Indeed, the reference point can be totally arbitrary.

TABLE 16.5
Dependence of weighted index on basis for normalization and alternatives considered, for example materials

	Normalized by A				Normalized by B		
	Normal cost	Normal density	Index		Normal cost	Normal density	Index
A	1.0000	1.0000	1.0000	A	0.8333	1.2222	1.0278
B	1.2000	0.8182	1.0091	B	1.0000	1.0000	1.0000
C	1.6000	0.6364	1.1182	C	1.3333	0.7778	1.0556
D	2.4000	0.9091	1.6545	D	2.0000	1.1111	1.5556

	Normalized by C				Normalized by D		
	Normal cost	Normal density	Index		Normal cost	Normal density	Index
A	0.6250	1.5714	1.0982	A	0.4167	1.1000	0.7583
B	0.7500	1.2857	1.0179	B	0.5000	0.9000	0.7000
C	1.0000	1.0000	1.0000	C	0.6667	0.7000	0.6833
D	1.5000	1.4286	1.4643	D	1.0000	1.0000	1.0000

	Normalized by Maxima				Normalized by Maxima without D		
	Normal cost	Normal density	Index		Normal cost	Normal density	Index
A	0.4167	1.0000	0.7083	A	0.6250	1.0000	0.8125
B	0.5000	0.8182	0.6591	B	0.7500	0.8181	0.7840
C	0.6667	0.6364	0.6515	C	1.0000	0.6363	0.8181
D	1.0000	0.9091	0.9545				

	Normalized by Averages				Normalized by Minima		
	Normal cost	Normal density	Index		Normal cost	Normal density	Index
A	0.6452	1.1892	0.9172	A	1.0000	1.5714	1.2857
B	0.7742	0.9730	0.8736	B	1.2000	1.2857	1.2429
C	1.0323	0.7568	0.8945	C	1.6000	1.0000	1.3000
D	1.5484	1.0811	1.3147	D	2.4000	1.4286	1.9143

TABLE 16.6

Dependence of rankings of materials on the basis of normalization and alternatives considered

Normalizing factors	Order of ranking
Alternative A's cost and weight	A < B < C < D
Alternative B's cost and weight	B < A < C < D
Alternative C's cost and weight	C < B < A < D
Alternative D's cost and weight	C < B < A < D
Smallest cost and weight among all alternatives	B < A < C < D
Average cost and weight of all alternatives	B < C < A < D
Largest cost and weight among all alternatives	C < B < A < D
Largest cost and weight without considering D	B < A < C

Summary. Each of the five primitive models for "decisionmaking under uncertainty" is strongly deficient. Each in its own ways fails to meet the standards we should expect from a sound engineering procedure: intelligent, unambiguous use of all the relevant information about the problem. They should all be rejected.

16.3 COMPLEXITY OF CHOICE

The first contribution of decision analysis is to organize the problem for the analyst or planner. This may seem insignificant but is actually of great practical importance. Without structure to organize one's consideration of the possibilities, people tend to polarize around only a few, and they therefore miss important aspects of the problem. Experience also indicates that the elements of the problem which the structure brings into focus are often the most interesting and desirable solutions.

Correctly stated, any design of a system involves a very great number of alternatives. Even a relatively simple problem involves thousands of different possibilities. This is because each different combination of the design parameters leads to a different configuration, and because the number of combinations of items is an exponential function.

In general, the development of most systems involves three basic parameters:

- *Size*—How big, or what kind of activity should it be?
- *Location*—Where will this system be installed? For whom?
- *Time*—During which period will this project be started?

When each of these factors is part of the design, which is the normal situation for a system that will evolve over time, the number of possible combinations is defined by:

$$\text{Possible Designs} = [(\text{sizes})^{(\text{locations})}]^{(\text{periods})}$$

Mexico City Airport: Possible Designs

This is the first of a series of examples that refer to one of our studies, for the government of Mexico in 1970. The issue was: what is the best evolution of the airport system for Mexico City through the end of the century?

The number of possibilities for such a system is limited, compared to other systems, because airports only make sense in a few different sizes and because there are only a few places where you can place such a facility in a highly populated metropolitan area.

For Mexico City, only four different types or sizes of airports were considered: for domestic, international, general, and military aviation. Likewise, only two locations were available. Finally, we looked at the design for three periods: 1970, 1985, and the year 2000. The number of possible configurations logically possible were thus:

$$\text{Possible Designs} = ((4)^2)^3 = 4096$$

Some of the possible designs are not worth considering in any detail: it would evidently not have been worthwhile to build a complete new airport at a new site in 1985, and then close this down and return to the old site in 2000. Even discarding such combinations leaves us with thousands of possible patterns of development for this fairly simple system.

This is a very large number indeed. Note carefully that it is exponential, not multiplicative as many people would guess it should be (see box and Section 7.1).

Faced with such a large number of choices, most people easily become confused. This difficulty is compounded by uncertainties about what may happen. The mind quickly boggles after a few thoughts along the lines of "If I do this, then that will happen . . . I could then do the other; on the other hand, that might not happen . . . and besides I could always do something else in the first place." Without some structure to help people grasp all these possibilities, they generally focus their attention on a few choices.

This polarization of attention is the normal human way to deal with complexity for people who do not have some structure that will organize the problem. This is unfortunate as it leads, almost inevitably, to inferior choices. The obvious difficulty is that any evaluation that systematically fails to look at a large fraction of the possibilities has a high probability of missing some attractive solutions. This difficulty is increased, moreover, by the way people polarize their attention.

The fact is that people tend to focus on simple, clear-cut solutions. They tend to avoid the ones that are complicated. Specifically, they tend to avoid designs that are combinations of the simpler solutions. This fact is important because, as discussed further in Section 16.5, the best solutions are often precisely those that combine the best features of several simpler designs (see following box).

Mexico City Airport: Polarization of Choices

The question of how Mexico City ought to expand its airport system had preoccupied planners for over a decade before our participation in the process. The issue had actually become quite controversial.

The nature of this debate illustrates well the kind of polarization that often occurs in system planning. When we arrived, just two alternatives were being considered; two out of the over 4000 that could easily be imagined.

Moreover, these two were definitely clear cut. They were based entirely on either of the two possible locations, the existing one at Texcoco or the new site of Zumpango. Specifically, the solutions were:

1. "All Texcoco," all services were to be concentrated at Texcoco for all time.
2. "All Zumpango," all services were to be moved as soon as possible, for all time, to the new site.

No combinations, such as a partial development of a new site or its gradual development, were being considered. After the analysis, these combinations were exactly the ones that turned out to be most desirable.

16.4 STRUCTURE OF DECISIONS

Decision analysis structures the problem to bring out all the relevant choices, as well as all the possible outcomes that can be imagined. The means for doing this is the decision tree.

The *decision tree* is a conceptual device for enumerating each of the possible decisions that can be made, and each of the possible outcomes that may occur according to each of the events or states of nature that may arise. Graphically, it branches out from an initial node, to subsequent nodes where there is further branching, hence the metaphor of a "tree." In practice, decision trees are only drawn for illustrative or textbook purposes; for real problems it is impractical to draw a tree and the concept is embedded in computer files.

The decision tree first of all represents a sequence. This is the pattern of actions that one can take concerning a problem. It consists of the alternation of two elements:

1. *Decision nodes*, which are the moments when possible decisions are considered and a decision made
2. *Chance nodes*, the periods after a decision in which outcomes are determined by prevailing events or states of nature

Graphically, the sequence is:

$$D - C - D - C -$$

where an initial decision is followed by chance events, after which the designers face another set of decisions, and so on.

The decision tree is a "tree" in that each node in the sequence has several branches, as many as needed to show the possible decisions or chance events and resulting outcomes. The decision node thus indicates which specific choices might be made at that time. Figure 16.1 illustrates this for the problem of the Mexico City Airport. For this situation there are 16 different designs that could be implemented during the first period, each of the combinations of four kinds of services at the two separate sites.

The chance nodes differ from the decision nodes. Since we propose to do an analysis, they are in the first place subject to the discipline of the laws of probability. This implies first of all that the several branches define all the events E_j that may occur. Secondly, these events should be distinct; they should not refer to the same thing. If they did, there would be double-counting. Formally, the events referred to by the branches of each chance node should be "mutually exclusive and collectively exhaustive," so that their probabilities, P_j, sum to 1.0 (i.e., something does happen).

The chance nodes differ further from the decision nodes in that they may have several stages of branches from each node. This is a device that allows us to represent joint probabilities of two or more events conveniently (a possibility which is rather awkward in a payoff matrix, for example). Figure 16.2 illustrates this. Section 16.5 shows how to calculate the joint probabilities.

The chance nodes also carry considerable information, in addition to the possible states of nature. A complete branch from a chance node has two tags on it:

1. The probability P_j of the event E_j of that branch occurring (these must sum to 1.0 for any stage).

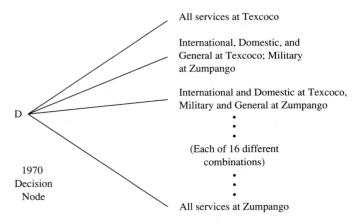

FIGURE 16.1
Initial decision node for the design of the Mexico City airport system: The possible decisions that could be made in the first period of 1970.

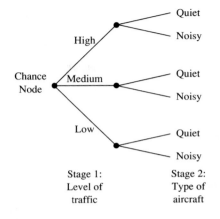

FIGURE 16.2
Structure of a chance node for the design of the Mexico City Airport System: Joint possibilities associated with the two different states of nature—level of traffic and type of aircraft—shown by stages of branches.

2. The outcome O_{ij}, measured in numerical terms, that results from the original decision D_i preceding the chance node and the state of nature or event E_j that prevails afterwards.

Graphically, these items of information are usually placed alongside and at the end of each branch from a chance node, thus

$$C - \textit{Probability, } P_j - \text{Outcome } O_{ij}$$

The complete structure of a decision tree for a real problem is thus quite complex, as might be expected for a complex problem. The beauty of the decision tree is that it can be constructed in a series of simple steps, each of which can be linked in computer files with little difficulty. The analyst can then appreciate the structure without having to draw it completely in detail. Figure 16.3 outlines the complete tree for the design of the airport system for Mexico City.

> **Semantic caution:** The tree metaphor pervades decision analysis. When the tree is complex, as for Mexico City, it may be referred to as a "messy bush." When we discard possible choices, we speak of "pruning" the "branches."

The structure of the decision tree is useful—indeed essential—to the analysis. A first contribution is that it educates the planners as to the real possibilities.

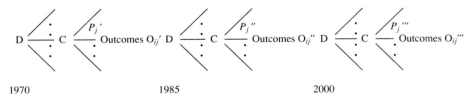

1970   1985   2000

FIGURE 16.3
Sketch of the complete decision tree for the analysis of the Mexico City Airport System.

Thus in the case of the work in Mexico City, simply developing and presenting the decision tree to the planners and the ministers opened up the problem: it helped them realize that their choices were not polar (see Section 16.3), but included a wide range of combinations. The structure thus opened the way to finding the most desirable solution. The decision tree also provides the basis for the actual analysis, as discussed in what follows.

16.5   CALCULATIONS (SINGLE PERIOD)

For ease of presentation, the calculations of decision analysis are first explained and illustrated for a decision covering only a single period. In this case the decisionmaker has only one opportunity to make a choice; there is no follow-on or contingencies that are being taken into account. Such a simple case is, of course, quite unrepresentative of the reality of designing a system. The calculations for the typical case involving many periods are shown in Section 16.7.

Principle for calculations. The essential principle of decision analysis is simple: choose the decision that offers the *best average value*. Each of these terms, "best," "average," and "value" requires careful definition, however.

Value represents the real worth of any outcome to the decisionmaker. This may not correspond in any simple way to size of that outcome. For example, the value of a first plate of food to a starving person might be extremely high because it represents the difference between life and death; the value of the fourth plate on the other hand might be insignificant if the person were now already fed. As Chapters 18 to 20 explain in detail, value can be—and in general is— a complicated, nonlinear function of the outcomes. In other situations, such as those represented by choices whose economic outcomes are relatively small for the company or person concerned, the values can be considered to be equivalent to the outcomes.

To facilitate the discussion of decision analysis itself, this section ignores the possibility that outcomes do not represent their real value to the decisionmaker. This complication is left to Chapters 18 and 19. Once the process of decision analysis and the methods of determining real value are understood, they are easily brought together as needed, as Section 19.8 illustrates.

The "average" value relevant to a risky decision, D_i, is simply its *expected value:* the outcomes weighted by their estimated probability of occurrence. Formally, the average value of a possible decision D_i is then

$$EV(D_i) = \sum_j P_j O_{ij}$$

where $EV(\cdot)$ is a standard notation to indicate expected value.

> **Semantic caution:** The term "expected value" has an established definition that can be confusing in decision analysis. In probability it indicates nothing more than the

probabilistic average defined above. It has nothing to do with whether the things being averaged are expressed in outcomes or in their real values, as discussed later in Chapters 18 and 19.

The "best" average value refers to how the decisionmaker sees the outcomes. It is the highest average value of the outcomes that are desirable, and the lowest if they are not.

The calculations necessary to determine the optimal decision are easy. The process requires nothing more than many repetitions of the simple formula for expected value. The calculations may become confusing, however, since risky decisions often involve thousands of possibilities as Section 16.3 indicates. This confusion will be avoided if one organizes the work carefully.

The calculations will be straightforward if one carefully follows the structure of the decision tree. Specifically, the process should consist of two steps for a single stage:

1. Calculate the probability of the outcomes
2. Calculate the best decision

Calculation of probabilities. When the outcomes are determined by two or more independent events, it is necessary to calculate their probability of occurrence. For example, consider the analysis of a new technology whose success depends both on its cost of production (high, medium, low, etc.) and the overall state of the economy (boom, stagnation, recession, etc.). The estimates of the probabilities of each of these two different kinds of events are typically obtained through a different process and different experts. A production engineer may have provided estimates of the cost of production, for instance, and an economist the economic forecasts. The actual outcomes will depend on the events that occur as combinations of these two events such as "high cost and boom economy," "high cost and recession," and so on. The probability of these outcomes is the *joint probability* of the relevant events.

The joint probabilities can be easily calculated only if the events are *independent*, that is, if their probabilities of occuring do not depend on each other. (In the previous example the probabilities might not be independent: the probability of getting high costs could conceivably depend on whether the economy were in a boom, or a recession with plentiful labor.) The joint probabilities of independent events are simply the factor of their individual probabilities. Thus the probability of "high cost and boom" is simply the probability of high cost of production times the probability of a boom economy.

In practice, the calculation of joint probabilities may be a really important step in the process. This is because the outcomes may depend on many factors leading to a great many possible combinations. The calculations then usually indicate that the distribution of the probability of the outcomes is much broader than decisionmakers otherwise imagine. The detailed calculations, naturally done by computer, thus educate the decisionmakers as to the real risks involved in any decision (see box).

Calculation of Probabilities

This example comes from the files of an electric power utility that was trying to identify the best way to conserve energy. Their analysis indicated that the outcomes, in terms of net benefits, were determined by five independent factors: the lifetime of the device; the company's future discount rate; and the escalation rates or rates of increase in required capacity, production costs, and revenues.

Schematically, their chance node after any possible decision was as in Figure 16.4(a). The total number of branches from the chance node were $(3 \times 3 \times 3 \times 3 \times 2) = 162$. Each branch, being a joint probability of all five different independent events, had a specific, distinct outcome. These constituted a probability distribution that could be summarized graphically for easy display. Figure 16.4(b) gives an example. This kind of result helped the directors of the utility appreciate that any decision could have a really wide range of outcomes.

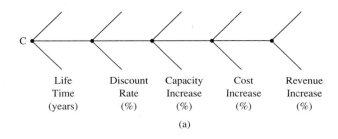

(a)

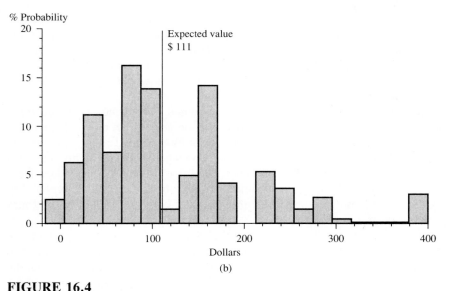

(b)

FIGURE 16.4
(a) Sequence of difference chance events. (b) Joint distribution of outcomes resulting from sequence of chance events.

Optimal decision for single period. The best decision is the one with the best average value. Insofar as the outcomes correspond to their real worth, the best decision is simply the one with the best expected value for the outcomes.

The expected value for each possible decision is easily calculated if there is only one period of possible decisions and chance nodes in the decision tree. It is simply the probabilistic average as defined previously:

$$EV(D_i) = \sum_j P_j O_{ij}$$

The optimal decision D^* is thus the decision with the best expected value.

To illustrate the calculations, consider this simple decision: should you take your raincoat or not, the next day you go to work or school? Suppose for simplicity that the risky events E_j are that it may either rain or be clear, and further that

- the probability of rain, $P(\text{Rain})=0.4$, so that the probability of no rain is $P(\text{Clear})=0.6$.
- the values of the possible outcomes, O_{ij} (such as being caught in the rain without a raincoat) are the numbers indicated on the right in the following decision tree.

Your decision tree for this single period is thus:

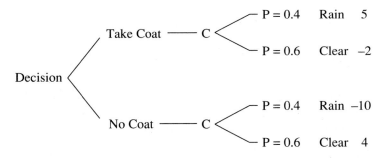

To calculate the optimal decision, we calculate the expected value of each choice:

$$EV(\text{Take Coat}) = P(\text{Rain})(5) + P(\text{Clear})(-2)$$
$$= (0.4)(5) + (0.6)(-2) = 0.8$$

$$EV(\text{No Coat}) = (0.4)(-10) + (0.6)(4) = -1.6$$

The best choice would be to take the raincoat:

$$EV(D^*) = EV(\text{Raincoat}) = 0.8 > EV(\text{No Coat})$$

16.6   CONTINUOUS PROBABILITY DISTRIBUTIONS

For ease of presentation, the decision trees have so far been shown with a finite number of branches emerging from each chance node. This should not be taken to imply that decision analysis can only handle a finite number of outcomes. On the contrary, the method can easily deal with the infinite number of possibilities associated with a continuous probability distribution.

The application of decision analysis to situations involving continuous probability distributions is essentially identical to the procedure just described. The only difference is that we must use integrals to evaluate the expected values. Thus, if the probability distribution is some function of the chance event, E_j:

$$\text{probability distribution} = \text{pdf}\,(E_j)$$

then the expected value of any decision is simply the integral of this distribution times the possible outcomes:

$$EV(D_i) = \int O_{ij} \bullet \text{pdf}\,(E_j)\ dE_j$$

See box for an example application.

Many kinds of risky situations are best represented by continuous probability distributions, as indicated in Section 15.4. These include all kinds of physical and social phenomena that are to occur repeatedly and for which a continuous distribution can be estimated. They include, for example,

- rainfall, needed for the planning of water resources systems.
- earthquakes, whose intensity must be estimated for the design of structures.
- traffic intensity, by time of day and season, useful for the management of all kinds of networks, from communications to highways.
- economic conditions, which play an important part in the success of business investments.

16.7   CALCULATIONS (MULTIPLE PERIODS)

The realistic situation for any system is that there are many stages of possible decision and chance nodes, as for the problem of the Mexico City Airport illustrated in Figure 16.3. To find the optimal choice, one must calculate the best decisions stage by stage, starting with the last period. The best decision for this last period is calculated as for a single period (Section 16.5).

The process of finding the optimal decision for multiple periods is similar to that employed in dynamic programming (see Chapter 7). The result of this procedure is a great economy in the number of calculations necessary, just as there is through the use of dynamic programming.

The problem of finding the best decision in a sequence of possible decisions is equivalent to finding the best paths through the decision tree. It thus has

Optimal Design Against Earthquakes

The definition of the optimal design against earthquakes was a classic application of decision analysis to a situation involving continuous probability distributions. Some years ago, we did this for the United States.

There were—and are in general—a discrete number of possible choices. These are represented by building codes that define consistent standards of strength for a structure. Naturally, designing according to a more stringent building code both provides more strength and costs more money. The issue is: which is the right code for any given locality?

The optimal choice depends on the kinds of earthquakes that occur. Where there are only insignificant earthquakes, it is not worthwhile to spend much money on protection against them, and vice-versa.

The possible intensity of earthquakes in any region is conveniently summarized by a probability distribution giving the frequency of occurrence of earthquakes of any given intensity. This information is routinely collected in earthquake zones, and reported either on the Richter scale or the Modified Mercalli Index.

The damage that may occur as a result of an earthquake, O_{ij}, depends both on the choice of the building code, D_i, and the intensity of the earthquake, I_j. The expected cost associated with any code is thus the cost of its implementation plus the expected damage due to earthquakes. This is:

Expected Cost of Building Code $=$ Construction Cost

$$+ \int (\text{Damage due to } I_j)(\text{Distribution of } I_j) dI_j$$

---

the same form as the sequential route problems discussed in Section 7.2, and can be solved similarly. In practice, a formal dynamic program is essentially never used, as it is easier to proceed through the decision tree than to set up the formal structure of a dynamic program. But the overall effect on the number of calculations is the same.

Consider the analysis of the development of the Mexico City Airport discussed in Section 16.3. At each period there were 16 possible decisions as Figure 16.1 shows. For the three periods there were thus $(16)^3 = 4096$ different combinations, and thus paths through the decision tree. This is the number of expected value calculations that would be necessary if we examined each possible sequence explicitly. By analyzing the problem period by period, however, we only considered 16 possible decisions at each of the three periods, and thus $16 \times 3 = 48$ in all. The size of the problem was thus multiplicative rather than exponential in the number of periods—(16×3) versus $(16)^3$.

The reason the analysis is so much easier when done stage by stage is that we determine a single best decision after the chance outcome of a previous period, and thus drop from consideration all the other possible decisions at that period—

as well as the combinations they would represent. This is the step known as "pruning" the decision tree.

The procedure is best illustrated by a simple example with only a very few branches. This kind of problem does not demonstrate the way the analysis reduces the number of calculations; it has few branches to begin with and thus few to prune. But one can fully graph a simple problem as one cannot a realistic problem such as that of the Mexico City Airport!

The example concerns the problem of deciding how best to plan for development. The idea is, as often occurs in practice, that one must first decide whether to reserve a site for expansion and then later decide whether to build. In between these decisions one gets a chance to see how fast ones' activities grow. The final outcome depends on this growth and some other chance events occurring after the decision as to whether to build. This situation is, in fact, a simplified version of the Mexico City case, as Figure 16.5 shows.

The analysis of the problem begins with the last period and consists of calculating the expected value associated with each of the possible decisions at the available decision nodes. From these analyses we can conclude which decision is best at each decision node in the last period. Knowing what is best at that time and what we could do if we were ever in the position defined by that node, we can drop from further analysis all the possible decisions we could avoid. Figure 16.6 shows the result so far. Note that since we now know what we would do as a result of each chance outcome in the preceding stage (for example, if we had reserved a site and there were growth, we would build), and knowing its

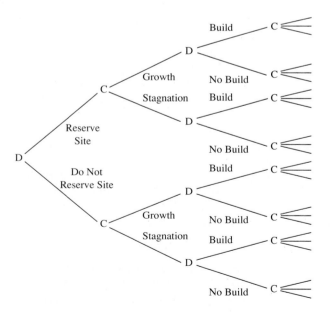

FIGURE 16.5
A decision tree for the example problem of trying to determine the best pattern of development for some group.

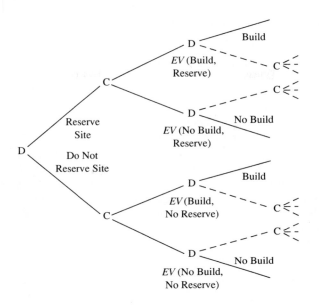

FIGURE 16.6
Example decision tree after analysis of last stage in which nonoptimal branches have been eliminated from further consideration.

expected value, we simply define the value of that outcome as the expected value of the best decision at that point.

The process continues with the next, that is, the preceding, period. At this point the problem is as shown in Figure 16.7. Expected values of each possible decision are again calculated and the decision with the best expected value is selected. Note how this analysis looks at simple outcomes of the chance nodes, rather than the really complex ones represented by all the possible decisions and branches that could be taken later.

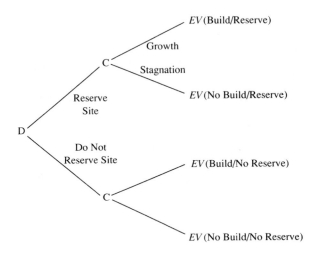

FIGURE 16.7
The example problem viewed from the next, preceding stage.

16.8   DECISION ANALYSIS AS STRATEGY

Results. The final result of a multistage decision tree is a strategy. Formally, a *strategy* can be considered a sequence of decisions contingent on all the possible outcomes. It is not a single sequence of decisions best for all occasions.

For example, let us say that the optimal decision at the first stage of a multistage site selection problem is to reserve a site. The decision at the next stage is not specified by this first decision; it depends on the intervening chance outcome. For our example, the final recommendation would be: First reserve a site; then build if there is growth or do not build if there is stagnation. This was, in fact, our final recommendation to the President of Mexico and his decision in 1971 concerning the capital's airport. Zumpango was reserved, but ultimately not built since traffic stagnated as a joint result of economic recession and development of direct flights to coastal resorts. We considered this a most successful decision: it preserved the options when needed, but avoided massive costs that ultimately were not necessary.

This kind of result is completely different than the "master plans" frequently encountered in practice. A *master plan* specifies a single sequence of development in each phase (such as to build a new airport at Zumpango, close the old airport, transfer all traffic, etc.). Master plans have been the typical result of most efforts to define the development of large-scale engineering products.

The definition of an optimal strategy of development is one of the real contributions of decision analysis. It permits and encourages the designer to deal effectively with the inevitable uncertainties. Master plans by contrast promote inflexibility and a resistance to doing the right thing for prevailing circumstances. Master plans are also inherently far less than optimal since there is always a reasonable chance that the proposed master plan (e.g., reserve site and build) is disadvantageous compared to some other pattern of development (e.g., reserve site but do not build—if there is no growth).

16.9   APPLICATION

The use of decision analysis was recently very effective in facilitating the design of a major national system. We used it to help the Australian government decide how to develop airports for their major hub, Sydney.

The advantage of using decision analysis in this case is particularly evident when contrasted to the standard alternative of benefit-cost analysis, which had been repeatedly used quite unsuccessfully on the same problem. This case also nicely illustrates how decision analysis

- educates the client, by structuring the problem to bring into focus the real range of risk and options.
- defines an optimal choice, particularly for the immediate first stage.
- identifies a preferred strategy for dealing with the inevitable eventual changes in the situation.

Background. Australian governments have long recognized the need to provide additional airport capacity for Sydney. The existing commercial airport, Kingsford-Smith, had—when we were called in to help in 1984—only two runways to serve a city of three million. Comparable cities, such as Boston, will have three or four major runways.

The situation was becoming increasingly urgent because the few plausible sites were being engulfed by metropolitan development. For Sydney, this situation was particularly acute. The Kingsford-Smith Airport sits on restricted landfill in Botany Bay, surrounded by both hills and densely inhabited communities. Furthermore, the Sydney region is ringed by substantial mountains and cut up by rivers. The options were quite limited as the need pressed.

Previous governments had made several major attempts to decide how to expand the airport system for Sydney. Each had tried to define the best master plan for the region, either to extend the existing site by filling in a major portion of the Bay or to acquire another site and build a new airport. None of the previous efforts had been successful in defining an acceptable solution, despite millions of dollars worth of first-class work in engineering and planning.

The preceding studies had each evaluated the alternatives using some form of benefit-cost analysis. Basically they would attempt to estimate future costs and benefits of any candidate design over the next 20 to 30 years; based on some forecasts of growth. Inevitably, by the time the final recommendations came to be debated, some two years or so after the forecasts were factored into the analysis, these predictions were already wrong. These analyses were thus simply not credible.

The proponents of each master plan were always in the unfortunate position of "defending the indefensible." To demonstrate that their chosen plan was the best alternative they had to assert that their forecasts were correct. This is quite impossible; no amount of technical knowledge can predict popular trends over 20 or 30 years (see Section 15.1). Air travel itself changes so rapidly that the fallacy of their logic was evident almost immediately.

Education of client. The first step in any evaluation is to pick the right form of analysis for the situation at hand, as Chapter 10 stresses. Specifically, it is necessary to determine whether risk is an important factor for the problem.

Previous analysts had in effect assumed that risk was insignificant. They had based their evaluations on specific forecasts of what would happen, and had gone to great pains to defend these predictions when it came to justifying their recommended master plan. At the time our team arrived on the scene, the Australian government had an official forecasting bureau. This agency was confidently predicting an annual rate of growth of air traffic of 2%, maximum, and the government wished us to base our evaluation on this forecast.

The fact is that 20 to 30 year forecasts must be regarded as highly inaccurate. Section 15.1 makes the point. Long-term predictions concerning developing industries, such as air transport, are especially uncertain since they both grow rapidly and fluctuate substantially. This reality had to be brought home to the client.

Demonstrating that the official forecasts were unreliable was easy, as it generally should be. All we had to do was to contrast the current predictions with the previous ones made 5 and 10 years earlier, with the historical record and, for extra reinforcement, with experience in comparable situations elsewhere. These comparisons showed that growth rates could be as high as 10% for many years, were about 7% over the previous 20 years, and that previous forecasts had recently asserted that long-term rates would be about 5%! Naturally, the professional forecasters were upset that this evidence was brought forward: it effectively dismissed their work. Yet the client had to recognize, as anyone should, that the future outcomes are highly uncertain.

Secondly, we had to help the client appreciate the complexity of the decisions. Previously the problem had been presented as a stark, polar alternative: build a major facility either at the current or at a new site. The reality of course is that any large system requires many stages, each involving many possible decisions, leading to a very great number of alternatives. Drawing out the decision tree graphically illustrates the issue. We stressed the point verbally by emphasizing that the only immediate decision the government had to make was to select a site; decisions about whether any airport should be built, or at what size, only had to be made many years later, after the actual growth in traffic had been observed.

Evaluation. Decision analysis was the appropriate form of evaluation because of the many possible outcomes of any decision. It is the only method that can deal adequately with risky alternatives. It is unquestionably better for this problem than the benefit-cost analyses, which have no reasonable way of dealing with contingencies.

The analysis itself proceeded normally. It clearly showed that the best immediate step was to acquire a site for a new airport—however the traffic might develop and whatever decisions the government might eventually want to take. This is because securing the site provides insurance against the chance of growth, and good decisions almost inevitably provide means to deal with risks.

We did not use a decision tree when it came time to present the results to the Minister for Aviation, the government generally, and ultimately the public-at-large through the environmental impact statement. One cannot expect that this concept, which requires considerable study, will mean anything to most people. We therefore used a simple payoff matrix to summarize the analysis. Table 16.7 reproduces our presentation.

This display makes it obvious that the optimal choice, for the first stage of the process, is to secure a site for a new airport. Whereas a new site is not the better choice if we absolutely knew that air traffic would stagnate (at 2% a year), the reality is that we cannot be so sure. By acquiring a new site the government has at least an adequate solution whatever happens.

Strategy. A strategy of development is the only reasonable solution when there is risk, as decision analysis indicates. Once one recognizes that long-term predictions are unreliable, master plans for what should be done are indefensible—as

TABLE 16.7
Consequences of alternative first stage decisions for Sydney

Action	High forecast	Median forecast	Low forecast
Select site	Good decision: site available to meet demand	Good decision: site available to meet demand	Neutral decision: temporary sterilization of site; land put to alternative use until required
No action	Poor decision: congestion at Kingsford-Smith Airport; site at higher cost or greater distance subsequently selected	Poor decision: congestion at Kingsford-Smith Airport; site at higher cost or greater distance subsequently selected	Neutral decision: proposed sites put to higher priority use: site at higher cost or greater distance subsequently selected

previous planners for Sydney's airport had discovered. Our recommended strategy was simple:

- First, acquire a new site.
- Then, depending on how fast traffic grew, either build to the appropriate size or not.

Results. The most important result is that decision analysis led to an acceptable decision. Within a year after we submitted our recommendation and environmental impact statement, uneventful public hearings had been concluded and the government began to acquire the site. Three years later the job was more than half done.

The reason decision analysis succeeded where benefit-cost had failed so miserably is that the recommendation made simple common sense. Our key argument was that we could not predict the future and *therefore* had to take adequate precautions. Rather than trying to "defend the undefensible" idea of omniscience, we made a strength of the reality of risk.

REFERENCES

Behn, R. D., and Vaupel, J. W., (1982). *Quick Analysis for Busy Decision-Makers*, Basic Books, New York.

de Neufville, R., and Keeney, R. (1972, 1974). "Use of Decision Analysis in Airport Development for Mexico City," Chapter 23 in *Analysis of Public Systems*, A. W. Drake, R. Keeney, and P. M. Morse, eds., MIT Press, Cambridge, MA; and Chapter 24 in *Systems Planning and Design*, R. de Neufville, and D. H. Marks, eds., Prentice-Hall, Englewood Cliffs, NJ.

de Neufville, R., (1990). "Successful Siting of Airports: the Sydney Example," *Journal of Trans-portation Engineering*, American Society of Civil Engineers, Vol. 116.

Raiffa, H., (1970). *Introductory Lectures on Choices Under Uncertainty*, Addison-Wesley, Reading, MA.

PROBLEMS

16.1 *Election Campaign*

As a politician you can end your campaign for election either in City A or B. You estimate that a speech in A will gain you either 2000 votes or, if local students protest, 4000 votes more than your opponent. However, if your opponent also comes to A you will have to cancel the speech and debate, in which case you will get 1000 votes less than your opponent. Your manager estimates that the probability of your opponent showing up is 0.5. The probability that the students will protest is 0.3.

Alternatively, you can go to B, where there are no students and your opponent has already been, where you may either gain 2000 votes (probability 0.3) or 600 votes (probability 0.7).

(*a*) Which city would you go to if you are trying to maximize your votes?

(*b*) Which city should you go to if current polls show you are losing by 800 votes?

16.2 *Money Bags, Take 2*

Welcome back (see Problem 15.1) to the "Money Bags" TV show. You have won $600. Then Monty, the MC, offers you, for your $600, a wallet in which there are either ten $100 bills (making $1000) or one $20 bill and three $100 bills (making $320). He also gives you the option, for a cost of $100, to pull one of the bills out of the wallet before choosing whether or not to take the contents (which will be either $1000 or $320) at the additional cost of $600.

(*a*) Structure the decision tree for determining whether you should keep your $600, take the wallet without pulling a bill (at a cost of $600), or look at a bill before deciding whether or not you should buy the wallet. Calculate the appropriate consequences and probabilities for the tree.

(*b*) What is the strategy that maximizes the expected monetary value?

16.3 *Assembly Robot*

An industrial assembly robot is being used to join two machine parts. A peg from Part 127 must be inserted into a hole in Part 34A. The robot may be programmed either to pound Part 127 into Part 34A, or to nudge it in gently. The pounding process is faster if Part 34A was presented to the robot in the proper alignment, but slower otherwise.

	Part 34A presentation	
Robot action	Aligned	Not aligned
Pound	0.2 s	1 s
Nudge	0.4 s	0.6 s

The conveyor belt seems to align correctly about 70% of Part 34As that are fed to this robot.

The robot is also equipped with a laser and a set of photocells that can be used to test that alignment "visually." Correct alignments will give "okay" test results 80% of the time, while misalignments yield "not okay" readings 90% of the time. The laser-bearing head takes 0.001 s to make the test itself, but 0.05 s are required for the head to swing into test position and then back out of the way, so that Part 127 may approach without hitting the laser.

(a) Structure the decision tree for the choice of pound, nudge, or test.

(b) Find P(aligned/"okay"), P(aligned/"not okay") using Bayes' Theorem.

(c) Assign appropriate probabilities and outcomes to the branches of the tree. Find the expected time of each alternative strategy by folding back the tree. Which strategy will be the fastest?

16.4 *Mars Probe*

A group of researchers has leased space on a Mars probe for an experiment to be run once the probe lands. They have limited grant money available, but if their experiment succeeds, they will receive a grant for $10 million to continue their research. If their experiment fails they will get nothing. The experiment to be conducted can be run in one of two ways, but can only be run once. Scientists in the group have two theories about the Martian surface which they deem equally likely. The validity of the theories affects the probabilities of success of the two methods as indicated in the following table.

True theory	Probability of success	
	Method X	**Method Y**
A	0.8	0.4
B	0.4	0.7

(a) Calculate the probability of success if method X is used; if method Y is used.

(b) Draw the decision tree for deciding how to conduct the experiment.

(c) Which method should be used?

16.5 *Software Development*

You are president of Celestial Software company, and have enough money to buy an exclusive license to produce software for one of the two personal computers due to be released next summer. You are convinced that only one of these will be a hit, but you do not know which. You must act soon or another company will purchase the license before you do. If you own the license for the PC that becomes a hit, you will make a profit, but if your PC flops, then you will suffer a loss:

License purchased	Financial outcome ($1M)	
	Hit	**Flop**
A	10	−1
B	8	−0.5

(*a*) Assuming that both PCs are equally likely to become hits, draw the decision tree and label its branches with the appropriate probabilities and outcomes.

(*b*) Which license should you buy?

16.6 *Traffic Department*

As head of the Traffic Department you are planning a new system of traffic lights. Your experts are divided into two groups. One believes in theory A and one in theory B (A or B is true, not both). At present you consider the two theories equally plausible. You have two options for your light system—systems X and Y.

If theory A is true and you adopt system X, then your payoff will be 1 with probability 0.8, and 0 with probability 0.2. If theory B is true and you adopt system X, then your payoff will be 1 with probability 0.1, and 0 with probability 0.9. Your payoff to system Y is 0.5.

You have a two-period time horizon. You can choose system Y now for the two periods or you can experiment for the first period (i.e., use system X) and then choose a system for the second period depending on your payoff in period 1.

(*a*) Draw the decision tree. Label carefully.

(*b*) Put the payoffs at the ends of the branches.

(*c*) Put the probabilities you can write down immediately on the appropriate branches.

(*d*) Explain how to compute the other probabilities.

(*e*) Assuming that you wish to maximize the expected value of the payoff, what strategy should you follow?

16.7 *Oil Exploration*

An oil company has the option of exploring for oil at only one of three sites. The company estimates that the three sites have approximately the same productive lifetimes and costs and that their probable production is as in the table:

Site	**0**	**20K**	**100K**	**1000K**
	P(output), barrels per day			
A	0.05	0.4	0.5	0.05
B	0.1	0.75	0.1	0.05
C	0.7	0.05	0.05	0.2

At which site should the company explore?

16.8 *Earthquake Protection*

Your friend, Phil Vallee, is going to buy a $300,000 house on the West Coast. However, the site is on a 45° slope and is susceptible to landslides caused by earthquakes. During the 10 years Phil plans to live in the house, there is a 10% chance that a damaging earthquake (which would cause a slide and destroy the house) will occur. The probability of having more than one earthquake during the next 10 years can be neglected. If such an earthquake occurs, it will be "moderate" with 90% probability and "severe" with 10% probability. Your friend can take one of three actions: (1) do not provide earthquake protection (and spend exactly $300,000 initially), (2) design the foundations of the house, at an additional cost of \$15,000, so that it can take a moderate earthquake but not a severe one, or (3) spend an additional \$120,000 and design the house so that it will survive even a severe earthquake.

(*a*) Draw a decision tree showing all possible actions, outcomes, and consequences (in dollar terms).

(*b*) If money were the only consideration, which alternative should you recommend?

16.9 *Sonny's PV's*
Sonny Reyes (see Problem 15.6) must decide how to manufacture the PV panels. He has three choices:

- Develop a new method
- Alter existing methods
- Get an outside firm to produce them

Developing the new method would yield a profit of \$11 million if successful, and if it cannot be developed, the outside firm must be used for a profit of \$2M. There is a 70% chance that the new method will be successfully developed.

Altering the existing method successfully will yield a profit of \$7M, and there is a 90% chance of the alterations being successful. If not successful, the outside firm must be used for a profit of \$3M. If used immediately, the outside firm will definitely be able to produce the panels and this would lead to a profit of \$5M.

Neglecting any time considerations,

(*a*) Structure the decision tree.

(*b*) Solve and select the best strategy.

16.10 *PY-RIC Enterprises*
M.T. "Vic" Torrey heads the division of PY-RIC that launches communications satellites. Vic has to decide whether to go ahead with today's launch or delay it for more favorable conditions. At present the probability of a successful launch is estimated at 0.90. The resulting profits would be \$20M. If the launch fails, the loss of the payload costs \$120M. A month's delay would increase the probability of success to 0.95, but the profit would drop to \$10 M due to penalty fees paid to clients. If the launch is totally aborted, PY-RIC must refund clients \$10M.

(*a*) Draw the decision tree.

(*b*) What should Vic do if he decides only according to expected values of profit?

16.11 *Marian Haste*
Marian Haste is a painter under contract to paint the exterior of a building for \$225,000. Unfortunately for her, the outside temperature may drop below freezing. If it does, the paint will not stick well and may peel off. The paint may also peel off even it does not freeze. Either way, Marian would have to repaint the building, at a cost of \$150,000.

The radio forecasts a 60% chance of freezing. Marian also believes there is a $\frac{1}{3}$ chance the paint may peel if it freezes, but a 10% chance if it does not. Her choices now are to go ahead and paint, or to defer until there is no chance of frost. Deferring the job would require her to pay \$30,000 in overtime and penalties. What would you advise Marian Haste to do? (For your own amusement, the question is should Marian Haste go ahead, and repaint at leisure?)

16.12 *P. O'Toole*

Paddy O'Toole makes outdoor furniture that sells in the summer (the Paddy O. Furniture line). Production starts in January, however, right after the holidays. That is when Paddy must decide on whether to hire 1, 2, or 3 assistants at $14,000 each for the season. He could then produce Low (1200 units), Medium (1800 units), or High (2400 units). His product sells for $30/unit on average in June. Units not sold in June must be sold at half price. Based on experience, he estimates $P(N)$, the probability that the demand for his furniture next June will be N, as:

N	:	1000	1500	2000	2500
$P(N)$	:	0.2	0.3	0.4	0.1

How many assistants should Paddy hire to maximize expected profit?

CHAPTER 17

INFORMATION GATHERING

17.1 THE ISSUE

New information about a situation provides us with the opportunity to base our decisions on more current, better estimates of the consequences of any choice. We may expect that new information thus leads to better decisions. This logic suggests that any decision analysis should consider spending some effort gathering information.

Any decision problem has opportunities for gathering new information. It is collected through deliberate efforts to test the situation. For example

- An oil company may run detailed geological surveys before deciding whether to drill a test well.
- A manufacturer can build a prototype machine or even a factory before committing to full-scale production.
- A distributor may test market a new product before deciding if and how to sell it.
- A planner may use forecasting models to project future demand for a service.

In general, professionals are always engaged in some explicit forms of information gathering, so that they can improve their decisions.

Information can also be obtained simply by waiting. Indeed, the best way to determine what will happen N years hence is to wait until then and find out. If a decision must be taken earlier, one can at least wait awhile and see how some of the uncertainties about the future are resolved. There is thus a good reason to defer decisions.

In practical terms, the decisionmaker must decide how much information to obtain, if any. We must expect that additional information will be less and less useful. The cost of obtaining it will at some point exceed its benefits. To determine this point, and thus to define the optimum amount of information to collect, it is necessary to define the value of the information. This chapter shows how the analyst can calculate the value of information, and use this result to improve decisions and, more generally, the strategy for a system.

17.2   CONCEPT

The *value of information* in decision analysis is: The increase in expected value to be obtained from a situation due to the information, without regard for the cost of obtaining it. This definition is usefully explained by example. Consider a risky situation, L. (This would also frequently be called a "lottery," a term defined precisely in Section 18.5.) The analyst can calculate the sequence of decisions which maximizes the expected value to be obtained from the situation. Call the value of the optimum strategy $EV^*(L)$. Consider next the same risky situation, altered by the influence of new information which has revised the estimated probabilities of various consequences. Call this new version LI, and the value of its optimum strategy $EV^*(LI)$. The definition is then:

$$\text{Value of Information} = EV^*(LI) - EV^*(L)$$

This definition is explicitly devised to fit the needs of the analyst. It first of all focuses directly on how the information affects the problem being analyzed. Second, it is defined before costs are considered so that it can be compared directly to these costs. This distinction permits the analyst to address such practical questions as

- Is this information worth its cost?
- What is the benefit-cost ratio of getting this new information?
- How much can I afford to pay for the information?

Because the value of any information as defined is intrinsic to a problem, whereas its cost may be negotiable, the separation between the value and cost in the definition provides the manager with a good basis for discussing what to pay for information.

Decision analysts generally refer to a *test* in discussing this problem. A test simply refers to any specific process of collecting information. It may be as simple as what we normally think of as a test, that is, a one-shot verification of a system, or it may be quite complicated. Note carefully that tests cannot, in general, conclusively demonstrate exactly how a system performs (see the discussion of "false positives" in Section 17.3).

Decision tree after test. To calculate the value of any information, it is necessary to understand the decision tree that results from a data-gathering activity or test. This is as follows. Any data-gathering activity will produce one of a set of k observations, or test results, TR_k, out of many possibilities. Each of these possibilities has some probability of occurring, P_k. The decision to collect information thus leads to the chance node illustrated (see box) as

The Decision Tree for the Test Results

To illustrate what happens after a test, consider the simple decision problem discussed in Section 16.5: Should you take your raincoat or not the next day you go to work or school? Suppose again that the risk is that it may, for simplicity, either rain or not, and that the value of the various possible outcomes (such as being caught in the rain without a raincoat, etc.) are the numbers indicated on the right, below. Your original decision tree is thus:

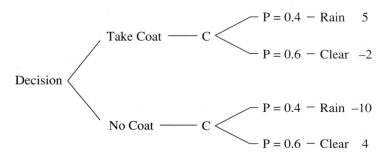

Suppose further that your data-gathering activity is to turn on the news to hear the weather forecast. For simplicity, suppose you might only hear either of two reports: rain predicted or not. From experience you could know the probability, P_k, of getting either report, TR_k, on a given day. Your decision tree for the test results would then be:

Decision ———— Test ⟨ Probability ———— Rain Predicted

Probability ———— Clear Predicted

$$D \;\text{——— collect information ———}\; C \;\text{———}\; P_k \;\text{———}\; TR_k$$

Each observation leads to a revision of the probabilities of events associated with the original risky situation, L. Call this revised risky situation, after test result TR_k, L_k. Graphically, as further explained in the next box,

$$L_k \equiv D \;\text{————}\; C \;\text{————}\; P(O_{ij} / TR_k) \;\text{————}\; O_{ij}$$

| | Original Alternatives | Revised Probabilities | Original Outcomes |

The risky situation represented by the decision to obtain information, LI, is the combination of the preceding two elements, the chance node for the test results,

Consequence of Test Results

Once you have the test result, either that rain is predicted or not, you have to revise your original decision tree. You of course have as many revisions as possible test results. For example, if the news report is "Rain Predicted," or RP, the subsequent decision tree is

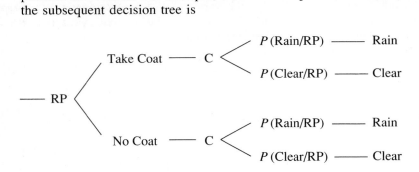

The complete decision tree after the test is simple, conceptually. It is the aggregation of the above. Graphically it is a messy bush, which we only sketch. Using CP for "Clear Predicted," it is

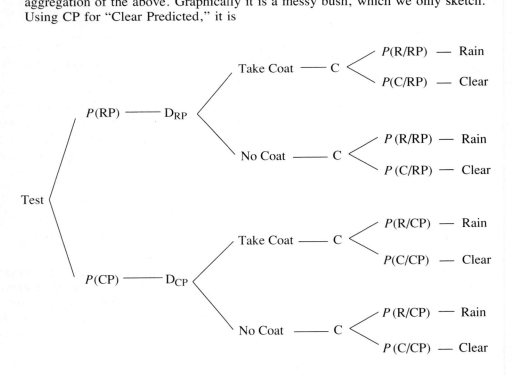

and a second stage of decisions consisting of k different new versions of the original decision tree:

$$\text{LI} \equiv \text{D} \text{——— collect information ——— C ——— } P_k \text{ ——— } L_k$$

The expected value of this situation is the expectation of the maximum value obtainable from each L_k and its probability of occurrence:

$$EV^*(\text{LI}) = \sum P_k \, EV^*(L_k)$$

Thus the value of information is:

$$\sum P_k \, EV^*(L_k) - EV^*(\text{L})$$

Complete decision tree with test. The total problem facing the analyst considering whether to collect some particular kind of information, that is, to do a specific test, is the original decision tree augmented by a single test branch leading to as many revisions of this original decision as there are possible outcomes of the test. Graphically, it is

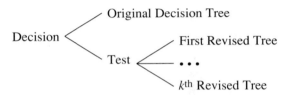

The value of information is the increase in value of the decision due to the addition of the test option. It is simply the difference between the expected value of the best sequence of decisions associated with the test compared to that associated with the original decision tree.

Events versus outcomes. It is important to notice that the result of any information-gathering activity or test is some knowledge about events E_j which are different from the outcomes O_{ij} that result from any decision. For our simple raincoat problem, for example, the information concerns whether it will rain or not; these are the two possible events. The outcome O_{ij} are the results that occur after making a decision and being subject to a chance event: for instance, deciding not to take a raincoat and being in the rain (event E_j) and getting wet (outcome O_{ij}, equaling -10 in the example).

Further examples of the differences between the events observed and the outcomes are

- An oil company might look for salt domes (event) to help them improve their forecast of oil reserves (outcome).
- A manufacturer would observe the productivity or sales (event) of a prototype, to make more realistic estimates of the profitability of full-scale production (outcome).

- A distributor would use the results of a test market (event) for a product in a particular city to estimate the market share that could be obtained from national sales (outcome).
- A planner would use a prediction made by a forecasting effort (event) to recalibrate the future loads on a system (outcome).

17.3 SAMPLE AND PERFECT INFORMATION

Two concepts of information must be considered: sample and perfect. Sample information is what you actually get from a test; its value is complicated to calculate. Perfect information is a totally hypothetical idea; its value is both easy to estimate and provides an upper bound to the value of information. Perfect information is thus a really useful artifact. Each type is discussed in detail below.

Sample information. Sample information is a set of actual observations as obtained in practice. It is inevitably a sample of the entire set of observations that might have been obtained if we had the resources to collect data indefinitely. It is necessarily incomplete.

Real, sample information also contains errors. Generally, these fall into two categories, either false positives or false negatives. A *false positive* is an erroneous report that an effect exists when it does not in fact. A "false alarm" for a fire is an example. False positives also occur routinely in medical examinations (see box). Conversely, a *false negative* is the false report that an effect does not exist when it actually does. An inspection that fails to detect a malfunction and thus reports that a system is in good order is an example of a false negative.

Because our instruments, our means for gathering data, are imperfect, we always have the possibility of both false positives and negatives. The probability of getting a specific test result, for example that an effect exists, is thus different from its actual probability of existence: $P(TR_k) \neq P(E_k)$ for sample information.

To calculate the probability of any test result, we must thus estimate the total probability of all the ways it may occur. These consist both of correct reports of an event when it occurs—a fraction of the whole since sometimes the event is not

---

Medical False Positives and Negatives

In many parts of the United States, teachers have been traditionally required by law to pass periodic tests for Tuberculosis (TB). This is a public health measure designed to protect children from contagion. TB or not TB? That is the question.

Screening for TB is routinely done by chest X-rays. Unfortunately, the dark spots on the lungs associated with TB can also be caused by other minor or noncommunicable diseases. Technicians may also of course either misread the photographs or transcribe the results erroneously. False positives are thus common with these X-ray examinations.

---

reported to exist when it really does, a false negative—and of the false positives. The reliability of the test, the degree to which it generates false positives and negatives, is a key element of this calculation.

The general formula is

$$P(TR_k) = \sum_i P(TR_k/E_i)\, P(E_i)$$

where (TR_k/E_k) is the correct report of an effect E_k when it occurs, and (TR_k/E_i), $i \neq k$ is the false positive report of E_k when actually E_i exists. Note that the summations of true and false positives are weighted by both the reliability of the test, $P(TR_k/E_i)$ and the frequency of occurrence of each case, $P(E_i)$. (See following box for example calculation.)

Probability of Test Result

Suppose that the X-ray examination for TB in some lab has a 90% chance of being correct. That is, 9 times out of 10 TB will be reported (TBR) when the person has it, and conversely that a clean report (CR) will be given when the person is healthy:

$$P(TBR/TB) = P(CR/C) = 0.9$$

There is then a 10% chance of false positives and negatives:

$$P(TBR/C) = P(CR/TB) = 0.1$$

Note that this is a simple case. In general the probability of a test result, the reliability of our measuring device, may depend on what is to be found. For example, the X-ray technician may be more likely to miss TB spots than to exaggerate them.

Suppose additionally that TB is a rare disease among the population being tested, say that only 1% of the group has it. The rest of the people are "clean," thus:

$$P(TB) = 0.01 \qquad P(C) = 0.99$$

In this situation, the chance that anyone in the group will be reported as having TB is:

$$\begin{aligned} P(TBR) &= P(TBR/TB)P(TB) + P(TBR/C)P(C) \\ &= (0.9)(0.01) + (0.1)(0.99) \\ &= 0.009 + 0.099 = 0.108 \end{aligned}$$

Note that in this particular case the incidence of false positives, $P(TBR/C)\, P(C) = 0.099$, far outweighs the incidence of true positives, $P(TBR/TB)\, P(TB) = 0.009$. This is because the error rate applies to the bulk of the population, which is so much greater than the small number of individuals with the TB condition.

One point needs to be carefully noted in connection with the results of real tests: no test can prove that any theory is correct. When a test result is compatible with theory it merely increases the probability that the theory may be correct. This is because no real test, with its imperfections, can exclude false positives and negatives. The change in credibility can be calculated by applying Bayes' Theorem (see Section 15.3 and following box). This point needs to be stressed because it confuses most people, who naturally—but wrongly—believe that a positive result confirms theory.

This confusion over the interpretation of test results is especially significant when we are trying to detect relatively rare conditions (such as AIDS) with imperfect measurements. What happens is that positive test results may easily be mostly due to the false positives from the bulk of the population that does not have the condition.

Positive tests on rare events should thus be repeated. This is standard procedure in medicine: positive results on TB, for example, are followed up with more precise (and more costly) tests. Similar procedures should be applied to all information gathering on important rare events.

Perfect information. This is an artificial concept that is most useful in practice. It represents the test results that would come from a hypothetical process that identifies exactly which event is true or what will happen. For example, perfect information about the incidence of TB would specify exactly which individuals had it and which did not; no false positives or negatives. Perfect information would give us exact knowledge about the environment and the consequences of decisions we might make.

The concept of perfect information provides an upper bound on the value

---

Misinterpretation of Test Results

A positive report from the X-ray test, that someone has TB, does not demonstrate that the person is actually affected, contrary to one's immediate impression. We can calculate the new probability of having the disease, given this new information, by Bayes' Theorem. Using our previous data,

$$P(TB/TBR) = P(TB)[P(TBR/TB)/P(TBR)]$$

$$= 0.01[0.9/0.108]$$

$$\sim 0.09 << 1.00$$

In this case, as so often with rare phenomena, the number of false positives dominates the test results (see previous box). Even though the test is relatively accurate, and revises the probability by an order of magnitude, it is still far from proving the condition.

of information from any test. Since perfect information—were it to exist—would be the best possible set of observations, it must have the highest value.

The value of perfect information is easy to calculate, far easier than the value of real, sample information. The next section describes this in detail. This feature, together with the fact that perfect information provides an upper bound, means that perfect information provides a practical basis for initial estimates of the value of any information-gathering process.

17.4 VALUE OF INFORMATION

We can calculate the value of both perfect and sample information. We consider the value of perfect information first because it is easier to calculate, more widely used, and often all that is necessary.

Expected value of perfect information (EVPI). The value of perfect information is easy to calculate. Perfect information both radically simplifies the decision tree after the test, and makes it trivial to assign the probabilities throughout. Neither revised probabilities of events nor the probabilities of the test results have to be calculated.

First, every test result, TR_k, from the perfect test will tell us exactly what will happen subsequently, and its associated outcome, O_{ik}, will have probability one in the revised decision tree following the test result, L_k: $P(O_{ik}) = 1.0$ and all other outcomes, (non-O_{ik}), will have probability zero, $P(\text{non-}O_{ik}) = 0$.

The optimal decision for each L_k, (D/TR_k), should then be obvious: one simply takes the choice with the highest expected value, which is then $EV^*(L_k)$.

Second, the probability of making any observation TR_k is obvious when we are dealing with perfect information. The estimated probability of making a perfect observation that a test result indicating that event E_k will occur is identical to our prior probability of E_k itself: a perfect test would by definition predict that E_k would happen exactly as many times as it does.

The value of perfect information follows directly from the two simplifications described above. The expected value after the information-gathering process is:

$$EV^*(LI) = \sum P(E_k)EV^*(D/TR_k)$$

The expected value of perfect information is then:

$$EVPI = \sum P(E_k) EV^*(D/TR_k) - EV^*(L)$$

For most practical problems, where we already have estimates of the probabilities of events, this calculation can practically be done by inspection (see Section 17.5).

The EVPI upper bound on the value of information is often all that is required in practical situations. It constitutes a minimum test any proposed data-gathering project should meet, and generally eliminates many alternatives from consideration. Indeed, if the project—a prototype plant, a geological exploration, or whatever—costs more than the maximum conceivable benefits, then it is clearly not worth doing. In practice, it is reasonable to impose more stringent standards, since no real information is likely to be near perfection. As a rule of thumb, providing a reasonable maximum to the value of sample information, we may usefully require the cost of any data-gathering project to be less than half the expected value of perfect information.

Expected value of sample information (EVSI). The expected value of sample information is calculated as outlined above—without any simplifications! Even for trivial textbook situations it is hard work.

The calculations involve several complications. First, revised probabilities of the outcomes, $P(O_{ik}/TR_k)$, must be calculated for each possible set of observations TR_k: k modifications of Bayes' Theorem. Then, each new risky situation L_k must be analyzed to obtain the best sequence of decisions for L_k and thus $EV^*(L_k)$: k modifications of the original decision analysis for L. Next, the probabilities of making any observation TR_k must be calculated:

$$P_k = P(TR_k) = \sum_j P(TR_k/E_j)\, P(E_j)$$

Finally, all this must be put together to obtain $EV^*(LI)$. The expected value of sample information is then

$$\text{EVSI} = \sum_k P_k\, EV^*(L_k) - EV^*(L)$$

The example in Section 17.5 illustrates what is involved. Even when computers are available, the effort is sufficiently complex to be avoided if possible. This underlines the usefulness in practice of the concept of perfect information.

17.5 EXAMPLE CALCULATIONS

This section shows how to calculate the expected values of perfect and sample information for the example problem given in Section 17.2. The information, in this case, consists of the weather forecast heard on the news, which can either be "Rain Predicted" or "Clear Predicted."

Expected value of perfect information (EVPI). Perfect information would mean—in this hypothetical case—that the weather forecast would predict exactly what will happen: if it says "Rain Predicted," it will rain.

Perfect information simplifies the decision tree after the test in two ways. First, it makes it possible to know the probability of getting any test results. In our case, our best estimate of the probability of getting a "Rain Predicted" forecast exactly equals our prior estimate of the probability of rain:

$$P_{RP} = P(\text{Rain}) = 0.4$$

The hypothetical perfect forecast would say "Rain Predicted" every time it would rain and only those times. Similarly for the probability of other possible test results. In that case,

$$P_{CP} = P(\text{Clear}) = 0.6$$

The second simplification provided by perfect information concerns the best decision after you hear the test results. These would tell you what will happen, and it then should be obvious what choice to make. In our case, if you heard "Rain Predicted" from the perfect forecast, you would know it will rain and that taking your raincoat was the best you could do at that point. Likewise, if the perfect forecast said "Clear Predicted" you would know not to take your raincoat.

The decision tree after the perfect forecast is thus very simple. In our case it is

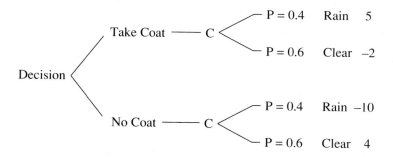

The expected value of having the test is thus

$$EV^{*}(\text{LI}) = 0.4(5) + 0.6(4) = 4.4$$

To find the expected value of perfect information, we must compare the expected value after the test with the expected value we would have had without the test. Our decision tree without the test was, from 17.2,

The expected values of the alternatives are, as shown in Section 16.5,

$$EV(\text{Take Coat}) = 0.8 \qquad EV(\text{No Coat}) = -1.6$$

Taking the raincoat is the better decision, with the highest expected value, which is the expected value of the situation without the test:

$$EV^{*}(\text{L}) = 0.8$$

The expected value of perfect information is, by definition, the difference between the value with and without the test:

$$EVPI = 4.4 - 0.8 = 3.6$$

Expected value of sample information (EVSI). Calculating the EVSI requires 5 steps:

1. Obtain the probabilities of the test results, P_k.
2. Revise the prior probabilities of the outcomes, based on the test results TR_k, to get the posterior probabilities $P(O_{ij}/TR_k)$. Note this requires you to apply Bayes' Theorem for each $P(O_{ij})$ for each TR_k.
3. Identify the best decision you could make after each test result, D_k^*. Note that this requires you to repeat k times the original analysis of the decision without test information, each time with different probabilities.
4. Calculate the expected value after the test, as the expected value of each optimal decision after a test result times the probability of that test result:

$$EV(\text{after test}) = \sum_k P_k EV^*(L_k)$$

5. Finally, find the expected value of sample information as the difference between the above and the expected value without the test.

The whole process is a big job—especially as compared to the ease of calculating the expected value of perfect information.

To obtain the probabilities of the test results, we need to know something about the reliability of the test. This we can usually obtain from an analysis of the past performance of the test. Suppose for simplicity that the weather forecast has a 70% chance of being correct:

$$P(RP/R) = P(CP/C) = 0.7$$

and conversely, then, a 30% chance of predicting something different:

$$P(RP/C) = P(CP/R) = 0.3$$

The possibility of each test result is calculated directly from the information on the reliability of the test, as described in Section 17.3. Thus for our case,

$$P(RP) = P(RP/R)\ P(R) + P(RP/C)\ P(C)$$

$$= (0.7)\ (0.4) \quad + (0.3)(0.6) \quad = 0.46$$

and in this simple case of two possibilities,

$$P(CP) = 1 - P(RP) = 0.54$$

Second, we must revise our prior probabilities of the outcomes depending on each of the different test results. In our case this is twice. If the forecast says "Rain Predicted,"

$$P(R/RP) = P(R)\left[\frac{P(RP/R)}{P(RP)}\right] = 0.4\left(\frac{0.7}{0.46}\right) = 0.61$$

$$P(C/RP) = 1 - 0.61 = 0.39$$

If, however, the forecast says "Clear Predicted,"

$$P(C/CP) = 0.6(0.7/0.54) = 0.78$$

$$P(R/CP) = 1 - 0.78 = 0.22$$

Third, we must identify the best decision we could make given the test result and the consequently revised probabilities. Thus if we have "Rain Predicted," we can calculate the expected value of each alternative as

$$EV(\text{Take Coat})_{RP} = (0.61)5 \quad + 0.39(-2) = \quad 2.27$$

$$EV(\text{No Coat})_{RP} = (0.61)(-10) + 0.39(4) \quad = \; -4.54$$

The best choice for "Rain Predicted" is to take the raincoat, and the value of that optimal decision is:

$$EV^*(L_{RP}) = 2.27$$

If, however, we have "Clear Predicted" we have

$$EV(\text{Take Coat})_{CP} = (0.22)5 \quad + (0.78)(-2) = \; -0.46$$

$$EV(\text{No Coat})_{CP} = (0.22)(-10) + (0.78)(4) \quad = \quad 0.92$$

The best choice here is not to take the coat, so

$$EV^*(L_{CP}) = 0.92$$

Now, finally, we can calculate the expected value after the test as the sum of the probability of each test result times the value of the best decision after that result:

$$EV^*(LI) = \sum P_k EV^*(L_k) = 0.46(2.27) + 0.54(0.92) = 1.54$$

The expected value of sample information can now at last be found:

$$\text{EVSI} = EV^*(LI) - EV^*(L)$$

$$= 1.54 - 0.8 = 0.74$$

This result and process should be carefully compared to those of the expected value of perfect information. First, perfect information provides an upper bound. Furthermore, as a rough rule of thumb indicated earlier, perfect information is generally at least twice as valuable as what you might actually get in a real test. In our case we have:

$$\text{EVPI} = 3.6 > \text{EVSI} = 0.74$$

The process for getting the expected value of perfect information is also very, very much simpler—even for the trivial case just presented. This reality underlines the advantage of calculating the value of perfect information and using it, where possible, at least as a first means for evaluating the desirability of any test or information-gathering procedure.

17.6 APPLICATION

Developers in the San Francisco area planned to build on about 350 acres or 1.4 km^2 of land reclaimed from the Bay. Their problem was to decide among some combination of three alternatives:

1. Immediate construction, without waiting for the soil to consolidate
2. Preloading of the site, to accelerate the consolidation
3. Waiting until consolidation occurred naturally

The risk they faced was that the soil might not have consolidated sufficiently, and might then settle excessively under the buildings, causing cracks and other damage. This risk depended on the compressibility of the soil, which may be considered the chance event for this decision analysis.

New information relevant to the analysis would come from samples of soil obtained from borings. The general question is whether it is worthwhile to carry out a test program (however boring). Specifically, it is appropriate to ask how many borings to make, in other words, which test program maximizes the value of information.

The value of the information naturally depends on the quality of the information already available, that is, the prior probability distribution. That in turn depends on the experts who provide it. In this case, three types were available: Senior professionals with an average of 15 years experience, junior engineers with 3 years on the job, and current graduate students.

Colleagues at Stanford University calculated the value of information for each type of expert and for tests involving different numbers of soil samples. They used continuous probability distributions such as those referred to in the box in Section 15.4. Once they had the value of information, they calculated the net gain associated with any program by subtracting off the cost of the borings. Their results are as shown in Figure 17.1.

The value of information in this case was minimal for experienced local engineers. It was significantly less than the cost of the test programs, which were thus not worthwhile. As frequently happens, in this and other fields, two complementary factors were at work: the experts understood the situation and the new information did not noticeably change the prior estimates. These factors combine to reduce the value of information.

Contrarily, the value of information increases as the priors degrade. It is worth more for junior than senior engineers, and the most for students. Because it is worth more, more tests are optimal for the less experienced. The optimal sample size for the three groups goes from 0 to around 5 to 15.

The fact that new information about soils has little or no value to soils experts in an area is well known to practicing professionals. Yet we can also

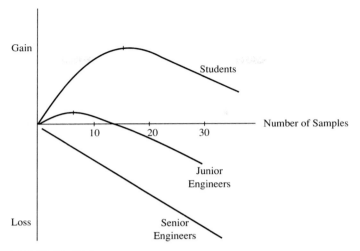

FIGURE 17.1
Expected net gain (value of information less cost of samples) from soil tests in example.

observe that they continue to collect it routinely. Why is this? They do so to protect themselves from lawsuits and claims of negligence. Even though the information may have no influence on the design, it may be necessary documentation for display in court. This kind of wasteful effort is an unfortunate, but common, result of a litigious society. It is known as "defensive" engineering, similar to "defensive" medicine of doctors.

17.7 CONSEQUENCES FOR STRATEGY

Whenever substantial risk is involved, the best approach to systems design involves a strategy, as Chapter 16 indicates. This consists of an optimal choice for the first phase of implementation, which incorporates sufficient flexibility so that the designer can alter the development to correspond to how the future unfolds.

Information gathering is important both to the choice of the first phase and to the implementation of the strategy. The collection of relevant additional information, that would clarify major uncertainties about a system, should often in fact be the first phase.

The first step in the design of a system should often be a major "testing" program. The information will have value for the optimal design, and should be obtained. As indicated in the beginning of this chapter, these tests may involve all kinds of surveys, investigations, trials, or prototypes. They each have the same common element: they establish progress in the development of a system with a minimum commitment.

The advantage of this approach can be appreciated by imagining how differently the U.S. utilities would have fared if they had consciously planned to develop nuclear power using information gathering as a major component of their plans. They would have soon appreciated that nuclear plants were far more expensive to build and operate than they had thought, and could have altered their plans accordingly. Having failed to do so, several major U.S. utilities faced bankruptcy.

In implementing a strategy, the practical question is: When should one proceed with the next phase of development? Here again, a conscious program of information gathering, directed toward revising the assumptions and estimates of risks on which the initial phase was built, is the key to timely, appropriate decisions.

The analysis of the value of the information will, in each phase of the system development, indicate how extensive a test program should be. It is thus an integral part of good systems design in risky situations.

REFERENCES

Behn, R. D., and J. W. Vaupel, (1982). "Compound Decision Dilemmas," Chapter 10, *Quick Analysis for Busy Decision-Makers,* Basic Books, New York.

Folayen, J., K. Hoeg, and J. R. Benjamin, (1970). "Decision Theory Applied to Settlement Predictions," *Journal of Soil Mechanics and Foundations,* American Society of Civil Engineers, Vol. 96, pp. 1127–1141.

de Neufville, R., and R. Keeney, (1972, 1974). "Use of Decision Analysis in Airport Development for Mexico City," Chapter 23, *Analysis of Public Systems,* A. W. Drake, R. Keeney, and P. Morse, eds., MIT Press, Cambridge, MA; and Chapter 24, *Systems Planning and Design,* R. de Neufville and D. H. Marks, eds., Prentice-Hall, Englewood Cliffs, NJ.

Raiffa, H., (1970). "More About the Economics of Sampling," Chapter 7, *Introductory Lectures on Choices Under Uncertainty,* Addison-Wesley, Reading, MA.

PROBLEMS

17.1. *Money Bags, Take 3*

Welcome back (see Problem 16.2) to the "Money Bags" TV show. Determine the value of information about the contents of the wallet.

(a) The EVPI.

(b) The EVSI. Is it greater or less than the amount Monty wants you to pay for a look at the bills?

17.2. *Assembly Robot (Revisited)*

See Problem 16.3. Examine the value of information of the laser test.

(a) What is its EVSI? What is the longest time the test could take and still be worth doing?

(b) What is the EVPI of a perfect test?

17.3. *Mars Probe Simulation*

The scientists described in Problem 16.4 have the option, at a cost of $1 million, of placing a remote sensing device on the probe to collect data about the Martian surface while the probe is still in orbit. The data could be used to simulate perfectly a method X experiment, which could then be used in chosing the method for the actual experiment.

(a) Calculate the probability that theory A is correct if (1) the simulation is a success; (2) the simulation is a failure.

(b) What is the probability that the experiment will be a success given that the simulation fails and the scientists choose method Y?

(c) Draw the decision branch for deciding to run the simulation. Calculate the remaining probabilities and label the branches.

(d) Should the scientists pay for the remote sensor if their objective is to maximize expected monetary value?

(e) What is the maximum they should pay for this device?

(f) What is the EVPI about the correct theory about the Martian surface?

17.4. *Software Development, Part 2*

As a member of the board of directors of Celestial Software, (see Problem 16.5) you are reviewing their proposed decision to buy a software license.

(a) What is the EVPI about the success of the computers?

You can hire an industry analyst to predict which PC will be a hit. By comparing the analyst's record for choosing hits from machines similar to A and B, you have determined that if A actually becomes a hit, there is a 60% chance that the analyst will have predicted this. Also, if B turns out to be the hit, there is an 80% chance that the analyst will have said so. The analyst's services may be purchased for $100,000.

(b) Calculate the probability that the analyst will predict A to be the hit.

(c) Calculate the probability that A will be the hit given that the analyst picks A; and that B will be the hit given that the analyst chooses B.

(d) Draw the decision branch for deciding to hire the analyst, and label all probabilities and outcomes.

(e) Should you hire the analyst?

(f) What is the maximum you would pay the analyst?

17.5. *PY-RIC, again*

Vic's lab (see Problem 16.10) suggests that the booster be checked by a procedure that predicts correctly if today's launch is successful or not 80% of the time. $P(\text{predicts success}|\text{success}) = P(\text{predicts failure }|\text{failure}) = 0.80$.

(a) Calculate the probability of a successful launch today if the test "predicts success;" if it "predicts failure." Use Bayes' Theorem.

(b) Calculate the probability of a successful launch today if two independent tests contradict each other: one "predicts success," the other "predicts failure."

Vic must now decide whether to test.

(c) What is the upper bound on the economic value of a test?

(d) Since the countdown is progressing, Vic does not have time to calculate the value of the proposed test. What is the maximum he might reasonably commit to it?

17.6. *Tax Shelter*

Ten years from now, having made your first $10 million in the engineering specialty of your choice, you must decide how to dispose of a tract of land originally purchased to avoid taxes. Your options are

- Spend $3M to develop resort (option R)
- Spend $1M to open a strip mine for coal (option M)
- Sell the property for $0.1M (option S)

The outcomes from options R and M depend on whether a coal seam runs through your property. A geologist friend estimates a 75% probability that there is a coal deposit. He believes that if coal is present it will be on your neighbor's land as well.

If there is no coal, the resort would return $12M in revenue, the mine would make nothing. If there *is* coal, your neighbor will eventually find out about it and start mining, spoiling the view and forcing you to convert the resort to a school worth just $1M in revenue, but the mine would have made $1M profit.

(*a*) Structure the decision tree. Select your best strategy.

One of your friends recommends a geological testing service whose test results will indicate either HIGH probability of finding coal, or LOW. Coal-bearing deposits will result in a HIGH test report 76% of the time; noncoal-bearing strata yield HIGH results in only 12% of the cases.

(*b*) What is the most you would pay to test for coal?

(*c*) Construct the decision tree for the test, and find the expected value of the test. Is it worth $1M?

17.7. *Lost Records*

You have the opportunity to purchase one of two plots of land for $4M. Their value depends on what you can build on them. Last year engineers took a set of 10 borings from each plot. In one set, 3 borings showed a hard rock base and 7 showed compressed soil, indicating that this plot will support a highrise building, making it worth $6.5M. In the other set 5 borings showed loose soil and the other 5 compressed soil, indicating that this plot will only support houses, making it worth $3M. The difficulty is that someone has lost the record of which set of samples goes with which plot.

The owner offers you the opportunity to obtain—at a cost of $0.5M—one more boring from either plot, provided you commit to buy at least one plot that you can choose afterwards. From experience, you estimate the probability of getting a boring of a specific type is directly proportional to the number in the original set of samples. For example, the probability of getting a boring showing compressed soil is 0.7 from the $6.5M plot.

(*a*) What is the expected value of perfect information on the plots?

(*b*) What is the most you would pay for a new boring?

(*c*) What is your best strategy?

17.8. *Bill Durr*

Bill Durr, president of a construction firm, proposes to set up a subsidiary. He estimates that he has an equal probability of making an $800,000 profit or a $400,000 loss. His friend, Pat Ronach, says to him: "By interviewing people at City Hall, I can determine whether or not the public works program will be expanding, staying the same, or cutting back. This should help you decide if you want to start the new business. For you, I'll only charge $40,000 for the service."

(a) What is the most he should conceivably pay for information about whether he would make a profit or loss?

(b) Bill supposes that he has an 80% chance of making a profit if the city expands public works, the same chance of losing if it contracts, and an even chance of winning or losing if the level stays the same. He also estimates each situation is equally likely. What should he do, if he has no help from Pat?

(c) Bill hires Pat and gets told: "There's a 40% chance of expansion—if that doesn't happen, it's equally probable that the public works program will contract or stay the same. Please pay $40,000." Is Bill ahead or behind?

17.9. *Sonny and Ex Reyes*

Sonny's former wife, Ex, comes along and says she can do research that will investigate the probability of success for the new method of producing PV panels (see Problem 16.9). Ex wants $1 million for her research.

(a) Draw the decision after the test.

(b) Should Sonny pay Ex Reyes's price? Explain.

17.10. *Penalty Clause*

Scientific Instruments Inc. (SII) has received an order with the stipulations that if the system arrives late, SII will pay $1000 for each late day; if it is defective, the client will not pay for it.

SII will make $40,000 if the system is delivered on time, but will lose $17,000 if it is defective. SII can easily deliver the system on time. However it may, with $P = 0.5$, be defective. This deficiency can be removed by an adjustment that costs $2000, and would delay delivery 10 days. SII can also test if the component needs adjustment. However, this test is fallible and costs something. Bob Ability estimates that there is a 0.6 probability that the test will be favorable (the component does not seem to need adjustment). He also thinks that if the test is favorable, there is one chance in four that the component does need adjustment; if the test is unfavorable, this probability increases to seven chances in eight.

(a) Draw the decision tree for SII, indicating probabilities.

(b) What is the highest amount SII should pay for a perfect test on the component?

(c) What is the highest amount SII should pay for a test?

(d) What strategy would you recommend SII follow?

17.11. *Mine Shaft*

A mine shaft has collapsed. Twenty miners were in the shaft, all in a single elevator. All may still be alive; or all may have died, either crushed by falling rock or poisoned by gas.

You have to decide whether to send in a rescue team. Excavating the rubble fast enough to help the victims is dangerous—an average of 5 rescuers would die. In addition, you believe that there is only one chance in five that the miners are alive.

(a) Structure this problem as a decision tree.

(b) What should you do to minimize expected deaths?

It would be less dangerous to send a few volunteers down to test the air. If they find poison gas, the miners are dead; if not, there is a 50% chance that the miners are alive.

(c) What is the absolute maximum number of rescuers you should sacrifice to find out if the miners are alive?

(d) What is the expected value of the gas test? Should you do if it would cost one life?

17.12. *Bridge Design*

You are designing a bridge for an area in which experts believe that there is a 50-50 chance that a single major earthquake will hit the area in the next 30 years. The choice is between a conventional design, sure to collapse under the stress of a major earthquake, and a new design.

A scale model of the new design has collapsed in several laboratory tests simulating a major earthquake. The engineers attribute the weakness to either the steel or the concrete. Both theories are equally plausible. They agree, also, that the bridge's probability of failure due to a major earthquake is 20% if the fault is in the steel, and 60% if in the concrete.

A conventional bridge costs $3M, and one with the new design $3.5M. The cost of rebuilding the bridge has a present value of $2.0M. Early warning systems for earthquakes will prevent any loss of life due to collapsing of the bridge.

(a) Structure the decision tree for deciding which design should be used. Label the branches and indicate the consequences of each path. Calculate the probabilities of each chance event occurring and place these on the appropriate branch.

(b) Assuming the client wants to minimize expected cost, which design is preferred?

An engineer discovers a unique field experiment, costing $0.02M, that simulates the effects of an earthquake on the new design exactly, and the model will either collapse or not.

(c) Draw a tree for deciding whether they should conduct the new experiment. Label the branches.

(d) If the model collapses, what is the probability that the the steel theory is correct? What if there is no collapse?

(e) Calculate the revised probability that the earthquake results in a collapse.

(f) What is the expected value of the field experiment? Explain this result. Should this experiment be conducted?

(g) Redo (h) assuming that the new bridge design costs $3.6M rather than $3.5M. Explain why the result is or is not compatible with the previous explanation.

(h) What is the expected value of perfect information about the correct theory? Assume the cost of the new design is $3.6M.

17.13. *Oil Well*

An oil explorer must decide whether to drill on a site before her option expires or to abandon her rights to the site. Drilling a well costs $100,000. If oil is struck, the explorer will sell and make a $500,000 profit.

The explorer can hire a geologist to take a seismic sounding of the site at a cost of $10,000. Such soundings reveal, with certainty, whether the geophysical substructure of the land is of type A, type B, or type C, where each type has a different degree of favorability for the existence of oil. From past experience, the probability that a certain substructure will occur, given that oil exists, is

$$P(\text{type A/oil}) = 14/28$$
$$P(\text{type B/oil}) = 9/28$$
$$P(\text{type C/oil}) = 5/28$$

The *a priori* probabilities for substructures at this site are

$$P(\text{type A}) = 0.20$$
$$P(\text{type B}) = 0.30$$
$$P(\text{type C}) = 0.50$$

Given that $P(\text{oil}) = 0.28$,

(a) Draw a fully labeled decision tree for deciding whether (1) the explorer should make the seismic tests and (2) should drill for oil or abandon the site following the decision to test or not. In taking the seismic test, the decision about drilling will be made knowing the substructure that exists.

(b) Calculate the monetary outcomes (use the explorer's change in assets) of each path on the tree and place each at the end of appropriate path. Remember that taking the seismic soundings incurs extra costs.

(c) Taking the seismic soundings improves knowledge about the existence of oil. Calculate the probabilities of striking oil in each of the three types of substructures (i.e., $P(\text{oil/type A})$, and so on).

(d) Label each chance branch in the tree from (a) with its probability of occurring.

(e) What strategy should the explorer follow? To pay for the seismic test? To drill for oil without taking the test? What decision should be made following the test?

(f) What is the maximum amount the explorer should pay for the seismic soundings? (i.e., what is the expected value of sample information?)

(g) What is the expected value of perfect information about the existence of oil?

17.14. *Poker Game*

Brette is in the middle of a poker game and the pot is now $175. Brette must either pay $25 into the pot to "see" Bart's hand, or fold and pay nothing. Brette has a fair hand and knows she can win if Bart is bluffing. If Bart is not bluffing, Brette knows she cannot win.

Brette believes that Bart is bluffing with probability of 0.2. Therefore, if Brette "sees" and wins, she will get $200. If she folds, she will lose nothing above what she has already paid into the pot.

Brette makes poker decisions on the basis of expected value.

(a) Draw a decision tree for Brette, showing decision nodes and branches, chance nodes and branches, the relevant probabilities, and the outcomes.

(b) What should Brette do?

(c) What is the maximum Brette would pay to know whether Bart is bluffing or not?

Brette knows that Bart has strange habits when drinking and playing cards simultaneously. She has noticed from past experiences that Bart often drinks more quickly when he is bluffing. Brette believes that the probability that Bart is bluffing, given that he is drinking quickly, is 0.9. She believes the probability that Bart is bluffing, given that he drinks slowly, is 1/20. Brette is debating whether to buy Bart a drink.

(*d*) If Bart has a drink, what is the probability that he will drink it quickly?

(*e*) What is the maximum Brette should pay to buy Bart's drink?

17.15. *House for Sale*

You must sell your house by the end of the month. You now have an offer of $200,000, but you think that by the end of the month there is a 60% chance that you will get an offer of $240,000 (and a 40% chance that you will not get any new bids). If you turn down the offer of $200,000, and do not get any new bids, you have a standing offer of $160,000.

Alternatively, you can have a real estate broker sell your home for you. The charge would be $12,000. For this you also get the broker's estimate of the sale price. You would then have to tell the $200,000 bidder whether you accepted that bid or whether you were going to let the broker find a buyer. Before you pay, however, the broker tells you it is equally likely that he will predict that he will be able to find you a bid of $240,000 or a bid of $160,000. Experience shows that the broker is correct half the time.

Assume that your objective is to get as much money for the house as possible.

(*a*) Structure your situation as a decision tree.

(*b*) What is the best decision you can make without hiring the broker?

(*c*) What is the expected value of perfect information? (Think of the broker's predictions as a "test" of the future.)

(*d*) Calculate the expected value of sample information. Explain your result.

17.16. *Procter N. Gamble*

Procter, president of a food company, must decide whether to market a new breakfast drink which the R and D division has developed. A special meeting devoted to this topic yields the following information:

- The marketing vice-president has defined two possible outcomes for the success of this product; either the public will accept the product or it will not. She believes that the product will be accepted with probability 0.1.
- The cost engineers believe that if the product is marketed and accepted, the company will net $100,000 yearly. If the product is rejected, however, the company will suffer a net loss of $20,000 yearly. If Procter decides not to market the product, her company will neither accrue more cost nor make any profit on this product.
- Procter always makes decisions based on the expected value of the outcomes.

(*a*) What is the best strategy in this case?

(*b*) What is the value of a test which would reveal perfectly whether the public would accept or reject the breakfast drink?

Before she can implement the strategy found in part (*a*), the marketing VP informs Proctor that she has developed a market test for the product. She proposes to test a sample population to determine its preference for the breakfast drink. Based on histories of similar tests, she estimates that the *sample population* would not accept the drink with a probability 0.2, when in fact the product would be accepted by the general public. She also believes that one time in forty the drink would be accepted by the public when the test group rejects it. Finally, she informs Procter that the probability that the public accepts the drink when the test group accepts is 0.4.

(c) Sketch the decision tree for the market test.

(d) Calculate the probability that the test appears favorable.

(e) What is the maximum Procter should pay for this test?

17.17. *Marian Haste, Again*

(a) See Problem 16.11. What is the maximum Marian should pay for better information about the weather?

(b) See Problem 15.8. What is May's advice worth to Marian?

17.18. *P. O'Toole, Again*

See Problem 16.12. What is the most Paddy should pay for a better forecast of June sales?

CHAPTER
18

VALUE
AND
UTILITY
FUNCTIONS

18.1 THE ISSUE

As indicated in the introduction to evaluation, Chapter 10, people's valuation of benefits and costs are often distinctly nonlinear. When this is the case, the evaluation of alternatives cannot properly use the methods of Chapters 11–13. Indeed, if the value of units of a product of a system varies according to its total quantity, we cannot legitimately add them to calculate total benefits or costs. (For example: $X^a + X^a = (2X)^a$ only if the expression is linear, $a = 1$.) When values are nonlinear, we need new procedures of evaluation.

This chapter begins the sequence presenting the ways to evaluate systems when values are nonlinear (Chapters 18–21). This chapter lays the theoretical foundation. The following two chapters indicate how nonlinear values can be measured over first one and then many dimensions. Chapter 21, finally, extends the analysis to the most complex situation of all, collective decisionmaking among groups with nonlinear values over many dimensions.

In practice, nonlinear values are routinely integrated with decision analysis, Chapter 16. This is because significant projects involving risk also normally require this treatment. Most texts on decision analysis in fact combine these two elements. They are separated here to make the presentation clearer. Section 19.8 illustrates their combination.

18.2 OBJECTIVE

This chapter describes the theoretic basis for representing the relative intensity of the nonlinear values that a person or organization places on consequences. These are collectively referred to as preference functions, $PF(\cdot)$, which assign a value to the quantity $(\cdot)$. These mathematical functions permit the analyst to estimate the value of possible choices, and then to advise his client, a single decision-maker or some group, as to the best choice.

There are two basic means of representing nonlinear preferences for possible benefits or losses: the value and the utility functions. These closely related concepts differ principally in the generality of their application. Value functions are based on just a few basic assumptions and are valid for almost any circumstances; they are so general, however, as to be useless for practical analyses (see Section 18.4). Utility functions result from a further set of assumptions and are thus less general; they are in fact particularly applied to situations involving uncertainty (see Section 18.5). Utility functions are most useful in practice and routinely used in decision analysis. Each concept is presented in detail, starting with the set of axioms that constitute its basis. These sets of axioms have practical consequences for the use of the function and its measurements which are described.

> **Semantic caution:** The definition of utility differs between economics and the field of decision analysis within operations research. The economics literature generally refers to all preference functions as utility functions, whereas in decision analysis this term has a specific, limited meaning. As the distinction between value and utility functions is useful, it is maintained here.

18.3 NONLINEARITY OF PREFERENCES

People in general do not attach the same value to each unit of benefit they receive or of cost they pay. For example, when you are hungry you are most interested in the first plate of food, less in the second, and even less in the third or fourth, when you are getting full. The relationship between a set of consequences, $\mathbf{X}$, and the *measure of preference, PM*, is in general nonlinear and possibly highly complex. Mathematically, we can think of

$$PM = PF(\mathbf{X})$$

where $PF(\mathbf{X})$ is the preference function.

A common form of nonlinearity of preference is that referred to as *diminishing marginal "utility"* by economists (see preceding Semantic Caution). It reflects the fact that people commonly attach less and less value to each additional unit of a benefit they might receive. The way you probably react when hungry illustrates the phenomenon: you will place a high value on your first plate of food and then, as the need for food decreases, your value per plate of food decreases. At some level of benefit, X_s (pronounced "ex-ess"), saturation may occur. The marginal increase in value then decreases toward zero. The total measure of preference correspondingly increases at a decreasing rate. Figure 18.1 suggests the relationship.

A parallel form of nonlinearity is suggested by a person's typical response to uncertain situations. In choosing between alternatives with different degrees of risk, people often select the option with a lesser benefit on average, but which is more certain. For example, imagine yourself evaluating two possibilities for investing $10,000 of your savings for a year: you may either put it in a bank and receive $900 interest, or put it in the stock market, a possibility that you estimate is equally likely (probability, $P = 0.5$) to earn you $0 or $2000. On "average," the riskier investment is more profitable: the expected value of its gain is $1000 ($= \$0(0.5) + \$2000(0.5)$). But when you make the choice only once you of course do not see the average, only the particular outcomes. In this situation most people usually prefer the more certain choice, although less profitable on average (see box). This behavior is generally described as *"risk aversion."*

Exploring Nonlinear Preferences

The concept of nonlinear preferences can be made vivid by some simple experiments. These can be organized either in class or as exercises. Any number of persons can be involved. One person should be the organizer of each game.

The object of the exercises is to show the diversity in preferences that routinely occurs among individuals, and some of the factors that change the preference functions. This is done in two complementary steps.

At the start of the procedure, everyone should have two pieces of paper and the organizer some cash. The participants will submit bids for money that the organizer offers to give away. The results consist of histograms of the frequency of offers at different levels, compared with the expected value of the money offered.

In the first part, the organizer offers to give away a small amount—say $1— on the toss of a coin: the organizer gives the dollar to a bidder if the coin shows a head, but keeps it on tails. The organizer then asks each participant to submit a bid for the opportunity to receive the money. If the organizer accepts the bid, the participant pays the bid and hopes for the best. The participant is equally likely to net $(1 − Bid) or $(−Bid). The expected value of the net monetary gain is $(0.50 − Bid).

The organizer plots the distribution of the bids before selecting the highest bidder (this increases the interest). The results are typically as on the top of Figure 18.2. Points to be noted are:

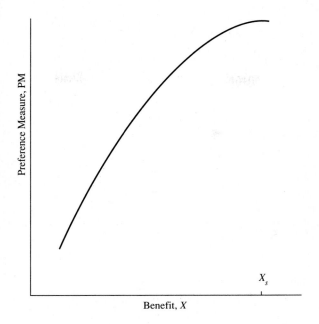

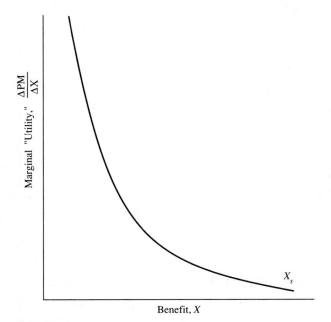

FIGURE 18.1
A nonlinear preference function with diminishing marginal "utility."

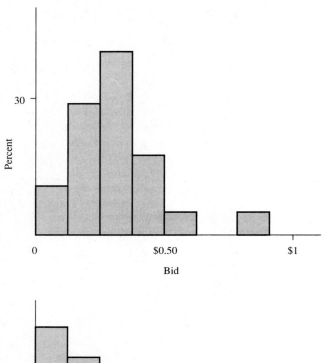

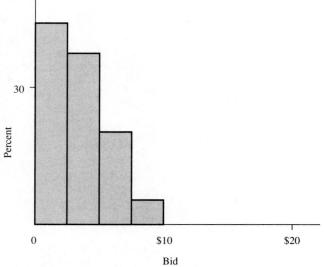

FIGURE 18.2
Typical distribution of bids for 50:50 chance on $1 (top) and $20 (bottom).

1. There is great diversity among the individuals.
2. Most offers reflect "risk aversion" in that the individuals bid less than the average of the offer.
3. Some individuals may show "risk preference" in that they bid more than the average.

The second exercise differs from the first by the size of the prize. A much larger amount, say $20, is offered. The results are as at bottom in Figure 18.2: people appear much more "risk averse." This and subsequent discussion among the participants brings out the fact that risk aversion and preferences generally depend on the amounts at stake, the particular circumstances of each individual (cash on hand, when they last received money, and so on), as well as personal preferences.

Note: No bid is more correct than any other. People differ, and legitimately and appropriately make different choices. The analyst must respect these choices.

The phenomena of diminishing marginal "utility" and "risk aversion" are closely related. This is illustrated with the help of Figure 18.3. We suppose that a person's preference function exhibits diminishing marginal "utility," similar to that of Figure 18.1, and show that it implies "risk averse" behavior. For each of the consequences of the choice with the uncertain outcomes, given in the preceding example ($0 and $2000), we can identify the measures of preference (PM_0 and PM_{2000}) and calculate the average measure of preference of the choice, $EV(PM)$. This is simply the expectation:

$$EV(PM) = PM_0(0.5) + PM_{2000}(0.5)$$

We can see from the shape of the preference function that the benefit that is equivalent to this average measure of preference,

$$X_e = PF^{-1}[EV(PM)]$$

is less than the average consequence, $1000. For most people, it is typically also less than $900. In this case $900 has a higher measure of preference than X_e and is preferred to it. The "risk averse" behavior, being the choice of the lesser benefit that is certain ($900) over the higher expectation of the risk situation, is thus associated with the nonlinearity of the preference function similar to that represented by diminishing marginal "utility."

> **Semantic caution:** The term "risk aversion" is often used in a most misleading way. The decision analysis literature measures "risk aversion" by the extent to which the preference function is nonlinear (See Section 19.7). The implication is that all nonlinearity is due to the presence of uncertainty. This is false because, as the previous discussion shows, "risk aversion" is compatible with and partially explainable by the decreasing marginal "utility" associated with saturation. The same remark applies to "risk preference" discussed in what follows.

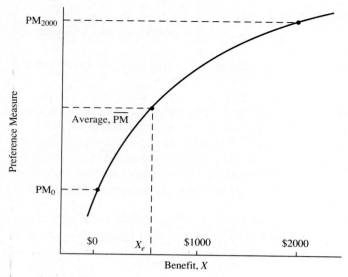

FIGURE 18.3
Representation of risk averse behavior: The measure of preference for the example risky situation, X_e, is less than the $1000 expectation of the situation.

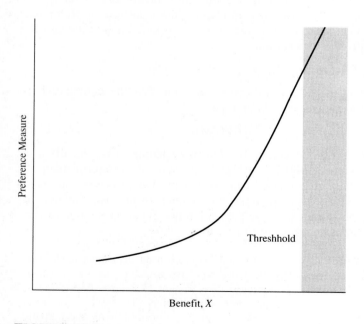

FIGURE 18.4
Preference function compatible with a threshold effect or risk preference.

People's preferences are not always compatible with diminishing marginal "utility" or "risk aversion." The inverse behavior, although less common, occurs frequently enough to be ordinary. Graphically, the preference function would be as in Figure 18.4. It would be likely to occur when there is some threshold to the consequences, above which they really matter and below which they are much less significant. For example, one might have such a preference for the speed of response to an emergency: if the police arrive fast enough, for example, they may prevent a crime—worth a great deal—if not, they can only record the event— worth relatively little.

Similarly, people faced with risky choices may show "*risk preference*." The contrary of "risk aversion," it means that they choose options that on average are less profitable, but that have the possibility of obtaining significant rewards. Entrepreneurs drilling for oil have been documented to behave in this way. Individuals buying lottery tickets, where the average total prize money paid is about 30% of the money collected, also exhibit "risk preference." The interpretation is that the people believe that winning the big prize would lift them above the threshold of their usual standard of living to a totally new life—for instance, one in which they might not have to work—and attach great importance to this possibility.

Preference functions need not be all one way or the other. They can easily be mixed (Figure 18.5). The inflection in the curve is associated with the thresholds.

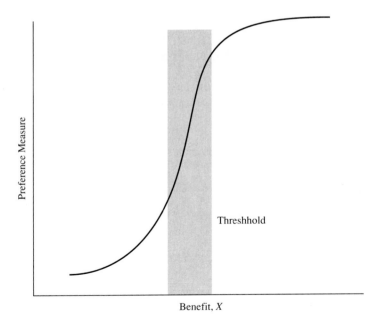

FIGURE 18.5
Preference function reflecting two different patterns of choice above and below a threshold.

Taking up the example of the speed of the police response to an emergency, one might attach only decreasing importance to the number of minutes they arrive in advance; what really counts is that they arrive in time. People confronted with risky choices may likewise exhibit "risk preference" for small amounts and "risk aversion" for larger ones. This behavior has been particularly documented for contractors who normally operate with a budget for unforeseen contingencies: so long as their choices fall within this budget, they may accept risks that they would avoid if the sums were larger.

Preference functions are usually assumed to be monotonically increasing with benefits. Strictly speaking, this need not be the case. One's valuation for the quantity of salt in one's food is an example of a preference function that first increases and then decreases. Some salt is appreciated, but beyond the right amount, more salt becomes increasingly distasteful (Figure 18.6). The justification of monotonic increases in practice lies in the idea that a person can avoid excess amounts of a consequence that would decrease his or her preference. One can, for example, simply not use any more salt than one wants, even if one has it available.

The problem for evaluation is to determine the form of the preference function, and to do so as analytically as possible. This is where value and utility functions are useful.

18.4   VALUE FUNCTION

A *value function*, $V(\mathbf{X})$, is a means of ranking the order relative preference between sets of consequences, of benefits and costs, $\mathbf{X}$. It assigns a number to every $\mathbf{X}$ such that for any two sets, $\mathbf{X}_1$ and $\mathbf{X}_2$, one is preferred to the other ($>$),

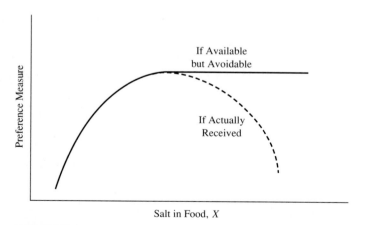

FIGURE 18.6
Preference functions for a benefit that is eventually undesirable.

only if its value is greater than the other's:

$$X_1 > X_2 \text{ only if } V(X_1) > V(X_2)$$

Similarly, X_1 will be indifferent to or preferred by $X_2 (X_1 \sim X_2$ or $X_1 < X_2)$ depending on their relative values.

Axiomatic basis. The existence of a value function depends on three basic axioms, that is, assumptions about the situation. Mathematically two other technical axioms are also required, but these have little significance for the analyst. Each important axiom is described in turn, together with the several names by which it is called in economics and operations research.

The most basic axiom concerns the existence of relative preferences for all outcomes. It asserts that

> For every possible pair of consequences, X_1 and X_2, in the domain of interest, a person will either prefer one to the other or be indifferent between them:
>
> $$X_1 > X_2, \qquad X_1 \sim X_2, \qquad \text{or} \qquad X_1 < X_2$$

It is referred to as the axiom of completeness or complete preorder. It represents a reasonable assumption. Although in general a person may confront many situations involving choices which have quite different attributes and may, thus, find it impossible at the moment to state his or her relative preferences, that does not mean that the person does not ultimately have relative preferences. The axiom is equivalent to the assumption that people do, in the end, make choices and can thus express their preferences.

The second axiom is that of transitivity. It assumes that

> For any three possible sets of consequences, X_1, X_2, and X_3, if $X_1 > X_2$ and $X_2 > X_3$ then the preference is transitive such that $X_1 > X_3$.

This is reasonable for any individual or group with a common set of preferences. It may, however, not be true for groups in general. This is because different individuals may rank choices in different orders and this fact, combined with the way the group organizes or votes upon its collective choice, may lead to intransitive choice by groups. This phenomenon is discussed in detail in Chapter 21.2.

The third important axiom is that of monotonicity. It simply assumes that more of a good thing is better (or more of a bad thing is worse). For reasons indicated in the previous section, when the desirability of salt in food was discussed (Figure 18.6), this is a reasonable assumption in most practical situations.

The monotonicity axiom is equivalent to the Archimedean Principle that the value of any item in a series can be represented as a weighted average of the value of the extremes. That is, expressing the greatest and least X_i as X^* and X_*, respectively,

For all $\mathbf{X}_i, \mathbf{X}_j$ within the range of interest, $\mathbf{X}^* \geqslant \mathbf{X}_i$, $\mathbf{X}_j \geqslant \mathbf{X}_*$, there is a number between zero and one, $0 \leq w \leq 1$, such that some other $\mathbf{X}_K$ lying between $\mathbf{X}_i$ and $\mathbf{X}_j$ can be expressed as

$$V(\mathbf{X}_K) = wV(\mathbf{X}_i) + (1 - w)V(\mathbf{X}_j)$$

This can only be true if preferences are monotonic.

Consequences. If the assumptions implied by the preceding axioms are acceptable, then it can be demonstrated that a value function exists. The nature of a value function should be understood carefully. The value function defines which possibilities are preferred to which others: it defines the *order* of preferences. Unless additional assumptions are made, it says nothing about the intensity of the preferences.

The units of the value function have no intrinsic meaning. Any value function can be transformed by a monotonic function, $MF(\bullet)$, and the result will represent exactly the same preferences as before because:

$$MF(V(\mathbf{X}_0)) > MF(V(\mathbf{X}_1)) \text{ only if } V(\mathbf{X}_0) > V(\mathbf{X}_1)$$

For example, the value function over two dimensions:

$$V_1(X_1, X_2) = X_1^2 X_2$$

will give exactly the same ordering over combinations of X_1 and X_2 as

$$V_2(X_1, X_2) = 2 \log(X_1) + \log(X_2)$$

even though the units would be quite different. Value functions such as V_1 and V_2 which are monotonic transforms of each other and thus lead to the same ordering over $\mathbf{X}$ are said to be *strategically equivalent*.

Because the units of the value function are meaningless, little attention is paid to describing its functional form. Attention is focused instead on the one aspect that can be defined unambiguously: indifference between different sets of consequences, $\mathbf{X}$. Zero difference in value function is not altered by any monotonic transformation and is something definite. The effort is thus to identify sets of consequences which are equally preferred or indifferent to each other.

The structure of the value function is commonly portrayed by contours of equal preference between sets of consequences. These contours may be called *isovalue lines* in general (the economics literature calls them *isoutility lines*). Strategically equivalent value functions have identical isovalue lines. Figure 18.7 illustrates the situation.

You should note the resemblance between the value functions in Figure 18.7 and demand functions, representing the quantity of an item that will be purchased as a function of its price, typically as illustrated in Figure 18.8. There is a close connection between them. Formally, the demand function represents the quantity of goods a person or group will purchase at various prices. The demand

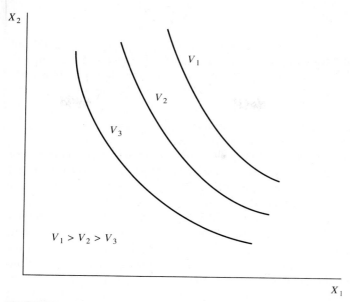

FIGURE 18.7
Isovalue contours representing the structure of a value function for two variables.

FIGURE 18.8
A demand function can be viewed as a representation of diminishing marginal "utility."

function represents the amount that a person will pay for each incremental unit of an item. This amount, the *willingness to pay*, can be viewed as the change in value associated with each extra unit. The typical demand function thus represents diminishing marginal "utility."

Measurement. Value functions are not measured directly, as a practical matter. This is only attempted in special circumstances, generally in research programs, and when additional assumptions are believed to hold. This is a consequence of the observation that quite different functions may be strategically equivalent and that units of value have no intrinsic meaning. There is thus much controversy about the significance of any attempt to measure value functions.

For the purpose of evaluation, the information contained in a value function can be obtained indirectly. This is done by estimating the demand function using a statistical analysis of choices people actually make. This analysis portrays revealed preferences, revealed in the sense that the choices a person makes define to some extent that person's underlying preferences. As a practical matter, value functions are never estimated for use in a decision analysis or an evaluation.

18.5 UTILITY FUNCTION

The *utility function*, $U(\mathbf{X})$, is a special kind of value function with a noticeable advantage: its units do have meaning relative to each other, unlike value functions. The utility function exists on a particular cardinal scale, on which values can be calculated meaningfully. It is then possible, within the limits defined by the axioms of utility, to measure the utility function.

This advantage has a most important practical consequence. It means that, provided always that the axiomatic assumptions are valid, it is possible to evaluate choices analytically, even when people have nonlinear preferences. The procedures for doing this are those of decision analysis, Chapter 16, and the way they can be combined with utility functions is illustrated in Section 19.8.

Lotteries. The discussion of utility relies heavily on the concept of a lottery. This is a simple risky situation, which can be visualized as a one-stage chance node as presented in the presentation of decision trees (Section 16.4). The different kinds of lotteries are defined as follows.

A *lottery* is characterized by the set of possible outcomes, $\mathbf{X}_i$, which will occur with probability P_i. Graphically, it is usual to show a lottery as a set of branches, as in Figure 18.9. The lottery can also be written as $(X_1, P_1; X_2, P_2; \ldots)$, being the sequence of pairs of outcomes and associated probabilities. The order in which these pairs are given has no particular significance.

When there are only two possible branches to the lottery, and where P_2 must be complementary to P_1, a more compact notation is used: $(X_1, P; X_2)$. This is called a *binary lottery*.

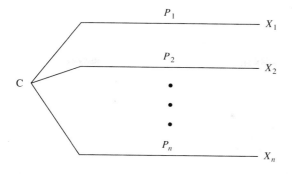

FIGURE 18.9
A lottery represented as a set of branches.

When one of the outcomes of a binary lottery is the status quo, and thus equals zero, we have the *elementary lottery*: (X, P).

Axiomatic basis. The assumptions underlying the utility function are all those required for value functions, plus some others. These consist of two assumptions concerning probability, and a key assumption about the nature of a person's preferences for probability. This last axiom is central; it is also quite controversial and the subject of much research. It represents the main limitation on the applicability of utility functions.

The axioms concerning probability are straightforward. The first concerns existence: that probabilities exist and can be quantified. This is a reasonable proposition, however much difficulty there might be in obtaining good estimates of probability in any specific case (see Section 15.1).

The second axiom on probability can be viewed as the monotonicity axiom for probability. It says, in effect, that a higher probability of a benefit is better. Formally, it states that a person prefers a greater chance of getting a desirable prize to a lesser chance.

> Given two choices, each with the same uncertain outcomes X_1 and X_2 where X_1 is preferred to X_2, a person will prefer the choice with the greater probability of getting X_1 (and the complementary, lesser probability of getting X_2).

As a specific example, this axiom assumes that you would prefer a 10% chance of getting a $1000 to a 5% chance, and that the greater the chance of the prize, the more valuable it is to you.

The key axiom of utility theory concerns the nature of a person's preferences with regard to probability: it assumes, in effect, that a person's preferences are linear in probability. The axiom is usually stated in different terms, however, and is referred to as the *substitution* or *independence axiom*. Either way, the axiom leads to the assertion that a person's preferences for an item should vary linearly with the probability of its occurrence. This is a testable proposition that can be compared to actual behavior, as is done a few paragraphs onwards.

This *substitution* axiom simply states that

> If a person places an equal value on two possible outcomes, A and B, then these can be substituted for each other in any choice involving uncertain outcomes without changing that choice. Thus, if $A \sim B$, then $P(A) + (1 - P)C \sim P(B) + (1 - P)C$.

It asserts, in effect, that equals can be substituted for each other. Stated this way, the axiom seems absolutely obvious. There is a subtlety, however, which is at the heart of the controversy concerning this axiom.

The subtlety of the substitution axiom lies in the idea that the outcomes that can be substituted are not necessarily identical kinds of items but are items that can be quite different in character. One may be a certain outcome, and the other may be a lottery. The substitutions supposed by the axiom may thus radically change the risks faced by a person, for example from certainty to uncertainty or in general from one probability distribution to another. The axiom implies that the substitutions can occur regardless of the other opportunities in front of a person and, thus, regardless of how these substitutions alter the probabilistic distribution of the consequences. For this reason the substitution axiom is also called the *independence axiom*.

The conditions called for by the substitution/independence axiom will only be met if the person's preferences are linear in probability. If they are not, changing the probability distribution could change the preference over choices involving uncertain situations.

The controversy about this axiom arises because repeated experiments demonstrate that people often act as if their preferences were nonlinear in probability. A classic instance of this is the "certainty effect" evidenced by individuals prepared to pay disproportionate amounts to achieve certainty in an uncertain situation. The experiment, simply stated, confronts the individual with the idea that he or she holds a certain number of lottery tickets to win a prize and asks how much the person would be willing to pay to obtain another ticket. The results are typically that the respondent would pay some average sum, except if there were the opportunity to buy the extra tickets to complete the set and thus guarantee the prize. A famous example of behavior contrary to the substitution/independence axiom is the Allais "paradox"—which is only a paradox if your premise is that the axiom is correct (see box).

The essential practical questions raised by the controversy are: do we assume that the substitution axiom is so obviously rational that any behavior contrary to it is a mistake, however well informed and intelligent the person may be? If so we should somehow disregard some of the person's stated preferences, and substitute ones we deem correct. (This can be taken as being presumptuous, if not arrogant.) Or do we suppose that the axiom is sometimes deficient for some subtle reason and reject it—and consequently the utility function which depends upon this axiom—when people express contrary preferences? Logic by itself does not resolve this question.

The Allais "Paradox"

This is a classic example of a situation in which many people choose as if their preferences were nonlinear in probability. This is contrary to the premise of the substitution/independence axiom. For those who believe this axiom must hold, the example is a "paradox."

For others, the author included, this case is simply an example of the complexity of human behavior. The author's own position is that there is nothing unusual about acting contrary to any norm or axiom which, when seen by itself, appears obvious: there are numerous situations when different norms conflict and it is impossible to satisfy all of them simultaneously. For example, we may agree that two important norms for behavior are truthfulness and kindness. Yet, when someone confronts us with the question "How do I look?" do we always manage to be both absolutely truthful and kind? Probably not: If we are absolutely truthful we may be unkind and vice-versa. It simply may not be possible to conform to all norms simultaneously.

The example can easily be run as an individual or classroom demonstration. It consists of two sets of choices. The organizer presents each set and asks the participants to express their preference on a piece of paper. The observation is that many participants, typically over half, indicate combinations of choices which are inconsistent with the substitution axiom.

The first choice is between a definite fortune and a gamble for a greater or equal amount but with a small but perceptible probability of getting nothing:

$$A = \$1 \text{ million}$$

or

$$B = (\$5 \text{ million}, 0.10; \quad \$1 \text{ million}, 0.89; \quad \$0, 0.01)$$

In practice, almost everyone responds: $A > B$.

The second choice is between two similar gambles:

$$C = (\$1 \text{ million}, 0.11; \quad \$0, 0.89)$$

or

$$D = (\$5 \text{ million}, 0.10; \quad \$0, 0.90)$$

People normally divide in their preferences between C and D. For a majority, though, $D > C$. Their reasoning apparently is that the great difference in prizes outweighs the small difference in probability.

The number of participants making any choice can be presented in a simple matrix as in Figure 18.10. Only the pairs of choices AC and BD are consistent with the substitution/independence axiom.

That the predominant pair of preferences, AD, is inconsistent with the substitution axiom is demonstrated as follows. By the monotonicity/Archimedean axiom we know that there is some w such that

$$\$1 \text{ million} \sim (\$5 \text{ million}, w; \quad \$0)$$

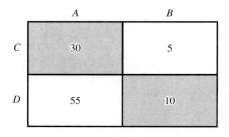

FIGURE 18.10
Typical distribution of participants by pairs of choices. Shaded combinations are consistent with utility axioms, others illustrate Allais "paradox."

We then substitute the lottery for the $1 million where it occurs. Thus $A > B$ implies:

$$(\$5 \text{ million}, w; \quad \$0) > (\$5 \text{ million}, 0.89w + 0.10; \quad \$0)$$

Since we presume more is better regarding probability, this means that

$$0.11w > 0.10$$

Likewise, $D > C$ implies:

$$0.10 > 0.11w$$

In short, the pairs of choices AD and BC represent situations for which the substitution axiom does not hold; it leads to contradictory inferences about w. The explanation of the phenomenon appears to be that many individuals are nonlinear in their valuation of probability, especially toward certainty: they weigh the extra 1% chance of success highly when it is the difference between a sure thing and a gamble (A vs. B) but only lightly when it merely changes the gamble slightly (C vs. D). This is the essence of the "certainty effect."

As a practical matter, recent research we have conducted indicates that the substitution axiom holds, at least as a first-order approximation, except when the probability of some great consequence is either very small or close to certain. Consequently it would seem reasonable to use utility functions except in those cases. Unfortunately those "low probability, high consequence" situations, such as those associated with nuclear reactors say, are fairly common.

Consequences. The axioms that distinguish utility from value functions lead to two important practical results:

1. The utility of a consequence can be measured on a special cardinal scale (see Section 18.6), which allows calculations and analysis.
2. Measurement of utility is a balancing procedure in which probabilities serve as the weights (see Chapter 19).

These results depend particularly on the substitution/independence axiom and the linearity of value with respect to probability it implies. Indeed this linearity permits us to state that the utility of any chance at a prize $(\mathbf{X}, P)$ as a multiplication of that probability and utility of the prize:

$$U(\mathbf{X}, P) = PU(\mathbf{X})$$

The value of an entire risky situation, or lottery, is then

$$U(\text{Lottery}) = \sum P_i U(\mathbf{X}_i)$$

This relationship leads both to the cardinality of the utility function and to the possibility of measuring it.

18.6 SCALE FOR UTILITY

The scale on which utility can be measured is a special form of the cardinal scale: the ordered metric. To understand what it implies, consider first the standard cardinal scale, the ratio scale, which is used to calibrate phenomena such as distance and time. The *ratio scale* has two features:

1. Its units are constant, identifiable amounts (such as meters or hours) which can be combined linearly by addition, subtraction, or averaging. For example: 1 mile plus 2 miles is 3 miles; a speed of 30 mph for a day plus 60 mph for 2 days averages to 50 mph.
2. Zero on the scale indicates an absence of the phenomenon being observed. This implies that ratios between measures have meaning. Thus, if an adult is 6 ft (1.8 m) tall and a child 3 ft (0.90 m), we can say that the adult is twice as tall as the child.

This second feature is the reason the standard cardinal scale is known as a ratio scale.

The *ordered metric scale* differs from the ratio scale in that it does not have the second property. Zero on an ordered metric scale has no absolute meaning; it is simply a reference point that could as well be any other number, such as 32 or whatever. The concept of the ordered metric scale is little known although it is widely used in practice, specifically to measure temperature (see box).

Ratios between measures on the ordered metric scale do not have any meaning. Thus if one object has a centigrade temperature of 100°C and another a temperature of 25°C, we cannot validly say that one is four times as hot as the other. Indeed, the Fahrenheit temperatures of these objects are also 212°F and 77°F, and not a 4:1 ratio.

All measurements on an ordered metric scale can be transformed into equivalent measures in an important way, known as a *positive linear transformation*. To understand this, start with the idea that ratio scales can be transformed into equivalents by straight multiplication: we can convert meters into feet and dollars into francs by applying the appropriate positive conversion factor. For example,

$$(\text{distance in feet}) = \left(\frac{10}{3}\right)(\text{distance in meters})$$

Since there is no absolute zero on an ordered metric scale, we can also obtain equivalent scales by adding or subtracting any amount, which simply changes the reference point. We then have the positive linear transformation (*PLT*):

$$PLT(\cdot) = a(\cdot) \pm b \qquad a > 0$$

This is what we use to convert from degrees Fahrenheit to Centigrade and vice-versa (see box).

Measurements of utility, being on an ordered metric scale, can also be transformed into equivalents by a positive linear transformation:

$$U'(\mathbf{X}) = aU(\mathbf{X}) \pm b \qquad a > 0$$

More precisely, $U'(\mathbf{X})$ and $U(\mathbf{X})$ are strategically equivalent, as defined in Section 18.4, in that they would lead to the same results in an evaluation.

Any two utility functions related by a positive linear transformation are said, in the jargon of operations research, to have a *constant shape*. This term is used extensively with the analysis of utility functions over many dimensions (See Section 20.3).

Temperature: An Ordered Metric Scale

Temperature is traditionally measured on an ordered metric scale, either degrees Centigrade or Fahrenheit. (The Kelvin scale, which rests on the relatively modern concept of the absence of heat at absolute zero, is a ratio scale.)

Temperature scales permit proportional averaging, and are thus cardinal. Thus two units of a fluid at 60° plus one unit at 90° equals three units at 70°.

Conventional temperature scales do not imply an absence of heat at 0°; their zero points are simply convenient references. Ratios of temperature therefore have no particular significance; to say that "it's twice as hot today as yesterday" is a meaningless statement—unless one is referring to degrees Kelvin.

Temperatures scales are "constant up to a positive linear transformation." For example,

$$(^\circ F) = \tfrac{9}{5}(^\circ C) + 32$$

or, vice-versa,

$$(^\circ C) = \tfrac{5}{9}(^\circ F) - 17.77$$

Conventional temperature scales were each defined with respect to two absolutely arbitrary reference points. All other points on the scale were determined proportionally to these two. As a matter of convenience these two reference points were labeled 0° and 100° on both scales. For the Centigrade scale, these represent the freezing and boiling points of pure water, at standard atmospheric conditions. For the Fahrenheit scale these represent the freezing point of water saturated with salt and the human body temperature (they did not get the latter quite right in the early 18th century). Although the Fahrenheit scale looks odd, when one is thinking of freezing at 32°F, it is as rational as the Centigrade scale.

Semantic caution: Graphically, the notion of utility functions with constant shape can be confusing. When you plot such curves their slopes are generally different in fact. This is because of the a factor in the positive linear transformation. What is really constant is not the shape but the implications for choices: utility functions with constant shape, being strategically equivalent, always indicate the same order of preference among consequences or lotteries.

The above property implies that utility, and ordered metric scales in general, can be defined with respect to any two points one wishes to select. These can furthermore be assigned any convenient value. The ability to define the value of the ends of our scale of utility turns out to simplify the measurement of utility considerably. Conventionally, we thus set the utility for the worst set of consequences, X_*, at zero:

$$U(X_*) = 0$$

and the utility for the best consequences, X^*, at 1:

$$U(X^*) = 1$$

Sometimes utility is also scaled from 0 to 100 or, for undesirable outcomes such as fatalities, from -1 to 0. These choices are a matter of personal preference.

At this point we have all the essential theoretical basis for proceeding with actual measurements of utility. Chapter 19 shows how to do this for one dimension, and Chapter 20 shows how we can build on this capability to obtain utility functions over several dimensions, the *multiattribute* utility functions.

REFERENCE

Kahneman, D., Slovic, P., and Tversky, A., eds., (1982). *Judgement and Uncertainty: Heuristics and Biases*, Cambridge University Press, Cambridge, England.

PROBLEMS

18.1. *Diminishing Marginal Value*

Assume that on your next quiz in systems analysis, a grade between 60 and 69 is just passing, D; between 70 and 79 is a C; between 80 and 89 is a B; and over 90 is an A. Consider that at this stage your grade on the quiz would be 60. How many hours would you work to get 70? 75? 80? 85? 90? 95? 100? Plot results and discuss.

18.2. *Cornering the Market*

Suppose that your local organization is having a raffle for a college scholarship worth $5000, and is selling off 1000 tickets. How much might you pay for one ticket? For a 51st ticket, if you already had 50? For the 1000th ticket if you already had the 999 others? Discuss your answers.

18.3. *Assembly Robot (A Third Time)*

See Problem 17.2. Is the criterion of minimizing expected time the right one for the factory manager? Would it be equally good for decisions in other areas (for example, the time required for open heart surgery, for the arrest of an epidemic, or the interception of an enemy missile)?

18.4. *Threshhold*

(*a*) As the founder of a new engineering company you must earn $10,000 a month to pay rent, salaries, and the bank loan. Anything over this is your own salary. Anything under must be added to your debt. Think about and plot the form of your utility for a monthly income of $5000 to $20,000.

(*b*) As an employee in a big company, you know that the average salary increase for your colleagues is 5%. Variations depend on your bosses' assessment of your performance. Plot the form of your utility for a salary increase of 0 to 15%.

18.5. *Strategic Equivalence*

The sales, *S*, of a new high-tech product are estimated to depend on price, *P* (measured in $ $\times$ 10^3) and quality *C* (measured by an index):

$$S = 300P^{-0.5}C$$

(*a*) Plot price versus quantity (the demand function) for $C = 1, 2, 3$. Interpret the meaning of these curves.

(*b*) Suppose we introduce a new index of quality: $C' = 3C^2$. How would we change the formula for sales? How would the new index affect the analysis?

18.6. *Scales*

(*a*) What are the positive linear transformations that give °C as a function of °F? K as a function of °C?

(*b*) Suppose a utility function for *X* is a linear interpolation between the following points:

X	:	$0	$20	$50	$100
U(X)	:	0	0.1	0.8	1.0

Plot $U(X)$. Then plot $U'(X)$ as the positive linear transformation with a range of 0 to 0.4; 0.8 to 1.0; 0.5 to 0.8.

(*c*) The utility for response time, *T*, to an emergency is

T (min)	:	0	5	10	15	20
U(T)	:	1.0	0.8	0.5	0.1	0

Plot $U'(T)$ as the positive linear transformation with a range of 40 to 80.

(*d*) The utility for deaths, *D*, due to industrial accidents is

D(units)	:	0	1	2	5	10
U (D)	:	0	−0.01	−0.05	−0.30	−1.0

Plot $U'(D)$ as the positive linear transformation with a range of 0 to 100.

CHAPTER
19

MEASUREMENT
OF UTILITY

19.1   ORGANIZATION

This chapter presents the basic procedures for measuring utility: the Certainty Equivalent (CE) and the Lottery Equivalent/Probability (LEP) methods. The CE approach has been the standard and is still widely used in practice. It suffers from a broad range of practical defects, however. This has led to the development of the LEP, which experts in the measurement of utility now recommend.

Many other procedures are possible. As the next section indicates, we measure utility by solving a simple linear equation with one unknown and a minimum of three independent arguments. These can be permuted in many ways, leading to a variety of measurement procedures, each emphasizing different features. Research into these possibilities is active, and we can expect additional improvements in utility measurement.

The techniques for measuring utility blend two contrasting intellectual paths. First there is the theory of utility, presented in Chapter 18. Then there is *psychometrics*, the science of measuring behavioral responses of people (or animals). Psychometrics has been developed and applied extensively in behavioral research for nearly a century. It demonstrates the techniques that should be used to obtain good measurements of utility, those that are replicable with small margins of error or variance.

The proper presentation of utility measurement is thus inherently complex because we must both integrate psychometrics and cover alternative methods. To simplify matters, we have adopted the following organization. Sections 19.2 and 19.3 provide the theoretical and psychometric basis. Sections 19.4 and 19.5 describe the CE and LEP methods and place them in the overall step-by-step procedure. Sections 19.6 and 19.7 cover special situations. Sections 19.8 and 19.9 illustrate the measurement itself and the application of utility to decision analysis.

19.2   GENERAL CONDITIONS

Measurement of utility is based on the central result of the axioms of utility:

$$U(\text{Lottery}) = \sum P_i U(\mathbf{X}_i)$$

The utility of a risky situation is the sum of the utility of each of the possible outcomes times their probability of occurrence. This provides us with a simple linear expression that we can solve explicitly for the utility of any specific level of X.

The methods for determining utility have a common characteristic: they establish an equivalence between a stimulus and a response. The stimulus is provided in the measuring process to provoke a person's response, indicating the intensity of preference, the utility. The process is analogous to radar identification of objects: a signal goes out and the response interpreted.

The stimulus will be, in practice, a binary lottery of the form $(X_1, P; \quad X_2)$. It will thus have three independent parameters since the probability of X_2 must be complementary to that of X_1 (see Section 18.5). The stimulus is structured so that its utility is known, either by calculation or construction as described in Section 19.4.

The response provided by a person is designed to define a situation of equal value to the stimulus. The key factor is that it contains no more than one $\mathbf{X}_i$ whose utility is unknown:

Utility of Response (with one Unknown Utility $\mathbf{X}_i$)

$$= \text{Utility of Stimulus (of Known Utility)}$$

Solution of this equation provides the utility of $\mathbf{X}_i$. In principle, the procedure can be continued indefinitely to obtain as many readings on $U(\mathbf{X})$ as desired. The limits on the process are practical.

There are many ways to obtain the utility function. These are associated with the many ways one can define the stimulus and the response. The sequence of observations can be obtained by keeping the probabilities in the stimulus lottery constant and varying the outcomes, or by varying the probability while keeping the outcomes constant. The size and sequence of the gradations in the outcomes or the probabilities can be taken in any convenient order. Finally, the response can be either a deterministic quantity (a *certainty equivalent*) or another lottery (a *lottery equivalent*).

Measuring utility is a process similar to triangulation used in surveying. Here one seeks to define an unknown utility function over $\mathbf{X}$ by some chain of observations based on the assumed utility of two values of $\mathbf{X}_i$ that define the scale for utility. Triangulation similarly attempts to define terrain, a shoreline for example, based on bearings taken from two positions whose location is assumed to be known.

Theoretically, if the axioms are correct, all these procedures should lead to the same utility function for an individual, constant to a positive linear transformation. If the base pair of outcomes is assigned the same arbitrary values, the utility functions should be identical. It is the same with triangulation: no matter which way you go about it, you should end up with the same trace for the shoreline. The difficulty, as we will see in the discussion of the standard certainty equivalent method in Section 19.4, is that the theory sometimes fails. These situations have to be recognized and avoided.

As a practical matter, the procedures for measuring utility functions apply to situations in which the outcomes have only one dimension, that of money, for instance. The subsequent discussion in this chapter therefore focuses on $U(X)$. The procedures for assessing multiattribute utility functions, $U(\mathbf{X})$, in which the outcomes have several dimensions (money, safety, pollution, etc.), are presented in Chapter 20. The multiattribute utility functions are usually constructed from one-dimensional utility functions.

Since both value and utility functions are unique to individuals, as indicated in Section 18.3, the measurement of any utility function must be done in some kind of personal way. This can be through individual interviews or by questionnaires administered collectively. Because the methods are so personal, doing them well requires some special psychometric skills.

19.3 PSYCHOMETRIC CONSIDERATIONS

At least five issues need to be considered in the measurement of human response. These concern:

1. The nature of the interview
2. Its context
3. The scale of the response
4. The way it is obtained
5. Consistency and replicability

Interview. The measurement of a person's utility function necessarily requires some sort of personal interaction with this individual. Measurement of personal choice and values is quite different from ordinary engineering measurements of materials and things. People tend to respond to their interviewer on a personal basis, as materials evidently do not. A person feeling tested or threatened will normally distort his or her truthful responses to socially acceptable ones, suitable to the occasion. For example, if the tax service asks people about their income, they normally tend to minimize it. Care must be taken to avoid biases that this kind of behavior introduces into the measurements.

A basic rule for the measurement process is thus to put the person being interviewed at ease with the process. It is important to stress that

1. The analyst requires and values the interviewees' opinion. They are the only ones who can provide it, and are thus the experts.
2. There are no wrong answers (the interviewees are entitled to their preferences, even when these do not accord with the axioms—the simplifying assumptions—that are the basis of the theory).

The second point is particularly important because people being interviewed by analysts tend to feel that they are being tested to see if they are correct or as smart as the analyst. This may lead them to distort their answers toward what they think the analyst wants to hear. It certainly may put them on the defensive and hinder the measurement process.

Context. It is important to recognize that people's utility functions depend on their situation. For example, your valuation of food is different when you are starving or have just eaten. Similarly, people's valuation of money clearly depends on their current financial position. After you have just been paid, or received a generous holiday gift, you might feel more inclined to take a financial risk than if you were trying to make ends meet at the end of the month. The utility function for losses is also generally different in intensity and curvature from the utility function for gains.

The extent to which utility functions depend on context is a matter of current research. Meanwhile, it is good practice to measure a person's utility in a context that is relevant to them and the decisions they may take.

One way to place the questions in a relevant context is to suggest professionally or personally familiar situations to the interviewee. Another is to present scenarios similar to the projects or strategies that will be evaluated with the person's utility function. It is best if both these variants can be merged.

The questionnaires used in a recent evaluation of ways to mitigate against damage to buildings from earthquakes illustrate the context issue. In this case, the ultimate question was how much expensive reinforcement should be put in buildings to protect the public. The optimal choice naturally depended on whether you were a tenant and had to pay higher rent; a designer, interested in making sure your building never collapsed; and so on. To define the optimal design from the perspective of different groups, we had to obtain their utilities for money. To get these, we recognized their different backgrounds, and prepared questionnaires that asked the same mathematical questions, but in a customary context for members of each group (see box).

Scale. The scale of the utility function is defined by means of two arbitrary points. This is as for any ordered metric scale such as temperature (see Section 18.6). Since the points are arbitrary, they might as well be convenient.

Practitioners usually find that the best points to define the scale are those at the extremes of the range of X with which they are concerned. Conventionally, the worst level of X is labelled X_*, and the best X^*. It is typically most convenient to assign these the utility values of

Placing Questions in Different Contexts

In our study to determine the best level of protection against earthquakes, we wanted to find people's utility for extra costs. To make them comparable, these were expressed as percentage increases over normal costs, from 0% to +10%. Our stimulus was thus to be a lottery of the form:

$$(0\% \text{ extra}, P = 1/2; \quad 10\% \text{ extra})$$

This situation was presented in an appropriate context for each group. For engineering contractors we stated:

> "Suppose you are in charge of the construction of some building. Early results on the tests of concrete from the foundation indicate that it is understrength. On the best expert advice, you perceive that you have two choices, either to rip out the apparently weak spot (Choice A) or to leave it in. If you leave it in, you may never have to touch the foundation (Outcome B) or you may have eventually to go back, rip out some completed work, and pay a lot (Outcome C). You estimate that B and C are equally likely to occur if you leave the suspicious concrete in. The cost of B is 0% extra on the total cost of the building, and the cost of C is a 10% increase."

To tenants we interviewed we said, however:

> "Suppose you are forced to give up your sublet and look for another apartment. As you hunt around, you see you have really two choices, either to take what is immediately available elsewhere in your apartment building (Choice A) or to move. If you move you may find something at your current rental (Outcome B) or may have to pay considerably more (Outcome C). You estimate that B and C are equally likely to occur if you decide to move. The cost of B is 0% more than your current rental, and the cost of C is a 10% increase in rent."

In both cases the person being interviewed faced the same choice:

Choice A   versus   The stimulus

$$U(X_*) = 0 \qquad U(X^*) = 1.0$$

If X is some undesirable outcome, for example the number of accidental deaths, X_* might not be the lowest amount. This implies a utility function decreasing to the right. If this seems bothersome one can simply redefine the axes, for example by making X a desirable quantity such as accidental deaths prevented. If one does not like the idea of assigning a positive utility to undesirable outcomes, one can also run the utility scale from -1.0 to 0 so that

$$U(X_*) = -1.0 \qquad U(X^*) = 0$$

Bracketing. A special procedure should be used to obtain equivalents from people: bracketing. This is a way to help people define equivalents, a task which many ordinarily find difficult. The essential idea is for the interviewer to help the person focus on the equivalence gradually. The interviewer does this by first suggesting an equivalent that is less than the maximum but almost certainly too high, and to ask if the person being interviewed prefers the equivalent or the test lottery. The answer is easy. The interviewer next suggests an answer that is probably too low. Again an easy answer. The result so far is to narrow the possible range of response by "bracketing" the equivalent which lies somewhere in between. The interviewer continues the process until the interviewee settles on the equivalent. This is illustrated by the example from the earthquake questionnaire (see box).

Bracketing works in two ways. One is to focus on the answer gradually, helping the respondent exclude the easy cases and concentrate on the answer. The other is to reach the answer both from above and below. This avoids the phenomenon known as *anchoring*, the tendency people have to give a high answer when it is approached from above, and a low answer when approached from below. Good psychometric practice mitigates this bias by taking measurements from both directions. Tests of hearing are generally conducted in this way. Bracketing achieves the same result.

Computer program. An experienced interviewer can avoid introducing biases into the measurement of utility, can be consistent in the way of phrasing questions and presenting choices, and can thus obtain reliable results with low error. In

---

Application of Bracketing

The questionnaires used in the earthquake study used bracketing to get the equivalence of the response and the stimulus. The following kinds of questions came after the situations presented in the previous box:

Would you choose A if it cost

1% extra?	yes	no
8% extra?	yes	no
3% extra?	yes	no
7% extra?	yes	no
5% extra?	yes	no
6% extra?	yes	no

What is the maximum you would be prepared to pay for Choice A before you would be prepared to take the risk?

The respondent would, by answering each question, be closing in on the value appropriate for this person.

---

general this requires skills not ordinarily available. Many measurements of utility thus contain mistakes made by the interviewers.

Interactive computer programs provide the means to avoid these errors and insure consistency and reliability in the measurement of utility. Properly done, they incorporate the significant skills of an experienced interviewer, and are thus expert systems in some sense. They also have many additional features that improve the measurement. They are, obviously, totally consistent and cannot bias the responses by the different ways a person might present the stimuli. People being interviewed also tend to feel more comfortable working with a machine than with a person, whom they suspect may be judging them.

Computer programs for utility assessment provide great analytical advantages over oral or written interviews. They encode the data instantaneously, avoiding the tedious task of transcribing responses. They also can process it immediately to provide feedback as appropriate, for example with plots of the utility function. Overall, research has demonstrated that interactive computer programs for measuring utility reduce the band of error, the variance, significantly. One example of an interactive computer program for measuring utility is available for educational and research purposes from the author at MIT. This ASSESS program is written in Fortran and C.

19.4 ALTERNATIVE RESPONSES

This section discusses two kinds of responses that can be solicited to obtain utility functions: the certainty equivalent and the lottery equivalent/probability. The certainty equivalent has been the standard and must therefore be known. Its numerous defects have motivated the search for a replacement. The lottery equivalent/probability is the recommended alternative.

Certainty equivalent (CE). The conventionally standard method for measuring utility uses certainty equivalents. To start, the stimulus is the binary lottery whose possible outcomes are the extremes of the range, as defined in the previous section. The first point on the utility function is defined by the certain amount that a person values equally to the stimulus. This quantity is the *certainty equivalent*, X_1 :

$$X_1 \sim (X^*, P; \quad X_*)$$

Given our definitions, $U(X_1) = P$, as indicated in Figure 19.1.

The next two points on the utility function are obtained by substituting the certainty equivalent X_1 for each of the extreme levels of X in the binary lottery and obtaining new certainty equivalents, X_2 and X_3. Thus,

$$X_2 \sim (X_1, P; \quad X_*)$$
$$X_3 \sim (X^*, P; \quad X_1)$$

giving $U(X_2) = P^2$ and $U(X_3) = P(2 - P)$. Subsequent points are obtained by substituting X_2 and X_3 in the binary lottery for X^*, X_1, and X_* in turn. The process can be repeated as often as desirable or practical.

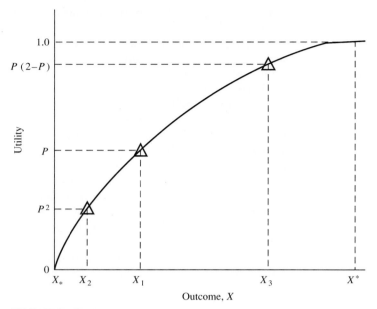

FIGURE 19.1
Measurement of the utility function $U(X)$ by the fractile method.

This approach, using the same probability in all stimulus lotteries, is also called the *constant probability* method. This is in distinction to the *variable probability* method, which seeks the certainty equivalents to binary lotteries in which the interviewer provides different probabilities as a stimulus. The latter method is really only used in research.

The procedure is particularly simple if $P = 0.50$. Then the certainty equivalents divide the range of utility into halves, quarters, and so on. Indeed, $U(X_1) = P \quad U(X^*) = 0.5$, and then $U(X_2) = P \quad U(X_1) = 0.25$ as well as $U(X_3) = P \quad U(X^*) + (1 - P) \quad U(X_1) = 0.75$. For this reason the approach is also called the *fractile method*. This division into equal parts has a particular advantage: it makes it possible to check the measurement of the utility function for internal consistency. Since $U(X_1)$ is halfway in value between $U(X_2)$ and $U(X_3)$ by construction, consistent measurements should find that the certainty equivalent to $(X_3, 0.5; \quad X_2)$ is X_1. This can be verified by asking whether

$$(X_3, 0.5; \quad X_2) \sim X_4 = X_1?$$

With a little practice, analysts find it easy to obtain consistent responses ($\pm 5\%$) for measurements.

Most people also are more ready to respond to questions put in terms of 50:50 lotteries. They are usually familiar with the idea of bets on the toss of a coin, as in "heads or tails?" This certainly makes the measurement easier. It does not, however, necessarily make it better. It is possible that people get into a rut about 50:50 lotteries and give distorted responses. This is an open question for research.

Most unfortunately, the certainty equivalent method of assessing utility has numerous, major defects. Extensive recent experiments indicate that, for reasons that are not yet clear, measurements made with this method appear to be systematically distorted.

The empirical fact is that measurements of the utility function using different probabilities in the fractile method translate into quite different results. All applications of the fractile method should by theory lead to the same utility function when applied to an individual, just as triangulation should trace the same shoreline regardless of the angles of the lines of sight. The problem is that they do not: utility functions obtained using higher probabilities in the stimulus lottery are systematically above the utility functions obtained with lower probabilities (see Figure 19.2). This family of curves is easily different by ±25% on the ordinates. The reason for this difficulty has not been determined, but a certainty effect has been suspected (See Section 18.5 and box on Allais paradox).

Additionally, the standard certainty equivalent method has other defects that encourage and propagate errors in measurement. By construction, for example, the stimulus constantly changes the range of choices presented to a person; it varies from $(X^* \text{ to } X_*)$ to $(X^* \text{ to } X_1)$ to $(X_1 \text{ to } X_*)$, and so on. This is confusing, and is likely to induce errors. Compounding this effect, the process inherently propagates errors since each reading depends on previous results. This chain of measurement passes any error on to all subsequent measurements. This is contrary to good practice, which would insist on independent readings for each value.

These theoretical and practical difficulties with the certainty equivalent method have motivated the development of alternative procedures. The most likely candidate as a replacement now appears to be the lottery equivalent/probability method.

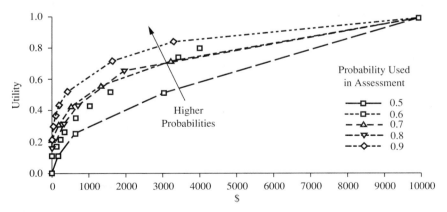

FIGURE 19.2
Empirical demonstration that utility functions obtained by the fractile method are layered according to the probabilities used in the assessment.

Lottery Equivalent/Probability (LEP). This new procedure uses lottery equivalents instead of certainty equivalents. It thereby simultaneously avoids difficulties associated with the certainty effect and the chaining of error.

The lottery equivalent method uses a binary lottery for the response. In the recommended version, the outcomes are fixed at the extremes of the range of X, and the probability varies in each measurement. Formally, it uses $(X^*, P_e; \quad X_*)$. This lottery is made equivalent to the binary lottery by adjusting the probability P_e, which is the response in the LEP method.

In practice the LEP method works as follows. The binary lottery with P_e is compared to another binary lottery with $P = 0.50$ and one outcome set at the worst end of the range of X, X_*, and the other at the variable X_i. Formally,

$$(X^*, P_e; \quad X_*) \sim (X_i, 0.50; \quad X_*)$$

Successive (X_i, P_e) pairs define the utility function.

The arithmetic of the LEP method is direct. With the conventional assumptions that $U(X^*) = 1.0$, $U(X_*) = 0$, each lottery equivalent leads to

$$U(X_i) = 2P_e$$

Figure 19.3 illustrates the procedure.

The obvious advantage of this approach is that it avoids all reference to certainty and thereby absolutely excludes the possibility of certainty effects. A

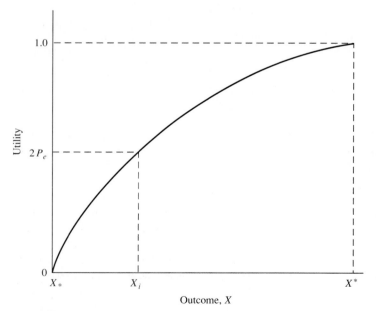

FIGURE 19.3
Measurement of the utility function $U(X)$ by probability equivalents.

secondary advantage is that it avoids error propagation: each measurement of the utility function is independent of others.

Experiments to date with the lottery equivalent/probability method indicate that it provides a much tighter set of measurements of the utility function than the fractile method. The results are, however, not yet conclusive.

There is another lottery equivalent method, the lottery equivalent/outcome approach. This fixes the probability of the response and varies one of the outcomes. Research indicates that this method leads to a family of utility functions that depend on the probability, rather as the certainty equivalent method does. The lottery equivalent/outcome method is thus so far only used in research.

19.5 STEP-BY-STEP PROCEDURE

The practical process of measuring utility consists of five distinct steps:

1. Defining X
2. Setting Context
3. Assessment
4. Interpretation
5. Functional Approximation

1. Defining X. To start the process we must first define what it is we want to measure: the nature of X, its range, and thus its scale. Because utility functions depend on their context, as indicated in Section 19.3, we must therefore determine how we will be using the utility functions and in which decision analyses they will be used.

Normally, the choice of X and its range follow directly from the problems in which the utility function will be used. The nature of X will be determined by the way the decision problem has been formulated. The extremes of the range, X^* and X_*, will simply be the extreme outcomes of the problem.

2. Setting context. We must next develop a way to present the interview to the person whose utility we are measuring. Specifically, we must prepare a scenario that puts risky choices over X in a context appropriate to the decision analysis and to the person.

For example, consider the problem of choosing the right level of earthquake protection for buildings, as sketched out in Section 19.3. In this instance the decision analysis concerned costs and utility functions for money were required. The problem itself was about housing. Merging these two situations, we developed a context that referred to housing costs. This concept was further adjusted to the people being interviewed: design engineers were asked about costs in the construction of buildings; consumers were asked about rental costs for apartments.

3. Assessment. The assessment itself proceeds as described in the previous Section. This is illustrated in detail, for both the certainty equivalent and lottery equivalent/probability methods, in Section 19.8.

4. Interpretation. The pairs of equivalences between stimulus and responses must be solved for values of $U(X_i)$. This is done as indicated previously. Normally, $U(X)$ is then plotted by interpolation between the measured points.

5. Functional approximation. This step is optional. It consists of fitting an analytic function to the measurements so that the utility function can be used more easily in the decision analysis. Two kinds of functional forms are usual.

The exponential function has been favored in the past. It is

$$U(X) = a + be^{-cX}$$

This function has some nice properties mainly to do with the obsolescent concept of "risk aversion." These are irrelevant for practical problems.

The alternative is the power function

$$U(X) = a + bX^c$$

In practice it appears to be as effective as the exponential. Either is fitted to the data in the same way: by adjusting the functional parameters so that the function generates the values of $U(X)$ assumed at the endpoints of the range and gives the best fit of intermediate points.

19.6   BUYING AND SELLING LOTTERIES

The interviewer should be careful about the way the stimulus lottery is presented and interpreted. The issue centers on whether the person being interviewed sees the situation as "buying" or "selling" the lottery. These conventional terms generally cause problems because the interviewer is trying to determine whether a person is indifferent between two quantities, not to buy or sell anything. The issue is nevertheless real: it concerns the interpretation of the X. It thus directly affects the assessment of the utility function.

The problem is best explained by example. Consider a lottery ticket for a prize, $(X^*, P; \quad 0)$, and its equivalents. Keep the arithmetic simple; consider only certainty equivalents, although the issue is general.

Selling the lottery. One possibility is that you have the ticket. You can then exchange or sell it for a certain amount (presumably somewhere in between X^* and 0). Your *selling price*, X_s, is the price at which you are indifferent between keeping the risk and selling it; it is the certainty equivalent for the lottery: $X_s \sim (X^*, P; \quad 0)$. Note that in this case your three possible outcomes are

$$0, \quad X_s, \quad X^*$$

You either walk away with the certain amount, X_s, or end up with or without the prize (X^* or 0).

Buying the lottery. The other possibility is that you do not start out by having a ticket but can buy one. In this case you either refuse the possibility and stay as you were (outcome $= 0$); or you buy the ticket and end up either with the prize *less* the purchase price, or win nothing and lose your purchase price. Your *buying price*, X_b, is the amount for which you are indifferent between buying the lottery or not. If you buy the lottery, you either win $(X^* - X_b)$ or lose this purchase price $(-X_b)$. The three possible outcomes are

$$-X_b, \quad 0, \quad (X^* - X_b)$$

The indifference statement is then properly written as

$$0 \sim (X^* - X_b, \quad P; \; -X_b)$$

Note that the buying price is not the certainty equivalent to the lottery in this case.

Comparison. The difference between buying and selling the lottery is that a person starts with a different reference point, either with or without the risk. Consequently, the person faces a different range of outcomes. Because the utility function is nonlinear, this means that the buying and selling prices are not equal.
  In the buying case we have

$$U(0) = PU(X^* - X_b) + (1 - P)U(-X_b)$$

  In the selling case,

$$U(X_s) = PU(X^*) + (1 - P)U(0)$$

When $U(X)$ is a nonlinear function, these two situations are quite different and thus $X_b \neq X_s$. Consequently the person measuring utility must be quite careful in how the questions are posed.
  Many practical examples of buying and selling lotteries exist. A person making an investment can be considered to be buying a lottery: the investor exchanges a certain sum for a property with uncertain returns. Someone who buys insurance is, on the other hand, "selling" a lottery: in exchange for premiums of fixed amount, somebody else takes the risks.

19.7 SPECIAL DEFINITIONS

The literature on utility in operations research uses a number of phrases to describe the shape of the utility function. They are worth knowing since they are widely used. Unfortunately they are also misleading.
  The first concept is that of "risk aversion" (see Section 18.3). A person is said to be "risk averse" when indifferent between a certain amount, CE, and an uncertain situation whose expected value equals $EV(L)$, where CE is less desirable than $EV(L)$. Formally

$$\text{CE} \sim (X_i, P_i; \; \ldots) \text{ for CE} < EV(L) = \sum P_i X_i$$

When people are "risk averse" their certainty equivalent to a lottery will be less beneficial than the certain amount equal to the expected value of the lottery ("less beneficial" rather than "less" because, if X is an undesirable quantity, it would be "more").

For example, suppose there is a ticket for a 50:50 chance to win $20, as in the box in Section 18.3, with an expected value of $10. Any person who prefers to receive $9 or any CE < $10 for sure rather than have the ticket, is said to be "risk averse" under these circumstances. This means that a person's utility function would be as shown in Figures 19.1 and 19.3.

The concept of "risk aversion" is misleading because, as indicated in Section 18.3, it may have nothing to do with any attitude toward risk. The shape of the utility function may simply represent diminishing marginal utility that exists regardless of whether there is risk or uncertainty.

In practice, "risk aversion" is an alternate means of referring to concave utility functions. Yet this is not quite right either. A person may be risk averse for a choice, within the definition given above, over a range of X for which the utility function is both concave and convex, as it normally is when there are thresholds for major changes in value. See Figure 19.4.

Following in the track laid by "risk aversion," a person who chooses according to expected values is said to be *"risk neutral"*:

$$CE = EV(L) \sim (X_i, P_i, \ldots)$$

Likewise a person exhibits *"risk preference"* when preferring the lottery to some

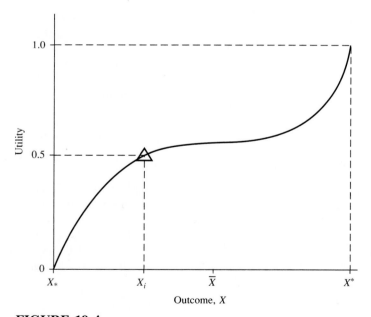

FIGURE 19.4
A person may be "risk averse" toward a lottery spanning concave and convex portions of the utility function, for example: $X_i \sim (X^*, 0.5; X_*)$ $X_i < EV(X)$.

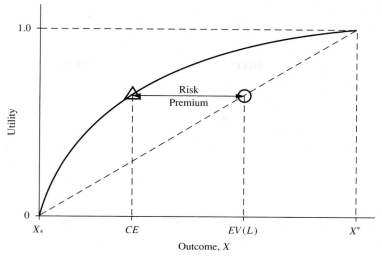

FIGURE 19.5
Definition of "risk premium," using the lottery $(X^*, P; X_*)$.

certain amount better than the expected value. A person with "risk preference" is sometimes said to be "risk prone." This is a particularly unfortunate phrase as it suggests someone who is accident prone, which has nothing to do with the matter.

Finally, the term *"risk premium"* is used to describe the difference between the equivalent to a lottery and the expected value:

$$\text{Risk premium} = EV(L) - CE$$

Figure 19.5 illustrates the concept. As with "risk aversion" it is a misleading phrase. The distance to which it refers may simply be caused by a person's diminishing marginal utility and have nothing to do with the uncertainty.

19.8 EXAMPLE MEASUREMENT

This example replicates a process we routinely use in class to illustrate the step-by-step process for measuring utility, as presented in Section 19.5. In what follows, we illustrate the use of both the certainty equivalent and lottery equivalent/probability methods by repeating the assessment and interpretation, steps 3 and 4, for each case.

1. Defining X. We start with the assumption that we are interested in evaluating investments in different consumer items likely to interest the class, stereo sets for instance. The utility function for money is thus required. For this example, consider the range from $X_* = \$0$ to $X^* = \$1000$ (but any other can be assumed).

2. Setting context. Building on the context of the purchase of something for enjoyment, as a stereo, it is appropriate to suggest a situation in which the person being interviewed is receiving a gift of money as a present.

My own practice is to ask the person to imagine that he or she has an eccentric relative who likes to play games—and has perhaps been influenced by a recent trip to Las Vegas. This relative supposedly offers lotteries as gifts rather than simply cash.

3. Assessment (CE). With the certainty equivalent method the person is asked to provide the certain amount which is (for them) of equal value as the lottery. We determine this by bracketing, asking the person to choose between certain amounts and the lottery until he or she is indifferent between the two.

A typical starting question is:

"Suppose your relative offers a choice for your holiday present: either a 50:50 chance at $1000 or nothing, or a certain amount. Would you take the certain amount if it were $900?"

Most people find this easy to answer and prefer the $900.

The subsequent questions vary the certain amount in the question. First to $100, say. Again, most people find this easy; they prefer the lottery. Their indifference point must therefore lie in between $100 and $900; it is the point their preference between the lottery and the certain amount switches. To find this we try certain amounts of $700, $200, and so on until the range is really small and the person can provide the certainty equivalent directly. For this example, suppose that it is $320.

4. Interpretation (CE). The above certainty equivalent defines the equation:

$$U(320) = 0.50U(1000) + 0.50U(0)$$

With conventional definitions of the best and worst extremes for the range

$$U(1000) = 1.0 \qquad U(0) = 0$$

we obtain

$$U(320) = 0.50$$

This is easily plotted on a graph of $U(X)$ versus X.

Using the standard terminology discussed in the previous section, this utility function would be said to show "risk aversion." The "risk premium" for the ($1000, 0.5; 0) lottery would be $180, the difference between the certainty equivalent and $500, which is the monetary expectation of the stimulus lottery.

3. Assessment (LEP). Repeating the process for the lottery equivalent method, we simply alter the response suggested to the person being interviewed. The person must choose between two lotteries.

A typical starting question would thus be:

"Suppose your relative offers a choice for your holiday present, either a 50:50 chance on getting \$500 or nothing, or a 45% chance of getting \$1000 or nothing?"

Notice that the probability in the second lottery, $P = 0.45$, is less than in the first. If it were larger, the second lottery should always be preferred as it would have the greater chance of the greater prize. For most people the above question is easy and they would prefer the second lottery.

Subsequent questions vary the probability in the second lottery. First to another easy choice, $P = 10\%$, and then to increasingly difficult ones such as $P = 35\%$, 15%, and so on. Finally the person will be able to supply the lottery equivalent/probability. For this example, suppose that it is 35%.

4. Interpretation (LEP). The equivalence now is

$$(1000, 0.35; \ 0) \sim (500, 0.50; \ 0)$$

which translates to the equation

$$0.35U(1000) + 0.65U(0) = 0.50U(500) + 0.50U(0)$$

The solution when the conventional values are assigned to the extremes of the range are, as indicated in Section 19.5,

$$U(500) = 2(0.35) = 0.70$$

Again, this defines a "risk averse" utility function.

5. Functional Approximation. Using the above result for the LEP assessment, we can now approximate the utility function by a formula. Taking the power function by way of example, we have, for each of the three known points,

$$U(0) = 0 = a + b(0)^c$$
$$U(500) = 0.70 = a + b(500)^c$$
$$U(1000) = 1.0 = a + b(1000)^c$$

The first equation implies $a = 0$. This means that we can get an expression in c alone by dividing the last two equations. The result is

$$0.70 = (0.5)^c$$

so that

$$c = 0.514$$

and then

$$b = (1000)^{-c} = 0.0287$$

The power approximation to this utility function is

$$U(X) = 0.0287X^{0.514} \approx 0.03X^{0.5}$$

19.9   USE IN DECISION ANALYSIS

This section illustrates how utility functions are integrated in decision analysis. The basic idea is simple: substitute the utility of the outcome for the outcome and do the analysis. The result will be the preferred decision once a person's utility is considered.

Consider that the person whose utility we assessed and fitted in Section 19.8 has in fact received a $1000 holiday present. Imagine further that this person intends to buy a $500 stereo and has to decide whether or not to buy the $100 service contract that would guarantee all repairs at no further cost. With this warranty, the total cost of the system would be $600 so our friend would end up with $400 left. Without it, the total cost depends on the reliability of the system. The records show that there is a 70% chance of no problems and no extra cost, a 20% chance of a $100 repair, and a 10% chance that the whole system must be replaced at an extra cost of $500. In that case, our friend would have no money left. The decision tree for our problem, stated in terms of money left, is

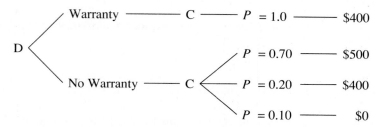

Looking only at the money outcomes, it would seem better not to have the warranty. The expected money left would be

$$\text{Expected \$, No Warranty} = 430$$

This is more than what our friend would have with the warranty.

Integrating utility in the analysis, we transform the decision tree by substituting the utilities. Thus

D

Warranty ——— C ——— $P = 1.0$ ——— $U(400) = 0.625$

No Warranty ——— C — $P = 0.70$ ——— $U(500) = 0.70$
$P = 0.20$ ——— $U(400) = 0.625$
$P = 0.10$ ——— $U(0) = 0$

The better choice, considering utility, is to take the warranty. Indeed,

$$\text{Utility, No Warranty} = 0.7(0.7) + 0.2(.625) = 0.615$$

This is less than the utility when one has the warranty. As should be expected, the person who is "risk averse" similarly may be expected to weigh safer choices more favorably in practice.

The purpose of measuring a person's utility in a controlled setting is to provide insight into how that individual would choose. The utility function enables the analyst to incorporate that person's values into complex situations, and to determine which strategies are best for that person—a task that person would normally not be able to do, unless skilled in decision analysis.

REFERENCES

Hogarth, Robin, (1987). *Judgement and Choice: The Psychology of Decision*, 2nd ed., Wiley, New York.

McCord, Mark, and de Neufville, R., (1986). "Lottery Equivalents: Reduction of the Certainty Effect in Utility Assessment," *Management Science*, Vol. 32, pp. 56–60.

PROBLEMS

19.1. *Utility Manipulation I*

(a) Given the lottery ($16, 0.75; $0) and the utility function $U(X) = (900 + 100X)^{1/2}$, determine the lottery's expected value; expected utility; selling price; buying price. Does $U(X)$ show "risk aversion"?

(b) Repeat (a) for the lottery (100, 0.5;   0) and $U(X) = (100 + 3X)^{1/2}$.

19.2. *Utility Manipulation II*

(a) A person is found to have the utility function: $U(X) = (400 + 100X)^{1/2}$, X in $. For each of the lotteries ($21, 0.5;   −$3) and ($16, 0.5; $0) find the expected value, expected utility, and selling price.

(b) Repeat (a) using the utility function $U(X) = (400 + 20X)^{1/2}$ and the lottery ($125, 0.4; $0).

19.3. *Utility Manipulation III*

Ms. Thomas has the utility function $U(X) = [(100 + X)/200]^{1/2}$. For what probability P would she have a selling price of -50 for the lottery $(28, P ; -68)$?

19.4. *Probability Equivalents*

Given the following utility function:

X	:	-100	-90	-80	-65	-50	-35
$U(X)$	:	0	3	4.5	6	7	8

X	:	-20	0	20	45	70	110	150
$U(X)$	:	9	10	11	12	13	14	15

(a) Calculate the probabilities P_1 and P_2 such that 45 is indifferent to the lotteries $(20, P_1; 150)$ and $(-20, P_2; 110)$.

(b) Calculate the selling price and risk premiums of the lotteries: $(-90, 0.5; -20)$; $(-65, 0.8; -20)$; $(-100, 0.2; -50, 0.3; -20, 0.4; 70)$.

(c) Calculate the buying price for: $(70, 0.5; 150)$; $(150, 0.4; 45)$.

19.5. *Jones*

Suppose Jones tells you his selling prices for the lotteries $(-\$40, 0.2; \$70)$ and $(-\$40, 0.75; \$30)$ are 30 and 0 respectively. Note, Jones is not "risk averse" between $-\$40$ and $\$30$. He is "risk averse" between $\$30$ and $\$70$.

(a) Plot a plausible utility function for Jones indicating key points.

(b) If $U(70) = 25$ and $U(30) = 15$, what would $U(0)$ equal?

19.6. *Table*

Consider the table below. Does this utility function show the respondent to be "risk averse," "risk seeking," or "risk neutral"?

Travel time (min)	Utility
0	1.0
10	0.8
20	0.5
30	0

Explain.

19.7. *Utility Functions*

Which of the following utility functions represent an "expected value maximizer," a "risk positive" individual, or a "risk averse" individual?

(a) $U(X) = X$ (d) $U(X) = X^2$

(b) $U(X) = 2X + 4$ (e) $U(X) = X^{0.5}$

(c) $U(X) = -e^{-3x} - e^{-x}$

19.8. *Workstations*

Lee O'Tard, President of Munskin clothes, needs to acquire computer workstations to design new fashions. The salient criteria are cost and speed. Through interviews, Lee indicates that:

• where costs are concerned: $\$4000 \sim (\$6000, 0.5;\ \$1000)$

• for megahertz of speed: $10 \sim (24, 0.2;\ 4)$ and $18 \sim (24, 0.75;\ 10)$

(a) Plot the utility function for cost.

(b) Is Lee "risk averse" for money?

(c) Plot the utility function for speed.

19.9. *Fire Chief*

A fire chief who wants to minimize response time to answering fire calls indicates indifference between 1.6, 2.25, and 0.5 min for sure and the following lotteries, respectively:

(2.5 min, 0.4; 0 min)   (2.5 min, 0.5; 1.6 min)   (1.6 min, 0.75; 0 min)

Is the decisionmaker "risk averse" or not? Explain.

19.10. *Charles Chancy*

Suppose you wanted to construct a utility function for Charles who tells you that 320 and 850 are respectively his certain monetary equivalents for the lotteries ($600, 0.5; $0) and ($1000, 0.5; $600). Assuming Charles exhibits "risk preference," draw a graph that indicates how the above information restricts Charles' utility function in the region $X = 0$ to $X = 1000$.

19.11. *Lottery Construction*

Write the lotteries defined by the following statements:

(a) A manager is willing to invest no more than $4 million in a project that is equally likely to gross $10 million or nothing.

(b) Another manager is willing to sell for no less than $1 million the plans to a new process that would make $3 million with probability of 0.7 and nothing with a probability of 0.3.

(c) A third manager is willing to pay no more than $2 million to avoid a 75% chance of losing $5 million and a 25% chance of making $1 million.

19.12. *Smith*

You are told that Smith could be willing to sell for no less than $20 the lottery ($50, $\frac{2}{3}$; $-$100); to pay up to $30 to get the chance to play the lottery ($50, $\frac{3}{4}$; $-$70); and has a "risk premium" of $-$22.5 for the lottery ($50, 0.05; $0, 0.10; $-$100, 0.85).

Sketch Smith's utility function over the range for which you have information. Clearly label axes and the coordinates of the important points.

19.13. *Bob*

Given that Bob is willing to sell the lottery (100, 0.8; $-$50) for no less than $50; to pay up to $40 to avoid the lottery (50, 0.25; $-$50); and to buy the lottery (75, 0.5; $-$15) for no more than $25,

(a) Sketch Bob's utility function between $-$50 and $100.

(b) What is Bob's selling price and risk premium for (100, 0.75; $-$40)?

19.14. *Cathy*

Suppose that Cathy is willing to pay a maximum of $50 to get out of playing the lottery ($100, 0.5; $-$100), to pay up to $10 to buy the lottery ($110, 0.5; $-$40), and to sell for no less than $60 the lottery ($100, $\frac{2}{3}$; 0). Assuming that Cathy is consistently "risk averse":

(a) Sketch her utility function between $-$100 and $100.

(b) For Cathy to be consistent, what should her selling price be for the lottery: ($0, $\frac{2}{3}$; $-$100)?

19.15. *John*

John would be willing to sell the lottery ($500, 0.5; $-$100) for no less than $100. He would pay up $50 to play the lottery ($150, 0.6; $-$50). He would also give up the lottery ($500, 0.6; $100) for no less than $300.

(a) Write John's indifference statements for the above three lotteries.

(b) Sketch his utility function. Clearly label the axes and points.

(c) What factors may account for a utility function that is "risk averse"? Classify John's utility function as either "risk averse" or "risk seeking."

19.16. *Petra*

Petra would sell the lottery ($80, $\frac{2}{3}$; −$20) for $70; the lottery ($70, 0.6; $0) for $50; and would pay $20 for ($100, 0.1; $0).

(a) Write her indifference statements for the three lotteries.

(b) Sketch her utility function, clearly labelling axes and points.

(c) What factors may account for a utility function that is "risk averse"? Classify her utility function as "risk averse" or "risk seeking."

19.17. *Andy*

Given the lottery: (100, 0.5; 0) and the utility function $U(X) = (100 + 3X)^{1/2}$, calculate its expected value; expected utility; selling price; and buying price.

19.18. *Georgia*

By interviewing Georgia you find that she would sell the following lottery for $50 : ($100, 0.9; −$80); would pay $50 to get ($100, 0.8; −$30) and $60 to avoid ($0, $\frac{1}{3}$; −$80).

(a) Write Georgia's indifference statements for the three lotteries.

(b) Sketch the utility function, clearly labelling axes and points.

(c) For Georgia to be consistent, find the probability for the statement $0 ~ ($50, P; −$60).

19.19. *Meredith*

Meredith's utility function for money is $U(X) = (5 + .01X)^{1/2}$ for all X from −500 to 1000 dollars. Calculate Meredith's selling price, buying price, and risk premium for the lottery ($900, 0.4; $400).

19.20. *David*

David is willing to sell the lottery ($40, 0.6; 0) for a minimum of $22. He will pay a maximum of $10 for the lottery ($32, $\frac{5}{8}$; −$20). David is always "risk averse" and prefers increasing amounts of money.

(a) Draw a graph that shows how the above information restricts David's utility function in the region from −$30 to $40.

(b) David's utility function can be approximated by a positive linear transformation of $U(X) = -e^{-0.01x}$. Write an expression for his utility function with $U(40) = 1$ and $(U − 30) = 0$. (Hint: $e^{0.4} = 1.5$.)

19.21. *Toothpick*

Your friend who has made a fortune with the invention of the piezoelectric toothpick asks your advice in planning some investments. By interview you find that your friend:

• Would spend up to $3M to develop a new automotive emission control, which would, with probability 0.50, be worth $10M.

• Has a new invention, a bike lock, that will make $7M except if (one chance in five) it does not catch on; and would be willing to sell the rights to the lock for $5M or more.

• Has a batch of piezoelectric toothpicks with potential malfunctions. If they actually fail, penalties would be $3M. There is a 60% chance of this and your friend would spend up to $2M to correct the defects.

(*a*) Formulate the above as indifference statements.

(*b*) Sketch your friend's utility function.

(*c*) List 2 questions you could ask to test your friend's consistency, and indicate what answers would be appropriate.

19.22. *Vegas Bus*

The mayor of Vegas has to decide whether to spend $1M on a bus experiment along the entertainment strip. The local gamblers estimate that there is a 50-50 chance that the system's total revenues will be $0.2M, a 0.3 chance of breaking even, and a 0.2 chance of $1.4M profits. Your evidence of the mayor's attitude is her behavior last year on a $0.8M budget. She was then prepared:

- To invest the city's money in a "cavalcade of stars" which was 4:1 (0.2 chance of success) to profit $1.2M; otherwise Vegas would lose the whole budget.
- To trade, when approached by the governor's office intent on dispersing patronage, a grant of $0.8M for the opportunity to host a national convention equally probable to have $1.2M or zero profits.

(*a*) Draw the mayor's utility function, stating any necessary assumptions.

(*b*) You now find that last month the mayor decided to spend $0.9M on a beauty contest that would either gross $1.7M (probability 0.4) or $0.1M (probability 0.6). Is the mayor consistent in her general attitudes toward risk?

(*c*) What should she do about the bus experiment?

19.23. *International Exploitation*

The record of International Exploitation, Inc. indicates that the following decisions represent its attitude toward risk-taking:

- If a project is equally likely to boom (revenue = $8M) or bust (revenue = $0), I. E. will implement the project if the project costs $2M or less.
- If a smaller project is equally likely to succeed (revenue = $3.5M) or bust (revenue = $0), I. E. will not spend more than $1.5M on the project.
- The company seems indifferent among any of the three choices: $0.5M certain or ($2M, 0.4; $0) or ($6M, 0.3; $0,0.2; −$0.5M, 0.5).
- Corporate policy indicates a willingness to spend as much as $0.5M to avoid a 20% chance of losing $2M.

(*a*) Construct the lotteries outlined.

(*b*) Approximate and plot I. E.'s utility function (seven points can be inferred from the data).

(*c*) Assuming I. E. is consistent, for what cash payment would I. E. sell the lottery ($6M, $\frac{1}{3}$; −$1.5M)?

(*d*) For what probability would I. E. be indifferent between −$0.5M and ($2M, P; −$1.5M)?

CHAPTER
20

MULTIATTRIBUTE UTILITY

20.1 CONCEPT

This chapter presents Keeney-Raiffa multiattribute utility $U(\mathbf{X})$ as the recommended analytic method for measuring preferences of consequences with many different dimensions, $\mathbf{X} = (X_1, \ldots, X_i, \ldots, X_N)$. This approach is a direct extension of the one-dimensional utility presented in Chapter 19.

Keeney-Raiffa multiattribute utility is appropriate for practical analyses because it provides a good balance between convenience and ease of use on the one hand, and accuracy on the other. Compared to the elementary models, it is relatively fast while incorporating the kinds of interactive effects between dimensions that exist in interesting situations. Section 20.2 discusses the deficiencies of the alternative models in detail, setting the context for the subsequent presentation of the theory on which the preferred approach is based.

The essence of the theory lies in two assumptions, similar to axioms, about the nature of the preferences of a person or organization. These have a significant consequence: they reduce the number of calculations exponentially from the number required by a direct application of the methods for measuring utility presented in Chapter 19. Section 20.3 presents these assumptions and discusses their limits in detail. The following sections indicate how multiattribute utility should be used in practice, and illustrate its application.

Multiattribute utility complements the procedures presented in Chapter 8 for multiobjective analysis. Those methods, which seek to identify noninferior solutions, have the great advantage of not requiring any explicit measure of preference. They are therefore much simpler and should be used whenever possible.

The multiattribute methods should be used when there are no clearly dominant choices and when a more detailed, analytic method is required. In practical situations it is often most efficient first to use the multiobjective methods to screen out dominated, clearly unattractive possibilities and identify the noninferior alternatives as defined in Section 8.2. Then, if necessary because there is no dominant choice, the next step is to use multiattribute utility on the set of noninferior alternatives.

20.2 ELEMENTARY METHODS

There are two obvious ways of defining the preference function for a set of distinct objects or attributes. One is to add up the preference functions for the individual objects; the other is to extend the measurement of utility as described in Chapter 19. The first method often simplifies the situation excessively, thus neglecting many of the interesting features of the problem. The other requires far too much effort for practical use. Additionally, three other methods for evaluating multiattribute alternatives are popular because they are easy to use on personal computers. Yet these contain serious deficiencies. This section covers each of these approaches in detail, as a motivation for the recommended procedure.

Additive approach. This is the traditional method. It simply expresses:

$$U(\mathbf{X}) = \sum w_i U(X_i)$$

where the w_i are some scaling factors or weights between the values of the different dimensions.

This is the approach implicit in most practical economic analyses such as engineering economy (Chapter 12). In those cases the weights between the different objects are simply their prices, p_i. Since these approaches also assume that value is linear in quality, they express:

$$U(\mathbf{X}) = \sum p_i X_i$$

This simple formula is useful in the limited situations for which the assumptions hold, that is, when one is dealing in a strictly commercial environment, in which all X_i have prices; when these prices are constant regardless of the level of any X_i; and when these prices do in fact reflect the real value of the X_i. These situations occur in many routine operations. They are, however, quite atypical of the most interesting situations, particularly those involving large-scale systems.

The more sophisticated approach, of defining $U(\mathbf{X})$ as the weighted sum of the utilities for individual attributes $U(X_i)$, has a fundamental limitation that makes it unattractive in practice: the additive model cannot express the value of any interaction between the different objects. This is a major weakness because, as it happens, there is generally considerable value (either positive or negative) to the interaction between the several attributes of a system.

People value the interaction between the attributes of a system because these effects are frequently complementary: one or more attributes may have little value without others being present. Conversely, the attributes may also be antagonistic in that the presence of one attribute negates the value of the other. The whole may be either greater or less than the sum of its parts. Formally, any attribute X_i may have one value $U(X_i)'$ if another attribute X_j is present, and quite another, $U(X_i)''$ if X_j is absent (see box). It is in the nature of systems that the values of the attributes interact.

Additive models of utility cannot represent the broad range of common situations, and are therefore inadequate for general use. As the analysis for the two-dimensional case in Section 20.3 indicates, additive multiattribute utility is truly exceptional.

Extension of utility measurement. In principle, the utility over many attributes incorporating all relevant interactions, $U(\mathbf{X})$ can be measured just as the utility for any simple characteristic, $U(X_i)$. One could define the utility of two arbitrary reference points and then estimate the utility of all others with respect to them. This last step would require some special effort because one would be changing

---

Values for Complementary and Antagonistic Attributes

As an example of complementary attributes, consider a computer program that prepares graphic displays. It has two attributes that would obviously be interesting to any user:

$$X_1 = \text{Speed} \qquad X_2 = \text{Resolution}$$

A utility function can be defined for each of these attributes. These functions, $U(X_1)$ and $U(X_2)$, may be quite typical: a person will place considerable emphasis on the initial improvements in either speed or resolution, and will have diminishing marginal utility for ever better performance.

The additive model of value for both speed and performance is not appropriate, however:

$$U(\text{Speed, Resolution}) \neq w_1 U(\text{Speed}) + w_2 U(\text{Resolution})$$

Why? Because any graphics program must have both speed and resolution together; a program with great speed and no resolution is probably of little use, for example.

Examples of antagonistic attributes abound, although they may be less obvious. For example, you may value both spending time with your parents and going to parties. However, having your parents with you at a party with your peers may dampen your enjoyment considerably. Likewise, a community may value the acres available for bird sanctuaries and the land for airport development. Having the two together is rather worthless—the aircraft disturb the birds and the birds have the unfortunate tendency to get sucked into jet engines, causing crashes.

---

several attributes simultaneously and one would want to be careful to do so systematically. Yet there is no theoretical reason this could not be done.

The difficulty with this approach is practical. It requires such a large number of measurements that it is hardly feasible even for just two attributes, and certainly not for more. Indeed, the number of points that would have to be assessed by the direct application of utility measurement increases exponentially for any given degree of resolution with the number of attributes to be valued. Thus if one wants each single-dimensional utility function, $U(X_i)i = 1$ to N, to be defined by M points, the N-dimensional utility function $U(\mathbf{X})$ will have to be defined by about M^N points. More precisely, since we always assume the utility for two reference points, the number of points to be assessed by the direct extension of utility measurement is $(M^N - 2)$. (See box.)

Dimensionality of Direct Measurement of Multiattribute Utility

Suppose we wish to measure the utility of a graphics computer program considering the two attributes of speed and resolution. Suppose further that we will be satisfied with a crude measurement dividing the range of each dimension into quarters. The total number of points that must be defined is thus 25, as the display indicates:

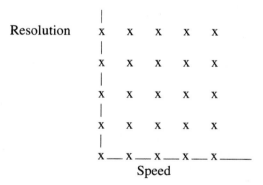

Points, x, to be defined for two-dimensional utility.

As the value of two points could be assumed, such as $\mathbf{X}^*$, the best performance, and $\mathbf{X}_*$, the worst, the utility of 23 points $(= 5^2 - 2)$ would have to be measured.

Both greater resolution and more dimensions would be impractical. Six points per dimension would require 34 points in all, at the limit of practicality; and a three-dimensional utility function would require $(5^3 - 2) = 123$ points, well beyond what is possible.

The practical limit to the number of points that can be measured in a utility function would appear to be about 30 if the assessment is conducted verbally. This limit may be as great as 50 if the assessments are done with an interactive computer program (see Section 19.3.) Beyond these limits the person being interviewed is too tired to respond meaningfully. These limits mean that only a two-dimensional multiattribute utility function can be measured by this method. The direct extension of utility measurement is therefore not a practical method for measuring multiattribute utility.

Lexicographic ordering. This approach to ranking consequences with many attributes derives its name from "lexicon," the name for a book that arranges things alphabetically, such as a dictionary or a telephone directory. This method operates on much the same principle.

The procedure involves two phases. The first is to rank the attributes in order of importance. The second is to rank the consequences one is evaluating in terms of their most important attribute, using the second most important to break ties between the rating on the first attribute, and so on (see box). This process is trivial to automate and thus commonly available on computers.

This mindless procedure is worthless for analysis. It ignores all possible trade-offs in values between the attributes. It implies that any advantage on the first attribute, however small, outweighs all advantages on the other attributes, no matter how large. It thus implies that all secondary attributes are worthless. If this is so, one might as well simply worry about one-dimensional utility. If we really do care about the many attributes of a consequence, this approach is totally unrealistic. The only reason to discuss it is to put you on guard against something that, looking easy, is seductive.

Lexicographic Ordering

Consider a series of graphics programs defined by their speed, in megahertz, and resolution, in terms of numbers of pixels to a side of the screen. Suppose that the (speed, resolution) characteristics of four of them are:

$$(16, 1000) \quad (9, 500) \quad (9, 250) \quad (6, 1000)$$

If speed is identified as the more important attribute, the lexicographic ordering would rank the programs in the order just given: the fastest first; the next fastest (9 MHz) according to their secondary attribute of resolution; and the slowest last.

Note that this procedure does not admit the possibility that the slow, high resolution program (6, 1000) could be better than the thoroughly mediocre program (9, 250). No trade-offs are considered and secondary attributes are virtually disregarded.

Conjunctive and disjunctive methods. These two methods are quite similar. Again, they proceed through two phases. The first is to define minimum criteria for each attribute. The second is to use these standards to define the set of things worth considering. Note carefully that, by itself, neither approach ranks the items in the set or defines the preferred choice—unless the set has only one element.

The *disjunctive* approach defines the set as all the elements that meet at least one criterion. It is the union of all the possibilities that have not been systematically rejected by each minimum standard. In terms of Figure 20.1, this is the set of elements that lie in the areas A, B, and C, between the minimum standards and the maximum possibilities as defined by the noninferior alternatives (see Section 8.2).

The *conjunctive* approach defines the set more narrowly as the conjunction of the possibilities that meet the criteria, that is, those in area B. This would seem the better method in that it could seem to define the preferred alternative more tightly.

Both approaches are easy to automate because they simply require a mechanical sort of alternatives according to their attributes, as with the lexicographic approach. Both are thus also readily available on computers and seductively easy to use. Both, however, fail equally to consider trade-offs between attributes and are of little value in practice.

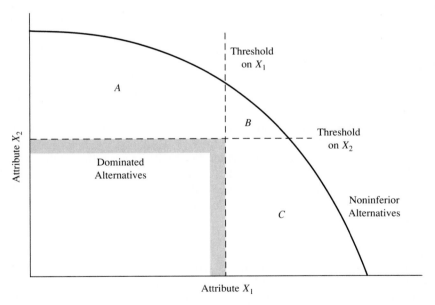

FIGURE 20.1
The disjunctive approach to multiattribute analysis includes alternatives in A, B, and C; the conjunctive approach focuses narrowly on alternatives in B.

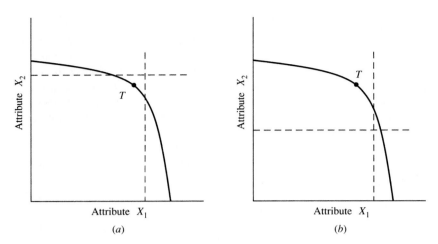

FIGURE 20.2
Situations in which the disjunctive (*a*) and conjunctive (*b*) approaches to multiattribute analysis miss the alternative *T*, which represents the best tradeoff between the different attributes.

The difficulties with these methods is easily seen by example. Consider the relatively common situation in which the curve of noninferior alternatives has a "knee" that defines the preferred choice at *T* (see discussion in Section 8.6). The first difficulty is that both the conjunctive and disjunctive methods may exclude the best choice, as Figure 20.2(*a*) shows. One might imagine that this problem could simply be resolved by lowering the standards and enlarging the sets. Such is not the case. Figure 20.2(*b*) provides such a situation: here the conjunctive approach does define a nonzero set of choices, but excludes the preferred one at *T*; the disjunctive includes *T*, but along with so many others as to not be especially useful.

In short, both the conjunctive and disjunctive methods are rather ineffective ways to define the set of alternatives one should focus on. This set consists of the noninferior alternatives as defined in Section 8.2 and is best defined by analysis or, if necessary, by sorting directly for noninferior alternatives.

20.3 THEORY

The theory of multiattribute utility is based on two assumptions about the structure of preferences. These assumptions refer to the way a person values the interaction between attributes. They lead to a considerable reduction in the number of calculations that are necessary. If the assumptions are acceptable for a person faced with a particular situation, we thus have a practical means to obtain the multiattribute utility while still accounting for the interaction between attributes.

The two assumptions are similar to axioms in that they define the nature of the analysis. They differ from axioms in the following way. Axioms are taken to be statements about how people should behave rationally. The special assumptions of multiattribute utility on the other hand do not have any ethical content, they are merely descriptive. The question to be asked concerning the assumptions is thus: Do these two assumptions describe the preferences of a person for a situation within a tolerable degree? If the answer is yes, then the multiattribute utility can be measured by the method to be described.

The two assumptions are those of

- preferential independence
- utility independence

The reason they simplify the measurement process is that they lead to ways to decompose the N-dimensional utility functions into N one-dimensional portions that can subsequently be recombined. The number of calculations is therefore changed from an exponential to a linear function of the number of attributes. Each assumption is described as follows.

Preferential independence. This assumption concerns the order of preferences. Specifically it is that the ranking of preferences over any pair of attributes is independent of the other attributes. Preferential independence is important because it permits us to decompose a multidimensional problem.

Formally, the assumption of preferential independence is that

- If for any pair of attributes, say X_1 and X_2, one combination is preferred to another

$$(X_1', X_2') > (X_1'', X_2'')$$

for some level of the other attributes, say X_3 to X_N,
- then the order of this preference will be maintained for all other levels of the other attributes.

Symbolically, this can be written as (where a/b indicates conditionality and is to be read as "a exists when conditions b prevail")

If	$[(X_1^a, X_2^a)/(X_3, \ldots, X_N)] > [(X_1^b, X_2^b)/(X_3, \ldots, X_N)]$
implies	$[(X_1^a, X_2^a)/(X_3', \ldots, X_N')] > [(X_1^b, X_2^b)/(X_3', \ldots, X_N')]$,
then	X_1 and X_2 are preferentially independent of $(X_3, \ldots, X_N)$.

People are quite commonly preferentially independent between attributes (see box). Note however that being preferentially independent does not mean that one does not care about the other attributes. One probably does value them significantly. Preferential independence only implies that the order of ranking

Example of Preferential Independence

Again consider the computer graphics program. Most people would be preferentially independent between speed and resolution of the program on the one hand, and its cost on the other.

Thus a person interested in digital maps might prefer (medium speed, high resolution) to (high speed, low resolution) regardless of cost; the resolution would be particularly important. Thus,

If   [(medium,high)/high cost] $>$ [(high,low)/high cost]

implies   [(medium,high)/low cost] $>$ [(high,low)/low cost]

then the person is preferentially independent for speed and resolution versus cost.

The person presumably values cost as an important attribute of the choice, and would distinctly prefer a lower cost program. Preferential independence in this case implies that for any given price, the order in which pairs of levels of speed and resolution are ranked will stay the same.

---

between two attributes does not change because of changes in the level—and value—of the other attributes.

Situations in which preferential independence does not hold are not common, but common enough that decision analysts should watch out for them carefully. Most people for example are not preferentially independent over the various attributes of their diet (see following box). More generally, there are many instances in which the ranking of one's preferences do depend on the level of some other attribute, particularly on whether it is above or below some threshold.

Analysts should investigate whether a person's preferences are in fact reasonably described by preferential independence between attributes. This must be done case by case, for each different person and for each specific kind of situation. The standard way to check for preferential independence is to ask a person at the start of the interview whether their ranking between attributes (such as speed and resolution for the computer graphics program) might depend on the other attributes. This should be done for all possible pairs of attributes (e.g., speed and resolution versus cost; speed and cost versus resolution; and so on.). This process is fairly tedious, but should be done as there may well be combinations for which preferential independence does not hold. For the computer graphics program it may not, for instance, if there is a minimum level of resolution that is required.

Situations in which preferential independence does not hold can often be circumvented once detected. This can be done either by eliminating all alternatives with levels of an attribute that fall below a required threshold, as by eliminating from consideration all graphics programs with insufficient resolution; or by refor-

Counterexample to Preferential Independence

Consider attributes of a diet measured in terms of the weight of each element of the diet:

$$X_1 = \text{Steak} \qquad X_3 = \text{Bread}$$
$$X_2 = \text{Potatoes} \qquad X_4 = \text{Desserts}$$

A person with enough money to have plenty of bread and desserts each day, ($X_3 = 5$, $X_4 = 6$) say, is likely to prefer a high-meat main dish with fewer calories to one with low meat and high calories. Thus,

(slices of meat, few potatoes) > (no meat, many potatoes)

when you have:

(much bread, much dessert)

If this person becomes poor, however, and cannot generally have enough calories, then the preferences would change. The high calorie, low-meat meal would now be preferred to the other:

(no meat, many potatoes) > (slices of meat, few potatoes)

when you have:

(no bread, no dessert)

this person is thus not preferentially independent over the attributes as defined.

The decision problem might be reformulated so that the person might be preferentially independent over a new set of attributes. This could be the case if the diet were expressed in terms of more fundamental elements such as calories, bulk, percent of fats, sugars, and so on.

---

mating the problem into one with attributes that are preferentially independent (see box).

Utility independence. This assumption concerns the intensity of preferences, not just their relative order as does preferential independence. It is a cardinal condition rather than an ordinal condition. It is thus much more demanding—and also much more useful—than preferential independence.

Specifically, the utility independence assumption is that the indifference between a lottery and a certainty equivalent for any attribute does not depend on the levels of the other attributes. This is a most valuable condition because it implies that it is possible to measure the way the utility changes over one dimension, independent of all other attributes. These independent measurements can then be combined to give the multiattribute utility function.

Formally, the assumption of utility independence is that:

- If for any given level of attributes X_j other than X_i, there is an indifferent statement between several levels of X_i:

$$X_i' \sim (X_i'', P; X_i''') \text{ for one set of } X_j, j \neq i$$

- then this indifference holds for all levels of $X_j, j \neq i$.

Symbolically, this can be written as (where / again indicates conditionality)

If $\qquad (X_i'/X_j) \sim (X_i''/X_j, P; X_i'''/X_j)$

implies $\qquad (X_i'/X_j') \sim (X_i''/X_j', P; X_i'''/X_j')$

then X_i is utility independent of $X_j, j \neq i$. (See box for an illustration of this definition.)

People are quite commonly utility independent among different attributes. This assumption does not noticeably limit the way the multiattribute utility function can define the value of interactions between attributes. Paradoxically, it is the assumption that causes the least difficulty for the analyst even though it is

---

Example of Utility Independence

Consider the evaluation of the computer graphics programs again. Assume that when considering GRAF-ITTY, a particular release with known levels of speed and resolution, a professor is indifferent between buying the program at the discount introductory price of $450 or taking the risk with probability $P = 0.8$ of getting a review copy at no cost and probability $P = 0.2$ of having to pay the full price of $600. Thus,

$$\$450 \sim (\$0, 0.8; \$600)$$

This statement of course defines a relationship between the utility of three levels of cost for the GRAF-ITTY program. Specifically,

$$U(\$450) = 0.8U(\$0) + 0.2U(\$600)$$

The professor would be utility independent for cost if the same statements applied for any other graphics program, with different levels of speed and resolution.

It is important to note that these kinds of indifference statements can hold regardless of the level of the other attributes. Thus even if a particular graphics program is poor and not worth $450 to the professor, the statement can hold: the professor might be indifferent between having to pay $450 for sure for the junky program (if it were required by a consulting client, say) and of having an 80% chance of getting it for free and a 20% chance of having to pay $600.

---

more demanding analytically: A person who is preferentially independent over attributes is almost certainly utility independent.

Utility independence of an attribute is often interpreted as meaning that the *"shape" of the utility function* over that attribute is the same, independent of the level of the other attributes. This is a useful shorthand, but one that must be interpreted carefully. Most obviously the statement that two utility functions have the same "shape" in this context means that if it is "risk averse" for one set of the other attributes it is not "risk positive" for some other set of those attributes. More precisely, the statement that two utility functions have the same "shape" is to be interpreted as meaning that they are positive linear transformations of each other as defined in Section 18.6:

$$U'(X_i) = aU(X_i) \pm b \qquad a > 0$$

Since such transformations can change the vertical scale considerably while keeping the X_i scale constant, utility functions with the same "shape" may look quite different (see box).

Utility Functions with the Same "Shape"

Consider the professor's indifference statement for the cost of graphics programs, given in the previous box:

$$\$450 \sim (\$0, 0.8; \$600)$$

One interpretation of this statement is that, considering less cost to be preferable:

$$U(\$600) = 0 \qquad U(\$0) = 1.0$$

$$U(\$450) = 0.8$$

This utility function is sketched in Figure 20.3(a).

Many other utility functions for money match the above indifference statement. For example consider one in which $U(\$600)$ is raised by adding 0.5, and the vertical scale shrunk to 0.2 of what it is above:

$$U'(\text{cost}) = 0.2U(\text{cost}) + 0.5$$

Then we have:

$$U'(\$600) = 0.5 \qquad U'(\$0) = 0.7$$

$$U'(\$450) = 0.66$$

This utility function for cost, which might be appropriate for another program with different levels of speed and resolution, is sketched in Figure 20.3(b). It looks quite a bit different from the other, being much flatter; nonetheless it has the same "shape" within the meaning of the phrase used in the context of multiattribute utility.

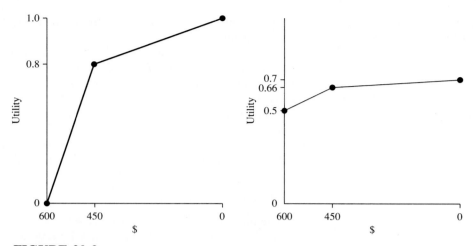

FIGURE 20.3
Two utility functions with the same "shape." Although visually dissimilar they both satisfy the same indifference statement: $450 ~ ($0, 0.8; $600) so that $U(\$450) = 0.8U(\$0) + 0.2U(\$600)$.

Consequences. A practical method for measuring multiattribute utility is possible if both the preferential and utility independence assumptions are acceptable. This method both represents the value that people place in the interactions between attributes and is sufficiently efficient as regards calculations to be feasible in real situations.

When the preferential and utility independence assumptions hold, the multiattribute utility function $U(\mathbf{X})$ is defined by:

$$KU(\mathbf{X}) + 1 = \prod (Kk_i U(X_i) + 1)$$

where

- $U(\mathbf{X})$ is scaled from $U(\mathbf{X}_*) = 0$ to $U(\mathbf{X}^*) = 1.0$ when all X_i are respectively at their worst and best levels.
- $U(X_i)$ are likewise one-dimensional utility functions for each X_i, scaled so that $U(X_{i*}) = 0$ and $U(X_i^*) = 1.0$ for the worst and best levels of X_i.
- k_i are individual scaling factors for each dimension of attribute, measured in a way to be defined subsequently.
- K is a normalizing parameter that insures consistency between the definitions of $U(\mathbf{X})$ and the $U(X_i)$. It is commonly referred to as "big kay," to distinguish it from the k_i factors.

The crux of the equation for the N-dimensional multiattribute utility is that this function is defined entirely by

- N one-dimensional utility functions
- N scaling factors

This means that the number of points to be measured for any specified level of detail is a linear rather than an exponential function of the dimensions.

The computational advantage of this approach becomes apparent when it is compared to the requirements for measuring the multidimensional utility by the direct extension of utility theory discussed in Section 20.2. In that case, the number of calculations required is $(M^N - 2)$ where each $U_i(X_i)$ is defined by M points. Using the formula above, the number of points required is $(M - 1)$ for each dimension, being $(M - 2)$ for each utility function plus 1 for the scaling factor. The computational advantage of the multiattribute utility function is thus that:

$$N(M - 1) << (M^N - 2)$$

With this approach it is thus practical to measure six-dimensional utility functions; using the same level of detail as in Section 20.2, $M = 5$ and 24 points must be measured, well within the practical limits for measuring utility. We in fact measured six-dimensional utility functions for the government of Mexico to help them determine a strategy for developing the airport system for their capital.

The nature of the formula for multiattribute utility becomes more evident when we examine the two-dimensional case. We then can also obtain an explicit solution for both $U(\mathbf{X})$ and the normalizing factor K. For two dimensions then,

$$KU(X_1, X_2) + 1 = [Kk_1U(X_1) + 1][Kk_2U(X_2) + 1]$$

Multiplying this expression out and eliminating common terms thus gives:

$$U(X_1, X_2) = k_1U(X_1) + k_2U(X_2) + Kk_1k_2U(X_1)U(X_2)$$

We can thus see that the multiattribute utility is the weighted sum of the one-dimensional utilities, modified by terms accounting for the interaction between the attributes.

The one-dimensional utility functions, $U(X_i)$ are measured just as described in Section 19.5. In doing this we need not be concerned with the level of the other attributes because, with the assumption of utility independence, we know that the "shape" of each $U(X_i)$, is the same for all levels of the other attributes. The only new factor we need to pay attention to in the measurement of the $U(X_i)$ is to be sure to scale them so that $U(X_{i*}) = 0$ and $U(X_i^*) = 1.0$, to be consistent with the formula for multiattribute utility.

The normalizing factor K, that insures consistency between the definition of $U(\mathbf{X})$ and the $U(X_i)$, can be calculated from these definitions. Note carefully that by definition for the equation $U(\mathbf{X}^*) = 1$, and each $U(X_i^*) = 1$ when all the X_i are at their best levels. Substituting these values into the formula for multiattribute utility we obtain an implicit expression for K:

$$K + 1 = \prod (Kk_i + 1)$$

In general this expression, an $(n - 1)$-dimensional polynominal, must be solved for K by trial and error.

The determination of K is facilitated by the fact that its value is bounded by the sum of the k_i scaling factors for each dimension. Thus,

$$\sum k_i < 1.0 \qquad \text{implies} \qquad 0 < K$$

$$\sum k_i > 1.0 \qquad \text{implies} \qquad -1 < K < 0$$

For the special case when $\sum k_i = 1.0$, the solution for K degenerates and the multiattribute utility is the simple additive model:

$$\sum k_i = 1.0 \qquad U(\mathbf{X}) = \sum k_i U(X_i)$$

In practice, the k_i that one obtains from people rarely add up to 1.0. This fact underlines the limited value of the additive model, already stressed in Section 20.2.

For the two-dimensional case there is an explicit solution for K. Thus:

$$K + 1 = K^2 k_1 k_2 + K(k_1 + k_2) + 1$$

so that

$$K = (1 - k_1 - k_2)/k_1 k_2$$

The solutions for this expression are summarized in the box.

This solution in turn leads to a simple solution for the two-dimensional $U(\mathbf{X})$. By replacing the above solution for K in the formula, we obtain

$$U(X_1, X_2) = k_1 U(X_1) + k_2 U(X_2) + (1 - k_1 - k_2) U(X_1)U(X_2)$$

This formula clearly indicates how the interactive terms disappear when $\sum k_i = 1.0$, resulting in the exceptional additive case.

Finally, the scaling factors k_i need to be obtained by a special procedure. To appreciate this step, it is helpful to understand what the k_i represent. Each k_i is the multiattribute utility of the best level of its attribute i, when all the other attributes $X_j, j \neq i$, are at their worst levels. Figure 20.4 illustrates the situation in two dimensions. In general, these special combinations of (X_i^*, X_{j*}) are referred to as "corner points," by analogy to this figure.

The k_i are thus obtained with respect to the reference points for the multi-attribute utility:

$$U(\mathbf{X}_*) = 0 \qquad U(\mathbf{X}^*) = 1.0$$

Solutions for K in Two Dimensions

k_1	$k_2 = 0.1$	0.2	0.3	0.4	0.5	0.6	0.7	0.8	0.9
0.1	80	35	20	12.5	8	8	2.9	1.2	0
0.2		15	8.3	5	3	1.7	0.7	0	−0.55
0.3			4.4	2.5	1.33	0.55	0	−0.42	−0.74
0.4				1.25	0.5	0	−0.38	−0.63	−0.83
0.5					0	−0.33	−0.57	−0.75	−0.88
0.6	Symmetric					−0.56	−0.71	−0.83	−0.93
0.7							−0.82	−0.89	−0.95
0.8								−0.94	−0.97
0.9									−0.99

Note that

- For $k_1 + k_2 < 1.0$ $K > 0$
- For $k_1 + k_2 > 1.0$ $-1 < K < 0$
- For $k_1 + k_2 = 1$ $K = 0$ leading to the additive form as a special solution

$$U(X_1, X_2) = k_1 U(X_1) + k_2 U(X_2)$$

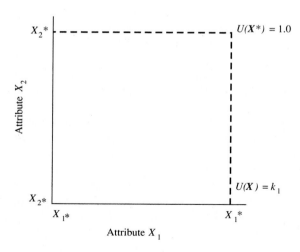

FIGURE 20.4
The scaling factors k_i represent the multiattribute utility of the corner points, where X_i is at its best level and all other X_j, $j \neq i$, are at their worst level.

Specifically, the object is to find an indifference statement that defines the multiattribute utility of each corner point:

$$(X_i^*, X_{j*}) \sim [\mathbf{X}^*, P_i; \mathbf{X}_*]$$

So that

$$k_i = U(X_i^*, X_{j*}) = P_i U(\mathbf{X}^*) + (1 - P_i)U(\mathbf{X}_*) = P_i$$

Since the indifference statement defines all possible levels of X_i, the only element that can be changed is P_i. The indifference statement is thus determined by the lottery equivalent/probability method described in Section 19.4.

20.4 MEASUREMENT

The measurement of a person's multiattribute utility function for a given situation is a straightforward implementation of the theory. It consists of the following steps:

- Specification of the Attributes
- Verification of Assumptions
- Measurement of One-dimensional Utilities $U(X_i)$
- Measurement of Scaling Factors, k_i
- Calculation of Normalizing Parameter, K
- Determination of Multiattribute Utility, $U(\mathbf{X})$

Each step is discussed in turn with reference to specifics given in boxes.

Specification of attributes. The analyst must first of all determine which are the most important attributes of a particular problem. This may require a certain amount of initiative and care. Many people are not used to thinking in many dimensions, and may not have already formulated their problem this way. The analyst should then help them identify the essential features—and thus attributes—of the problem (see box). Further, the analyst must consider and try to avoid the possibility that a person will not be preferentially independent for a specification of attributes, as in the diet example of the previous section.

Once the analyst and the client—an individual or an organization—agree on the attributes, they have to define the upper and lower ranges of interest for each attribute. They must also identify which level of each is the most and least preferred. This is as for one-dimensional utility.

Verification of assumptions. As people tend to be preferentially independent between attributes unless there is some particular kind of interaction between them—as in the diet preferences of the rich and poor given in the example of Section 20.3—the analyst should be on the watch for such possibilities. It is thus important for the analysts to understand the problem in some detail. If they

Specification of Attributes for Mexico City Problem

When we were approached by the government of Mexico to work on the decision about a possible second airport for Mexico City (as discussed in Section 16.3) our first task was to structure the problem and define the attributes of interest.

In thinking about the attributes, we had to recognize that this decision could have a major effect on the structure of the city and would thus affect groups with many different kinds of concerns. Three major groups seemed salient:

- The government, as promoter of the project
- The air travellers, as users
- The city residents, as bystanders affected by the airport

Our first suggestion to the government was that the attributes should reflect the essential features, and thus the main concerns of these groups. The attributes we selected for the analysis were then:

- "Airport Cost" and "Airport Capacity"
- "Safety" and "Access Time"
- "Noise" and "People Displaced"

These were acceptable to the government and we proceeded to measure six-dimensional utility functions.

It turned out that some of the attributes were not really significant. For example, the noise caused by aircraft was, at that time, of little concern in Mexico City, which was very noisy in any case due to buses and cars. In retrospect we should have chosen a different set of attributes which more accurately reflected the issues important to our client. As a general rule, any analyst working with a person or group should be alert to the desirability of changing the specification of the attributes to conform to the needs of the persons they are trying to help.

---

do not, they may overlook fundamental difficulties, in particular that preferential independence is not acceptable for a certain situation.

The general procedure for verifying that the preferential independence assumption is acceptable for any two attributes is to ask the client

- to rank a few pairs of these two attributes.
- to ask if these rankings would be changed by variation in the levels of the other attributes, particularly changes that the analyst suspects might cause difficulties. If the answer is no, then the preferential independence assumption is acceptable for those two dimensions. The process should be repeated for each two pairs of attributes.

The procedure for checking the utility independence assumption is similar: the analyst asks the person whose utility is being assessed if the indifference statements being provided would be changed if the level of the other attributes were changed. Because the verification of the utility independence thus requires at least portions of the one-dimensional utility functions, it is frequently most convenient to check this assumption as part of the assessment of these utility functions.

Measurement of one-dimensional utilities. This is done in the standard ways, as described in Section 19.4. No change is necessary for the multiattribute case.

Measurement of scaling factors, k_i. The method for finding each scaling factor is to obtain an indifference statement of the form:

$$(X_i^*, X_{j*}) \sim (\mathbf{X}^*, P_i; \mathbf{X}_*) \qquad j \neq i$$

This indifference statement must be developed by varying the probability P_i, instead of the certainty equivalent (X_i^*, X_{j*}), which we want to keep fixed at the corner point.

The probability P_i is found by the Lottery Equivalent/Probability method (see Section 19.4) using bracketing (see Section 19.4). The analyst thus first proposes a high value of P_i and then a low one, iteratively narrowing the gap until the person whose multiattribute utility is being measured accepts a specific P_i. This is then the scaling factor k_i (see box).

Calculation of normalizing parameter K. The normalizing factor, K, is determined from the formula

$$K + 1 = \prod (Kk_i + 1)$$

except if $\sum k_i = 1.0$, as pointed out in Section 20.3. If we have only two dimensions, an explicit expression for K is available:

$$K = (1 - k_1 - k_2)/k_1 k_2$$

For three or more dimensions, K must be determined iteratively. Analysts who have to do this frequently will develop a small computer routine to do so, using a standard search technique such as the Newton-Raphson method available in most large computer libraries.

Determination of multiattribute utility. The obvious way to obtain $U(\mathbf{X})$ is by using its formula

$$KU(\mathbf{X}) + 1 = \prod (Kk_i U(X_i) + 1)$$

This works well whenever the one-dimensional utilities $U(X_i)$ are defined accurately for each X_i that might be of interest.

Scaling Factors in Automobile Industry

In the automobile industry, designers can now choose between many different materials: a variety of alloys of steel, of aluminum, and a range of plastic composites. For many parts of the car, their concern focuses on the cost and the weight, the latter being important because it influences fuel economy.

In working with the industry, our group at MIT found that multiattribute utility functions over cost and weight are really helpful to the designers. Specifically, we develop utility functions for the range of attributes suitable for the particular part or system being designed, such as a bumper.

For a bumper, the weight might range from 20 to 50 kg, and the manufacturing cost from \$50 to \$150. Least amounts are of course preferred so that

$$\mathbf{X}_* = (50 \text{ kg}, \$150)$$

$$\mathbf{X}^* = (20 \text{ kg}, \$50)$$

To find the scaling factor for weight, we need to obtain

$$(X^*_{\text{weight}}, X_{\$*}) = (20 \text{ kg}, \$150) \sim (\mathbf{X}^*, P; \mathbf{X}_*)$$

We did this by asking designers questions such as:

> "Suppose you were engaged in a research and development program. You know you could certainly make bumpers out of Alloy X with characteristics (20 kg, \$150). You could also choose a process that has a probability P of giving you the wonder alloy you have been looking for ($\mathbf{X}^*$) or which, with probability $(1 - P)$, might leave you with unimproved current material ($\mathbf{X}_*$). Would you opt for Alloy X if $P = 90\%$? 5%? . . . and so on."

This process works well. By putting the person being interviewed into a familiar, realistic context, it leads to an easy measurement of the scaling factors.

In practice we find that the k_i found by this kind of process do quite clearly reflect the relative weighting anyone would expect. For example, in considering the relative merits of industrial development and the environment, the "greens" clearly give a much higher k_i to the environment than industrialists.

In practice, it often occurs that we want $U(\mathbf{X})$ for combinations of X_i whose utility lies somewhere in between the points measured explicitly. It is then necessary to interpolate. This may be done either by formula or linearly.

If the interpolation is done by using standard formulas (see Section 19.5) of the form

$$U(X_i) = a + be^{-cXi} \quad \text{or} \quad = a + bX^c$$

Then these expressions can be directly introduced into the formula for the multi-attribute utility.

Often, however, linear interpolations must be used. This would be because the one-dimensional utility functions are too irregular to fit a smooth formula. This requires a careful extension to the multidimensional utility.

The essential concept in applying linear interpolations to $U(\mathbf{X})$ is that the "shape" of the one-dimensional changes in utility—parallel to any X_i axis—remain the same. As defined in Section 20.3, this means that the relative difference in utility $U(X_i)$ between its two extreme points, $U(X_{i*})$ and $U(X_i^*)$ is constant throughout the domain of $U(\mathbf{X})$. To find the utility along any X_i dimension we therefore simply effect a positive linear transformation on the original $U(X_i)$, scaled from 0 to 1, of the form

$$U'(X_i) = aU(X_i) + b \qquad a > 0$$

In doing this it is most important to be careful about the definition of a and b.

Linear interpolation for $U(\mathbf{X})$ is almost exclusively done for two dimensions due to the complexity of visualizing higher order spaces. It is therefore explained and illustrated for two dimensions. The procedure is

- Assign the known utilities to the corner points of the space defined by the range of attributes. These are $U(\mathbf{X}_*) = 0$, $U(\mathbf{X}^*) = 1.0$ for the worst and the best levels of all attributes; and $U(X_i^*, X_{j*}) = k_i$ for each corner point.
- Interpolate one-dimensional utilities from the "origin" of $U(\mathbf{X})$, $\mathbf{X}_*$ where $U(\mathbf{X}_*) = 0$, to the corner points. In this case,

$$U(X_i, X_{j*}) = k_i U(X_i)$$

- Interpolate one-dimensional utilities from the corner points to the apex $\mathbf{X}^*$ where $U(\mathbf{X}^*) = 1.0$. The positive linear transformations are

$$U(X_i^*, X_j) = (1 - k_i)U(X_j) + k_i$$

since we now must interpolate from a starting utility equal to that of the corner point, that is k_i, and scale the utility of the other dimension to the range available, $(1 - k_i)$, as shown in the box.
- Interpolate, on lines parallel to either the X_i or X_j axis, to obtain $U(\mathbf{X})$ for any point inside the range of the attributes, being careful to define the transformation so that the base and scale are correctly defined: the base, b, is the end of the line with the lowest $U(\mathbf{X})$, the scale is given by the difference between the lowest and the highest $U(\mathbf{X})$ on that line (see box).

Interpolation for Two-dimensional Multiattribute Utility

A designer in the automobile industry, responsible for bumpers, has the one-dimensional utility functions for weight and cost shown in Figure 20.5. For simplicity, we assume that the designer's utility for dollars is a straight line

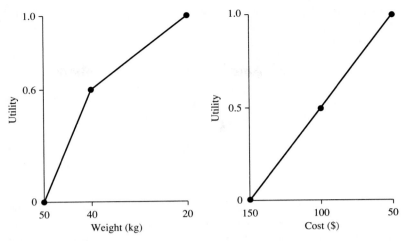

FIGURE 20.5
One-dimensional utilities used for interpolation of multiattribute utility function.

(perhaps because the amounts are small compared to the total cost). Suppose that we have already found that the designer's scaling factors for weight and cost are

$$k_w = 0.7 \qquad k_\$ = 0.4$$

The first step of the interpolation process is to assign the utilities to the four corners of the space defined by the range of attributes:

$$50 \text{ kg} \geq \text{weight} \geq 20 \text{ kg}$$

$$\$150 \geq \text{cost} \geq \$50$$

This is done in Figure 20.6.

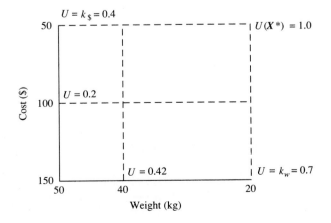

FIGURE 20.6
Utilities assigned after the first two steps of the interpolation process.

Now we interpolate the one-dimensional utilities along the axes from the "origin" of $U(\mathbf{X})$ at $\mathbf{X}_*$. For weight we thus have, always at the worst level of cost, $X_\$ = \$150$:

$$U(50,150) = 0 \qquad U(20,150) = 0.7$$
$$U(40,150) = 0.7(0.6) = 0.42$$

Likewise for cost we have, with weight at its worst level, $X_W = 50$ kg:

$$U(50,150) = 0 \qquad U(50,50) = 0.4$$
$$U(50,100) = 0.5(0.4) = 0.2$$

These numbers also appear in Figure 20.6.

The interpolation on the remaining sides now proceeds as above, except that we must remember that the linear transform of $U(X_i)$ involves a change in the base. Thus, along the top of the region, where $X_\$ = \$50$, we have

$$U(50, 50) = 0.40 \qquad U(20, 50) = 1.0$$
$$U(40, 50) = (1 - 0.4)(0.6) + 0.4 = 0.76$$

Likewise for cost, along the right where $X_W = 20$ kg:

$$U(20, 150) = 0.7 \qquad U(20, 50) = 1.0$$
$$U(20, 100) = (1 - 0.7)(0.5) + 0.7 = 0.85$$

These utilities are indicated in Figure 20.7.

Finally, the utility of points interior to the domain are interpolated from the knowledge of the utilities along the edge. The utility of point A in Figure 20.7 with $X_W = 40$ and $X_\$ = 100$ can thus be found by varying $X_\$$ along $X_W = 40$ kg:

$$U(40, 150) = 0.42 \qquad U(40, 50) = 0.76$$

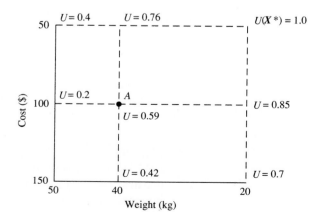

FIGURE 20.7
Utilities assigned by end of interpolation process.

$$U(40, 100) = (0.76 - 0.42)(0.5) + 0.42 = 0.59$$

It can also be found by varying X_W, along $X_\$ = \$100$:

$$U(50, 100) = 0.2 \qquad U(20, 100) = 0.85$$
$$U(40, 100) = (0.85 - 0.2)(0.6) + 0.2 = 0.59$$

20.5 APPLICATIONS

This section discusses two applications of multiattribute utility analysis, first to the Mexico City Airport and second to the selection of new materials. The Mexico City case is the classic: it was the first major application of the Keeney-Raiffa approach, it was done with those principals, and has been extensively reprinted. It also seems appropriate to bring closure to the many references made to it throughout the text. This discussion focuses on the actual results of the multiattribute utility analysis.

A set of applications to the evaluation of materials comes next. These represent the results of the latest work being done, and illustrate the range of uses to which this analysis can be put.

Mexico City airport. This case concerns the location of new airport facilities for Mexico City. The issue as presented to us by the government of Mexico was polarized around two locations, Texcoco and Zumpango. One faction wanted to keep all activity at the existing site, the "All Texcoco" alternative; the other faction wanted to move everything to a new facility, the "All Zumpango" solution.

As all such problems, the situation is really much more complex. Looking at the ways the different possible sizes of the facility combine with the different locations and can be phased over time, the number of logical possibilities was:

$$[(\text{Sizes})^{(\text{Locations})}]^{(\text{Periods})} = 4096$$

as indicated in Section 16.3. Further, as stated in Section 20.4, it seemed reasonable to consider six major attributes to the problem. We thus performed a decision analysis on this basis. The assessment of the multiattribute utility function was straightforward, even on this the first major application. The major difficulties were in fact not technical but concerned our mutual problems in translating between Spanish and English. In detail, we assessed utility functions for each of the major directors of the Ministry of Public Works. These were relatively homogenous, as they often are in a work unit that has grown to share common values, so that we felt comfortable in averaging their parameters to obtain a collective multiattribute utility function for the Ministry itself.

Integrating this function with the decision analysis we could obtain the optimal choices. Both of the salient choices, the "All Texcoco" and the "All Zumpango," ranked right near the top—as indeed they should have since these were preferred solutions.

The salient result of the multiattribute utility analysis was that it also ranked a wide range of compromise solutions right at the top. In fact, the difference in value between the top 10 to 20 choices were down in the second and third decimal places, way beyond the accuracy of any utility assessment. The multiattribute utility analysis made clear, by recognizing the trade-offs between attributes and incorporating them into the analysis, that there were many possible compromise choices that were acceptable. The common feature of each was that it provided insurance against risks and flexibility to adapt as necessary. As practitioners we have now come to recognize this discovery of compromise alternatives as a standard result of the use of multiattribute utility.

This analysis thus provided the effective basis for developing a strategy for development for Mexico City's airports. This was much along the lines presented for Sydney's Airports in Sections 16.8 and 16.9. The difference between that application and the earlier one for Mexico City is that, having learned that multiattribute utility systematically identifies compromise solutions, and knowing what kind of insurance makes sense for airports, we could skip the multiattribute utility analysis for the second situation, a virtual replay of the Mexico City case.

Materials selection. The choice of materials has become a considerable problem for engineers. The number and type of materials available has grown rapidly in recent years, and vastly expanded the possibilities that a designer should consider seriously. In designing cars for example, one only used to have to consider several grades of rolled steel; now it is realistic to evaluate also the potential of other materials, such as aluminum, powdered metals, and an extraordinary range of plastics, each having quite different characteristics. Materials selection is now truly a multiattribute utility problem.

The Materials Systems Laboratory at MIT has been developing the many different ways multiattribute utility analysis can be useful to designers. By doing this in close collaboration with major international producers and users of materials, they have been able to document which applications are truly practical.

The most obvious application is to the selection of the preferred designs for a part or an assembly. This implies a choice of materials in fact since different designs will be best executed with different materials. For example, one automobile bumper may involve honeycomb plastics to absorb energy, another a solid steel beam, and a third structural thermoplastics.

In practice, the decision analysts will assess the multiattribute utilities of the members of the design team, and apply them to the possible choices. If the designers have relatively similar utility functions, this process will lead them to the design that offers them the best combination of their desired characteristics. Often this choice will be a compromise—as in the case of the airport applications—between initially polarized views. Typically, the design that is ultimately favored was far from obvious at the start, so that multiattribute utility analysis makes a significant contribution.

When the designers turn out not to share the same preferences, the analysis will identify the fundamental reasons for their disagreements about design. We have found that this process can be most helpful in design groups. It clarifies their objectives and permits a clearer understanding of choices to be made.

A second application concerns research management. Major laboratories can estimate the kinds of achievements they might obtain from a given effort in various directions. The management task is to identify which lines of work give the highest value in terms of all the attributes of interest. Should the lab focus on one material that could significantly reduce weight at some cost and loss of its capability to reduce dents; or on another that promises cost reductions and extended service life, for some increase in weight? The analysis focuses on ranking the alternatives.

Another significant area of application concerns the producers of materials, who must constantly decide whether to introduce a new material and, if so, at what price. To resolve this question, producers obtain their customers' multiattribute utility functions. (Realistically, this may have to be done indirectly through independent consultants, to avoid the potential bias buyers may introduce when talking to sellers.) The analysis then constructs an isovalue line (see Section 18.4) through the properties of the material currently used for some application, as in Figure 20.8. They can use this information to decide what to do.

We have observed several instances in which the analysis demonstrated that a new, technically superior material simply could not be produced at a competitive price. Graphically, its minimum cost (at A) was too high; its advantages in lower weight, for example, did not compensate for the extra costs required to produce it. In another instance, the analysis permitted a producer to estimate how high one could price a new material so that, at B, it would be about as high as it could be while still offering greater utility to the potential users of the material.

Overall, the application of multiattribute utility analysis provides, for really the first time, a rational method of evaluating materials which fully incorporates the many simultaneous, nonlinear trade-offs designers do make among the characteristics of a system. The experience in materials selection can and has been extended to many other fields.

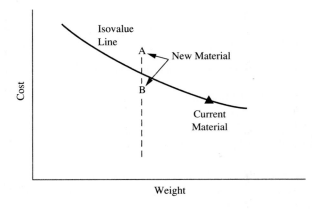

FIGURE 20.8
Use of multiattribute utility analysis in decisions about introducing and pricing new materials.

REFERENCES

de Neufville, R., and R. Keeney, (1972, 1976). "Use of Decision Analysis in Airport Development in Mexico City," Chapter 23, *Analysis of Public Systems*, A. W. Drake, R. Keeney, P. Morse, eds., MIT Press, Cambridge, MA; Chapter 24, *Systems Planning and Design*, R. de Neufville and D. H. Marks, eds., Prentice-Hall, Englewood Cliffs, NJ.

Field, F., and R. de Neufville, (1988). "Materials Selection—Maximizing Overall Utility," *Metals and Materials*, May, pp. 378–382.

Keeney, R., (1978). "Utility Independence and Preference for Multiattributed Consequences," *Operations Research*, Vol. 19, pp. 875–893.

Keeney, R., and Raiffa, H., (1976). *Decisions with Multiple Objectives*, Wiley, New York.

PROBLEMS

20.1. *General I*

Given
$$U_x(X) = \frac{1}{32}(X^2 - 4) \qquad 2 \le X \le 6$$

$$U_y(Y) = \frac{1}{6}(Y + 36)^{1/2} \qquad -36 \le Y \le 0$$

and
$$k_x = 0.5 \qquad k_y = 0.6$$

(a) Give the value of $U(X,Y)$ for all four corner points for which the multiattribute utility is defined.
(b) Find by interpolation $U(4, -36)$; $U(4,0)$; $U(4, -20)$.
(c) Write the general formula for $U(X,Y)$.
(d) Solve for the value of K in the formula.
(e) Calculate $U(4, -20)$ by using the formula.

20.2. *General II*

Given
$$U_x(X) = \frac{X(X + 6)}{160} \qquad 0 \le X \le 10$$

$$U_y(Y) = \frac{(Y^{1/2} - 5)}{5} \qquad 25 \le Y \le 100$$

and the following indifference statements:
$$(10, 25) \sim [(10, 100), 0.6; (0, 25)]$$
$$(0, 100) \sim [(10, 100), 0.6; (0, 25)]$$

(a) Give the value of $U(X,Y)$ for all four corner points for which the multiattribute utility is defined.
(b) Find by interpolation $U(4, 25)$; $U(4, 100)$.
(c) Write the general formula for $U(X,Y)$.
(d) Solve for the value of K in the formula.
(e) Calculate $U(4,100)$ by using the formula.

20.3. *Workstations, again*
The original interviews (see Problem 19.8) also revealed that, when confronted with the possibility, Lee was indifferent between the low price, slow model, and a strategy which led to an even chance of getting the best or worst combinations.

But when she could have the high price, fast model, a strategy with only a 30% chance of getting the best would be just as acceptable.

$$(\$1000, 4) \sim (\text{Best}, 0.5; \text{Worst})$$

$$(\$6000, 24) \sim (\text{Best}, 0.3; \text{Worst})$$

(a) Identify the best and worst cases in terms of ($, Speed) pairs.
(b) Sketch the (Cost, Speed) plane indicating the utility values you can identify from the preceeding information.
(c) Using the information from previous problems, what is the utility of Workstation A = ($4000, 24)? Workstation B = ($1000, 10)?
(d) State the formula for the two-dimensional utility and use it to obtain the utility of Workstation C = ($4000, 18).
(e) Help Lee by ranking the workstations from most to least desirable.

20.4. *Basketball & Movies*
Bobby West likes to spend his leisure time playing basketball or going to movies. His utility functions for basketball games and movies per month are given in the tables below.

Basketball games per month	One-dimensional utility	Movies per month	One-dimensional utility
0	0	0	0
2	0.1	1	0.2
4	0.6	3	0.6
6	0.9	5	0.9
8	1.0	8	1.0

Bobby has expressed the following indifference statements:

$$(8B, 0M) \sim [(8B, 8M), 0.7; (0B, 0M), 0.3]$$

$$(0B, 8M) \sim [(8B, 8M), 0.4; (0B, 0M), 0.6]$$

(a) Draw a graph with axes labeled basketball games per month and movies per month. Indicate multiattribute utilities at the four corner points.
(b) Define and explain the significance of utility independence.
(c) Assuming utility independence, calculate the multiattribute utility of the following points by interpolation and label them on the graph from (a):

$$U(4B, 0M) \qquad U(0B, 5M) \qquad U(4B, 8M) \qquad U(8B, 5M)$$

(d) Based on your results in (c), interpolate to find $U(4B, 5M)$ and label this on the graph from (a).
(e) Write the general formula $U(X, Y)$.
(f) Solve the formula for $U(4B,5M)$ and compare answer to your results in (d).

20.5. *C. Eric Lubb*
C. Eric Lubb, environmental lobbyist, has utility functions for birds and trees as shown in the table.

Item	Number of species	Utility (one-dimensional)
Birds	0	0
	5	0.5
	15	0.75
	40	1.0
Trees	0	0
	5	0.1
	10	0.3
	15	0.75
	30	1.0

(a) In considering the Rat Race National Park, the Congress seems to be headed toward approval of a Pesticide Treatment Plan (PTP) that will allow a total of 30 tree species to be established, at the expense of killing off all of the birds. Eric is undecided whether to try to get the bill back into committee, which has a 30% chance of approving the Environmentally Sound Management Plan (ESMP), which would give the park 40 kinds of birds and 30 of trees, but a 70% chance of allowing strip mining (no birds, no trees). Express as an indifference statement.

(b) In some consistent way, assign values of U(PTP), and U(ESMP), and U(strip mining).

(c) Eric says "That blasted Pesticide Plan is as bad as having 15 bird species and no trees." What is U(15 birds, 0 trees)?

(d) What assumptions must you make to facilitate the construction of a utility function from the information given? What sort of questions would you ask to test these assumptions?

(e) Sketch $U(0, T)$, $U(15, T)$, and $U(40, T)$ as functions of T.

(f) Would you expect Eric to prefer $(15,10)$ or $[(15, 30), 1/3; (0, 15)]$?

(g) From the formula: $KU(B, T) + 1 = (Kk_t U_t(T) + 1)(Kk_b U_b(B) + 1)$ find an analytical expression for U(B, T) as a function of $U_b(B)$ and $U_t(T)$ and obtain $U(15, 15)$ and $U(5, 5)$.

20.6. *Auto Bumper*

Sloane Iaocca, an automobile executive, must select an appropriate material for an automobile bumper. The cost and weight are the criticial features of this problem. According to Sloane, "In order to stay within our EPA weight class, the bumper cannot weigh more than 50 pounds. Naturally, in the interests of fuel economy, we would like to keep the weight of the bumper down. However, as the weight of our feasible designs drops, the cost rises."

You are able to determine that Sloane is indifferent between:

- A 25 lb bumper and the lottery (50 lbs, 1/2; 15 lbs)
- A 35 lb bumper and the lottery (50 lbs, 1/2; 25 lbs)
- A bumper costing $60 and the lottery ($40, 1/2; $100)
- A $50 bumper and the lottery ($40, 1/2; $60)

(a) Fill in the following tables:

Bumper utilities—Sloane Iaocca

Cost ($)	U(cost)	Weight (lbs)	U(weight)
40		15	
50		25	
60		35	
100		50	

You now determine that Sloane is also indifferent between:

- A bumper that weights 15 lbs and costs $100 and the lottery [(15 lbs, $40), 4/10; (50 lbs, $100)].
- A bumper weighing 25 lbs and costing $40 is as valuable as the lottery [(15 lbs, $40), 3/4; (50 lbs, $100)].

(b) What assumptions must you make to construct Sloane's multiattribute utility function?

(c) What is $U(15$ lbs, $100)$, $U(25$ lbs, $40)$, $U(15$ lbs, $40)$, and $U(50$ lbs, $100)$?

(d) What is $U(50$ lbs, $40)$?

(e) What is the value of K?

(f) Assuming that Sloane is consistent, would she prefer bumper A (35 lbs, $50) or B (25 lbs, $60)?

20.7. *Developer*

A developer reviewing the design of a $20M building faces a tradeoff between construction costs and energy consumption. The current design requires 10 million btu/yr of heating and cooling power. Many modifications such as the addition of awnings, improved insulation, or solar panels could save up to 7 billion btu/yr, at a cost of $4M. Since the range of possibilities and the uncertainties are rather confusing, she wants you to help sort out her preferences.

From interviews you determine that, for building costs alone, she is indifferent between

$22.5M and ($24M, 0.5; $20M)
$23.4M and ($24M, 0.5; $22.5M)
$21.5M and ($22.5M, 0.5; $20M)

regardless of the level of energy used. Similarly, for energy measured in millions of btu/yr, she is indifferent between

5 and (10, 0.5; 3)
3.75 and (5, 0.5; 3)
7 and (10, 0.5; 5)

regardless of the level of costs. For combinations of costs and energy, she is indifferent between

($20M, 10) = the current plan
and [($24M, 10), 0.2; ($20M, 3)]

and also

$$(\$24M, 3) = \text{maximum energy conservation}$$
$$\text{and } [(\$24M, 10), 0.3; \quad (\$20M, 3)]$$

(*a*) Solve the indifference statements for their implied utility.
(*b*) Determine which plan the developer is apt to prefer:

Plan	Cost ($M)	Energy use
Current design	20	10
High insulation	21	7
Solar heating	22.5	5
Sheltered windows	23	4
Maximum conservation	24	3

(*c*) Would the developer prefer the current design or the alternative [(22.5, 7), 0.6;   (22.4, 3.75)]?
(*d*) Find K by applying the general formula and check the results from part (*b*).

20.8. *Earthquake Code*

A research team investigating the desirable level of earthquake protection for apartment buildings obtains the following information from an apartment dweller:

- If the rent control board were reviewing the rent on her apartment, with equal chances of setting rents of $100 or $250, she would settle with her landlord for any monthly rent up to $200. If she thought she had an 80% chance of getting the $100 rent from the board, she would not settle for more than $150.
- Given the choice between one building code that would result in X earthquake deaths per 100,000 residents over the next 10 years, and another equally likely to result in 0 or 70 deaths per 100,000 residents, she prefers the fixed code for $X < 40$.
- If she were apartment hunting, expecting to find either a most desirable apartment ($100/month, 0 lives lost/100,000) or a least desirable apartment ($250, 70) depending on her luck, she would accept a cheap-but-risky compromise apartment ($100, 70), if her probability of getting the most desirable is less than 0.5. She would also accept an expensive-but-safe compromise apartment ($250, 0) if the probability of finding a most desirable apartment fell below 0.4.

(*a*) On a cost vs. lives graph, plot the utilities directly identified by the information given. Assume utility independence.
(*b*) Assuming linear interpolation, comment on the apparent desirability to our subject of the building codes with the following outcomes:

   A. ($125, 70)   B. ($150, 40)   C. ($200, 20)

   D. [($100, 70), P; ($225, 0)] as a function of P.

(*c*) Use the general formula to determine K.

(*d*) Use *K* to find $U(\$150, 40)$ and $U(\$200, 20)$. Check against your answers in (*b*).

20.9. *Chip Wright*

Chip Wright frequently flies between Boston and St. Louis, a trip that can take as little as 3 hours on a direct flight, or otherwise up to 5 1/2 hours. Chip likes to round up poker games. As he plays against strangers, he is never sure how well he might do, although he does expect a less conservative player out of Chicago than out of Boston. He has difficulty deciding which flight to take.

(*a*) In talking to Chip, he tells you that he once, during a 3 hour flight to St. Louis, paid a dollar to drop out of a game on which he had a 50-50 chance of winning $10 and losing $5. Sketch his utility function over money. Does Chip really seem like a gambler to you? Why?

(*b*) You also find that he just came home on a 4 hour flight from St. Louis, which he chose in preference to an even chance to make either the quickest flight back by placing himself on the waiting list or to have to catch a backup flight that would arrive 2 1/2 hours later. Anyway, he felt certain to lose $5 because this was his unlucky day. Sketch Charlie's utility function over travel time.

(*c*) You find, in the end, that Chip is indifferent between the following situations, given in terms of (time, money earned):

$$(4, -1) \sim [(4, -5), 0.6; (3, -1)]$$
$$(4, -1) \sim [(3, -5), 0.8; (5.5, -5)]$$
$$(4, -1) \sim [(4, 10), 0.5; (4, -5)]$$

How many indifference statements are necessary to scale the two-dimensional utility function? Which of the preceeding provide(s) the necessary information?

(*d*) Calculate $U(5.5, 10)$ on a scale with $U(3, -5) = 0$ and $U(3, 10) = 1$.

(*e*) Sketch isoutility lines for $U = 0.5, 0, -1$.

20.10. *Highway Project*

A highway project will have two serious effects on a town: commuter time savings and residential displacement. Their range appears to be

$$\text{commuter time savings:} \quad 0 \le S \le 300 \text{ hrs/day}$$

$$\text{residential displacements:} \ 0 \le D \le 140 \text{ families}$$

You find that:

- In comparing the null alternative, $(S = 0; D = 0)$, to a hypothetical alternative that has probability P of yielding (300,0) and probability $(1 - P)$ of producing (0, 140), The mayor seems to be indifferent between the two when $P = 0.7$.
- When choosing between (300, 140), the maximum impact project, and the hypothetical project the mayor seems to be indifferent between the alternatives when $P = 0.6$.
- Ignoring the level of D, the mayor is indifferent between $S = 100$ and a 50/50 lottery between $S = 0$ and $S = 300$.
- The mayor is indifferent between $D = 80$ and the lottery (0, 0.5; 140).

(*a*) What is the utility of (0, 0)?

(*b*) What is $U(300, 140)$?

(*c*) Assuming linear interpolations between assessed points, sketch $U(S, 140)$ and $U(0, D)$.

(*d*) Assuming mutual utility independence, sketch $U(S, 0)$. What is the utility of (100,0)?

(*e*) Sketch $U(100, D)$. What is the utility of (100, 80)?

(*f*) If the mayor is offered a choice of (100,80) or the lottery $[(0, 80), 0.5; (200, 0)]$, which choice would you expect?

20.11. *Muckraker*

The editor of Exposé Publications is discussing with an agent a book that claims to be a true, behind-the-scenes view of State A and M.

"Although we have a 90% chance of netting $\$10^6$ from this book, there's a 10% chance that SAM could sue us while we only recover costs. While a little publicity is good for business, a SAM lawsuit would be a biggie (versus a small or average), which would be more than we can handle. I'm afraid your price is too high."

"But," replies the agent, "I know you took a chance on a biggie lawsuit last month."

"Yes, but we talked to the lawyers and had our 10% chance of a biggie (with a 90% chance of no suit) changed to a guarantee of a small suit. That was some negotiation session. Had the chance of the biggie been 20%, we would have taken an average suit instead."

"Okay," says the agent, "I see your point. But the money here is very good. I know you were between a 25% chance of netting 10^6 and a 75% chance of netting 0 last month and you took a guaranteed 2×10^5 overseas licensing contract instead. Surely a 90% shot at 10^6, lawsuit or no, is worth it."

"Let me think it over. I'll call you tomorrow."

(*a*) Describe as a lottery the choice facing the editor.

(*b*) Formulate the lotteries that describe the editor's attitude toward lawsuit size.

(*c*) What is U (lawsuit size)?

(*d*) What is the editor's utility function for net return on a book? Be sure to write the lottery.

In reviewing past business decisions, the editor finds two similar ones that can be described as:

$$(10^6, \text{Biggie}) \sim [(10^6, \text{no suit}), 0.96; (0, \text{Biggie})]$$

$$(0, \text{no suit}) \quad \sim [(10^6, \text{no suit}), 0.8; (0, \text{Biggie})]$$

(*e*) Calculate the editor's utility function and prepare a table of values for all computable points of U (\$, suit size).

20.12. *Great Western Children's Museum*

The Great Western Children's Museum is building new quarters, and the trustees must decide how much earthquake protection should be built into the structure. If there is a quake and the museum collapses with children inside, the trustees will be held responsible. The best estimates the trustees have been able to obtain have set the probability of a major earthquake in the next 20 years (the design horizon for the museum) as 40%. Three basic design options have been proposed:

Design	Extra cost	Probability of *L* deaths, given major quake			
		L = 0	*L* = 30	*L* = 50	*L* = 100
Standard	0	0.1	0	0.3	0.4
Super-rigid	$2M	0.4	0.5	0.1	0
Flexible	$5M	0.7	0.25	0.05	0

In negotiations the board of trustees has indicated the following indifferences:

For Lives: $75 \sim (100, 0.5;\ 0)$; $50 \sim (50, 0.5;\ 0)$; $30 \sim (50, 0.5; 0)$

For Extra Building Costs: $\$3M \sim (\$5M, 0.5; 0)$; $\$2M \sim (\$3M, 0.5; 0)$

For Combinations of Lives and Costs:

$(0, \$5M) \sim [(100, \$5M), 0.6; (0, \$0)]$ $(100, \$0) \sim [(100, \$5M), 0.2; (100, \$0)]$

(*a*) Sketch the board's utility functions for lives and for costs.
(*b*) Formulate the two-dimensional utility function over lives and cost.
(*c*) Set up decision tree and determine optimal choice.

20.14. *Work and Play*
Here you are, looking for a job. Assume that, to a first approximation, your two dominant criteria are salary and days of vacation (S, V). You feel you really ought to get at least $30,000/year, to justify the expense of education. As regards vacation, you feel you need some at least, and would really like to have a lot so you could travel. Your one-dimensional utility functions thus are:

Salary ($K)	*U*(S)	Weeks off	*U*(V)
20	0	0	0
25	0.1	1	0.3
30	0.5	2	0.4
35	0.8	3	0.5
40	0.9	4	0.8
50	1.0	5	1.0

You find that you are indifferent between the job as a lifeguard in a holiday resort, (S, V) = (20, 5), and a 50:50 chance that you will get that super job (50, 5) or end up at the dreary grind (20, 0). On the other hand, you are also indifferent between the offer of a high-priced grind (50, 0) and a 50:50 chance between the lifeguard and the super job.
(*a*) By formula, determine whether you prefer (35, 2) or (30, 4).
(*b*) Verify (*a*) by interpolation, showing all work.
(*c*) Sketch isovalue lines on the S, V plane.

CHAPTER
21

COLLECTIVE DECISIONMAKING

21.1 OBJECTIVE

Many different groups of people must often jointly agree on the design of a system. The towns in a metropolitan area, for example, may have to select a subway design that best meets their various needs for service; or a consortium of companies may have to select an industry standard for their products. This kind of collective decisionmaking represents the most difficult form of systems analysis and design.

This final chapter addresses this ultimate question. It indicates how planners can most effectively organize the analysis to assist their clients in selecting the system that will be best for them. This procedure, given in Section 21.6, pulls together the important elements of both system optimization and system evaluation, Parts I and II of this text. An application illustrates the recommended procedure.

The design that is best overall for groups with different interests cannot be found analytically, unfortunately. As a matter of principle, no such procedure will ever be universally valid or acceptable. Section 21.2 covers this theory. This fact does not mean, of course, that analysts do not propose many analytic procedures that purport to define the optimum collective choice for groups. These procedures are, at best, only acceptable under quite limited conditions. Whatever their appeal, they are ultimately flawed by resting on unacceptable assumptions. Section 21.3 makes the point with reference to the most common approach proposed as a solution for collective decisionmaking in design: the naïve idea of product maximization.

The reason there cannot be any universally acceptable analytic solution is simply that the way different people or groups value products differs enormously. As indicated in Chapters 1 and 2, the fact that people have values means that purely technical considerations cannot define the optimum. Sections 21.2 and 21.4 discuss these issues in the context of collective decisionmaking.

The approach recommended for group design of systems is collaborative negotiation (Section 21.5). Negotiation permits the different groups to progress toward mutually beneficial improvements, as must almost inevitably exist. Collaboration further facilitates the exploration of economies of scale (see Chapter 4) for mutual advantage.

21.2   THE ISSUE

The basic difficulty in collective decisionmaking is that there is no way a universally acceptable utility function can be defined for all groups in a decision. If such a function were available then the selection of the optimal design would be obvious: we would simply choose the system that maximizes the expected utility for the group. This section discusses the concept of a group utility function, examines some of its difficulties, and then proceeds to the demonstration why such a function cannot be defined in any uniquely acceptable way.

Concept. The utility function for a group is known formally as either a group utility function (in operations research) or a *social welfare function* (in economics). We use the second term because it ties in most directly with the standard theoretical literature on the nature of choice for group.

> **Semantic caution:** "Social Welfare" does not refer to charity in the sense used currently. It simply means the common good of society.

The social welfare function, SWF, is usefully thought of as some kind of expression of the utilities of different individuals or members of the groups, U_i:

$$SWF = f(U_1, \ldots, U_n)$$

The immediate question is what this aggregation should look like.

A little thought indicates that the nature of the social welfare function should depend on the ethical concepts of the group. If we were to suppose that society valued every individual equally, one might imagine that the social welfare function were some kind of summation. Is it then

$$SWF = \sum U_i \ ?$$

But a society might, as often happens, value some people more than others. The ancient Roman republic, for example, explicitly gave its aristocrats more votes than the plebians in elections. Closer to home, we might discount the desires of some individuals; children for instance typically get no votes and their childish desires are substantially ignored. These ideas would imply an alternative social welfare function, in which individual utilities were somehow weighted. Could it be

$$SWF = \sum w_i U_i \ ?$$

We need not suppose, however, that the social welfare function is necessarily a summation of individual utility, in which the great joy of some counterbalances the misery of others. A sense of social justice may lead us to conclude that the social welfare function should at least reflect some concept of equality; it may also naturally give some weight to ensuring that everyone achieves some minimal level of satisfaction, and thus discount greater individual levels of utility. Would a more realistic version then be

$$SWF = \sum w_i e^{-(U_i - U_{\text{average}})} \ ?$$

This discussion has two implications. First, no simple addition of individual utilities is likely to define a plausible group utility function. Secondly, it is very difficult to imagine what a satisfactory functional form might be.

For discussion purposes, the shape of the social welfare function for most groups can be imagined as in Figure 21.1. Were we able to define it, it would be something rather like that of an individual valuing several benefits. It would favor some kind of balance, reflect the group's diminishing marginal utility for excessive benefits to individuals, and thus curve inward toward the origin.

Interpersonal comparisons. In thinking about the social welfare function, we need also to ask how we can combine the utilities of different people. We can certainly add them up; but to what extent does any such addition make sense?

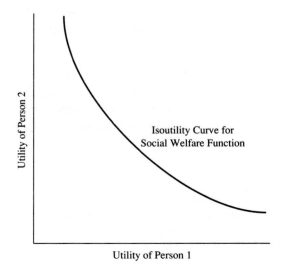

Isoutility Curve for
Social Welfare Function

Utility of Person 2

Utility of Person 1

FIGURE 21.1
Plausible nature of a social welfare function.

Are individual utilities measured in comparable units that can legitimately be summed?

Economists and philosophers have thought hard about this question of interpersonal comparison of utility. Their conclusion is that such comparisons simply do not make sense. The problem is that there is no way to transform everyone's utility into a common denominator. Even for an individual, utility is a relative measure; we have no way of measuring any person's absolute degree of happiness. By extension there is no way we can establish comparable degrees of happiness among individuals.

The short of it is that even if we could persuade ourselves that we have devised the right mathematical form for the social welfare function, we could not calculate it in any meaningful way from individual utilities. We would not know how to define the personal utilities on a common scale, and thus could not use the function in practice.

Arrow paradox. Logically, there is an alternative to constructing a social welfare function from the utilities of individuals. We could think of identifying a group's utility from the choices it makes, just as we construct an individual's utility from the choices a person makes. This aggregate approach has the appeal of being direct. Unfortunately, this approach is not satisfactory either. Kenneth Arrow demonstrated this fact and received the Nobel Prize for his investigations of this issue. His essential results are that

1. The choices a group makes depend on its internal rules of decisionmaking; for example, its voting rules.
2. No one voting rule or decisionmaking process is intrinsically best.
3. The choices made by a group are therefore necessarily an ambiguous reflection of its preferences, so that we cannot rely on a group's choices to construct its social welfare function.

The "Arrow Paradox" illustrates the situation. It demonstrates by simple example the kind of ambiguity of choice that may result from voting procedures. Consider a group of three persons evaluating three different design options. Their individual preferences are quite different, as Table 21.1 shows.

Suppose that the group agrees to select its final design by successively comparing pairs of options until it has ranked them all. This is a natural way to search for dominant choices; it is also rather like selecting the president of the United States after a set of primaries.

Let us proceed to apply the rule to the case at hand, starting by comparing A and B alone. We find

$$A > B \quad \text{(C excluded)}$$

by a 2:1 majority. If A is thus retained as a preferred option and compared to C, we find

$$C > A \quad \text{(B excluded)}$$

TABLE 21.1
Individual Rankings of Options A, B,
and C for Arrow Paradox

Ranking of option	Individual		
	Tom	Dick	Harry
First	A	C	B
Second	B	A	C
Third	C	B	A

also by a 2:1 majority. Having compared all three options, can we then conclude

$$C > A > B \quad ?$$

The Arrow Paradox is precisely that this ranking is not valid. We can check the result by comparing B and C alone, and find

$$B > C \quad \text{(A excluded)}$$

also by a 2:1 majority. The net result is intransitive. If we chain the results we obtain

$$C > A > B > C \quad !$$

The interpretation is that we cannot rely on the choices expressed by a group to reflect its social welfare function. The actual choice may depend critically on the precise way a voting procedure is applied. It may depend even more on the voting rules themselves. We thus cannot presume that we can interpret the choices expressed by a group as their clear preferences.

Impossibility of the social welfare function. The point of this discussion has been that it is simply not possible to construct a valid group utility function that we can apply to collective decisionmaking. Recognizing this impossibility provides the right starting point for dealing with collective decisionmaking.

21.3 DISTRIBUTION PROBLEM

What makes system design for a group so difficult is that it involves a complex problem entirely different from the kind we have been discussing throughout the text. In collective decisionmaking we must consider the distribution of the products of a system to each member of the group. This distribution defines the utility of each member and, thus, the social welfare of the group.

The text has so far treated system design as a *production problem*. The issue has been to specify how the system will be configured, and thus what it produces. The entire analysis is based on a combination of good technical design (the technically efficient production functions in Chapter 2), and the prevailing values that may either be interpreted as costs (as in Chapters 4 to 14) or as utilities.

System design for a group could also be viewed simply as a production problem if we could define the utility of the group, the social welfare function. That is impossible, however, as the previous section indicates. The only way to define value for the group is to consider the values of its members. That implies that we have to focus on the distribution of products of the system. This is the *distribution problem*, the determination of what each member of the group will get.

Naïve approach. A popular procedure for dealing with system design for a group is simply to deal with the production and distribution problems separately. The idea is "first, make the pie as big as possible, and then worry about how it's divided." Specifically, this is interpreted in practice as maximizing economic value and letting politicians worry about the rest. This is the underlying concept when development economists focus on maximizing the gross national product of a country, or engineers justify a new highway on the basis of its economic stimulus. This approach has considerable superficial appeal, but unfortunately is naïve and deficient.

At first, it does seem logical to concentrate on "maximizing the pie." It would seem obvious that the more pie we had, the easier it would be to make everyone happy. The more we had to distribute, the easier it would be to give everyone enough. The separation of the problems also is professionally appealing: the production problem seems like a nice technical issue suitable for systems analysts, whereas distribution involves social and political issues one might prefer to leave to others.

The approach is naïve because no system produces only one product that we can unambiguously maximize. Life is not just a bowl of cherries we can only make into a pie. Every system involves multiple products and impacts. Without a unique way to compare them, without a social welfare function, we cannot define what it means to maximize product. In short we have apples and oranges in addition to cherries, and do not know how to compare them. Economic development of a country, for example, typically implies urbanization, disruption of the traditional social structure, and other effects not reflected in the statistics on gross national product. A new highway likewise has pollution and other impacts in addition to its economic benefits.

A simple example illustrates the issue. Consider a country that produces two types of products: exports and fresh food. We may suppose its best combinations of design at any time can be represented by a curve. These are the noninferior solutions described in Chapter 8, also known as the production possibility frontier in economics. If there are diminishing marginal returns in each product, the curve will bow away from the origin as in Figure 21.2. The issue is, what is the best design of the system; specifically, what is the best combination of exports and fresh food to produce?

Maximizing the "pie" consists in practice of maximizing economic value. This depends on the relative price of the products. Graphically, the maximum economic value, Z^*, is defined by the point on the production possibility frontier

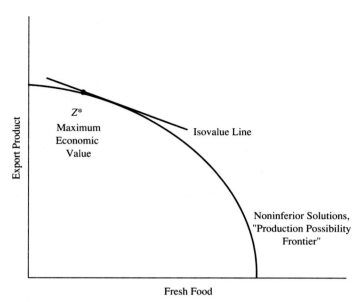

FIGURE 21.2
Maximizing the economic "pie" for example country.

that is tangent to the highest isovalue curve. If we assume, as is most often the case in developing countries, that the relative price of exports is high, maximum economic production will favor exports against local agriculture. This has been a typical result in Nigeria (petroleum, palm oil, and peanuts), Central America (bananas), Malaysia (tin and rubber), and so on. In each of these cases, focus on maximization of economic value has meant that some products, particularly local agriculture, have been neglected.

Maximization of economic value often does not and cannot lead to the best solution for the group. This is most obviously the case if the group's welfare requires minimum levels of products which have not been produced. Suppose for example that our country requires a minimum level of fresh food for its health, as shown in Figure 21.3. We may then imagine that its social welfare function, could it be drawn, would be asymptotic to this minimum as shown. The design that maximizes the social welfare, SWF^*, is quite different from the design that maximizes economic value, Z^*. Moreover, getting the economic maximum may make it impossible to attain the social welfare maximum insofar as money cannot buy some products—such as fresh food—if they have not been produced. In fact, malnutrition is often a common phenomenon of Central American and other countries that export cash crops. Maximizing the economic pie may thus not only be quite different from the social welfare optimum, but in fact preclude it.

The difference between the economic and social optimum is not just a phenomenon of simple examples or foreign countries. The same kind of results

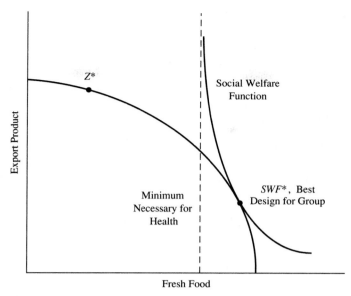

FIGURE 21.3
The economic maximum may be different from and preclude the best design for the group.

can obtain in industrialized nations. We may admit that every country requires an educated, healthy population to ensure its future. But if it focuses narrowly on immediate financial benefits, and neglects the training of teachers, doctors, and researchers, it may not be able to buy them when they are needed. Some attribute the decline in America's international competitiveness precisely to this focus on immediate rewards that neglected investments in the future.

Effect of prior distribution. The price of goods reflects the existing distribution of wealth in society, in the world. The price of 20 carat diamond rings reflects the number of multimillionaires, for example. If there are many, as in the capitalist world, the prices may be high because they can afford to pay a lot for these amusements. If there are no millionaires, for instance in an egalitarian socialist society, then the price of jewels cannot be high—no one can pay for them.

This is an important observation. It means that what we determine as the economic maximum must also depend on the existing distribution of wealth, and must be good or bad depending on how we view this distribution. If you believe that the current situation is unjust, then you will reasonably conclude that the economic maximum does not define an acceptable social optimum.

Put another way, the rich have more economic votes. Having more money, they can call for products to satisfy their desires more effectively than the poor. To the extent that we allow prices to determine the design of a system for a group, we imply that the social welfare function weights the utilities of the rich highly. Many may find this unacceptable.

Consider Figure 21.3 again. The high price of the export product, such as bananas from Central America or coffee from Brazil, depends on the existing wealth of the industrialized countries. Their good fortune gives them the economic power to define what is produced in the exporting country. Does this arrangement necessarily lead to the optimum for all? Only if you believe that the rich somehow have a right to their wealth, that they have earned it in some way.

The possible inequity of the prior distribution of wealth is thus another reason why the economic maximum may not be the social maximum. This reinforces the conclusion that we cannot solve the problem of systems design for a group by the naïve approach that separates the production and distribution problems. These issues must be addressed together.

21.4 ANALYSIS OF DISTRIBUTION

We must first understand how to analyze the distribution problem before we integrate it with production to arrive at the best design for a group. We do this in two stages. First we consider the simpler problem of distributing a fixed set of products to members of a group. Then we examine the larger question of deciding both what to produce and how to share it.

Fixed product. The analysis of the distribution of a fixed set of products to members of a group is best explained graphically. The device for doing this is the *Edgeworth Box*. This is a diagram that indicates the effect of any allocation of two products to two individuals. The lessons drawn from this case apply directly to the more complex situation of multiple products and many members of the group.

The Edgeworth Box displays the two products to be distributed on a rectangle in the X-Y plane. To make it easy to remember the arrangement, think of these products as two chemicals, Xenon and Yttrium. Starting from the origin, any point in the rectangle shows the amount of X and Y distributed to one individual. This varies from none of each at the origin, to all the available products, (X^*, Y^*), at the opposite corner of the rectangle.

The Edgeworth Box is special because it has two origins, one at each opposing corner. As Figure 21.4 shows, any point A in the space simultaneously shows the allocation to individual 1, (X_1, Y_1) and, viewed from the other origin, the allocation to individual 2, (X_2, Y_2). Naturally, these allocations must be complementary, and sum to the total amounts available:

$$X_1 + X_2 = X^* \qquad Y_1 + Y_2 = Y^*$$

Consider how each individual views the allocation of products. Assuming that these have been represented as benefits with diminishing marginal utility (see Section 18.3), we may presume that each individuals's utility function can be represented by isovalue lines bowed away from the origin, rather as shown

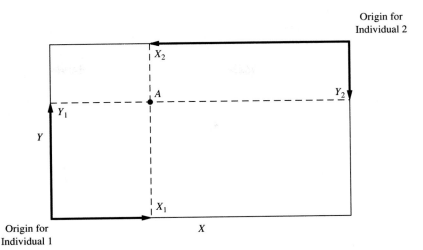

FIGURE 21.4
The Edgeworth Box: any point in the rectangle indicates the allocation of X and Y to two individuals.

in Figure 21.1 and Figure 18.7. Any allocation represented by point A will simultaneously be on two intersecting isovalue lines, one each for individuals 1 and 2, as Figure 21.5 shows. The Edgeworth Box thus also indicates the utility any individual gets from the distribution.

Now the important result: whatever the initial allocation of products to individuals, we should almost always be able to improve the allocation to *everyone's* benefit! To see this, consider the effect of changing the allocation from A to B, as shown in Figure 21.5. Given that each individual's isovalue curves bow away from their origin, then the move from A to B provides both individuals with higher utilities.

What is remarkable about this result is that we achieve *mutually* beneficial improvements in the distribution although the product, the "pie," is fixed. This deserves special attention because it is counterintuitive to most people. The general—but wrong—assumption is that since the "pie" is fixed then any advantage one person gets must be to the disadvantage of the other. (Such a situation is called a *zero-sum game* in operations research.) The simple analysis would be correct if we were only dealing with a single product. But we are generally not dealing with a zero-sum game when we have multiple products because the difference between these products provides mutually beneficial opportunities.

The reason we can usually achieve mutually beneficial improvements is that, at any point, each individual values each product differently. What one person values little, another may really want. There should thus be opportunities for trades that benefit both.

Figure 21.5 illustrates the situation. At allocation A, individual 1 gets little value from more Y, as shown by the steep isovalue curve. Individual 2, on the

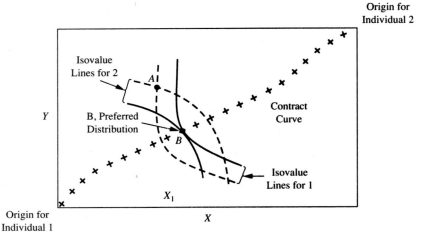

FIGURE 21.5
Any allocation A can, in general, be improved to the mutual benefit of all concerned.

other hand, values Y relatively highly, and is quite willing to trade some X to obtain it. This is what happens as they trade and change the allocation from A to B. Note that in this analysis we assume, as is generally the case, that any person's utility for a product is nonlinear, and depends on what is in short supply or surplus. Trading between individuals allows them to achieve balanced distributions that maximize their mutual utility. (See box for an example.)

There is a limit to the mutual improvements that can be achieved. In Figure 21.5, B is such a point. Any change in distribution from B necessarily decreases the utility of one or both individuals. Graphically, this is indicated by the tangency of the isovalue curves. Any movement away from this point must be to a curve of lower value.

The Edgeworth Box

For this example, the products are M and N, with the total amount to be shared, $(M^*, N^*) = (5, 5)$. Each individual values M and N differently. Assuming linear values for simplicity

$$U_1 = 4M + N$$

$$U_2 = M + 2N$$

Suppose the M's and N's are shared so that individual 1 gets (3, 2). Individual 2 would thus get the complement: [(5 − 3), (5 − 2)] or (2, 3). This is point A in Figure 21.6.

For the allocation represented by A, the value to each individual is:

$$U_1 = 4(3) + 2 = 14$$
$$U_2 = 2 + 2(3) = 8$$

The isovalue line for individual 1 can be expressed as

$$N = 14 - 4M$$

and for individual 2

$$N = (8 - M) / 2$$

These two lines pass through A as in Figure 21.6.

The fact that the isovalue lines intersect indicates that it is possible to reallocate the products to mutual advantage. Any allocation represented by the points in the shaded area would lead to increases in utility for both individuals, being further away from the origin than the isovalue line for each individual. For example, consider the allocation represented by B: this gives $(4, 1)$ to individual 1 and $(1, 4)$ to individual 2. The resultant benefits to each are greater than those of the initial allocation A:

$$U_1 = 4(4) + 1 = 17 > 14$$
$$U_2 = 1 + 2(4) = 9 > 8$$

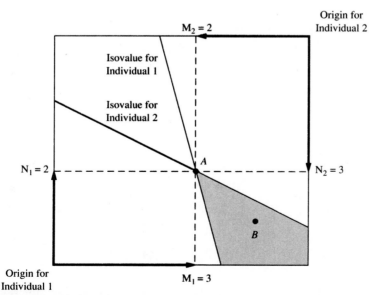

FIGURE 21.6
Illustration for Edgeworth Box analysis.

The locus of all allocations that represent the limit of mutually advantageous changes in distribution is the *contract curve*. Graphically, this is the locus of all points of tangency of the isovalue curves. Because we cannot effect the interpersonal comparison of utilities, we cannot define this curve numerically.

The important point about the contract curve is that it defines only a minuscule fraction of all the possible allocations of a fixed set of products. The probability that any initial distribution is on the contract curve is thus essentially zero. Consequently, we may assume as a practical matter that members of a group can always change any initial allocation of products to their mutual advantage.

Choice of product. The analysis of distribution when the amounts to be produced are not fixed is also best done graphically. This is because, given the impossibility of acceptable interpersonal comparisons of utility and social welfare functions, no analytic solution is possible.

We focus on noninferior designs, the ones on the production possibility frontier that define the maximum combinations of products we can achieve. Each particular noninferior design, Z_i, provides benefits that can be shared by members of the group. The maximum utility to these individuals is defined by the contract curve, so that each design implies a maximum level of utilities to the members. The case for two individuals can be plotted as in Figure 21.7.

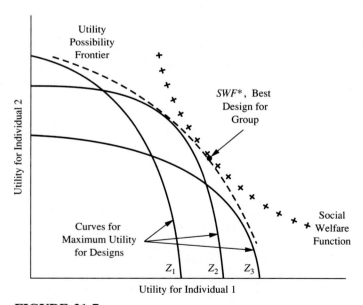

FIGURE 21.7
The best design for a group requires finding both the best system and the best way to allocate its benefits.

The set of all noninferior designs defines a *utility possibility frontier*. This is the maximum utility that individuals can receive from all possible productions and allocations, and is the outer bound of all the maximum utility curves for a fixed production, as Figure 21.7 shows.

The best design for the group, SWF^*, is the one that achieves the highest social welfare. Graphically it would be defined (if we could actually draw acceptable curves) as the point of tangency of the utility possibility frontier and the highest isoutility curve for the social welfare function.

This discussion indicates that achieving the best design for the group of members with different values requires us to do two things:

1. Move along the production possibility frontier of noninferior alternatives to find the design that can give all members the highest utility.
2. Find the allocation of products of this system which exploits all opportunities for increasing mutual advantage.

21.5 COLLABORATIVE NEGOTIATION

The best procedure for collective decisionmaking is collaborative negotiation. Negotiation is essential because there is no analytical way to proceed, given the impossibility of making interpersonal comparisons of utility. Some kind of bargaining, or exploration of each other's preferences and trade-offs has to be worked out. Collaboration is equally important because of the numerous possibilities for mutual gain.

This section discusses some of the characteristics of the negotiation process that system analysts ought to consider. Naturally, this is only an introduction. Negotiation is a subtle subject at the limit of where systems analysis leaves off and psychology, not to say diplomacy, begins.

Trade-offs. Changes in allocation are central to mutually beneficial improvements, as the previous section shows. These are achieved by exchanges between individuals. A key aspect of negotiation thus consists of finding opportunities for these trade-offs.

Trade-offs can most obviously be between products of the system. They can also be between their characteristics, such as cost, reliability, or quality. They can even be between characteristics of the system itself: its site, its configuration, its accessibility.

More subtly, trade-offs can be made between different levels of risk. Some members of a group may be quite reluctant to accept risks when others are not; this provides the opportunity for exchanges between the two. One group can provide insurance to the others. For example, if a community is extremely averse to the possibility of dioxin emissions from a proposed municipal incinerator that an entrepreneur proposes to build, they can come to an arrangement whereby the developer guarantees to close the plant if it does not perform as expected. The developer may then be able to build, at the cost of more risk; the community bears less risk but permits the facility.

Economies of scale. Economies of scale in a system provide an enormous additional motivation for collaborative negotiation. As indicated in Section 4.4, the cost function for a system is often

$$\text{Cost} \sim \text{Constant } (\text{Capacity})^{0.5}$$

This means that when many entities get together to establish a system, their total cost can be very much cheaper than if they each attempt to provide the services for themselves. If nine towns of equal size got together to build a metropolitan incinerator, for example, their total cost would be one-third (!) of what it would be if they each built an individual facility.

The tremendous savings possible by exploiting economies of scale can be used effectively to secure agreement for a large system, such as a metropolitan incinerator, an airport, or a power plant, that might otherwise be rejected by the community. Some of the financial benefits of the larger system can be traded off with other members of the group who may care more about other factors, such as safety, noise, and risk.

Exploitation of great by small. An almost inevitable characteristic of collective decisionmaking is that the smaller members of the group get a larger distribution of benefits than their proportional share according to size. This fact is counterintuitive; one might expect that the powerful members get their own way and exploit the weak.

The strong do dominate the weak when results are determined merely by brute force. But the reverse is true when we consider collective decisionmaking in which each member of a group has some kind of vote on the final design.

The reason the bigger members get exploited is that they have a great deal to gain from collective action, precisely because they are big. They therefore are often willing to trade these savings relatively generously to the smaller members, who may not have as much to gain, to ensure that a collective decision is made. A salient example of this phenomenon is the OPEC oil cartel. Saudi Arabia is by far the greatest producer and yet has consistently got far smaller production quotas relative to its potential than the other nations. Saudi Arabia has, in effect, paid other nations to maintain the cartel.

A numerical example of the exploitation of the great by the small is tabulated in Table 21.2. Suppose a potential group consists of four members, A, B, C, and D. A is the largest, and requires six units of product. The others need only one unit apiece. Assume that cost is proportional to the square root of capacity, the approximate situation with economies of scale. Their total costs are 5.45 if the members act independently, but only 3 if they collaborate, producing a savings of 2.45 or 45%. There is no way to predict how the members of the group would in fact distribute these savings, but the allocation shown in Table 21.2 would be a representative pattern. In this case the larger member, A, gives up some of its

TABLE 21.2
Example of Exploitation of Great by Small

Member	Capacity required	Cost if acting		Group savings	
		Alone	As group	Total	%
A	6	2.45	1.8	0.65	25
B	1	1	0.4	0.6	60
C	1	1	0.4	0.6	60
D	1	1	0.4	0.6	60
All	9	5.45	3	2.45	45

proportional share of the savings to ensure that they exist. The smaller members, B, C, and D, do get less than A, but more than their proportional share.

This result may or may not appear equitable to different people. The important fact is that it is frequently what happens normally. It should thus be anticipated.

Process. The process of negotiation is most important to its outcome, to the result of collective decisionmaking. Process is important at two levels. First, the result depends on the voting rules for the group; different arrangements translate the desires of individual members differently. Simple majority rule is different from proportional representation. The United States Senate is surely different, with its rule of two senators per state regardless of size, than it would be if senators represented equal districts.

Secondly, small procedural features can make a substantial difference to the outcome. The discussion of the Arrow Paradox in Section 21.3 illustrates this: the option that emerges as preferred from the paired comparisons depends absolutely on which pairs you consider first. This kind of phenomenon explains why experienced diplomats and negotiators pay great attention to the details of procedure.

Finally, personal styles influence the result of bargaining. Abrasive, aggressive approaches may seem to be effective but often fail utterly in achieving the significant gains that can result from collaborative negotiation. A full treatment of the subject being beyond this text, the interested reader is referred to an excellent introductory manual to effective bargaining: *Getting to Yes*, by Fisher and Ury, (see References).

21.6 RECOMMENDED PROCEDURE

As this chapter stresses, there is no analytic way to define the design, the system that best meets the desires of a group of different members. We can only recommend a process for dealing with the problem.

The recommended procedure consists of five steps:

1. Model the physical system
2. De̠   ̠.̠ noninferior options, the production possibility frontier
3. Determine individual preferences
4. Explore the possible trade-offs
5. Negotiate toward a collectively satisfactory solution

A model of the system is essential to understand the technical possibilities. This consists of developing either an analytic or a simulation model of the production function, as described in Chapter 2.

The production possibility frontier focuses our attention of the designs that clearly produce the most benefits. These are only a very small fraction of the total number of options. Considering only these keeps the analysis to a minimum. These noninferior solutions can be determined as described in Chapter 8.

Individual utility functions indicate what products or characteristics of the system are most and least important to each member of the group. This information provides the basis for exploring trade-offs. The appropriate multiattribute utility functions can be determined as described in Chapters 19 and 20.

The exploration of possible trade-offs is an information gathering activity. In order to find opportunities for trades we need to understand which products or characteristics are valued differently by different members, and which thus offer the possibility of mutually beneficial exchanges.

Finally, the individual members must negotiate between themselves. In doing this they proceed along two dimensions: the product and its distribution. In terms of the product, they move along the production possibility frontier, from the designs they would prefer themselves, to compromise designs that are collectively acceptable. Simultaneously, they should explore how the production itself should be shared. This process is not necessarily one in which the members lose; as shown in Section 21.4, this process may be mutually advantageous as they change the allocation of benefits. The final result should be an effective collective decision on the design of the system.

21.7   APPLICATION

At MIT we have successfully used the SUMIT case study of a hypothetical electric power system to illustrate the issues of collective decisionmaking. It has been applied in a wide range of situations, in graduate subjects, in summer institutes, and short seminars for senior professionals. Its details are available on request. SUMIT concerns a hypothetical electric company that must meet the demands of its clients while satisfying political and environmental constraints. The company must devise a plan to provide sufficient additional power for its service area, keeping costs within tolerable bounds, yet ensuring environmental quality.

The case is organized as a participatory exercise among the members of the class or seminar. They are divided into small subgroups representing: the company itself; its industrial customers; environmentally conscious consumer advocates; and the state agency that regulates the price of electricity. Each subgroup is given materials enabling it to play its role, and is provided with a diskette that enables it to calculate the consequences of any design. The subgroups are told that collective decisions can only be made when three out of the four subgroups agree. The entire group is then charged with developing a plan for the future.

The SUMIT case provides the participants with the model of the computer physical system, and so automatically fulfills step 1 of the recommended procedure. This is realistic as such models are, in fact, quite common.

The exercise of finding the noninferior solutions is often most revealing, notably to experienced professionals who participate. This is because the usual way to approach the design is to look for the optimum solution, not to define the frontier that includes all kinds of designs that are not optimal to them. The revelation is associated with the expanded set of solutions. It leads all participants to recognize that their preferred design is contingent on their own values, which are probably not representative of the group.

When the participants determine their preferences, they are usually surprised to find how complex they are. The nonlinearity of their utility functions forces them to recognize that, at some points, they are in fact prepared to sacrifice some of their preferred objectives in order to obtain a reasonable overall balance. This step both prepares them to consider trade-offs and helps them understand what kind of trade-offs might be acceptable.

At this point, in running the SUMIT case, we encourage the participants to engage in a lot of informal discussions between themselves. It is necessary for them, as it is in real life, to explore possible trade-offs in preparation for more formal negotiations.

The specific outcome of the final negotiation for any group is unpredictable. It depends on many factors, not the least of which are the skill and personalities of the participants.

Some general results of the SUMIT case stand out consistently. These are:

1. A collectively satisfactory design is possible. This is a big lesson for most participants who, when presented with the problem, assume that resolution can only come through power and at the expense of others.

2. The emergence of the satisfactory collective decision is not a matter of chance, it is systematically facilitated by the recommended procedure.

3. Collaborative efforts are necessary. Participants who adopt combative, unyielding attitudes miss the opportunities for exploiting mutual benefits and systematically end up with inferior solutions as compared to other groups.

4. Working on the distribution problem is essential. It is virtually impossible to determine the acceptable solution without simultaneously defining how the benefits will be shared.

Overall, we have found that the SUMIT case study provides an excellent integration of the range of issues of systems analysis.

REFERENCES

Arrow, K., (1963). *Social Choice and Individual Values*, Yale University Press, New Haven, CT.
Fisher, R., and W. Ury, (1981). *Getting to Yes*, Penguin, New York.
Olson, M., (1971). *The Logic of Collective Action: Public Goods and the Theory of Groups*, Harvard University Press, Cambridge, MA.

PROBLEMS

21.1. *Sharing the Crop*

Peter and Paul jointly grow rye and wheat (R, W) for their own use. They each have different tastes for these products:

$$U(\text{Peter}) = 4R^{0.5} + W^{0.5} \qquad U(\text{Paul}) = 2R^{0.5} + 3W^{0.5}$$

(a) Calculate Peter's utility if his share is (16, 16). Plot the isovalue line through this point. You may find it helpful to express $W = f(R)$.

(b) Repeat (a) for Paul when he also gets (16, 16).

(c) Suppose the crop yields (32, 32). Compare their utility if they share the crop evenly with that if Paul gets (9, 25) and Peter (23, 7). Are we robbing Peter to pay Paul? That is, does the advantage to one come at the disadvantage of the other?

(d) Draw the Edgeworth Box that illustrates the unequal distribution in part (c). Define the region in which Peter and Paul can mutually improve their positions from that defined by the "fair" distribution, in which each gets half of each product.

21.2. *Dividing the Pie*

Mother Evening has to divide her four apple and four blueberry pies between her children, Sam and Janet. She knows they have different tastes:

$$U_S = 10A^{0.5} + 2B^{0.5} \qquad U_J = 4A^{0.5} + 8B^{0.5}$$

(a) Calculate Sam's utility if he gets half of each. Plot his isovalue curve through this point.

(b) Repeat (a) for Janet.

(c) Draw the Edgeworth Box for Sam and Janet, showing their isovalue lines through an equal division of the pies. Identify the possibilities for a mutually more advantageous way for them to share the pies.

(d) Propose a better allocation and indicate how it increases the pleasure of Sam and Janet Evening.

21.3. *Share Cropping*

On a plantation that can grow either cotton or food, the owners have decided— in view of prevailing export prices—to concentrate on growing cotton for export, and only let the workers cultivate small plots for food. The resultant production is (C, F) = (40, 1). The utilities of the owners and workers for the products are:

$$U_o = C + F^{0.5} \qquad U_w = C + 10(F^{0.5})$$

(a) Calculate the utility of the owners and workers if the owners get all the cotton and the workers get all the food.
(b) Draw the Edgeworth Box for the allocation of (40, 1) and determine its optimal distribution between owners and workers.
(c) Suppose that it is possible to produce (30, 9) on the land: discuss whether you think this would be better? What do you mean by better? How do you weigh the importance of the preferences of the two groups?

APPENDIX

NOTATION

Symbol	Meaning	Chapter
A	Matrix of Constraint Parameters	5
A_0	Parameter of Cost Function	4
AC_Y	Average Cost of Product	4
a	Constant in Utility Function	18
	Returns to Scale Parameter	4
a_i, a_{ij}	Parameters of Constraint Equations	5
	Parameters of Production Function	2
B	Vector of Constraints	5
B	Discounted Benefits	13
b	Constant in Utility Function	18
b_j	Constraint	5
C	Vector of c_i	5
C	Discounted costs	13
°C	Degree Centigrade	18
$C(Y)$	Cost Function for Product	4
CE	Certainty Equivalent	19

451

C_c	Closure Costs	13
C_f	Fixed Costs	14
C_k	Initial Capital Costs	6; 12
C_r	Annual Recurring Costs	12
C_v	Variable Costs	6; 14
CLR_j	Conditional Likelihood Ratio for O_j	15
c	Constant exponent	19
c_i, c_{ij}	Parameters of Objective Function (often costs)	5
c_o	Fixed Charge	5
$c(\mathbf{X})$	Input Cost Function	4
crf	Capital Recovery Factor	15
D_i	A Possible Decision	16
E	Event	15
$EV(\cdot)$	Expected Value of $(\cdot)$	15; 16
e	Naperian number, 2.7183	11
F	Future Amount	11
°F	Degree Fahrenheit	18
$f(\cdot)$	Function of $(\cdot)$	5
$f_s(K)$	Cumulative Return Function for State S	7
$G(\mathbf{X})$	Objective Function for Dynamic Programming	7
$g(\cdot)$	Production Function	2
$g_i(X_i)$	Return Function	7
$h(\cdot)$	Constraint Equation	3
I_i	Inventory in Period or Stage i	7
IRR	Internal Rate of Return	13
i	Interest Rate	13
K	State, in Dynamic Programming	7
	Normalizing Parameter for Multiattribute Utility Function	20
k	Number of Observations in a Test	17
k_i	Scaling Factors for Individual Dimensions of Multiattribute Utility	20

R_i	Requirement for Period or Stage i	7
RTS	Returns to Scale	2
r	Returns to Scale parameter	4
	Discount Rate	11
r_{irr}	Internal Rate of Return	13
r_p	Return on Investment	12
S	Future Amount	11
	Number of Sizes	16
S_j	Slack Variable	3
SP	Vector of Shadow Prices	6
SV	Vector of Slack Variables	6
SWF	Social Welfare Function	21
s	Scaling factor	2
T	Number of Periods	16
TR_k	Test Result	17
$U(\cdot)$	Utility of $(\cdot)$	18
U_i	Utility to Individual i	21
u	Learning Curve Exponent	4
$V(\cdot)$	Value of $(\cdot)$	18
W	Vector of Dual Variables	5
w_i	Relative weight	2; 21
X	Vector of Resources Used in Design	2
X_b	Buying Price of a Lottery	19
X_s	Selling Price of a Lottery	19
X_i	Inputs to a Design	2
Y	Product of a System	2
Y_i	Product in Period i	7
Z	Dual Objective Function	5

Greek Symbol

λ_j	Lagrangean Multiplier	3

Special Mathematical Notation

$(\cdot)^*$	Best Value of $(\cdot)$
$(\cdot)_*$	Worst Value of $(\cdot)$
$\sim$	Is Indifferent to
$>$	Is Greater Than
$<$	Is Less Than
$>$	Is Preferred To
$<$	Is Preferred By

INDEX

Definitions are on pages marked with **boldface** type.

457